ISBN 978-1-390-90778-0
PIBN 11185658

1 MONTH OF
FREE
READING

at

www.ForgottenBooks.com

By purchasing this book you are eligible for one month membership to ForgottenBooks.com, giving you unlimited access to our entire collection of over 1,000,000 titles via our web site and mobile apps.

To claim your free month visit:

www.forgottenbooks.com/free1185658

English
Français
Deutsche
Italiano
Español
Português

www.forgottenbooks.com

Mythology Photography **Fiction**
Fishing Christianity **Art** Cooking
Essays Buddhism Freemasonry
Medicine **Biology** Music **Ancient
Egypt** Evolution Carpentry Physics
Dance Geology **Mathematics** Fitness
Shakespeare **Folklore** Yoga Marketing
Confidence Immortality Biographies
Poetry **Psychology** Witchcraft
Electronics Chemistry History **Law**
Accounting **Philosophy** Anthropology
Alchemy Drama Quantum Mechanics
Atheism Sexual Health **Ancient History**
Entrepreneurship Languages Sport
Paleontology Needlework Islam
Metaphysics Investment Archaeology
Parenting Statistics Criminology
Motivational

IRISH TEXTS SOCIETY

cumann na sgríbeann ngaedilge

VOL. XXXIV

(1932)

1938

PRINTED AT THE

BY PONSONBY & GIBBS.

LEBOR GABÁLA ÉRENN

THE BOOK OF THE TAKING OF IRELAND

PART I

EDITED AND TRANSLATED, WITH NOTES, ETC.

BY

R. A. STEWART MACALISTER, D. LITT.

DUBLIN:

PUBLISHED FOR THE IRISH TEXTS SOCIETY
BY THE EDUCATIONAL COMPANY OF IRELAND, LTD.
89 TALBOT STREET

1938

CONTENTS.

SECTION I: FROM THE CREATION TO THE DISPERSAL OF THE NATIONS.

CORRIGENDA.

p. xiii, line 23 : *after* R² *add*—traceable in some quotations in R³.

p. xv, line 20 : *add*—At the top of the first page of E there are two old library class-marks, A. 1. 8 and B. 35. Above the 8 there is the invocation *Emanuel,* faint but decipherable : between the two marks there is an illegible note, dia dui (?) . . . ib, with a date ending (1)753.

p. xvi, line 10 : *add*—P was probably meant to complete an acephalous copy already in its writer's possession : hence the abrupt ending.

p. xxiii, line 6 : *after* manuscripts *add*—I dare not flatter myself that these complex lists of variants contain no errors or omissions, but I feel confident that nothing of importance has been overlooked.

p. xxxiv, line 2 : for √A read √V.

p. 8, line 6, below the table : *for* eleventh *read* twelfth. In line 8, *after* Madrid, *add*—Σ^M, likewise at Madrid, is of the eleventh century.

p. 12, line 21 : *delete* whether . . . importance. In line 24, *after* edge, *add*— The tear would have run in the opposite direction if it had been inflicted in the original act of pillage ; it must have been a later misdemeanour, to remove from the leaf matter not germane to its new context.

p. 163, line 14 : *for* Dula *read* Dala.

p. 223, footnote (²⁹) : *after* version *add* of the Irenaeus text.

p. 239, line 15 : *add*—This poem is printed, *Todd Lectures,* iii, p. 46.

TABLE OF ABBREVIATIONS AND CRITICAL SYMBOLS.

1. *Notation for Redactions* :—

    R¹, **R²**, **R³**, the First, Second, Third Redactions.

    Min or μ, the version called *Mīniugud*.

    K, the modernised version of Micheāl ō Clēirigh.

2. *Notation for the Extant Manuscripts* :—

A : Stowe A.2.4.

B : Book of Ballymote.

β : H.2.4 in T.C.D.

β^1: H.1.15 in T.C.D.

β^2: Stowe D.* 3.2.

D : Stowe D.4.3.

E : E.3.5. no. 2 in T.C.D.

F¹ : Book of Fermoy.

F² : Stowe D.3.1.

H : H.2.15 no. 1 in T.C.D.

L : Book of Leinster.

Λ : Book of Lecan, first text.

M : Book of Lecan, second text.

P : P.10266 in National Library, Dublin.

R : Rawl.B.512 in Bodleian Library.

V¹ : Stowe D.5.1.

V² : Stowe D.4.1.

V³ : Stowe D.1.3.

    R¹ is contained in **L, F.**

    R² „   „   „   **A, D, E, Λ P, R, V.**

    R³ „   „   „   **B,** β**,** β^1**,** β^2**, H,M.**

    Min is suffixed to the copies of **R²** in **Λ, R,V.** To distinguish the portions of these MSS. containing the Min text from those containing the R² text, the symbols μ**Λ,** μ**R,** μ**V** are used for the former.

    K is contained in a number of paper MSS., but for purposes of reference the authoritative autograph (23 K 32 in R.I.A.) has been considered sufficient.

---

*For the sake of brevity the shelf-marks of the Stowe collection are here stated in Arabic numerals, though Roman numerals are used in the Library.

Where it is necessary to refer to any combination of two of the β MSS., or to all three of them, the formula β^{012} (varied as required) is used for brevity.

F[1], **F**[2], are parts of one dismembered MS. collectively denoted by **F**.

V[1], **V**[2], **V**[3], are parts of one dismembered MS. collectively denoted by **V**.

3. *Notation for Lost Manuscripts of Critical Importance* :—

*Q, ***X**, ***W**, ***Z.**

$\sqrt{}$ **B**, the exemplar from which **B** was copied.

$\overset{2}{\sqrt{}}$ **B**, the exemplar from which $\sqrt{}$**B** was copied.

$\overset{n}{\sqrt{}}$ **B**, a MS. in the ancestry of **B** at an unspecified number of steps back from it.

(Analogous symbolism for the ancestry of the other MSS.)

$\sqrt{}$**BH**, the common ancestor of **B** and **H**. [But **H**$\sqrt{}$**B** means the extant MS. **H** in combination with $\sqrt{}$**B**.]

∞ **R**[3], the *autograph* of the Third Redaction, or the *compiler* of the Third Redaction, according to the context.

∞ **L**, the Manuscript in which the tradition represented by **L** was differentiated from the other MSS. of the same Redaction.

$\sqrt{}$**R**[3], the Manuscript from which all the *extant* Manuscripts of the Third Redaction are derived (which may or may not be identical with ∞**R**[3]).

(Analogous symbolism for the ancestry of other MSS. and Versions.)

Note.—**R** *alone* denotes the Bodleian MS. ; **R** with a superscript numeral is to be read " Redaction."

4. *Miscellaneous abbreviations* :—

c : Correction, corrector (according to context).

g : Gloss, glossator ; a gloss *incorporated* in the text.

g^2: a secondary gloss, or gloss upon a gloss, also incorporated in the text.

3: a gloss which remains external to the text, superscript (**sprs**), subscript (**sbs**), or in the margin (**marg**) of the MS.

s: Scribe: s^1, s^2, the first, second, scribe of a MS.

y: Interpolation, interpolator. **yc M** is to be read "interpolated by a corrector of **M**." **y sprs s M** "interpolated, above the line, by the original scribe of **M**". (**y** is used in preference to i as being a more distinctive letter.)

LG: The name of the text, *Lebor Gabāla*.

s., d.: *in the translation*, to be read "son of," "daughter of."

om, ins, in the lists of *variae lectiones*, to be read "omit(s)," "insert(s)."

sec. man. = *secunda manu*.

R.I.A.: Royal Irish Academy.

T.C.D.: Trinity College, Dublin.

§: The *sections* of the book.

¶: The *paragraphs* of the book.

The glossarial or other interpolated matter in the text is denoted by the signs ‡ ... ‖ . secondary glosses being marked ‡¹ ... ‖¹: these symbols are more fully elucidated, where necessary, in the notes.

The columns on each folio of the MS. are denoted in the usual way by the Greek letters $a \beta \gamma \delta$, the *recto* and *verso* being numbered thus continuously. In most cases $a \beta$ are on the recto, $\gamma \delta$ on the verso. Except in the case of the MSS. H, β, β^1, β^2 the numeration is by folios, *not* by pages.

In the translation, glossarial matter is enclosed in square brackets [ ]; the restoration of lost matter in angled brackets < >.

INTRODUCTION.

Lebor Gabāla Ērenn, a title which we can best translate literally, "the Book of the Taking of Ireland," is a compilation which professes to narrate the history of the successive colonists of that country. The earlier Redactions have come down to us, in whole or in part, in fifteen MSS. (counting F, V, as one each, but counting separately the two versions in the *Book of Lecan*). These have been enumerated in the foregoing table, and are more fully described below.

For critical purposes, however, the number has to be reduced to eleven. A is a direct (and very poor) copy of D, and gives us nothing that D cannot supply: while β β^1 β^2 are all derivatives from B, and are thus of no use except to restore one folio, which B lost at some time after they were written.

Although these manuscripts agree, on the whole, in the facts, or alleged facts, which they set forth, the words in which they state them differ profoundly. They fall into redactional groups, essentially at variance in the selection and order of presentment of the narratives, and in the language in which these are expressed. The editor has no alternative but to print them *in extenso,* independently of one another.[1] A single composite text, with an unmanageably cumbrous sediment of *variae lectiones* at the bottom of the page, would be perfectly useless for any critical student of this important document and of its complex history. It may be said that this conclusion has not been reached without experiment.

---

[1] There are a few places in which this is not necessary, but these are exceptional.

b

INTRODUCTION.

The work is primarily paedagogic, for which purpose it is interspersed with mnemonic sets of verses, intended to be learned off by heart. To the modern reader these verses are an unmitigated nuisance, rarely adding anything to what he has already learnt from the prose text; nevertheless it is clear that they are the foundation on which the whole work, *in its present form,* is based. The *corpus* of historical verse became the common reservoir of knowledge upon which the prose compilers drew; and the selections which they made therefrom dictated the selection of facts which they set forth in the several redactions.

For this reason, the treatment of the verse has to be different from that of the prose: it has been found most convenient (again after experiment) to separate the verse texts from the prose, and to print them independently.

It is probable, indeed, that this is a return to the practice of the original prose redactors; that they did not write out the verse compositions in full, but merely jotted down as cues the opening words of each in the margins of their MSS., in the confidence that their readers would already have these texts securely in their heads, as they themselves had. In fact, the manuscript R gives us no more than such jottings, incorporated, it is true, in the text, but not extending beyond the first quatrain of any poem. It is conceivable that this is *not* the mere shirking of a lazy scribe, but that it is an actual survival of a traditional custom.[2] This suggestion is corroborated by the diversity of the formulae introducing the poems, even in MSS. which otherwise have close verbal similarity. *As dia chuimniugud-sain: de quibus hoc carmen:* [so-and-so] *cecinit*—these and similar expressions are used, even in nearly related MSS., at random, making it clear that in this matter the scribes had no stereotyped exemplars to keep their copies uniform. We infer, therefore, that in the autographs these formulae of introduction were not present; and that they were inserted only after the scribes had realized that human memory is untrustworthy, and that it was wiser to write out the poems in full. The same conclusion is

---

[2] Some few of the poems are written in full in μR.

indicated by the divergent forms of proper names sometimes appearing in the verse texts and in the associated prose. Thus in B, ¶ 156 *ff.*, we find several times the name "Caithear," but in the parallel poem no. XIV it appears as "Caicher."

THE EXTANT MANUSCRIPTS.

There are in all five redactions of the text: *Min,* R[1], R[2], R[3], and K, the last being O'Clery's[3] modernised version. Postponing the questions of their contents, origins, and mutual relationships, we may here briefly describe the manuscripts upon which an edition of the text has to be based.

Owing to the convenience of denoting a manuscript by a single letter only, I have taken the liberty of adopting symbols for certain well-known codices, different from those in ordinary use. Thus, I call the *Book of Leinster* L, not LL: the *Book of Ballymote* B, not BB: and for the two texts in the *Book of Lecan,* instead of *Lec*[1] and *Lec*[2] (which would be too clumsy for constant reference), I have adopted the symbols Λ and M. The latter may be read and explained (at the reader's pleasure) not as "em," but as "lambda two."

The First Redaction.

Only two MSS. of R[1] survive, namely, L and F.

L. *The Book of Leinster* (T.C.D. Library, H.2.18), c. 1150 A.D. In this codex, which is too well-known to need description, our text occupies folios 1–13.

The folios measure about $12\cdot7 \times 9$ inches[4]; and bear four columns, with about 51–53 lines of writing in each. The *recto* of the first folio must have for long remained unprotected by a binding, in consequence of which the writing is rendered partly illegible by dirt, wear, and other injury.

---

[3] I use the anglicised form here, because the genitive case of the native form cannot be accommodated to an English context: "ō Clēirigh's" is gibberish.

[4] In this and the other MSS. these measurements vary slightly from folio to folio; the vellum is not cut with mechanical uniformity.

The rest, as a whole, is readable enough; though the edges of some of the folios are frayed, and, throughout, many of the words and letters are thus damaged or lost. A transcript of the first 115 pages of the MS., line for line and page for page, was made in 1852 by Eugene O'Curry. (L.5.20 in T.C.D. Library). This is often useful in restoring writing that has become illegible since his time; but it cannot be trusted with full confidence, and he has shirked the task of trying to decipher the first page, where his help would have been of the utmost value.

F. *The Book of Fermoy* (R.I.A. Library, 23 E. 29). The connexion of this copy of LG with the Book of Fermoy is factitious and partial only. It is written upon twenty-two folios of vellum, of which the first eight form a gathering, bound into the front of the Book of Fermoy: the remaining fourteen I had the good fortune to identify in one of the Stowe MSS. (R.I.A. Library, D.3.1). The folios measure on an average $10 \cdot 5 \times 8$ ins. There are 31 lines of writing in each column, and two columns on each page. The Fermoy fragment, and the first two folios of the Stowe fragment, are written upon in a coarse, bold hand, using very black ink and a broad-pointed pen on which the writer leans heavily. Dr. Best identifies the handwriting as that of Adam ō Cianāin of Lisgoole, County Fermanagh, whose *obit* is recorded in the *Annals of the Four Masters* at A.D. 1373. On the third folio of the Stowe fragment (fol. 11 of the complete book), in column a, after line 27, the handwriting appears to change abruptly: but careful comparison shows that the same scribe continues to work, using a pen with a finer point. On the same folio, however, column δ, after line 4, there is actually a change of scribe. s^2 F has a rounder, and, on the whole, a better style of handwriting than s^1 F. At first he decorates his capital letters with blobs of colour, though not on the later pages: he is fond of ending them with crudely drawn animal heads, which s^1 F never does. After the change of the pen in the hand of s^1 F, the number of lines in the column increases to 39. The whole work ends abruptly at 22 γ 10, with the reign of Eochaid Uairches in the "Roll of the Kings." The remainder of column γ, and the whole of column δ, of this folio were left blank, suggesting that the copy stopped at this point because the remainder was lost from √F: an irrelevant anecdote about King David and a beggar has at some later time been scribbled into the empty space.[5] An additional leaf, possibly part of the earliest binding of the book, originally blank, is also now covered with scribbling. As in the case of L, the *recto* of the first folio of F is in a very bad condition from wear, tear, and dirt. It was cleaned chemically during the progress of the present work by Professor Ditchburn, of T.C.D., with the satisfactory result that most of the text, which I had abandoned as hopelessly illegible, proved recoverable. It should be noted that the folios in the Stowe MS., as at present bound, are misplaced. The first, which follows immediately after the last folio of·the Fermoy fragment, is bound in as the seventh folio of the Stowe book.[6] The text carries on from there to the present end of the volume (eight folios): then continues on the prefixed folios in this order— 6, 1, 2, 3, 4, 5.[7]

Of the lost MSS. of the First Redaction, *Q and *X, which are of considerable critical importance, we shall speak when occasion arises. *Q was the copy used by ∞ R³, *X was used by one of the glossators of R².

The redaction called *Mīniugud,* which is a form of R¹, is more fully discussed below.

The Second Redaction.

The majority of the MSS. of LG belong to R². These are V, E, P, R, D, Λ, and A.

---

[5] Edited by S. H. O'Grady from two other MSS.; see *Mélusine* iv (1888), col. 163. See also K. Meyer in *Arch. für Celt. Lex.* iii 321 for a different version.

[6] The bottom margin of this leaf has been clipped off, apparently to remove some scribbled matter: there is similar scribbling on the bottom margin of the following folio, *recto.*

[7] In references to this MS. in the present edition, the folios are numbered in their *true* order, not in the haphazard order in which they are bound.

V, a MS. in the Stowe collection (R.I.A. Library), now divided into three volumes (V^1 = D.5.1, V^2 = D.4.1, and V^3 = D.1.3). V^1 consists of nine folios, with four columns of writing on each; size of leaves 11.8×8 ins., 51–55 lines of writing in each column. At the beginning there is an elaborately coloured interlaced monogram of the word IN: and throughout there are well-drawn initial letters. The whole is written in a beautiful neat hand, which, however, is rather cramped, and not perfectly easy to decipher. The MS. has undergone extensive re-inking, and it is not always certain that the restorer has done his work accurately. At the top of folio 1a of V^1 there are two faint, worn lines of writing in Gothic lettering—apparently a library mark; under ultra-violet light they seem to read *Monasterii Insi Putraic*, but they are too far gone to yield with assurance even to that powerful solvent of palæographical difficulties. V^2 has eight, V^3 six folios: they are on the whole better preserved than V^1, which has suffered severely from wear. In V^2 the writing stops abruptly at 8 δ 9 (end of the poem *Fland for Ērind hi tigh*), after which the rest of the column is blank. We must infer that a gathering had been lost from $\sqrt{V}$, and that the scribe of V was unable to find means of filling the lacuna.[8] The gap extends to the end of the 13th quatrain of the poem *Gāedel glas* in Min: with the 14th quatrain the text resumes abruptly, on the first folio of V^3, and runs on to the end of *Ēriu ardinis na rīgh*, which finishes the MS. There are coloured initials in V^1 and V^2, but not in V^3: but the style of the writing, the size of the folios, and the number of lines in the column, leave no room for doubt that the three volumes originally formed one book. Fragments of other books, in vellum and in paper, quite irrelevant in contents, are now bound up with the two later volumes.

---

[8] The lacuna does not exist in the closely cognate copy A; the text here runs on intact over rather more than 8 leaves of A which have no equivalent in V. This clearly shows that A is not, as has been supposed, a transcript of V: it must be derived from $\overset{\circ}{V}$ V at latest. In μV the Roll of the Kings originally stopped at Sīrna Sōeglach, and has been continued in a different but contemporary hand: μA knows nothing of this, and breaks off at Sīrna—another demonstration that the two MSS. are not in ''mother-and-daughter'' relationship.

E, a manuscript once bound up in separate folios scattered through a miscellany of scraps class-marked E.3.5 in T.C.D. Library (Gwynn's *Catalogue*, no. 1433, p. 308): now collected once more into a single volume, and class-marked E.3.5., no. 2. It contains 16 folios, measuring 11·4 × 8·25 ins., with four columns of 48 lines of writing on each. There is hardly any ornamentation. The handwriting was recognised long ago by O'Curry (*Battle of Magh Leana*, p. 35, footnote) as that of Tōrna ō Maeil-Chonaire, poet and historian to the earls of Desmond at the beginning of the fifteenth century: and this is confirmed by a scribal note at the bottom of folio 2 γ. He wrote carelessly; haplographies are frequent, usually corrected in the margin by himself or by a later reader. Many of the lenited letters, which were not dotted by the original scribe, have been dotted by a later meddler. On the other hand, there are many good readings, and the MS. is of considerable critical importance. A note at the bottom of fo. 9 verso claims ownership of the book for Muirges *ruadh* ua Maoil-Chonaire (a different person from the scribe of D), "wherever it may be found."

P, formerly in the Phillips Collection at Cheltenham, now in the National Library of Ireland, class-marked P. 10266. It has been described by Whitley Stokes,[9] who has, however, not observed that the fragment of LG (which he does not appear to have identified as such) is only by accident a part of the book. It is a single quaternion, 10 × 7·3 ins., prefixed to a fragment from another MS. with folios of a rather larger size. Only the first two folios contain LG material, and there does not appear ever to have been any more of the text. The writing is minute, running across the whole page in a single column of 41 lines. Folio 1 *recto* is utterly illegible, the whole page having been reduced with gallic acid and dirt to a uniform dead brownish black. A large monogram of IN, extending down the whole height of the page on the left-hand side, and followed (apparently) by PRI, in unusually large characters, can be traced; but nothing further. The rest of

---

[9] *Martyrology of Oengus* (Henry Bradshaw Soc. edition), p. ix ff.

the text is clear, extending from ⁊ *nī derna fāilte* (¶ 5A) to *risin mac mbec rugad* (¶ 119), where the scribe ceased abruptly from his work. Some parts of Folio 1 *verso* (the first nine lines and the poem No. 1) have been re-inked, not quite accurately. Though so fragmentary, the text is useful, as it helps considerably in the decipherment of some obscure passages in VE, the only other MSS. which have preserved the first folio of the text of R². There is no colophon: but Arabic figures are freely used in the text, and this and other indications suggest a date of about 1480–1520.

R, the only MS. of the older versions not in Dublin, is an early fifteenth-century copy contained in the well-known miscellany, Rawl. B. 512, in the Bodleian Library. This MS. has been described, and its contents catalogued, by Whitley Stokes[10]; and it is here needless to go over the same ground. The text of LG occupies foll. 76 *recto*–100 *verso*. The beginning of the book is lost: calculation shows that two leaves are gone; possibly three, if (as is improbable) the text contained the Nel-Moses pericope (¶ 118 ff.) and the long poem V written out in full. Another leaf has disappeared between ¶¶ 272–288. These defects took place before the addition of pagination to the MS., which ignores them. Two folios are numbered 76, the second being distinguished as 76 A: the first two folios are transposed in the binding. There are two columns upon each page, with 37 lines of writing in each column. At the end of the text of R² there comes the copy of *Mīniugud* here called μR.

D, class-marked Stowe D.4.3 in the R.I.A. Library. This is a vellum MS., the pages being 9×7.5 inches, with two columns of writing upon every page except the *recto* of fol. 7, and the lower part of the *recto* of fol. 21, in which the writing runs across the page with about 56 letters in each line. The book seems to have been exposed to fire at some time: the lower and outer edges, and especially the lower

---

[10] *Tripartite Life of St. Patrick* (Rolls Series), vol. i, p. xiv ff.

outer angles, of most of the folios are badly scorched, and the writing on the parts affected is often difficult to read. The lines of writing are very irregularly disposed; so far as I have counted them, they range in number from 29 to 41 in the column. Appropriately to this irregularity, the handwriting is poor, sometimes not very legible. Forty-two folios remain: two have been lost from the beginning, and the end is also imperfect. The MS. is of considerable critical value, and has some remarkable readings[11]: the scribe's name, Muirges (or Muirgius) mac Pāidīn, appears in scribbles at 17 γ bottom, 25 β 14, and 35 δ bottom. In the last place only has he given his father's name, and this has been partly burnt away. He is a grumbler: at the bottom of 8 γ, in a note now difficult to decipher, he appears to complain that his ruler is too broad; on 11 γ he is troubled because his light is bad; at 17 γ he has mislaid his *cailc*, that is, presumably, the pumice with which he smoothed the surface of his vellum; and on 11 *recto* the shears of a bookbinder have silenced a reference derogatory, as we may suppose, to his parchment. In the present work the two lost initial leaves are counted in, in references to this MS.; the first extant folio being numbered "3," in accordance with the old pagination. In the MS. a new pagination, starting from the first extant folio, has been substituted in roughly written numerals, the old pagination being sometimes either scratched out or written over.

The scribe was certainly the Muirges mac Pāidīn ua Maoil-Chonaire who made the transcript of the Book of Fenagh in the R.I.A. Library in 1517, and who died in 1543. Though the writing in the Fenagh volume is much more careful, comparison of the two books leaves no room for doubt that they come from the same hand. This being so, we may infer that this MS. is the same as "The Book of

---

[11] Among these are a number of interpolations, evidently borrowed from a copy of R[1], and all marked in the margin of the page as *Slicht Libuir na Huidri*, "An extract from (literally, [following in] The track of) *Lebor na Huidri*." This records the fact that a copy of LG, in the R[1] Redaction, was included among the (now missing) contents of that MS.

Baile ui Maoil-Chonaire, written by Muirghes mac Paidīn
ui Maoil-Chonaire out of Leabhar na Huidhri,'' which
O Clēirigh specifies as one of the sources of his own work.
The marginal notes referred to in the footnote have misled
him into supposing that the whole book was copied from LU.
See further on the MS. A, below.

Λ, the first text in *The Book of Lecan* (R.I.A. Library,
23.P.2). The impending publication of a facsimile of this
important volume makes it unnecessary to describe it here:
in the published catalogue of the Royal Irish Academy's
collection of MSS. there is a full analysis of its contents.
This text is at the beginning of the book, and has lost the
first nine folios: they were already gone in 1724.[12] In
consequence the copy begins abruptly in the section relating
to the FirBolg (in the middle of the poem appended to
¶ 292). The complete text, including the copy of *Min.*
appended to R² (here called $\mu\Lambda$), covered 30 folios, with two
columns on each page, containing 41–55 lines of writing, so
far as they have been tested. It ends in the middle of
column 30 δ, with the following colophon, repeated immediately below by a later hand in a different ink: *Finit.
Adam o Cuirnin do sgrib do Gilla Isu mac Firbissigh .i.
d'ollam o Fiachrach, Anno. Do', M° CCCC° xuiij°.* "It
endeth. Adam ō Cuirnīn wrote it, for Gilla Isu mac Fir
Bisigh, the man of learning of the Ui Fiachrach, A.D. 1418.''
This is the most exactly dated copy of the text which we
possess. Many of the folios have become semi-transparent
by contamination with some greasy substance, and the writing
on the one side shows through to the other, making decipherment difficult.

A is the only extant paper MS. (excluding some eighteenth
century copies, mentioned below) of any of the pre- O Clēirigh
redactions. It is Stowe A.2.4 in the R.I.A. Library, and

---

[12] Bishop Nicolson, *Irish Historical Library*, p. 38. The leaves from
this MS. now bound into H 2 17, in the library of T.C.D., are not
those missing from the beginning of the codex, as is stated by an
oversight in the catalogue of the T.C.D. Irish Manuscripts, p. 112.

apparently belongs to the seventeenth century.   There are
47 leaves, $7 \cdot 8 \times 5 \cdot 8$ ins., some of them much tattered.   I
have collated this copy sufficiently to assure myself that it is
a direct transcript of D.   It reproduces slavishly the ortho-
graphical and other peculiarities of D, except for the not
infrequent mistakes of its own copyist.   Some of these mistakes can be explained, on reference to D, by obscurities in
the script of the earlier MS.   A is imperfect at both ends,
and has no independent value for the criticism of the text:
it has just the slight importance that in a few cases it does
not reproduce corrections that have been made *secunda manu*
in D, suggesting that these may have belonged to a time later
than its own transcription.   But *s*A was so incompetent that
we cannot be sure even of this: he may have overlooked them,
or omitted them intentionally.   In the present edition of LG,
A has been left out of consideration altogether.

Assuming that D was one of the sources followed by
O Cléirigh, A was probably prepared for his use—not, however, *by* him, as it is not in his handwriting.   Some leaves
of a different text, which though roughly scribbled appear
actually to be in O'Clery's writing, are bound up in the same
volume.

A lost MS. of this redaction, *Z, will be referred to as
occasion arises.   It was the copy of R^2 used by a *glossator*
of R^3 (*g* R^3).   The Manuscript of R^2 used by the *compiler*
of R^3 (∞ R^3) we shall call *W.

The Third Redaction.

R^3 is contained in two MSS., B and M; and an important
fragment of a third, H, is extant.

B, *The Book of Ballymote* (R.I.A. Library, 23 P 12).   In
this codex LG occupies folios 8–34: on each page there are
two columns of writing, with 55–57 lines in each.   Folios 9,
and 24–30 inclusive, are missing.   The latter defect is of long
standing; but folio 9 must have been lost after the middle
of the eighteenth century, when two transcripts of the text

were made from this MS. One of these, written in 1728 by Richard Tipper, here called β, is fairly good, though not perfect; and it is of great value for restoring the text of the missing folio. It is labelled on the binding "Book of Bally-mote," and class-marked H.2.4 in T.C.D. Library (Gwynn's Catalogue, 1295). The other is apparently lost, but two copies were made from it: β^1, in a MS. written by Tadhg O Neachtain, in or about the year 1745, and dubbed upon its title-page *Psaltair na Teamhrach,* "The Psalter of Tara," though the binding is more soberly labelled "Miscellanea Hibernica, transcribed by T. O'Naghtan"; also in T.C.D. Library (H.1.15, Gwynn's Catalogue, 1289): and β^2, a pitifully illiterate production, class-marked Stowe D.3.2 in the R.I.A. Library. These two MSS. share a considerable number of mistakes and peculiar spellings, showing their descent from a common more or less inaccurate original ($\sqrt{\beta^{12}}$) interposed between them and the ancestral B[13]; and they are both so much inferior to β, that their only use is to corroborate some of its peculiar readings, and to show that these were really to be found in the missing leaf of B. In very few cases can we accept a divergent reading of $\sqrt{\beta^{12}}$ in preference to β. Where we have B intact, these three copies are useless, and are here ignored. Folios 24–30 were lost from B before any of them was made: β does not attempt to supply the deficiency; but $\sqrt{\beta^{12}}$ has filled it by copying from the still extant μV, for collation shows beyond the possibility of doubt that $s\sqrt{\beta^{12}}$ has here and there been misled by peculiarities in μV (misspellings, a badly set-out *cor fā chasān*, imperfectly legible writing, etc.). The version of this missing portion in β^1 and β^2 is, therefore, of no value.

---

[13] I allow this to stand, because it is still possible as a statement of the facts: but on subjecting my collations to a final revision, when I considered the relationship between these two MSS. more closely, and noted a number of places where a peculiar error in β^2 could be accounted for by careless penmanship in β^1, I became more inclined to regard β^1 as a direct (though poor) copy of B, and β^2 a yet worse copy of β^1. The hypothethical $\sqrt{\beta^{12}}$ thus disappears altogether, and β^2 loses all the little value that it might have had.

M is the second text in *The Book of Lecan,* occupying folios 264–312.[14] It is a very peculiar text, having some interpolations (notably the story of Partholon's faithless wife Delgnat) not found in any other ancient version. √M was apparently imperfect : certainly the latter half of the "Roll of the Kings" was missing from it, and *s* M was compelled to supply the deficiency by a makeshift adaptation of a version of the saga of the *Bōrama* Tribute, differing in some respects from that in the Book of Leinster. The important lacuna in the first section of LG, to be described later, was also a serious imperfection in √M. The problems connected with this copy must, however, be considered as they arise.

The copyist of M was working against time. Even when he was called away for a few minutes, a deputy (s^2 M) took his place, and wrote during his absence. The text is, so to speak, punctuated by short groups of lines in the very distinctive handwriting of s^2 M, which alternate with the work of the main scribe (s^1 M), changing sometimes even in the middle of a line. There is never any crowding or overrunning, as would be the case if s^2 M were a later scribe, filling in gaps that for any reason had been left by a predecessor. Presumably the writers of M could not obtain the use of √M for more time than was just sufficient for their work. As in such a case they would not have leisure to hunt for extraneous matter, it seems probable that the interpolations and other peculiarities of M were all transferred to that MS. bodily from √M. It is further possible that they were deprived of it before they were able to copy the whole of the Roll of the Kings, and that this, rather than a deficiency in √M, is the explanation of the peculiarity noticed in the preceding paragraph.

H is a fragment of five folios, $13\cdot5 \times 9\cdot6$ ins., with two columns on each page, and 56 lines of writing in the column. It is bound into a volume of miscellaneous fragments (H.2.15, no. 1, in T.C.D., Gwynn's Catalogue, 1316).

---

[14] Throughout this edition the old *foliation* of the Book of Lecan, in the upper right-hand corner of the *recto* of each folio, is used for reference, instead of the more recent *pagination* in square brackets in the bottom margin.

Four of these folios belong to the first section of LG, and contain matter nowhere else extant. The fifth has a version of the end of the Nemed section, cognate with that in K, and differing profoundly from every other text of this part of the book. With this the H copy of LG appears to have ended, the remainder of the folio being occupied with other matter. At the end of this folio there is a colophon which would seem to date the MS. to some time before 1252 (see Gwynn's Catalogue, p. 91), but the interpretation of the note is uncertain, and the date seems, if anything, too early for the language and especially the orthography of the MS. It is the pages, not the folios, in this miscellany which are numbered (as under, in pencil).[15] The first portion of LG occupies pp. 97–104, but the folios are not in their right order—they should run thus, 103–104, 97–98, 101–102, 99–100. The Nemed fragment is in the first column of page 67. About one-third of the upper portion of folio 103–104 has been torn away and lost.

In preparing for publication the three prose texts, I have chosen L, V, and B as the standard copies of R[1], R[2], and R[3] respectively; and the book is printed as it appears in those MSS., except where some other fills a lacuna, or corrects an obvious error. Numerals, as well as the ordinary abbreviations and contractions, are expanded silently; and the marking of long vowels, which is quite haphazard in the MSS., is reduced to some sort of order (with horizontal strokes). In the tables of variants, and in places where a passage depends on one MS. only, the marking of prolongation (with accent-like strokes), is reproduced as in the original[16]: except on the

---

[15] There is an older, now obsolete, pagination in ink, which we may ignore.

[16] In a few cases marks of prolongation, inserted before I decided to give without such interference passages depending on a single MS., have evaded deletion and appear on the printed page. I have allowed them to stand, to avoid needless proof-correction: but these apart, the absence of such marks will be a useful indication to the reader that the text before him survives in one MS. only. In *English* contexts, meticulous accentuation has not been considered necessary.

letter *i,* where the accent-like mark is usually nothing more than a distinguishing mark, like the dot in ordinary print. This is here left out. I also omit the *punctum delens* placed over "eclipsed" letters. By repeated collations an effort has been made to attain to the ideal of recording every variant, however trifling, presented by the manuscripts. The three MSS. specified have been chosen, less because they are the best copies of their respective redactions than because they are the most complete. In fact, F probably is nearer to ∞ R^1 than L; and the late MSS. of R^2, DER, often give readings preferable to those in V. M is admittedly more complete than B, but it has too many eccentric readings and interpolations to justify its being selected as the standard for R^3.

The verse texts cannot be classified into "redactions," and they have to be treated in a different way. Of these I have endeavoured to construct a text, giving the reader as full an *apparatus criticus* of variant readings as possible, to enable him to test, and, it may be, to improve upon it. I have not, however, attempted to standardize the orthography, which would involve an interference with the testimony of the MSS. that I felt would be too drastic. The text does not need to be treated like a Greek classical composition, where it is of the first importance to recover the exact words of the literary master who wrote it. The ideal which I have set before myself is the humbler one, of making it possible for a scholar to whom the MSS. are inaccessible to reconstruct the text of any one of them, except in the matter of abbreviations and marks of vowel prolongation. To have attempted to reproduce all of these would have more than doubled the bulk of the lists of *variae lectiones,* with no very apparent advantage. This is not to say that they are unimportant: on the contrary, I have gleaned some valuable hints on the affiliation of MSS. from a comparison of such extraneous matters as the ornamentation of initial capital letters, and the abbreviations or other peculiarities of the caligraphy (or cacography) of individual words.

In this connexion it may be said here that it is especially interesting to compare the initial letters scattered throughout V with those in D. In V they are neatly drawn and coloured,

EXAMPLES OF INITIAL LETTERS FROM D AND V.

though in design they show only too clearly that the art to which they belong was already moribund or dead : in D they are badly drawn, in an ink outline only. But it is obvious that they are the same designs. As D cannot possibly be a copy of V, it is clear that the two MSS. derive their ornamentation, like their text, from a common original. This fact, which gives us a new criterion for determining the affinity of manuscripts, may be illustrated by the specimens here reproduced,[16a] from tracings made with the kind consent of the Council of the R.I.A.

O'Clery's Redaction.

K has already been published as far as the *Roll of the Kings,* and need not here be repeated. It is of little critical value, having been much manipulated editorially, but there is enough to show that its compiler had access to MSS. no longer extant. He has a long version of the Partholón-Delgnat story, differing from that in M almost throughout : and his Nemed text, though it has affinities with the unique text in H, displays a like independence. The chief importance of this version is its rich glossarial matter.

The last degeneration of the text is found in two nineteenth century MSS. in the British Museum (Egerton, 101, 105), which give us O'Clery's version with some of the difficulties cut out and easy bits of Keating's History substituted.

The Contents of the Book.

The book in its present form, in all the principal redactions, falls into ten separate and independent sections, as under—

I. From the Creation to the Dispersal of the Nations.
II. The Ancestors of the Gaedil.
III–VII. The successive invasions of Cessair, Partholón, Nemed, the Fir Bolg, and the Tūatha Dē Danann.
VIII. The invasion of the sons of Mīl, *i.e.* of the Gaedil.
IX. The Roll of the Kings before Christianity.
X. The Roll of the Kings after Christianity.

[16a] The small ᚷ, to the left, and the upper O, O, R are from V; the lower O, O, R and the large ᚷ are from the corresponding paragraphs in D. (Notice the broken lines and loose ends in the first of

—and notwithstanding the profound differences in detail between the different redactions, they agree in the main lines of their contents.

Prof. A. C. Clark, in a work to whose teaching I gladly acknowledge my indebtedness,[17] has laid it down as a principle that "a text is like a traveller who goes from one inn to another, losing an article of luggage at each halt." By this he means, that the text sheds passages piecemeal as it is copied from manuscript to manuscript; so that when delivered to its reader at the end of a succession of transcriptions, it is shorter—often considerably so—than when it left the author's hand, to run the gauntlet of scribal carelessness, sleepiness, incompetence, and laziness. Other things being equal, a longer text is, therefore, to be preferred, by the critical editor, to a shorter text. That this principle is sound when applied to classical literature no one who has made a careful study of Prof. Clark's work can doubt: but it breaks down when applied to Irish texts. In Ireland, the philomath, eager to air his stock of erudite inanity, early made his baleful appearance. To adapt the formula of Prof. Clark's analogy, an Irish text is like a traveller who, as he passes from inn to inn, stuffs his portmanteau with the china dogs, the waxen fruits, the crochet-work antimacassars, and all the other futilities with which his successive lodgings are adorned. It is quite possible that when LG was drawn up by its first compiler, it was not longer than what would fill three or four sheets of notepaper. It has grown to its present dimensions by an extraordinary accretion of glosses, interpolations, and other amplifications. Certainly the old canon of New Testament criticism, *brevior lectio praeferenda verbosiori*, is here applicable!

It does not require any great insight to see that the book is in reality a combination of two originally independent documents. The block of material, sections III to VII, has been interpolated; sections II and VIII run on continuously, and were no doubt at one time in immediate connexion. If we cut the interpolated sections out, we find ourselves left

---

these letters, showing that the artist, though a fair draughtsman, did not understand the principles which regulated designs such as this.)

[17] *The Descent of Manuscripts* (Oxford, 1918), at p. 23.

with a *History of the Gaedil,* based upon the history of the Children of Israel as it is set forth in the Old Testament, or (perhaps more probably) in some consecutive history para-phrased therefrom.   The parallelism, which can be displayed in tabular form as below, is too close to be accidental.

Old Testament.	*Lebor Gabāla.*

The biblical history from the Creation to the Sons of Noah is borrowed by the Irish historians : after which—

Shem is selected and his genealogy is followed out . . .	Japhet is selected and his genealogy is followed out . . .
until we reach Terah and his son Abram, upon whose family the historian specializes . . .	until we reach Nēl and his son Gāedel, upon whose family the historian specializes . . .
down to the two wives and the numerous sons of Jacob.	down to the two wives and the numerous sons of Mīl.
A servitude in Egypt begins with a friendly invitation from an Egyptian king . . .	An oppression in Egypt begins with a friendly invitation from an Egyptian king . . .
and the children of Israel are delivered by the adopted son of an Egyptian princess.	and the children of Nēl are delivered by the son-in-law of the Egyptian king. This deliverer meets and almost joins forces with his prototype Moses.[18]
They wander for a long time, beset by enemies . . .	They wander for a long time, beset by enemies . . .
and sojourn at a mountain (Sinai) where they receive the doom that not they but their children shall reach the Promised Land; so they wander . . .	and sojourn at a mountain (Riphi) where they receive the doom that not they but their children shall reach the Promised Land; so they wander . . .
till their leader sees the Promised Land from the top of a mountain afar off.	till their leader sees the Promised Land from the top of a tower afar off.

[18] Some portions of this incident are probably due to later inter-polation: it is in essence, however, at least as old as Nennius.

Old Testament—con.	*Lebor Gabāla*—con.
He dies: but his successor conducts the people to a subjugation of the former inhabitants of Canaan, amid circumstances of marvel and mystery . . .	He dies: but his successors conduct the people to a subjugation of the former inhabitants of Ireland, amid circumstances of marvel and mystery . . .
and to a successful colonization of the country.	and to a successful colonization of the country.
The history then concludes with a brief record of the successive kings (beginning with a partition of the country), allotting in most cases not more than a single paragraph to individual kings.	The history then concludes with a brief record of the successive kings (beginning with a partition of the country), allotting in most cases not more than a single paragraph to individual kings.

We infer that the book originally described only a single "taking"—that of the Celtic Irish, to whom the author himself belonged, and in whom he was chiefly interested. This is why *Gabāla*, in the singular number, still remains in the title of the book: it is not the "Book of Takings of Ireland," but "The Book of The Taking."

The intruded matter (§§ III–VII) may have had some historical basis, but much of it partakes rather of the nature of a *Theogonia*: see the introductions prefixed to each of the sections, where their relation to mythology and history is discussed. We shall see later that this group of sections is itself capable of further analysis into separate component elements.

These different histories appear to have been in existence, and (even if their combination had already been effected) to have been still available in their separate form, when Nennius wrote his *Historia Britonum*, about the end of the eighth century.[19] He must have been able to refer to a literary source of information about the Pre-Milesian invasions: but for the history of the Milesians themselves he apparently had

---

[19] *Historia Nennii*, ed. Petrie in *Materials for the History of Great Britain*, p. 56: ed. Faral in *La légende arthurienne* (Paris, 1929), vol. iii, pp. 11, 12. For convenience I assume the historical existence of "Nennius": after all, *someone* must have written the book which bears his name. Also for convenience I call him by the old-established form of his name, rather than by the less familiar "Nemnius."

to depend on the oral information conveyed to him by persons described as *peritissimi Scottorum* (and condemned by some of his glossators with the words, *nulla certa historia originis Scottorum continetur*). His abstract of the Pre-Milesian invasions is analysed at a later stage of our work; the only point about it which we need notice here is the single word "Damhoctor"[20]—which Nennius wrongly supposes to be a personal name, denoting the leader of one of the invading troops whose progeny was supposed to be still in Ireland at the time when Nennius wrote. But evidently it is nothing but the Irish for "a company of eight persons": this misunderstood word is a valuable testimony that for *this* part of the history Nennius had a written text in the Irish language at his elbow.

The Relation between the Redactions.

The relationship existing between (*a*) the Manuscripts and (*b*) the Redactions has been discussed by Thurneysen[21] and Van Hamel.[22] I may say that I refrained from making a close study of these most important contributions to the subject till I had formed my own conclusions, so as to arrive at an independent opinion.

The very simple *stemma* of the MSS. drawn up by Van Hamel (*op. cit.*, p. 115) is hardly an adequate representation of their inter-relationship. The facts, which are more complex, must be allowed to develop themselves as we proceed: for the moment it is sufficient to advise readers of Van Hamel's most valuable study, that the *Mīniugud* appendix of V (which Van Hamel calls "S") is *not* lost: and that Λ (which Van Hamel calls "Lec I") is not a daughter MS. of his S, but, if we may further develop the genealogical terminology, a sort of "niece." Two of the many proofs of this have been given already. Likewise, F cannot be considered a direct copy of L; in many places it

---

[20] We need not trouble ourselves with the variant reading *Clamhoctor* adopted in Petrie's edition.

[21] "Zur irischen Handschriften und Litteraturdenkmälern, zweite Serie": *Abhandl.* der k. Gesellschaft der Wissenschaften zu Göttingen, neue Folge, xiv, no. 3, 1913.

[22] "On Lebor Gabāla." Z.C.P. x (1915), p. 97.

preserves an older and purer text. Moreover, V (Van Hamel's S) is not an original text, but a faulty copy; in some places even the late MSS., E and P, give preferable readings.

As to the Redactions, both Thurneysen and Van Hamel recognise the five different versions, R^1, R^2, R^3, Min, and K, as they are here called. Thurneysen calls them A, B, C, B III, and D respectively (B II being the synchronistic matter appended to R^2). Van Hamel uses a similar symbolism—A, Ba, C, Bb, D. Their distribution of the MSS. among the redactions is the same as mine, except that Thurneysen counts F among the MSS. of C ($= R^3$). This Van Hamel corrects, and Thurneysen would probably himself adopt the correction after another examination of the text. But he is not without justification: for R^3 is based upon a lost MS. of R^1, here called *Q, and F is in many respects much more closely akin to *Q than to L, the MS. adopted by all of us as typical of R^1.

Van Hamel follows Thurneysen's notation to avoid confusion; but he objects to it on account of the secondary place which it assigns to the B-group (R^2). This redaction is, in his opinion, of primary importance for the history of the text, bringing us nearer to the original form than any other. "B" he considers to be fuller than "A"; and, although he admits that neither is a copy of the other, he regards "A" as a mere abstract of the common original, omitting, as irrelevant, details which from the first were included in the text, and which "B" preserves.

But on the principle laid down above (p. xxvi), in dealing with an Irish text, the fuller it is of extraneous detail, the more likely it is to be *remote* from the original version.

As for Min, appended to the three R^2 MSS. V, Λ, R, it is obviously cognate with "A" (R^1); but it is equally obvious that it is neither a copy nor an abstract of "A," but an independent version. Apparently it represents a stage of the R^1 tradition slightly earlier than that contained in the extant MSS. of R^1; but it certainly belongs to that group.

What, then, is the relation between these versions? As I understand it, it is as follows :—

We start with a *Liber Occupationis Hiberniae*, a sort of

quasi-historical romance, with no backing either of history or tradition; an artificial composition, professing to narrate the origin of the Gaedil onward from the Creation of the World (or the Flood), their journeyings, and their settlement in *their* "promised land," Ireland. This production was a slavish copy, we might almost say a parody, of the Biblical story of the Children of Israel. The germ which suggested the idea to the writer was undoubtedly the passage in Orosius (I. 2. 81), wrongly understood as meaning that Ireland was first seen from Brigantia in Spain, where (*ibid.*, § 71) there was a very lofty watch-tower. This suggested a reminiscence of Moses, overlooking the Land of Promise from Mount Pisgah : and the author set himself to work out the parallel, forward and backward. Incidentally Orosius gave trouble to Irish topographers, ancient and modern, by speaking of an Irish river *Scena*, setting them on a hunt for a non-existent *Inber Scēne*. As *sc* conventionally represents the sound of *sh* (compare the Vulgate Judges, xii, 6, where the Hebrew word *shibbōleth* is rendered *scibboleth*), we must pronounce this word as *Shena*, and it is then easily recognised as Orosius' version of *Sinann* (genitive *Sinna*) or "Shannon." Further, we must assume that this quasi-Israelite history was written *in Latin*.[23]

Next we must postulate a separate text, compounded out of a number of separate sagas (or rather a number of varieties of one saga), but with a much better claim to enshrine genuine traditional (though not necessarily historical) material. This document still existed as an independent entity in the time of Nennius—or, to be more exact, Nennius had access to a manuscript, possibly of some antiquity, which preserved it, or some of it, in its independent form. It was a brief treatise on the pre-Gaedilic inhabitants of Ireland : and as it contained the expression *dāmh ochtair*, "a troop of eight persons," which Nennius mistook for a proper name, it must have been written in Irish. It does not

---

[23] A clear proof of translation from Latin is presented by some of the place-names, which have been transferred unintelligently into their Irish context in the accusative case. Thus in ¶ 156, to cite but one of many examples, *sech Albaniam . . . sech Ghothiam* must have a Latin original behind them.

appear to have contained the stories of Cessair and the other antediluvian colonists.

Liber Occupationis soon began to be taken seriously : and it was inevitable that the small tract just mentioned should become combined with it, in order to make its historical record more complete. This changed its character, turning it into a history of Ireland, rather than a history of the people then dominant in the country. Nevertheless its title remained unchanged : it was still *Liber Occupationis*. The interpolation spoilt the logical form of the history : for its readers, having at last after many vicissitudes reached Ireland, were now obliged to jump suddenly back to the beginning, both in time and in space, in order to follow out the second strand which had thus been interwoven with the narrative. But the earlier invasions were still of subordinate interest, and for a time were most likely differentiated by their language from the main current of the Latin story. If we could be sure that the opening paragraphs of Min have not been drastically compressed, the scanty notice there found of the earlier invasions would very closely resemble the form of this part of the book when it had reached this stage of the development.

At about the same time, the Cessair narrative (an old flood-myth mixed up with some *Dindsenchas* material) was committed to writing, but whether in Latin or in Irish is not very clear : presently it found a place in front of the interpolation. See further the Introduction to that section.

The history of the text thereafter divided into two streams. Two schools of history, retaining its framework, each of them working independently of, and often at variance with, the other, added new material as they found it.

The next stage was inaugurated by translation from Latin into Irish. The first translation to be made was undoubtedly from the text underlying Min. The translator headed his work, very naturally, "An explanation of *Liber Occupationis*." By now the historical nature of the book was a fully accepted tradition : it was regarded as a true record of the past of Ireland and of her people : and in view of its importance it was considered desirable to make it accessible to students whose Latin was unequal to a study of the original text. The associated poems, at this stage not yet incorporated with the written text, were of course in Irish from the first.

A generation or two later, the ''A'' text, with the additional material which had accumulated in the interval, was translated again (R¹); as was also, now for the first time, the ''B'' text (R²).

This reconstruction explains all the phenomena completely :

(1) The parallel ''Israel'' and ''Ireland'' story.

(2) The short Nennius text, based on an original in Irish, enumerating the earlier invasions, but ignoring the Milesian colony.

(3) The mention of a single invasion in the title, though a large number of invasions are enumerated in the text.

(4) The general similarity of Min and R¹, though the verbal differences forbid us to regard either as a copy of the other.

(5) The word *miniugud*, ''explanation'' in the title of Min.

(6) The similarity of framework in R¹ and R², though the two texts are so profoundly different that they can never have had a common Irish original.

It may be further suggested that the Latin preface to Min, where a parallel is drawn between Ireland and Adam's Paradise, and where there are obvious reminiscences of Orosius, is actually the preface of the original *Liber Occupationis*, at least in the form to which it had evolved at the time when the translation of Min was made. It was a preface, not an intrinsic part of the text: and subsequent translators passed it over altogether.

The next phase began when some owner of an R² text, no longer extant, got hold of a copy of Min. Though R² contains matter not in Min or R¹, the contrary is also true: and R² is especially unsatisfactory (from the point of view of a historian who wants to know everything) in the section containing the Roll of the Kings. I do not agree that this section, in its earliest form, is an addition to the original text. I believe that a germ of this record formed an essential part of the text from the first, and that it developed with the rest. The postulated scholar sought to remedy the defects of his version by appending an abbreviated version of Min to his copy of R². Where Min contained matter already in R², he left it out, merely writing *ut supra dixi* or the like: this is enough to show that Min, as we have it, is not independent

d

of the text to which it is appended. The MS. to which this addition was made we may call $\sqrt{A \wedge R}$. There is no evidence that either E or D was within its family, or ever possessed this supplementary appendix.

R^3 is the pastepot-and-scissors work of a man who anticipated the systematizing labour of Ō Clērigh. Vexed at the discrepancies between the two traditions, and having a considerable library at his disposal, he took a text of R^1 (*Q) and wrote it out with many interpolations, partly derived from R^2 (*W), partly from other sources. As we shall see, his MS. of R^1 was imperfect; it had lost the first page, as well as the Partholōn and Nemed sections.

K is also an artificial re-handling of the text. The biblical introduction is, of set purpose, swept away, and the successive invasions are arranged in a more logical order. This redaction is based on R^2 (D), though it shows some affinities with M; but the compiler *certainly* used a different copy of R^3, no longer extant, and he took arbitrary liberties with the text. There are many genealogical and other interpolations from sources outside the tradition.

It is my pleasant duty to express my acknowledgements to the Librarians and other officials of the Libraries in which the MSS. are preserved, for unfailing help and courtesy: to Professors Bergin and Eoin Mac Neill, Dr. R. I. Best, the Rev. Paul Grosjean, S.J., Dr. Myles Dillon, and Miss M. Joynt, for permitting me to consult them on various linguistic and other questions that arose during the progress of the work; to Professor R. W. Ditchburn, Trinity College, Dublin, for his unfailing interest and patience in the troublesome task of photographing illegible passages; to the lamented Provost M. R. James of Eton College, and to the Venerable Archdeacon Seymour, for valuable help in some of the questions on Apocrypha which arose in the criticism of the Biblical prolegomena in Part I; and to the Very Rev. Canon Boylan, LITT.D., for his great kindness in putting at my service a copy of the *Genesis* volume of that magnificent monument of scholarship and of typography, the Vatican edition of the Vulgate text of the Bible.

SECTION I.

FROM THE CREATION TO THE DISPERSAL OF THE NATIONS.

Introduction.

In accordance with the artificial scheme of *Liber Occupationis,* the history of the world from the Creation to the Tower of Babel is first recapitulated. The original form of the text was probably something like this :—

> "In the beginning God made heaven and earth. He gave the bailiffry of Heaven to Lucifer, of earth to Adam. Lucifer sinned and was cast into Hell. He was envious of Adam, for he was assured that Adam would take his place in Heaven. Whereupon he came and tempted Eve to sin, and Adam was driven out of Paradise. The children of Adam sinned thereafter, in that Cain slew Abel. Seth, the third son of Adam, is the ancestor of all the men of the world, for the Flood drowned the whole seed of Adam except Noah and his three sons, Shem, Ham, Japhet. Shem settled in Asia, Ham in Africa, Japhet in Europe. We Gaedil are descended from Japhet."

As we read the text in its present form, and compare the divergent versions, we realise that everything not contained in this bald summary must be a glossarial accretion.

This summary was drawn up before the Vulgate text of the Old Testament had become familiar in Ireland : certainly not later than the eighth century. The Biblical quotations are from an earlier text, as is shown in detail below, in the notes appended to each paragraph. The abbreviator of Min left out the Biblical portion of that version, so that it is lost to us : but it is still possible to recover something of the history of its evolution. We may safely presume that an early intrusion was ¶ 2 (in the form of a bare list of the works of Creation). ¶ 5 entered later; ¶ 6 was at first shorter than it is now; and the genealogical matter ¶ 7–10 developed gradually from very small beginnings. The document upon which two of the interpolations in ¶ 9 are based was early in existence, but they did not enter the text till a late stage of its formation.

Besides LF, the extant MSS. of R¹, I recognise two important MSS., now lost, which have had an influence on the development of the text. These are *Q, *X. Both of these were good copies: *X, I am inclined to think, on the whole the better of the two. *Q began with a highly ornate initial IN, which occupied a large part of the front page: and the lettering of the remainder of the page, if not of the folio, was of extra large size. Some reminiscences of this arrangement, which may be ultimately derived from *Q, appear in VP. LB also have the large initial IN, and M has got large letters in its first column: but as will appear presently, these latter are *not* survivals of the *Q tradition. *Q existed in a mutilated form down to the time of ∞ R³, and it formed the chief foundation of his work.

The history of the mutilation is very interesting. It is evident that √R² had lost its first folio. One of the owners of that MS., to repair the deficiency, tore out and appropriated the first folio of *Q: this made possible the palæographical influence suggested in the preceding paragraph. By a chance, this produced continuous sense with the beginning of the second folio of √R²; though the sense is absurd. Only in this way can we explain the fact that R¹ and R² are practically identical for the first few paragraphs, and then, with startling suddenness, fly apart rather than diverge, and never again have a paragraph in common. Even the verse-extracts are often set in different contexts. It also explains the further significant fact that at the point where the texts part company, a statement is made in R², inconsistent with everything that follows, to the effect that the Flood was a punishment for the murder of Abel. This statement has been accidentally produced by the combination of the first half of a sentence at the bottom of the first folio of *Q with the second half of a sentence at the top of the second folio of √R².

The continuous use of *Q by ∞ R³ begins *immediately* after this mutilation, proving that *Q was actually the copy which he used. We shall see presently that ∞R^3, in his turn, repaired the damage to *Q by tearing out the opening folios of a translation of the Book of Genesis, and substituting it for the missing matter. When this act of pillage was performed, or subsequently, one of the Genesis folios was torn across: and this accident has made it possible, as is shown in the proper place, to arrive at some approximation to an idea of the size of the folios of *Q, and the amount of literary matter that would go upon each. Now, the first of these folios must have contained the matter at the beginning, common to the two redactions $R^1 R^2$ (in the present form of the latter): and it is insufficient to fill one of the ordinary folios of *Q. We infer, therefore, that much space must have been expended upon a large initial, and in letters of an extra large size upon the opening page.

The importation of "Iofer Niger" into ¶ 4, derived from the Latin Life of St. Juliana, gives us another chronological hint. If the Old Latin Biblical excerpts suggest an eighth-century date at latest for the compilation, the name of the demon suggests a ninth-century date for the beginning of glossation, the date of the Juliana text being about 800 A.D. As Iofer Niger exists in L (corrupted), *Q (first folio, transferred to R^2) and *X, a MS. which underlies some glossarial matter in R^2, he must have been found in $\sqrt{\overline{LF}\,*X\,*Q}$. This manuscript, therefore, contained the full text as we have it, except for such interpolations as were afterwards incorporated. (Though it will afterwards appear that *Q probably lacked the Partholōn and Nemed sections.) F knows nothing of Iofer Niger; he must, therefore, have been still glossarial in $\sqrt{F}$ and passed over by s F.

The history of the gloss in ¶ 1, of the Iofer Niger interpolation in ¶ 4, and of the interpolation ¶ 5, as summarized in the notes on these passages, is all self-consistent. It shows that three stems branched off from $\sqrt{\overline{LF}\,*X\,*Q}$, becoming respectively the parents of L, *X, and F *Q. The F* Q tradition is slightly the oldest of the three, but the *X tradition is nearly as old, and in some cases preserves better readings; it is a pity that we have so little of this MS. F is a curious text, a mixture of L and *Q; but though very closely cognate with *Q, it has too much in common with L to be divorced from it altogether. Though actually a later MS. than L, it preserves an older stage of the tradition, and has not travelled so far from it as L has done.

After the extant portion of the original form of R² begins, the two redactions have nothing in common. This can be shown by a summary in parallel columns :—

R¹.	R².
¶ 1. Genesis I 1.	
2. List of Works of Creation.	
3. Lucifer and Adam: revolt of Angels.	Taken over into R² with the first leaf of *Q.
4. Envy of Lucifer. The Fall.	
5. Sentence on Adam.	
6. Cain and Abel.	

7. Genealogy of Shem: the Flood mentioned.	¶ 11. The Flood.
8. Dispersal of Nations.	12. Details of the Flood.
9. Genealogy of Noah.	13. Effects of the Flood.
10. Genealogy of Magog.	14. The Raven and the Dove.
	15. Noah comes out of the Ark. Dispersal of Nations.
	16. Genealogy of Găedel Glas.
	17. Chronology.
	18. Nēl goes to Egypt.
	19. A poem on the foregoing history.

It must surely be evident that the brief mention of the Flood in R¹ is original, while the long and laboured paraphrase of the Biblical story in R² is imported. The details of the genealogies are taken from different and mutually contradictory sources. Without doubt, the lost beginning of R² differed in a like degree from the first six paragraphs of R¹ which were substituted for it: we can have no direct knowledge of what it may have contained, but we may be absolutely certain that it emphasized the divine command on the Sethites to abstain from intermarriage with the Cainites, and that this command, and the disobedience of it by the Sethites, came after the R² narrative of the death of Abel, and was the original antecedent to the Flood narrative— not improbably as we have it in ¶ 53, which may come, either from *Sex Aetates Mundi*, or from R² through *Z.

The redaction R³ is not, like R¹ and R², an independent work. It is essentially a composite, based on the two preceding redactions. The foundation of it is R¹, but it is swelled with large interpolations from R² and from other sources.

The manuscript of R¹ used by ∞ R³ was unquestionably *Q, after it had suffered the loss of its first leaf. For the text of R¹ as it appears in R³ begins, as we have said above, immediately after the lacuna thus caused. To supply the deficiency, ∞ R³ tore the opening leaves out of an Irish translation of the Book of Genesis,[1] thereby killing the translation, of which no other copy survives, and which would have been of enormous linguistic value. This, with its extensive interpolated glosses, occupies ¶¶ 20–85. The relation between the remainder of R³, § I, and the previous redactions is set forth in the following table :—

Paragraph.	Found in MSS.	Source.
86	H	Poem no. V.
87	MH	R². An appended interpolation from Comestor's *Historia Scholastica*.
*88	BMH	R¹. ¶ 7.
*89	BMH	R¹. ¶ 8. Interpolation from *Sex Aetates Mundi*.
90	H	Apparently a different but parallel text.
91	H	*Sex Aetates Mundi*.
*92	BMH	R¹. ¶ 8.
93	H	R². ¶ 15.
*94	BMH	R¹. ¶ 9.
95	H	*Sex Aetates Mundi*, with many interpolations from Isidore, etc.
96	H	Comestor.
97	H	Some other source, not identified.
*98	BMH	R¹. ¶ 9 (end).
*99, 100	BMH	R¹. ¶ 10 much interpolated.

The paragraphs marked with an asterisk, if read continuously (omitting interpolations) will give the text of this part of R¹ as it appeared in *Q.

---

[1] If not of the whole Old Testament, or even the whole Bible.

The Biblical Excerpt.

Reviewing the Biblical excerpt, and its relation to the text as a whole, we naturally ask first if it was prepared *ad hoc* by the compiler of R³, or borrowed by him from some translation previously in existence. To this question there can be but one reasonable answer. Much of the matter in the Biblical chapters was altogether irrelevant to the purpose of ∞ R³ : a short abstract, such as is given by R¹, would have served him as well, or better. The translator expended much trouble over his work; the evidence that he collated the Greek Septuagint with the Vulgate text cannot be set aside; to do this merely as a preface to a historical tract relating to Ireland would involve a heavy expenditure of time, trouble, and valuable parchment. Collation of texts in the Middle Ages, without the easily read printed page, and without alphabetical indexes and other apparatus, would have been a much more formidable task than it is to-day. Certainly the scribes who have transmitted R³ appear to have found much of this preliminary matter wearisome and out of place, as is shown by the reduction of the frequent repetitions of the original (as, for example, I 25, and the list of creatures preserved in the Ark). Another point is the difference in literary style that we feel between the Biblical excerpt and its present context. The translator has certain peculiar mannerisms, to which attention is drawn in the critical notes, and which give him an individuality.

On the other hand, it would be so easy to tear from another MS. the pages required, that we are obliged to accuse ∞ R³ of having committed this crime, to save himself the trouble of otherwise replacing the missing first page of the exemplar before him.

Some examination of the nature of the text which formed the basis of the translator's work now becomes necessary.

For purposes of reference we shall denote the Latin MS. which lay before the translator by the symbol Δ. (New Testament critics have appropriated this symbol to the ninth-century Greco-Latin Codex Sangallensis; but as we shall here have no occasion to refer to that MS., there will be no consequent inconvenience.) Δ was certainly a copy of the Vulgate; from the translation it is possible to restore some of its readings with sufficient assurance to determine its affinities. The chief passages in which Δ deviated from the Standard Text, as constructed in the Vatican Variorum edition, are enumerated below, with a list of the MSS. (not including early printed texts and editions) agreeing with it.[2]

I 2. *erant*: G^C Λ^H X Π ^CD Σ ^O B A Φ V* ⊙ ^AM* Ψ B D F2 Ω S M

I 2. *Domini*: Λ^H B

I 4. *Deus*: G^C T M¹ Φ ^RA* Z G V P Ψ M

I 4. *a tenebris*: G^C Λ^H Π ^CD Σ ^O B T Φ ^RA2 Z G V P P2 Ψ F2 M Ω M

I 12. *facientem*: Λ^H Π ^CD Ω S

I 14. *et*: C X Π ^CD Σ ^OM Φ ^VP ⊙ ^AM P Ψ B D F2 Ω S J M

I 16. omit *ut praeesset*: Σ^M

I 18. *a tenebris*: Λ^H Π ^CD Φ ^VP2

I 20. *reptilia*: C Φ ^RAZG

I 21. *motabilem*: C2 Λ ^L2H Π D* Σ ^O B T M Φ ^RAZG V Γ ^O2 ⊙ ^AM P Ψ B D F M Ω S J M

I 26. omit *que*: C X Π ^CD Σ ^TOM ^O Ψ F*

II 2. *sexto*: Σ ^T2 Ψ F*

II 2. *Deus*: O

II 4. *sunt*: Λ ^L2H X2 Φ ^V Ψ B D F

II 11. *Fison*: C Λ^H X Σ ^TOM B

III 8. omit *Dei*: X

III 9. ins. *Adam*: C X ⊙ ^AM

III 11. ins. *Deus*: C* Λ^H Σ ^TOM Ψ F2 Ω J

III 20. *Eua*: C Λ ^LX Π D Σ ^TOM B T Φ ^RAZG V P O ⊙ ^AM2 P Ψ D M Ω S J M

IV 1. *Euam*: C Λ ^LH X Π D Σ ^TOM B T Φ ^RAZG V P ⊙ ^AM Ψ ^DM Ω S J

IV 15. *Cain in signum*: Λ^H Σ ^OM B Φ ^RAZG V P P2 Ω S2 M

IV 17. ins. *filium nomine*: X Σ ^TOM

VI 8. *Deo*: Σ^M T M Φ ^RA G V P ⊙ ^M* Ψ M

VII 17. ins. xl *noctibus*: Λ^H X Σ ^T2 P Ψ ^M Ω S2 M

VIII 7. ins. *non*: Λ^H X2 Π ^C2D2 Σ ^OM2 B A 2 Φ Z2 V2 P P* Ψ M Ω S J M

VIII 17. ins. *-que*: G^C Λ^H X Σ ^TOM Ω S

XI 20. *Saruch*: X Σ ^TO* Ψ B D F M Ω S

XI 22. *Nachor*: Λ ^LH X Π ^C Σ ^OT2 M Φ ^RAZ2 G V P P Ψ B D F M Ω S J M

XI 26. *Nachor*: Λ ^LH Π ^D2 Σ ^OT2 M2 Φ ^RAZG V P P Ψ B D F M Ω S J M

XI 26. *Aram*: A K Ψ ^M Ω ^M

In the above and the following tables, an asterisk denotes a reading abolished by a corrector: these must be reckoned,

---

[2] For details about the manuscripts indicated by the symbols, reference must be made to the Vatican edition; it may be said, however, that the large letters denote families, the small letters individual MSS.

for they presumably belonged to the original tradition of the family to which the MS. belonged. Readings denoted by (^{1}), (^{2}) are corrections *prima manu* and *secunda manu*. Though they are noted here, they are not taken into account in classifying the MSS. for our present purpose. Some of the above readings may possibly be due to LXX influence. Disregarding, however, this possibility for the moment, we now arrange the Vulgate MSS. in the order of their frequency in the foregoing table, as follows :—

Σ^O 15 + 1*	Φ^R 10	C 7 + 1* (1^2)	GG 4
Λ^H 15	Φ^G 10	Π^C 7 (1^2)	M 3 ($1^1 1^2$)
X 13 (2^2)	B 9	Ψ^B 7	O 3 (1^2)
Φ^V 12 + 1* (1^2)	Ψ^D 9	P 6 + 1* (3^2)	A 2 (1^2)
Ψ^M 12	Π^D 8 + 1* (2^2)	Ψ^F 5 + 2* (4^2)	Θ^G 0
Ω^S 11. (2^2)	Φ^A 8 + 1* (1^2)	T 6 (2^2)	Θ^H 0
Σ^M 11 (1^2)	Σ^T 8 (2^2)	Θ^A 6	G 0
Φ^P 11	Φ^Z 8 (2^2)	Θ^M 4 + 2* (1^2)	
Ω^M 11	Ω^J 8	Λ^L 4 (2^2)	

The standard text of the Vatican editors is based chiefly upon three important MSS., lettered O, A, G : and it is a logical consequence that in a list of deviations from the Standard Text in any other MS., the number of agreements with these three copies should come at the bottom of the list.

Σ^O, which heads the list, is a Madrid MS., of the eleventh century. Λ^H, which runs it close, is a twelfth-century MS., also at Madrid. The "cousin" of the latter, Λ^L, though derived from a common source, is two centuries earlier, but evidently is much less closely related to Δ. If now we reckon these MSS. by families (counting in the *starred* readings) we shall find, as the average of agreements

Agreements with the Σ group $\frac{1}{3}$ (16 + 11 + 8) $= \dfrac{35}{3} = 11\frac{2}{3}$

„ Λ group $\frac{1}{2}$ (15 + 4) $= \dfrac{19}{2} = 9\frac{1}{2}$

„ Ω group $\frac{1}{3}$ (11 + 11 + 8) $= \dfrac{30}{3} = 10$

„ Ψ group $\frac{1}{4}$ (13 + 9 + 7 + 7) $= \dfrac{36}{4} = 9$

„ Θ group $\frac{1}{4}$ (6 + 6) $= \dfrac{12}{4} = 3$

This may be a rough-and-ready method of reckoning, but it gives us a definite and apparently satisfactory result. We may leave the Ω group out of account; it consists of three MSS. of French origin, now at Paris, and of the 13–14 century: later, therefore, than any probable date for Δ. The Ψ group is Italian, entirely 12th century—again rather late to have served as the model for the Irish text. The Σ and Λ groups are both Spanish: and we infer that Δ was also a MS. of Spanish origin.

But the translator did not adhere slavishly to the Latin text before him. He had access to, and could use, a copy of the Septuagint; and the influence of this is shown by the following readings :—

I 11. Insert ὁ θεός
I 22. do.
I 26. do.
I 29. τοῖς πετεινοῖς in plural
II 1. τῇ ἕκτῃ
II 8. καὶ ἤκουσαν
II 10, 13. Similarities indicated in the notes.
III 15. καὶ ἔχθραν
III 22. ὁ θεός
IV 8. διέλθωμεν εἰς τὸ πεδίον
IV 9. ὁ θεός
V The ages of the Patriarchs in this chapter.
VII 1. πρὸς Νῶε
VII 3. The insertion of the clean and unclean *birds*.
VII 6. Νῶε · ὁ κατακλυσμός
VII 16. κιβῶτον
VIII 1. καὶ ... ὁ θεός

Some of these, taken by themselves, are not very impressive: but their evidence is cumulative, and the reading in VII 3 is conclusive. The figures in chapter V are less so, for they could have come from Isidore (*Etym.* V. 39): but the unequivocal cases of reference to the Septuagint strengthen the probability of the use of this authority, even where an alternative source is possible.

It is at least a coincidence that this combination of a knowledge of Greek, with some Spanish connexion, meets us again, in the North of Ireland. In the cemetery which contains the few remaining relics of the Monastery of St. Mura at Fahan, Co. Donegal, there is a large slab, bearing beautifully-designed interlacing crosses on each face. On one side there is a pair of human figures, standing with the cross-stem between them, and bearing upon their vesture an Irish inscription which does not here concern us. On the edge there is an inscription in Greek uncials—

ΔΟΞΑ ΚΑΙ ΤΙΜΕ (*sic*) ΠΑΤΡΙ ΚΑΙ ΥΙΩ ΚΑΙ ΠΝΕΥΜΑΤΙ ΑΓΙΩ

"Glory and Honour to Father and to Son and to Holy Spirit."

This is the first versicle of the "Gloria Patri," *in a Spanish form*, though in the Greek language. The formula "Glory and Honour," without the second versicle (*sicut erat*, etc.), was sanctioned by the Council of Toledo, and adopted in the Mozarabic liturgy. Thus we find someone who was at least a superficial Greek scholar, cutting, on an Irish tombstone, a Spanish liturgical formula, in letters resembling those of a Greek uncial MS.: and someone else translating into Irish a Biblical text from a Spanish copy, and able to check his work with a copy of the Septuagint. We have no authority to go further, or to suppose that the translation was actually executed in Fahan. This is not impossible, though the translation could hardly be as old as the slab. But in any case the number of uncial MSS. of the Septuagint available in Ireland can never have been very large.

It is for us a fortunate circumstance that the matter of Genesis XI 10–32 is misplaced in our text, being inserted between the verses VIII 19 and 20. There is no logical reason for this: the cause must have been mechanical, and due to the misplacement of a loose folio.

It follows that the matter which now comes after these verses was contained in a folio which ran from VIII 20 to XI 9. As we do not possess the translation in its original form—there are both omissions and interpolations—a count of words would lead us to wrong conclusions about the size of the folios, or the extent of the matter upon each. But a count of the corresponding words in the Vulgate text will enable us to estimate this with tolerable accuracy. If I have counted aright,

A. Genesis VIII 20–IX 27 in the Vulgate text contains 503 words.
B. „ IX 28–X 31 „ „ „ „ „ 382 „
C. „ X 32–XI 9 „ „ „ „ „ 170 „

B is missing from the translation *as we have it*, but it must have been there originally. Its omission would leave C, the Tower of Babel story, as a small detached narrative, too short for a folio of any reasonable size. It is easy to believe that the LG copyists, who pared away the redundancies of the Flood story, would have "jibbed" at the task of transcribing the tiresome list of incomprehensible names in the "Table of Nations" (Genesis X), which has nothing to do with the Taking of Ireland, and would use up much costly parchment.

A B C together amount to 1,055 words. If the translation of this passage was written upon one folio of vellum, with two columns on each page, there would be the equivalent of about 264 words in each column: or what would fill about 35 out of the 55–60 lines in a column of the *Book of Ballymote*.

I have not counted words back to the beginning of Genesis. But taking a printed edition, not complicated with interspersed references, and omitting the chapter headings, I find that

Genesis I 1–VIII 19 covers 70⅔ inches of type.
Genesis VIII 20–XI 9 „ 22⅛ „ „ „

The number of words in this printed copy is not evenly distributed: one column in Chapter III, in which the verses are long, contains 252 words, and another, in Chapter V, of exactly the same spacial length, contains 232 words. There is thus a sufficient margin of possible adjustment to permit us to say that the material preceding VIII 19 could have been written on three folios similar to that which we have postulated for VIII 20–XI 9. We infer from this that the matter appropriated by ∞ R³ covered a complete gathering of four folios, or two diplomas (pairs of conjugate folios), and the detached first folio of the next gathering. When a man carries off such a gathering and one extra folio, nothing is more natural for him to do than to slip the loose leaf into the gathering, to prevent it from being lost : and if its proper place is just *after* the last folio of the gathering, he will slip it in just *before* that folio. And this is exactly what he has done, to the confusion of his copyists.

Numbering the five folios of this Biblical MS. 1, 2, 3, 5, 4, in the order in which they ultimately became incorporated in R³, we see that 4 must have ended with the words³ *Hae sunt generationes Sem* (XI 10), which, however, were dropped by the copyists, as they had no meaning in their new context. 5 *a* began *Sem erat centum annorum* (¶ 69) and ran on to *ueneruntque usque Haran et habitauerunt ibi* (XI 31). This is a little longer than the allowance of 264 words to the column ; but the matter of these verses contains many numerals and stereotyped repetitions, which could be much abbreviated : and in any case column β *must* have begun with (XI 32), *Et facti sunt dies Thare.* For we must now notice the further fact, that the lower part of folio 5 was torn away (whether in the original act of theft or by some later accident cannot be ascertained, and is of trifling importance). This tear ran upwards obliquely, from the bottom inner edge to the top outer edge. It carried away from the first column (5 *a*) parts of all the verses after XI 26, and it left nothing intact in the second column except this one verse, XI 32. The copyists could not, or at least made no attempt to, extract any sense from the remaining fragments of the mutilated lines ; and thus it comes about that the misplaced extract from Chapter XI, in ¶ 77, jumps from v. 26 to v. 32, and then stops abruptly. The verso of the folio must have contained, in the first column, a few lines of the story of Abraham hiding his relationship to Sarah in Egypt, and in the second column the end of the story of Lot in Sodom and the beginning of the Battle of the Four Kings with the Five. These fragments were so utterly disconnected with the matter in hand, and with each other, that the copyists left them out.

---

³ Meaning, of course, the Irish translation of these words ; and similarly for the other quotations in this paragraph.

This reconstruction of the original form of the Biblical translation is more than a mere curiosity; for as it was possible to attach the Biblical folios to *Q, we may infer that the sizes of the two manuscripts were much about the same. And every scrap of information that we can discover about *Q is of importance, for the history of R³.

The Chasm in B, M.

B has lost, as already stated, its folio 9, beginning after the words *ocus ro hoslaicit* (Gen. III 7, ¶ 32), and extending to ¶ 138 in § II. This mutilation took place after β and $\sqrt{\beta^1} \beta^2$ were copied; and a count of words shows that the matter with which they fill this gap would exactly cover a leaf of B. Therefore one folio has been lost, and no more, at this place; a conclusion which accords with the old pagination.

The fragment H almost exactly fills the gap. If the top of the first leaf of this fragment had not been torn away, it would have filled it with suspicious exactness. Suspicious, because it suggests the deduction that the leaves of H were actually torn, from the MS. to which they belonged, by an owner of B, anxious to make his own property complete. They certainly present the appearance of having been pulled out violently.[4]

But the matter in H is considerably longer than what would fill a folio of B, and it contains an extensive passage ignored by the derivatives of B. We infer that there was a lacuna in $\sqrt{B}$, due to the loss of leaves in an ancestral MS., of which s B was unconscious.

When we look up M at this place we find a similar lacuna. It is less extensive; there is some matter common to M and H but unknown to B. Unlike s B, s M was aware of the defect in his exemplar, and he left a half column blank in the hope,

---

[4] It is likely that copies of this lengthy and important text were few, and were much in demand: and that Irish book-collectors were not any more conscientious than the rest of the fraternity. The total disappearance of the copy in *Lebor na Huidri* (ante, p. xxi) was probably the result of someone having been left for a few moments alone with that precious codex.

never to be fulfilled, of finding a more perfect copy from
which to supply the missing matter.

We may represent the relative lengths of the missing
portion in tabular form thus: let a represent the quantity
of matter surviving in M, between the beginning of the lacuna
in B and the beginning of the lacuna in M. Then we have—

   i. A length of a, absent in B, present in M, present in H.
  ii. A length of $5a$, absent in B, absent in M, present in H.
 iii. A length of $2a$, absent in B, present in M, present in H.

The third of these sections is the poem *Athair cáich,* and
a few lines intervening between it and the resumption of B.

The explanation is perfectly simple. B, M, H all derive
from MSS. copied *independently* from an ancestor, √BMH.
There can, therefore, be no common ancestor of any two of
these MSS. excluding the third: this is an assured fact of
fundamental importance in the criticism of the MSS. of R³.
The first of the ancestral MSS. to be copied was ∞ H, the
second ∞ M, the third ∞ B. Between the transcribing of
the first and last of these a gathering of four diplomas disappeared from √BMH piecemeal. Each folio of √BMH
contained matter equal in quantity to a. Here is a diagram
of the gathering—

The whole gathering was intact when ∞ H was copied.
Then the diplomas 4–5, 3–6, as well as folio 2 disappeared;
after which ∞ M was copied. Folio 7 was now loose: it
contained the beginning of *Athair cáich,* which must have
begun at the top of folio 7 *recto* and ended near the end of
folio 8 *verso.* There are 57 quatrains in this poem, so that
the folios of √BMH must have been quite small: each page

could not have held more than 15 quatrains. Folio 7, as well as the last diploma 1–8, disappeared before ∞ B was copied.

The impression which a study of the language of the translation leaves is that the latter is not much earlier than R^3, with which it is incorporated. Like the O'Clerys and the Four Masters, the translator affects an archaistic style, which he presumably thought was more consistent with the dignity of the text on which he was working. His language, when he is natural, is Middle Irish; his archaisms are Wardour-street revivals rather than survivals. He uses a deponent form for the verb whenever he remembers to do so. He invents forms like *barnimdaigther*, ¶ 24, which he has forgotten in ¶ 25, where we find "dēntar *bar n-imdugad*." It is more than probable that the MS. which ∞ R^3 mutilated was actually the autograph of the translation, and that this was, as we have said, killed by the transaction.

It is clear that the glossators had no idea that they were dealing with a Scriptural text. One of them had to reassure himself that the reference to the Holy Spirit in ¶ 20 is not profane: and another (¶ 30 y^2) quotes "Holy Scripture" to corroborate the passage from Holy Scripture upon which he is working!

SECTION I.

First Redaction.

(L 1 *a* 1 : F 1 *a* 1) *(a)*

1. *In principio fecit Deus celum et terram,* .i.
[1]Doringne Dīa nem ⁊ talmain ar tūs, ‡ ⁊ nī [2]fil tossach
‡' nā forcend ‖' fair-[3]seom [4]fēin ‖.

2. [1]Doringne chētus in maiss [2]nem-chruthaig, ⁊
soillsi aingel, ‡ isin [3]cētna [4]Domnuch ‖.   [5]Doringne
[6]firmament ‡ isin Lūan ‖.   [7]Doringni [8]tal*main* ⁊ muire
‡ [9]sin Mairt ‖.   [10]Doringni grēin ⁊ ēsca ⁊ [11]renna Nime
‡ [12]sin Cētāin ‖.   [13]Doringni ēnlaithe ‡ ind āeoir ‖ ⁊
[14]tonnaitecha ‡ in mara ‖ ‡ [15]sin Dardāin ‖.   [16]Doringni
anmanna ‡ in talman ‖ [17]archena, ⁊ Adam do [18]follom-
nacht foraib, ‡ [19]isind Āine ‖.   Ro chumsain īarum
‡ Dīa ‖ ‡ [20]issin tSathurn ‖ [21]do foirbthiugud dūla nūa,
‡ ⁊ nī ō [18]follomnacht [22]itir ‖.

3. Dobert ‡ [1]īarsain ‖ [2]archinnchecht Nime do
[3]Lucifiur, co [4]nōi ngrādaib angel Nime.   Dobert
[5]archinnchecht talman do Adam ‡ ⁊ do [6]Eua cona
claind ‖.   [7]Imromadar ‡ īaróm ‖ Lucifiur (*sic*) [8]conid
būi (?) toesech trīn slūaig angel. [9]Rothimmarc (?) in Rī
ē co trian in slūaig angel leis.i nIfrinn; ⁊ asbert Dīa

---

1. *All variants from* F *unless otherwise stated.*   [1] dorindi   [2] fuil
tosach·   [3] sium   [4] fein *added sec. man* L
2. [1] dorigne cetus   [2] n-ecruthaig : *above very faint traces of a*
gloss nemfaics(ide) F   [3] *om.*   [4] -nach   [5] dorigne   [6] neam
.i. firmamaind isan   [7] dorigne : *this word is abbreviated to* D *in the*
following sentences in L   [8] talam ⁊ muir   [9] isan F; sin Mairt
om. and ins. cL   [10] dorigne grian ⁊ esga   [11] randa   [12] isin
Cedain F: *om. and ins.* cL   [13] dorigne enlaithi   [14] tondaitheacha
[15] isa Dardain F: *om. and ins.* cL   [16] dorigne   [17] at first written
chena, *and the* ar *monogram squeezed in before it sec. man.* F

First Redaction

1. *In principio fecit Deus caelum et terram,* i.e., God made Heaven and Earth at the first, [and He Himself hath no beginning nor ending].

2. He made first the formless mass, and the light of angels, [on the first Sunday]. He made Firmament [on the Monday]. He made earth and seas [on the Tuesday]. He made sun and moon and the stars of Heaven [on the Wednesday]. He made birds [of the air] and reptiles [of the sea on the Thursday]. He made beasts [of the earth] in general, and Adam to rule over them, [on the Friday]. Thereafter God rested [on the Saturday] from the accomplishment of a new Creation, [but by no means from its governance].

3. [Thereafter] He gave the bailiffry of Heaven to Lucifer, with the nine orders of the Angels of Heaven. He gave the bailiffry of Earth to Adam [and to Eve, with her progeny]. [Thereafter] Lucifer sinned, so that he was leader of a third of the host of angels. The King confined him with a third of the host of

---

[18] follam- (*bis*)   [19] dia Hainediden, et ro   [20] isan tSatharn*n*
[21] o oipriugad   [22] *ins. sec. man. in small capital letters in* L *marg. In the text in* *Q: *om* F
   3. [1] iarsin   [2] aircinchacht   [3] Luidsifir   [4] nai   [5] aircindacht
[6] Eaba   ╲   [7] imroimadar   [8] *obscure in both* L *and* F: *in* F *looks like* for nim cona sluag angel leis .i. na demna   [9] cor hindarbad *and om.* co trian sluaig angel

---

fri muintir Nime : ‡ Dīumsach inti Lucifer ‖, [10]*uenite*
[11]*ut confundamus consilium eius.*

4. Ro formtig [1]trā Lucifer fri Adam, ar derb lais
issē no bērtha, līnad Nime tar a ēisi, do.   Conid aire sin
doluid [2]‡ Iofer Niger ‖ [3]i ndeilb in athrach, [4]co ro
aslacht imarbus for ‡ Adam ᚕ ‖ [5]Euа, im [6]thumailt [7]ind
ubuill don chrund ergartha.   [8]Conid aire sin ro
[9]innarbbad Adam a Pardus [10]hi talmain coitchind.

5. [1]Dolluid in Comdiu cucca īarsain, ᚕ atbert fri Adam
.i. [2]*Terra es et in* [3]*terram ibis* ‡ .i.   Do thalmain [4]don-
ringned ᚕ [5]hi talmain raga ‖.   *In* [6]*sudore uultus tui
comedes* [7]*panem tuum* ‡ .i. Nī [8]fuigbe sāsam cen[8] sāethar ‖.
[9]Asbert dana frisin mnāi .i.   *Cum* [10]*dolore et gemitu*
[11]*paries filios tuos* [12]*et filias tuas* ‡ .i. [13]bid co ngalar . . .
doīulaing (?) tuisema do maccu ‖.

L

6. Ro   immarbāigestar
cland Adaim ‡ īarom ‖ .i.
sinser mac (n)Adaim, .i.
Cāin miscadach, ro marb a
derbrāthair Aibēl [. . tria
formud (?)] ᚕ tria saint,
lasin (?) cnāim chamaill,
mar adberat eōlaig . . . .
tinnscnadar (?) fingail in
domain.

F

Īarsin trā do feallsad
clann Adaim for ūail ᚕ
dīmus ᚕ imarbus ᚕ fingal, .i.
Cāin mac Adaim in sinser,
ro marb-sidi a derbrātair
.i. Abēl tria saint ᚕ formad,
co fid cnāma camaill. ‡ Con
aire sin dorad Dīa dīlinn
tarsin n-uili doman. ‖

---

[10] *illegible in* F: *apparently* et dixit Deus *is inserted before* uenite
[11] et
4. [1] iarsin   [2] Iarngir L *om.* Iofer Niger F   [3] a neilb nathrach
[4] coreaslaig   [5] for Eba   [6] thom-   [7] ind ubaill   [8] con de sin
[9] hinarbad   [10] isin

angels in his company, in Hell. And God said unto the Folk of Heaven : [Haughty is this Lucifer], *uenite ut confundamus consilium eius.*

4. Thereafter Lucifer had envy against Adam, for he was assured that this would be given him (Adam), the filling of Heaven in his (Lucifer's) room. Wherefore he [Iofer Niger] came in the form of the serpent, and persuaded [Adam and] Eve to sin, in the matter of eating of the apple from the forbidden tree. Wherefore Adam was expelled from Paradise into common earth.

5. Thereafter the Lord came to them, and He said unto Adam, *Terra es et in terram ibis* [*i.e.*, of earth was he made and into earth shall he go]. *In sudore uultus tui comedes panem tuum* [*i.e.*, he shall not obtain satisfaction without labour]. He said further unto the woman : *Cum dolore et gemitu paries filios tuos et filias tuas* [*i.e.*, it shall be with . . . insufferable pain that thou shalt bring forth thy sons].

6. The progeny of Adam sinned [thereafter], namely, the elder of the sons of Adam, Cain the accursed, who slew his brother Abel . . . (through his jealousy?) and through his greed, with the bone of a camel, as learned men say. (In this manner ?) began the kin-murders of the world.

But thereafter the progeny of Adam wrought treachery, by way of pride, of haughtiness, of sin, of kin-murder—Cain son of Adam, the elder, he slew his brother Abel through his greed and his jealousy, with the shaft of a camel-bone. [And therefore God brought a Flood over the whole earth].

---

5. [1] doluid in Coimdi chuca iarsin ⁊ adbert [2] tearra [3] tearaim [4] dorignid [5] a [6] sudoire [7] panam [8-8] fuigbed biad can [9] adbert dono [10] doloire [11] pairras [12] *om.* et filias tuas [13] bid congneid ⁊ galar dofuisema do claindi

7. ¹Seth imorro, in tres mac ²Adaim ³‡ aca mbāi
cland ⁊ ‖ is ⁴ūata atiat fir ⁵in domuin uile :

y¹ .i. Nōe mac ⁶Laimīach meic Mathusali meic ⁷Henōc
meic ⁸Iared meic Malalel meic ⁹Cainan meic Enos meic
¹⁰Seth meic Adaim :

ūair is ē Nōe in tAdam tānisi, cusa mbertar fir domain
¹¹uile. ¹²Ūair ro bāid in ¹³dīliu sīl Adaim ¹⁴uile, acht
Nōe cona trī macaib, .i. Sem, Cham, Iafet, acus a
cethri mnaa .i. Cobba ⁊ Olla ⁊ Oliba ⁊ Olībana.

y² ¹⁵Ō dorat īarom Dīa dīlind darsin uile ndomuin, nī
thērna di dōenib in domuin ōn dīlind acht mad lucht na
hairce sin .i. Nōe cona trī maccaib, ⁊ ben Nōe, ⁊ mnaa a
mac.¹⁵

Ut dixit poeta,

   Slūag nād chlōe cūa-chel . . . .

8. ¹Sem didiu ro gob i nAsia, Cham i nAfraic
Iafeth i nEoraip—

   Sem rogab i n-Aisia n-ait . . .

Tricha mac ²bātar ac Sem, im ³Arfacsad, im Asur, ⁴⁊
im Persius.   Tricha ⁵mac ⁶ac Cam, im Chus ⁷⁊ im
Chanan.⁷ A cōic dēc imorro oc Iafeth, im Dannai, im
Grēgus, im ⁸Hispāinius, im ⁹Goimarus.

¹⁰No is mōirfeisir ar fichid do macaib badar ic Sem.

---

7. ¹ Seth mac Adaim   ² airïgda da bi ac Adam   ³ *this gloss*
om. F   ⁴ uad ataid   ⁵ *om.* in : domain uili   ⁶ Lamiach
⁷ Enog   ⁸ Iareth   ⁹ Cainain   ¹⁰ Seith   ¹¹ uili   ¹² ar do   ¹³ dili
¹⁴ uili   ¹⁵⁻¹⁵ *om.* F, *and substitute* Imroimadar clann Adaim fri Dia (᷍)
co tard Dia dile tarsin uile domain co nach terno nech beo eisti acht

7. As for Seth, one of the three sons of Adam [who had progeny], of him are the men of the whole world :

Noe s. Lamech s. Mathusalem s. Enoch .s. Iared s. Malalahel s. Cainan s. Enos s. Seth s. Adam.

For it is Noe who is the second Adam, to whom the men of all the world are traced.   For the Flood drowned the whole seed of Adam, except Noe with his three sons, Sem, Ham, Iafeth, and their four wives Coba, Olla, Oliva, Olivana.

Afterwards, when God brought a Flood over the whole world, none of the people of the world escaped from the Flood except it be the people of that ark—Noe with his three sons, and the wife of Noe, and the wives of his sons.

Ut dixit poeta,
Poem no. I.

8. Now Sem settled in Asia, Ham in Africa, Iafeth in Europe—

Poem no. II.

Sem had thirty sons, including Arfaxad, Assur, and Persius.   Ham had thirty sons, including Chus and Chanaan.   Iafeth had fifteen, including Dannai, Gregus, Hispanius, Gomer.

Or it is twenty-seven sons that Sem had.

---

lucht na hairce .i. Nae cona tri macaib Sem, Cam, Iafeth, cona ceitri mnaib .i. Coba, Olla, Oliba, Olibana, amail asbert in file

8. [1] Sem dana rogab an Aissia, Cam isan Adfraic, Iafeth asa nEoraip
[2] badar ic   [3] Airfecsat   [4] *om.* ⁊   [5] *om.*   [6] aili co Cam im Cuss   [7-7] *om.*   [8] Esbainus   [9] -mer-   [10] *This gloss in F only*

Tricha mac mīn monar nglē . . . .

9. ¹Iafeth ‡ trā mac ²Nōe ||, is ūad ³tūaiscert-leth na Haisia, .i. ⁴Aisia Becc, Armenia, Media, Fir na Scitīa; ᚁ is ⁵ūad lucht na ⁶Haeorpa uile.

y¹ Grēcus mac Iafeth, is ūad in ⁷Grēg Mōr, ᚁ in ⁷Grēg ⁸Becc, ᚁ ⁷Grēg na Halaxandrach. ⁹Essbāinus mac Iafeth, ō tāit ¹⁰Hispāna. Goimerus mac Iafeth, dā mac laiss, Emoth ᚁ Ibath. Emoth, is ūadh fine thūascirt in domain. Ibath, dā mac leis, .i. ¹¹Bodb ᚁ Baath. Bodb, diar bo mac Dohe.

y² Elinus mac Doi, trī meic leis .i. Armen, Negua, Isacon. Armen ōn, cōic meic leis, Gotus, Cibidus, Uiligotus, Burgantus, ᚁ Longbardus. Negua, trī meic leis, .i. Saxsus, Boarus, Uandalus. Hisicon imorro, in tres ¹²mac Eline, ceitre meic lais, ¹³Romanus, Francus, Britus, Albus.

y³ Is ē in tAlbanus dogab Albin ar tūs cona chlaind, ᚁ is ūadh ainmnigter Albo: cor indarb a brātair tar Muir nIcht, conad ūad Albanaig Leatha Hoidia.

10. ¹Magoth mac Iafiath, is dia chlaind-sin na tūatha tāncatar Ērinn rīa nGāedelaib: .i. ²Parthalōn mac Sera meic Srū meic Esrū meic ³Bimbind meic ⁴Aaithecha meic Magoth meic Iafeth; ⁴ᚁ Nemedh mac Aghnumaid meic mPaimp meic Tait meic Sera meic Sriū; ᚁ clanna Nemid, .i. Gaileōin, ᚁ Fir Domnan, ᚁ Fir Bolg, ᚁ Tūatha Dē Danann. Amail isbert in fili,

---

9. ¹ Iafiath   ² Nae   ³ tuait siar-deise na Haisia L tuas-cert-leth na Aisia F   ⁴ Aissia Beg ᚁ Armen ᚁ Fir na Sgeiaithia ⁵ uadh   ⁶ Horpa uili   ⁷ Grec (*ter: in the first the scribe began to write Grec; but discovered his mistake and stopped half-way*) ⁸ beg   ⁹ Hispanus L. *From this point to the bottom of the page (down to and including Poem IV, quatrain 1) L is illegible save for faint traces, sufficiently decipherable to shew that except some ortho-graphical differences the text is identical with F, which is here followed.*

Poem no. III.

9. [With regard to] Iafeth [son of Noe], of him is the northern side of Asia—namely Asia Minor, Armenia, Media, the People of Scythia; and of him are the inhabitants of all Europe.

Grecus s. Iafeth, of him is Grecia Magna, Grecia Parva, and Alexandrian Greece.   Espanus s. Iafeth from whom are the Hispani.   Gomer son of Iafeth had two sons, Emoth and Ibath.   Emoth, of him is the northern people of the world.   Ibath had two sons, Bodb and Baath. Bodb, who had a son Dohe.

Elinus son of Dohe had three sons, Airmen, Negua, Isacon.   As for Airmen, he had five sons, Gutus, Cebidus, Uiligothus, Burgundus, Longbardus.   Negua had three sons, Saxus, Boarus, Uandalus.   Isacon, moreover, one of the three sons of Elenus, he had four sons, Romanus, Francus, Britus, Albanus.

This is that Albanus who first took Albania, with his children, and of him is Alba named : so he drove his brother across the Sea of Icht, and from him are the Albanians of Latium of Italy.

10. Magog son of Iafeth, of his progeny are the peoples who came to Ireland before the Gaedil : to wit Partholon s. Sera s. Sru s. Esru s. Bimbend (*sic*) s. Aithech s. Magog s. Iafeth; and Nemed s. Agnomain s. Pamp s. Tat s. Sera s. Sru; and the progeny of Nemed, the Gaileoin, Fir Domnann, Fir Bolg, and Tuatha De Danann.   As the poet said,

---

F *sometimes uses* " ; " *and sometimes* "u ; " *to represent final* us: *thus* "Got ; ", *but* "Uiligotu ; ". *It has not been thought necessary to preserve this trivial distinction in printing.*   [10] Hispania L
[11] *Written* Bod | db, *divided between two lines* F   ´   [12] *om.* mac F; *the word can be detected in* L   [13] *Written* Roman us, *the space large enough to hold an* n
    10. [1] *See* ¶ 9 note (9)   [2] Partholon L   [3] Bi(?)amin L
[4] Fatocht L   [4] *om.* ⊣ L

Magog mac an Iafeth . . .

Second Redaction.

(V 1 *a* 1 : E 1 *a* 1 : P 1 *a* 1 : D 3 *a* 1 *first two folios lost.*)

(The opening paragraphs are numbered to correspond with R[1], being derived from *Q, a lost MS. of that Redaction; and are distinguished by a suffixed asterisk.)

1*. [1]*In* [2]*principio fecit Deus celum et terram* .i. dorighne Dīa [3]Neam ⁊ [4]talmain ar tūs.

2*. [1]Dorigne [2]cētumus in [3]maiss [4]n-ēcruthaigh, ⁊ soillsi aingeal, ‡ [5]issin cētna Domnuch ‖. [6]Dorigne firmaimint ‡ [7]is'in' Lūan ‖. [8]Dorigne ta'lmain' ⁊ muir ‡ [9]issin Mairt ‖. [8]'Dorigne' grēin ⁊ [10]ēsca ⁊ 'renda' Nime ‡ [11]issin Cētāin ‖. Dorigne 'ēnlaithe' ‡ [12]ind āeoir ‖ ⁊ [13]tondaithechu ‡ na f'airrge' ‖ ‡ Dīa [14]Dardāin ‖. Dorigne anmanda ‡ 'in tal'man ‖ [15]olchena, ⁊ [16]Adam do [17]follomn'acht' foraib, ‡ [18]issin nĀendidin ‖. R'o chumsain' ‡ [19]Dīa ‖ īarom ‡ [20]issin [21]tSat'hurn'd ‖ ō [22]oipriugad a dūla nūa, ‡' ⁊ dorad bendachtain foraib ‖, ‡ ⁊ nī ō [23]ollomnacht etir ‖.

2 A. y[1] Is [1]amlaid [2]dorōna Dīa na dūile : [3].i. araile co [4]tossach ⁊ cen crīch, amail [5]aingliu; araile imorro [6]co tossach ⁊ co crīch, amail anmanda indlightecha ⁊ [7]toirrthe in [8]talman; araile [9]dana co [10]tosach ⁊ co [11]forcend ⁊ cen forcend, amail atat na [12]dāine, .i. tossach [13]for a ngencmain [14]corpdai ⁊ forcend for n-a corpaib-sin, ⁊ cen [15]forcenn for a n-anmandaib.[15]

1*. [1]*A space left in* E *for an initial monogram, never filled up* [2]prindcipio fecid VE   [3] nemh E   [4]talam*ain* E

2*. *All variants in these opening paragraphs from* E *unless otherwise stated.*   [1]*ins.* .i. V: doirighne E   [2]cedamus   [3]mais [4]*sic* VE *but changed by a re-inker to* re cruthaigh, V   [5]isin ced domh-   [6]dorigni fiormamiint (*doubled* i *due to change of line*) [7]*words marked* ' ... ' *lost by a tear in the vellum of* V   [8]dorighni (*bis*) [9]isin mh-   [10]esgai   [11]isin cedaoin   [12]an aoeoir   [13]-aīthecha na fairrghe   [14]-daoin   [15]olcena V   [16]Adamh *om.* ⁊nd *sprs.* cE

Poem no. IV.

Second Redaction.

1*. *In principio fecit Deus caelum et terram,* i.e., God made Heaven and Earth at the first.

2*. He made first the formless mass, and the light of Angels, [on the first Sunday]. He made Firmament [on the Monday]. He made earth and sea [on the Tuesday]. He made sun and moon and the stars of Heaven [on the Wednesday]. He made birds [of the air] and [marine] reptiles [on the Thursday]. He made beasts [of the earth] in general, and Adam to rule over them[, on the Friday]. Thereafter [God] rested [on the Saturday] from the accomplishment of His new creation[, and gave them a blessing, but by no means from its governance].

> 2 A. In this wise God made the creatures: some with beginning and without end, as Angels; some moreover with beginning and with end, as irrational beasts and fruits of the earth; some further with beginning and with termination and without termination, as are men—a beginning to their bodily birth and a termination to their bodies, and no termination to their souls.

[17] -amhn-   [18] isind ain-   [19] *om.*   [20] isin   [21] -arnn
[22] oipriudug V   [23] follamhnacht itir

2A. [1] amhlaid   [2] doroine   [3] *om.* .i.   [4] tossuch *apparently* V, *but in the handwriting of this MS. it is sometimes difficult to distinguish between* u *and open* a: tosach E   [5] ainghliu   [6] go tosach   [7] toirti an   [8] talmun V   [9] imorro   [10] tosuch V   [11] foircend *(second time abbreviated to* f̄cend)*   [12] daoine   [13] forainngenemain V *for a* ngeinemain E   [14] chorpda   [15-15] -cend: a n-an. *om. and ins.*

y² Is amlaid dana dorōnad ¹⁶in duine sin .i. ¹⁷Adam: a corp(a) do talmain ¹⁸choitchend . . . .

a chend do ¹⁹tīr Garad, a ²⁰bruindi a tīr Arabia, a ²¹brū a Lodain, a ²²cossa a tīr ²³Agoria:

. . . . a fuil ‡ ⁊ ²⁴a allus ‖ do ²⁵uisci ²⁶in āeoir, a anāl dond āeor, a ²⁷thes do ²⁸tenig, a ²⁹anam do ³⁰thinfiud De.

y³ Isin treas ³¹ūair īar ³²cruthugad Adhaim, ro ³³teipead Eua ³⁴assa tāeb. ³⁵I n-āess trichtaig ro cruthaiged Adam; ³⁶i n-āess dā bliadan dēc ro ³⁷cruthaiged Eua.

3*. Dobert ‡ Dīa ‖ ¹airc(h)indeacht Nime do ²Luicifiur, con nāe ³ngrādaib aingel ⁴imbe. Dobert ‡ ⁵īarsain ‖ ⁶aircindecht talman do ⁷Adam ‡ ⁊ do ⁸Eua, cona ⁹chlainn ‖. Ro ¹⁰immarbšaigestar ¹¹Lucifuir for ¹²Nim ar ¹³ūail ⁊ ¹⁴dīumus fri Dīa, co ro hindarbadh ¹⁵i cinaigh in ¹⁶dīumsa sin do ¹⁷Neimi, ‡ ¹⁸co triun slūaig aingeal ¹⁹laiss ‖, ²⁰in nIffrinn. Conid andsin ²¹asbert Dīa fri ²²muintir ²³Nime: ‡ Ro-²⁴dīumsaich ²⁵intī ²⁶Lucsifiur (sic) ‖: ²⁷*et dixit, uenite ut* ²⁸*uideamus* ⁊ ²⁹*confundamus consilium eius*, .i. ³⁰tāit co ro ³¹fēgum ⁊ co ro ³²melachtnaigium comairle ³³indī Lucifiur. ³⁴Issī cēt breath rucad ³⁵rīam sin.

4*. Ro ¹formtigh ²īarsain Lucifir fri Hadum, derb ³lais issē dobertha ‡ i ffochraic³ do ‖, ⁴līnadh Nime dar a ⁵ēsi. ⁶Conid aire sin doluidh ⁷‡ Iofer Nigher ‖ ⁸i ndeilb nathrach ‡ co curp ⁹sēim ‖, co ro aslacht ¹⁰in imarbus for ¹¹Eua, im ¹²tomailt ¹³ind ¹⁴ubaill don ¹⁵chrund aurgartha, ‡ ⁊ co ro ¹⁶aslaich ¹⁷Eua for Adum ‖ . . .

---

cE *in upper margin* ¹⁶ an   ¹⁷ Adamh   ¹⁸ coitcend   ¹⁹ thir
²⁰ bhruinne   ²¹ bruo   ²² cosa   ²³ -oir-   ²⁴ a luais V
²⁵ usci V uisgi E   ²⁶ ind   ²⁷ tes   ²⁸ tein-   ²⁹ anim V
³⁰ thinfuidh V teinfi-   ³¹ *om.* V   ³² crutugh-   ³³ teiped Eba
³⁴ asa thaobh   ³⁵ ind aois triochtaige   ³⁶ ind aois   ³⁷ -aigh- *here and above*

3*. ¹ -echt neimhe   ² Lucif.   ³ ngradh-   ⁴ immi   ⁵ iarsin
⁶ *sic* E, airecht V   ⁷ Adham *hic et semper* E   ⁸ Ebhe   ⁹ cloinn
¹⁰ immarbusaigestar iar sin   ¹¹ Lucifer   ¹² nimh   ¹³ uaill
¹⁴ diom-   ¹⁵ hi cion·   ¹⁶ dimusa   ¹⁷ nimh   ¹⁸ co dtriun
¹⁹ lais   ²⁰ and Ifernn conadh   ²¹ adbert   ²² muindt-   ²³ -mh-
²⁴ dioumsaid   ²⁵ anti   ²⁶ Lucifer   ²⁷ *om.* et dixit   ²⁸ uidiamus V

In this wise, further, was that man, Adam, made : his body of common earth,

> his head of the land of Garad, his breast of the land of Arabia, his belly of Lodain, his legs of the land of Agoria :

his blood [and his sweat] of the water of the air, his breath of the air, his heat of fire, his soul of the breath of God.

In the third hour after the creation of Adam, Eve was drawn out of his side. At the age of a thirty years' space Adam was created, at the age of twelve years Eve was created.

3*. [God] gave the bailiffry of Heaven to Lucifer. with nine orders of Angels about him. [Thereafter] He gave the bailiffry of Earth to Adam [and to Eve with his progeny]. Lucifer made an assault upon Heaven, by reason of pride and haughtiness against God, so that he was expelled, for the crime of that haughtiness, out from Heaven, [with a third of the host of angels in his company], into Hell. So that then God said unto the Folk of Heaven : [Over-haughty is this Lucifer] : *et dixit, Venite ut uideamus et confundamus consilium eius,* i.e., Come and let us see and put to shame the counsel of this Lucifer. That is the first judgement which was ever pronounced.

4*. Thereafter Lucifer had envy against Adam, (for) he was assured that this would be given him [as a reward], to fill Heaven in his room. Wherefore he [Iofer Niger] came in the form of a serpent [with a tenuous body] and persuaded Eve to the sin, in the matter of eating of the apple from the forbidden tree, [and Eve persuaded Adam] . . .

---

uidemus E   [29] confunndamus   [30] taoid   [31] fegham   [32] melachtem
comairli   [33] inti   [34] is hi ced breth rugad   [35] -mh

4*. [1] foirmtig   [2] -sin   [3-3] leis ise doberta hi bfochraic   [4] lionad
nimhe   [5] eisi   [6] -adh   [7] *initial* I *erased,* E   [8] a   [9] *ins.*
aieorda : *the text was originally* natrach (*sic*) aieorda seimh. cE *inserted* co curp seim *interlined, and then, observing that* seim *was already in the text, scratched this word out.*   [10] indiumurbus *a correction prima manu of* indium;. *The* ''m;'' *was scratched out, and* m *re-written in blacker ink with* v *sprs.*   [11] Ebha   [12] -mh-, *the final* t *erased*
[13] an   [14] -bh-   [15] -and argarta   [16] fasl-   [17] Ebha

---

(a) This word should of course be *chorp* : but here and elsewhere I have preferred to let the MSS. speak for themselves without fussy corrections.

5*. Ocus ¹isbert Dīa friu : *De terra ²es et in terram ibis*;
‡ .i. Do thalmain ³ataī-siu ⅂ hi talmain ⁴rega ‖. *Et dixit,
In sudore ⁵uultus tui comedes ⁶panem tuum*; ‡ .i. ⁷Bid a
⁸hallus do gnūisi ⁹domēla do bairgena. ‖ Asbert dana fri
¹⁰Eua : *Cum ¹¹dolore et gemitu paries filios tuos* ‡ *et filias
tuas* ‖: ‡ .i. Bid co ¹²crāit ⅂ ¹³galair tūisēma do ¹⁴maccu
‡′ ⅂ t'ingena ‖′ ‖.

5ᴀ. Ro thaisbenta na dūile ¹corpta do Adam, (*a*)⅂ nī derna ²failte
friu. ³Conid ⁴aire ⁵sain ⁶tarlaicedh ⁷cotlud fair. ⁸Isin cotludh sin
⁹iartain ¹⁰ro ¹¹delbud ¹²Eua, ¹³iar n-a teipe don tsechtmudh.¹⁴asna
¹⁵assa ¹⁶toeb. ¹⁷Conid ¹⁸andsin ¹⁹asbert ²⁰Adum: *Ecce ²¹os de
²²ossibus meis et ²³caro de ²⁴carne mea* ‡ .i. ‡′ ²⁵is cuma ‖′ ²⁶atchim-si
²⁷cnāim ²⁸dom ²⁹chnāmaib ⅂ feōil dom ³⁰feōil³¹. ‖ ‡ ³²In ³³chēt-
³⁴ghāire ³⁵dernad ³⁶rīam ³⁷indsin, ³⁸⅂ in ³⁹chēt-failte. ³⁸‖

4* *resumed* . . . ¹Iar ²cintaib ³ind ⁴iomarbais, ro
⁵hinnarbad īarsin Adam a ⁶Parrdus ⁷issin talmain
⁸coitchend, ‡ ar nā ⁹toimled ¹⁰tuirthe ¹¹in ¹²Chraind
¹³Bethad ¹⁴i Parrdus; ar dīa ¹⁵toimled, nī ¹⁶fuigbed
¹⁷bāss co brāth, ¹⁸acht ¹⁹slāinte ⅂ ²⁰cenn ²¹fri ²²cotlud ‖.

6*. Ro ¹imarbasaigestar ²īarsain ³clann Adaim .i.
⁴sinnser mac nAdaim .i. ⁵Cāin ⁶misgadhach, do
marbudh a ⁷brāthar .i. ⁸Abēl mac Adaim ⁹tria ¹⁰formud
⅂ ¹¹dīumus. ‡ ¹²Cēt ¹³fingal ¹⁴in domain ¹⁵sin ‖. Do
lecain ¹⁶chamaill ¹⁷dana ro ¹⁸marb Cāin a brāthair.

5*. ¹ adbert   ² eis VE   ³ ataoisi   ⁴ raga   ⁵ ultus
⁶ painim tuam   ⁷ bidh   ⁸ hollus   ⁹ -meala   ¹⁰ Hebha
¹¹ doloire ⅂ geimitu pairieis filieos   ¹² craid   ¹³ galur   ¹⁴ maca
    5ᴀ. ¹ corpda E   ² failti EP   ³ conadh EP   ⁴ airi E
⁵ sin EP   ⁶ tarluic- E : *the word changed by ignorant re-inking to*
tarbiset P   ⁷ codl. *hic et semper* EP   ⁸ is isin P   ⁹ iarom P
¹⁰ do P   ¹¹ dealb- EP   ¹² Ebha *hic et semper* EP   ¹³ ar P : theipedh E
¹⁴ assna E, esna P   ¹⁵ asa EP   ¹⁶ thaobh E taobh P   ¹⁷ -adh P
¹⁸ ansin P : *the re-inker has missed the stroke over the* n   ¹⁹ adbert E
aspert P   ²⁰ Adh- *hic et semper* E   ²¹ oss V   ²² oisibus E
²³ caireo E   ²⁴ carni V cairne EP   ²⁵ *om.* is cuma E   ²⁶ adcimsi E
docimsi P   ²⁷ -mh E : cnaim dom *dittographed* V   ²⁸ domh E
doma P   ²⁹ cn-EP, -mh P   ³⁰ feoil E feoilsi P   ³¹ *ins.* fein E
³² an P   ³³ ced EP   ³⁴ choibche V caibhgi E   ³⁵ *ins.* ⅂ an
cet failti P : dodoronda*d* (*sic*) E, doronnad P   ³⁶ riamh E   ³⁷ inisin
V andsin P   ³⁸⁻³⁸ *om.* P   ³⁹ ced-failti E

5*.   And God said unto them: *De terra es et in terram ibis*, [*i.e.*, Of earth thou art and into earth shalt thou go]. *Et dixit, In sudore uultus tui comedes panem tuum*, [*i.e.*, It shall be in the sweat of thy face that thou shalt eat thy loaves]. He said further unto Eve, *Cum dolore et gemitu paries filios tuos* [*et filias tuas, i.e.*, It shall be with torment and sickness that thou shalt bring forth thy sons and thy daughters].

> 5A. The corporeal creation was displayed to Adam, and he accepted them not. Wherefore a sleep was cast upon him. In that sleep thereafter was Eve fashioned, after being drawn from the seventh rib out of his side. And then said Adam: *Ecce os de ossibus meis, et caro de carne mea* [i.e. (*b*) it is as it were that (?) I see a bone of my bones and flesh of my flesh. That is the first laugh which was ever uttered, and the first welcome].

4*.   . . . After incurring the guilt of the transgression, Adam was then expelled out of Paradise into the common earth, [lest he should eat the fruits of the Tree of Life in Paradise; for were he to eat, he would never die, but have health and ease of mind(*c*) (?)].

6*.   Thereafter the progeny of Adam committed transgression, to wit, the elder of the sons of Adam, Cain the accursed, by the slaying of his brother Abel son of Adam in his envy and haughtiness. [That was the first kin-murder of the world]. With the cheek-

---

4*. [1] EP *are punctuated so as to append the first four words to the preceding* ¶: a E   [2] centaibh P   [3] and E an P   [4] imarb- P -uis P   [5] innarbad V hiondarbad E   [6] Pardus E Parrthus P   [7] isin EP   [8] -cend EP   [9] -mhl- EP: -dh P   [10] tor- E toirthi P   [11] an EP   [12] chroinn E cr- P   [13] irgairti pui i Parrtus P   [14] a Pardus air E   [15] dtoimh- E toimledh P   [16] fuig- E -bedh P   [17] bas EP   [18] ach P   [19] -nti EP   [20] cend EP   [21] fria P   [22] codl- EP

6* [1] imarbaigh*es*dais E imarb*aigh*sistair P   [2] -sin E *om.* P   [3] cland E clanna P   [4] sindser E sinser P   [5] Cadin *changed sec. man. to* Caim E Caidin P   [6] miscadac P   [7] bh- E   [8] Aibel E   [9] tri P   [10] -ad E, at P   [11] dio- E, diu- P   [12] ced EP   [13] -cc- P   [14] an P   [15] sain V *om.* E   [16] camh- P (E *here illegible*)   [17] *om.* P

(*a*) Here P becomes legible.
(*b*) *Is cuma* is meaningless: see the note on this ¶.
(*c*) See. the note on this ¶.

‡ [19]No mar [20]atberat araile, fō [21]intamail [22]marbtha na [32]n-idhbart, [24]issī a [25]glacc ro [26]īad immo [27]brāigid. ||

Here ends the matter on the leaf derived from *Q: the original text of R[2], as we have it, begins at this point.

11. . . . [1]conid desin [2]tuc Dīa [3]dīliu [4]dar in domain [5]imaille, [6]connach tērna beō dīb acht [7]Nōe [8]cona [9]mnāi, ‡ .i. a [10]šiur [11]fodesin ||, ꝭ [12]cona [13]thrīb macaib, ‡ ꝭ bātar [14]iat-sidhe fir a trī n-ingen, || [15]ꝭ cona [16]thrīb ingenaib, ‡ ꝭ [17]bādar [18]iat-side mnā na [19]trī mac ||.

12. Ocus ba hē [1]fochond a [2]sāertha sech cāch, ar [3]nīr chumascsat cairdes fri [4]clainn [5]Cāin; ꝭ [6]dīa [7]līnad [8]in [9]domain [10]doridissi. Cethracha [11]lāithe don [12]dīlind [13]ic sīlind. Sē cēt bliadan [14]āess [15]Nāe [16]in tan dochuaid [17]ina [18]aircc, ‡ in tan [19]tarnaic [20]do Nōe cumtach ꝭ [21]ecor na hairci īar [22]forcedal Dē ‡' .i. [23]dēda do [24]inglan, [25]trēda [26]imorro ‡" nō [27]sechta ||" do glan, [28]dāig [29]idparta dēis [30]na [31]dīlind ||' ||. Luid [32]dana [33]Nāe cona [34]macaib ‡ ꝭ cona ingenaib || ꝭ cona [35]sēitchib [36]ina [37]aircc[(a)], hi [38]sechtmad dēc [39]ēsca [40]Mai. ‡ For [41]nōn [40]Mai lotar isin [42]n-aircc. || Dā cubat dēg din . . . ūas na [43]slēibtib [44]atā [45]airdiu.

---

[18] marp P   [19] *om.* no . . araile P   [20] adberad E   [21] innamh- P
[22] marta *with* b *sprs.* V -bhth- P   [23] n-idhbartai P   [24] no asi P
[25] ghlac P   [26] hiadh ima P   [27] bradaid E br-aid P
    11. [1] conadh P   [2] tug E   [3] dili EP   [4] tars EP   [5] *om.* P
[6] E *illegible:* conach tucad beo (*changed by re-inker to* bed) diph P
[7] Naoi E Naei P   [8] -nai P   [9] mnaoi E   [10] s *not dotted* P
[11] badesin E fodeisin (*changed by re-inker to* -siu) P   [12] a (*om.* con) P
[13] tri mic P   [14] iadside E iad sidie P   [15] *om.* ꝭ P   [16] tri
hiɴɴgenaiph P   [17] batar E   [18] iadsidie P   [19] dtri E
    12. [1] *ins.* so P: fochand E focuī (*changed by re-inker to* focui) P
[2] saoɪtha E saorthai P   [3] -ad cairdes E: ni ro cumusca a gcairdus P
[4] cloind E   [5] Caidin P   [6] do P   [7] lion- EP   [8] an P
[9] domuin V   [10] -dhisi P   [11] -thi P   [12] dilinn E: dilin (*changed*

bone of a camel Cain slew his brother. [Or, as others say, after the likeness of the slaying of the sacrifices, it was his grasp which he closed around his neck] . . .

---

11. . . . so that it was on that account that God brought a Flood over the world altogether, so that none thereof escaped alive except Noe and his wife, [his own sister], and his three sons, [who were the husbands of his three daughters], and his three daughters, [who were the wives of the three sons].

12. Now this was the reason for their deliverance to the exclusion of all others, for that they mingled no friendship with the progeny of Cain; and for their replenishing of the earth again. Forty days was the Flood a-raining. Six hundred years was the age of Noe when he went into his ark, [when there came to Noe the construction and ordering of the ark in accordance with the teaching of God : pairs of the unclean, triple pairs (or sevens) of the clean, for the purpose of sacrifice after the Flood]. So Noe went with his sons [and with his daughters] and with their wives, into his ark, on the seventeenth day of the moon of May. [On the nones of May they went into the Ark.] Twelve cubits [was the water] above the highest mountains.

---

by re-inker to dilui) P   [13] hic E ag P   [14] aois EP   [15] Naoi E .ix. (*sic*) P   [16] an P   [17] *om.* -a P   [18] airc P   [19] tairnig E tra tairnic P   [20] *om.* E, do .ix. P : cumdadach E, cumhdach P   [21] ecor E egor P : hairce V   [22] bf- P foirc- E   [23] -da *erased* P   [24] ning- V   [25] treada E tredha P   [26] *om.* P   [27] secht EP   [28] -gh P   [29] iodbar- E idhb- P   [30] *om.* na E   [31] -end EP   [32] dono P   [33] Naoi E Naei P   [34] macaibh . . . ingenuiph P   [35] -cibh P   [36] *om.* -a P   [37] airc P   [38] secht P   [39] esga EP   [40] Maoi E (*bis*)   [41] noin P   [42] *om.* n- E : airc EP   [43] sleibi V sleibhti*bh* E sleipti P   [44] ita E   [45] hairdi E a hairdi P

(a) E inserts a full stop here, and begins a new sentence with the following *Hi.*

Dēcc [46]cubait don aircc [47]fo [48]usce, [49]ꝛ fiche ōs [50]usce : [51]ꝛ
is aire [52]is a dēcc fo [53]usce, [54].i. dā-dēg don [55]dīlin ōs [56]in
[57]tslēib as [58]airdi, ar dāig na [59]hairci, ar is dēcc cubat dī
fo [60]usce :[49] ꝛ nīr bo furāil [61]dā cubait [62]dana do usce [63]etir
druim na [64]hairci ꝛ mullaige na [65]slīab. [66]Conid aire sin
[67]itā [68]dā cubait dēcc [69]ind airdi [70]na huisci ōs [71]cech [72]slēib
[73]airdd.

13. Ro [1]bāidh [2]in [3]dīliu [4]na huile [5]dāine ꝛ [6]anmanna
[7]archena, acht lucht na [8]haircce, ‡ ꝛ [9]Enōg, fil [10]hi
Parrdus do [11]chathugud [12]ria [13]Hainnticrist, ꝛ [14]Findtan
mac [15]Bochra. [16]Issē [17]adfēda na [18]scēla-sa do cāch,
īar ndīliun. ‖

14. Hi [1]cind [2]cōicad lāithe ar cēt [3]rogabsat na
[4]husce [5]sercadh. Secht [6]lāithe [7]fichet ꝛ secht [8]mīss
[9]dind [10]aircc ō [11]thuinn do [12]thuind, [13]co ndesidh for
[14]slēib Armenia. Ro [15]sergsat na [16]husce [17]cosin . . . .
[18]dechmud [19]mīss [20]atchessa mullaige na [14]slīab. Hi
[21]cind secht lā cethrachat īar sin ro [22]oslaic Nōe senister
na [23]haircce ꝛ [24]fāitte [25]in fīach [26]immach; ꝛ nī [27]thānic
[28]i frithissi. Ro [29]lēic in [30]colum [31]īar na [32]bārach, ꝛ
[33]tānic [34]ar [35]cūlu, ar nī fuair airm [36]ind anadh.
[37]Fōidis [38]Nōe [39]doriss [40]hi [41]cind secht [42]lāithi, ꝛ [43]doluid
la [44]fescor, ꝛ [45]gessca [46]ola-chrainn cona [47]dhuillib ina

---

[46] cubaid E   [47] fon uns fo us (*bungled in re-inking*) E   [48] uisqe P
[49-49] *om.* V   [50] uisqe P   [51] *om.* ꝛ P   [52] as P   [53] uisqe P   [57] ꝛ for .i. P
[55] -inn P   [56] an P   [57] -eiph P   [58] airde P   [59] -ce P
[60] uisqe P   [61] *ins.* dana E coic *for* da EP   [62] *om.* dana do usce E:
dono do uisce P   [63] itir E   [64] -ce P   [65] sliabh P   [66] -adh E -ad P
[67] iata E, it P   [68] .u. for .ii. E: cupait P   [69] in airde P   [70] an us- E
ind us- P   [71] gach EP   [72] sleiph P   [73] aird EP

    13. [1] baid E   [2] an P   [3] dili E dile P   [4] ina P   [5] daoine E
[6] -nnai P   [7] -cena E   [8] -ci E -ce P   [9] Eneog E Enogh P   [10] ꝛ E
[11] cath- P   [12] fri E   [13] hancr V hainnticr E ain xp P   [14] Fint. E
-nnt- P   [15] Bocra P   [16] ise EP   [17] atfed E -eta P   [18] scel;a E
sccai so P

Ten cubits was the ark under water, and twenty above water : and this is why it was ten under water—the Flood had twelve above the highest mountain, for the sake of the ark, for it (the ark) had ten cubits under water. So that two cubits of water would not be excessive between the keel of the ark and the tops of the mountains. Therefore the waters were twelve cubits in depth above every lofty mountain.

13. The Flood drowned all the men and beasts together, except the people of the ark, [and Enoch, who is in Paradise to fight against Antichrist, and Fintan son of Bochra. He it is who should relate these stories to all men, after the Flood].

14. At the end of a hundred and fifty days the waters began to dry up. Twenty-seven days and seven months was the ark (moving) from wave to wave, till it settled on a mountain of Armenia. The waters dried up until the <tenth month : on the first day of the>. tenth month the tops of the mountains were seen. At the end of forty-seven days thereafter, Noe opened a window of the ark, and he sent the raven forth; and it came not back again. He let the dove out on the morrow, and it came back, for it found no place where it should stay. Noah sent it forth

14. [1] cinn E gcinn P [2] chaogad E .la. P [3] -a *changed to* -ad cE -bhsat P [4] huis- E -scedha P [5] serg- E sercc- P [6] -thi P [7] -at P [8] mis EP [9] don EP [10] airc P [11] tuinn EP [12] tuinn E thuinn P [13] con-deis- E -deisigh P [14] sliabh P (*bis*) [15] sergtsat V *apparently* -gsat *changed to* -gsad cE -gsat P [16] huis- EP [17] gusan E [18] decm. E [19] mis EP [20] adcesai E atceassa P [21] cinn P [22] fosgail Naoi seinistir E, fosloig Naei feinister P [23] hairci E hairce P [24] faiti EP [25] an P [26] amach EP [27] tainic EP [28] for cula a bfritisi E, i frithisi P [29] leig E leicc P [30] colaim E [31] ar P [32] marach P [33] tain- EP [34] for E [35] cula EP : fuair E [36] an an E, ar n-anfad P [37] faidis E [38] Nai E [39] doridisi P [40] a E [41] gc- EP [42] -the E [43] -dh P [44] fesgor E feascc- P [45] gesga E gescai P [46] alo-cr P [47] duill- P

⁴⁸bēolu. Ocus ro ⁴⁹fāid ⁵⁰hi cind secht ⁵¹lā doridissi,
⁊ nī ⁵²tānic ⁵³ar ⁵⁴cūlu.

15. Ro ¹rāid Dīa fri ²Nōe ³tiachtain ⁴assin ⁵n-aircc,
⁶hi sechtmad ⁷lā fichet ⁸ēscai ⁹Mai, ‡ for ¹⁰pridnōin ⁹Mai,
‖ isin ¹¹cētna bliadain ar sē cētaib ¹²āisse ¹³Nōe.

y¹ ¹⁴Tossach na ¹⁵hāeisse ¹⁶tānaiste ¹⁷in domain. ¹⁸Co
¹⁹gen ²⁰Abraim ro ²¹saich .i. dā bliadain ²²nōchat ar dib
²³cētaib īar ²⁴fīrinde na ²⁵nEbraide, īarsin ²⁶Septin imorro
is dā bliadain cethrachat ar ²⁷ocht ccētaib.

²⁸Dorōne ²⁹Nōe īarsin altoir do ³⁰chumtach do ³¹Dīa ‡
.i. in ³²cētna ³³altōir īar ³⁴ndīlind ‖. ³⁵Cōica ar ³⁶trī
cētaib bliadan ³⁷bāi ²⁹Nōe ³⁸i mbeth'aid īar ³⁹nd'ilind :
⁴⁰ocus ⁴¹ro ⁴²rand ⁴³Nōe ⁴⁴in domun ⁴⁵hi ⁴⁶trib rand'aib
⁴⁷itir' a ⁴⁸maccu.

y² ⁴⁹Anmand mac ⁵⁰Nōe, .i. ⁵¹Sem, ⁵²Cam, Iafet.
⁵³Anmand 'a' mban iarum, Olla, ⁵⁴Olībana, Oliua : *de
quibus dicitur* ⁵⁵*hoc carmen*

Slūag nād chlōe cūa-chel . . .

Cam trā, ⁵⁶ro gab-side in ⁵⁷nAffraicc ⊓ ⁵⁸deisscert-leth
na ⁵⁹Haissia. ⁶⁰Sem for ⁶¹medōn ⁶²Aissia, ō sruth
Eofrait co tracht airthir ⁶³in ⁶⁴bethad. Is ō ⁶⁵Iafeth

---

⁴⁸ -la E -lau P   ⁴⁹ faoidh E faidh P   ⁵⁰ a gcenn E hi cinn
⁵¹ la yc V *sprs*: doridisi E, -dhisi P   ⁵² tainicc P   ⁵³ for E
⁵⁴ gcula P
    15. ¹ raidh P   ² Naoi E Nai P   ³ teacht P   ⁴ assind E as
in P   ⁵ airc EP (*om.* n-)   ⁶ *om.* hi P   ⁷ *om.* la VE   ⁸ esgai E
escca P   ⁹ Maoi E (*bis*)   ¹⁰ prittnoin P   ¹¹ cedna E   ¹² aois EP
¹³ Naoi E .ix. P   ¹⁴ tossuch V tosach EP   ¹⁵ haoisi EP   ¹⁶ tanuste P
¹⁷ an E   ¹⁸ go E   ¹⁹ gein EP   ²⁰ Apraim P   ²¹ soich P
²² nochad E   ²³ -aiph P   ²⁴ bf- EP   ²⁵ nEabr- E nEpr- P
²⁶ Seibtin E   ²⁷ dcccc. P   ²⁸ -oine E   ²⁹ Naoi E Nai P (*bis*)
³⁰ cumdach E qmhdach P   ³¹ Dhia P   ³² cedna E   ³³ h-alt- P   ³⁴ -inn E
³⁵ caoga P   ³⁶ *written* tri .ccc. E   ³⁷ baoi E   ³⁸ ina E : *words*

again at the end of seven days, and it came with the
evening, having a twig of an olive-tree with its leaves
in its beak.   And he sent it forth again at the end of
seven days, and it came not back.

15. God said unto Noe to come out of the Ark, on
the twenty-seventh day of the moon of May, [on the
day before the nones of May,] in the six hundred and
first year of the age of Noe.

> The beginning of the second age of the world.   To the
> birth of Abram it reached, two hundred ninety and two
> years according to the Hebrew verity, but according to the
> Septuagint it is eight hundred forty and two years.

Thereafter Noe caused an altar to be builded to God
[, the first altar that was made after the Flood].   Three
hundred and fifty years was Noe alive after the
Flood : and Noe divided the world into three parts
among his sons.

> The names of the sons of Noe : Sem, Ham, Iafeth.   The
> names of their wives thereafter : Olla, Olivana, Oliva(a):
> de quibus dicitur hoc carmen:

Poem no. I.

As for Ham, he settled in Africa and the south side
of Asia.   Sem over the middle of Asia, from the river
of Euphrates to the eastern border of the world.   Of

---

and letters marked thus '. . . ' torn away V   [39] -inn E   [40] occus P
[41] do E   [42] rann EP   [43] Naoi E   [44] an P   [45] a E   [46] trip P
[47] etir P   [48] -ca E   [49] -nda E -ndai P   [50] Naoi EP : ins dana E
[51] Seimh E   [52] Camh E Camm P   [53] -nn EP   [54] Oilibai
Oilibana E : Oliua Olibanu P   [55] hocc cairm- P   [56] -bhsidhe P
[57] Affraicc E -aic P : (om. n-)   [58] deisc- E d̄q P   [59] Haisia EP
[60] Seimh EP   [61] -medhon EP   [62] Aissai E Aisia P   [65] om.
in E; an P   [64] betha EP   [65] Iathfedh E Iafeith P

(a) EP give the names of these women in the correct order: Olibana was the
wife of Iafeth.

trā tūaiscert-leth na ⁶⁶Haissia, ⁊ lucht na Heorpa uile :
⁊ dīa ⁶⁷clainn ⁶⁸duinde ⁶⁹in n-ar ⁷⁰nGāidelaib.

16. ¹Gāidel Glass ar sen-athair, mac-²side Niūil
meic ³Fēniusa Farrsaidh meic ⁴Eogein meic ⁵Glūnřind
meic ⁶Lāmřind meic ⁷Etheoir meic ⁸Thōe meic ⁹Boidb
meic ¹⁰Sem meic Mair meic ¹¹Aurthacht meic Abuith
meic Ara meic ¹²Iarra meic Srū meic ¹³Esrū meic
Baaith meic ¹⁴Rifaith ¹⁵Scut, ¹⁶ō tāit ¹⁷Scuit.   Ocus
¹⁸issē ¹⁹Rifath ²⁰Scot ²¹tucastar ²²Scotic ōn Tur, ar ba
²³sē in ₎sesed prīm-²⁴thaisech ro ²⁵bāi i ²⁶ccumtach ²⁷in
²⁸Tuir Nemrōith.

Is follus de sin nach ²⁹raibe ³⁰Fēnius ³¹hi cumtach in
Tuir, mar ³²atberat na ³³senchaide cen ³⁴comšīniudh
³⁵chomhaimseraid. Is aire ³⁶so ōn, ar ³⁷issē ³⁸Fōenu Farsaid
in ³⁹seised fer dēc do ⁴⁰šīl ⁴¹Riafaid ⁴²tuc ⁴³Scotic ōn
⁴⁴Tur.

17. Dā bliadain ¹sescat ō ²scāiliud ³in Tuir co ⁴flaith
Nin meic ⁵Peil.   Ceithre bliadna dēc ar ⁶trib fichtib ar
ocht cētaib ō thūs ⁷flatha Nin co ⁸deirid flatha Tutanes,
⁹rīg ¹⁰in domain.   ¹¹Fria lind-¹²side ro toglad ¹³Trōe
¹⁴din thogail ¹⁵dēdenaig.   Secht mbliadna īarsin thogail
sin, co ¹⁶tuc ¹⁷Aenias ‡ mac ¹⁸Anaciss ‖ ‡ ¹⁹Lauinia ‖
²⁰ingen ²¹Latin meic Puin :   ²²conid trī bliadna
cethrachat ar nōi cētaib ō ²³scāiliud in Tuir co ²⁴tuc

---

⁶⁶ Haisia EP   ⁶⁷ cloinn E   ⁶⁸ -nne EP   ⁶⁹ nar (*om.* i) P
⁷⁰ -eal- E nGaidheal- P

16. ¹ *ins.* .i. EP; Gaoid- E   ² -dhe VP   ³ Feiniusa Fars- EP
⁴ Eb*ir* E Eimhir P   ⁵ Gluin- EP, -nn E   ⁶ Lamhř- E Laimhř- P
⁷ Eothoir E Ei- P   ⁸ Taoi EP   ⁹ Bridliph P   ¹⁰ Seim E
¹¹ Urthacht E Aurtachtt P   ¹² Iara EP   ¹³ Essru E   ¹⁴ Rifbaidth
(d *expuncted*) E   ¹⁵ Scot E Sgot P   ¹⁶ odtait P   ¹⁷ Sguit P
¹⁸ ise E ase P   ¹⁹ -aith E   ²⁰ Sgot P   ²¹ *ins.* tucc (*an incorporated
gloss on* tucastar) V : tugustar EP   ²² Scotig E Sgoitic P   ²³ se in
seised E, he an seisedh P   ²⁴ -tuis- V -thoiss- E primh-tois- P   ²⁵ bui
EP   ²⁶ cumdach P   ²⁷ an P   ²⁸ Tur (*with subscript* i *added sec.
man.*) P   ²⁹ roibe E raiphe P   ³⁰ Foenius E Feinius P   ³¹ i ccumt-

Iafeth is the north side of Asia, and the people of all Europe : and of his progeny are we who are Gaedil.

16. Gaidel Glas our ancestor, he was s. Nel s. Feinius Farsaid s. Eogan s. Glunfhind s. Lamfhind s. Etheor s. Thoe s. Bodb s. Sem s. Mar s. Aurthacht s. Aboth s. Ara s. Iara s. Sru s. Esru s. Baath s. Rifath Scot, from whom are the Scots. Now it is Rifath Scot who brought the Scotic Language from the Tower, for he was one of the six principal chieftains who were at the building of the Tower of Nemrod.

From that, it is clear that Feinius was not at the building of the Tower, as the historians say who have not harmonized the synchronism. This is why we say so, for Feinius was the sixteenth in descent from Rifath, who brought Scotic from the Tower.

17. Sixty-two years from the dispersal of the Tower to the princedom of Ninus son of Belus. Eight hundred seventy and four years from the beginning of the princedom of Ninus to the end of the princedom of Tutanes, king of the world. Toward his time was Troy taken for the last time. There were seven years after that capture, till Aeneas [son of Anchises] took [Lavinia] daughter of Latinus s.

E hi cumdach P ³²adberad E (the d yc E) adberait P ³³uide E aidhe VP ³⁴chomsiniud E -sinedh P. ³⁵comaimsiraid E comhaimsire P' ³⁶seo E ³⁷ise EP ³⁸Foenius E Feinus (with *subscript* i *added sec. man.*) P ³⁹seissed E seisedh P ⁴⁰siol P ⁴¹-aith E : *ins.* Sguit P ⁴²tucc E ⁴³-icc E, Sgoitic P ⁴⁴Tor P
17. ¹-ccat E -lxx- *second* x *expuncted* P ²sgaoil- P ³an P ⁴dtucc Aenias *written here and expuncted* P ⁵Pheil E ⁶tri EP ⁷flaitusai P ⁸derid V deired E -edh P ⁹ri EP ¹⁰an P ¹¹*ins.* 7 P ¹²-dhe VP ¹³Troie V Trai P ¹⁴din tog- E don tocc- P ¹⁵-aigh E deighean- P ¹⁶tucc E dtucc P ¹⁷Aneas E Aeinas P The glosses following this word are *gg* in VP, ꝺꝺ in E. ¹⁸Anachis E Aincis P ¹⁹Lauina EP ²⁰ingin E ²¹Lathin P ²²conadh P ²³sgaoil- P : in Tuir *yc* V ²⁴tucc Aeneas ingin E : dtucc Aeinas P

Aeniass ingen [25]Latin, ⅂ [25]Latin [26]dorōne [27]a cuir [28]friss.

[29]Is follus as sin conach cert-[30]tiaghait [31]lucht [32]ind [33]Auraiccepta, [34]combad hē [35]Laitin in [36]seissed prīm-[38]thōisech [39]ind Tuir, ⅂ a [40]fot [41]anūass [42]etorru [43]cethracha bliadan, o [44]scāiliud in Tuir co [45]tānic [46]Foenius Farsaidh [47]atūaidh asin [48]Scithia cona [49]scoil, do [50]iarraidh na [51]mbērla : ar do-[52]rumenatar [53]fosgebtais [54]and, ar bīth [55]as ass ro [56]scāilit. [57]Dā bliadain īar [58]tiachtain do [59]Fēnius atūaid [60]corice Nin.

18. Is [1]ē Nēl mac [2]Feniusa Farsaid [3]asrubrumar forcongart [4]Forand [5]Cincris rī [6]Ēigipti [7]ar imad a [9]fesa ⅂ a [10]eōlais ⅂ a [11]fogluma : ⅂ [12]dobert [13]Forand [14]ferann do, ⅂ [15]dobreath a [16]ingen [17].i. [18]Scota a hainm.

[19]Ocus asberat araile [20]comadh aire [21]adbertha ''Scota'' [22]fria, ar ba [23]''Scot'' ainm a fir, ⅂ [24]''Scuit'' ainm na [25]tūaithe dia [26]rabe [27]in fer; *unde dicitur* [28]''Scotus'' ⅂ [28]''Scota.''

19. [1]Conidh [2]do sin [3]asberar [4]so [5]sīss—

[25] Laitin P (bis)   [26] *ins.* fein E: doroine P   [27] acuir *written as one word* VP, *but om.* a E   [28] fris P   [29] iss E   [30] -aid E   [31] luicht E: luᵽ *changed by re-inker to* ais (*the* ı *can still be traced faintly*) P   [32] na P   [33] auraicepta E nuraicp P   [34] comadh P   [35] Latin E   [36] insseiss- E .uii. mad P   [38] -tois- P   [39] in E an P   [40] fot E fod P   [41] -as P   [42] -orrai P   [43] .lx. E   [44] sgaoil- P   [45] dtanic P   [46] Feinius P   [47] -aid' assin E   [48] Sgeithia P   [49] sgoil P   [50] iaraidh V   [51] -lae E -lai P   [52] -att *changed to* -atar V ruimnetar P   [53] -dais P   [54] ann EP : ar *dittographed owing to change of column* V   [55] is E   [56] sgaoilsit P   [57] .u. V   [58] tichtain (*om.* do) E   [59] Foen- E Feinius P   [60] -ricce P

Faunus : so that there are nine hundred forty and three years from the dispersal of the Tower till Aeneas took the daughter of Latinus, and Latinus made his treaties with him.

From that it is clear that the authors of the *Auraicept* do not reach a correct conclusion, that Latinus was one of the six chief leaders of the Tower, seeing that the length downward between them is forty years, from the dispersal of the Tower till Feinius Farsaid came from the north, out of Scythia with his School, to seek for the languages : for they thought that they would find them there(*a*) inasmuch as it was from thence that they were dispersed.   There were two years after the coming of Feinius from the north until Ninus.

18. It is the aforesaid Nel son of Feinius Farsaid whom Pharao Cincris King of Egypt invited, for the greatness of his skill, his knowledge, and his learning : and Pharao granted him an estate, and his daughter, Scota her name, was bestowed.

Some say that the reason why she was called "Scota" was that "Scot" was her husband's name, and "Scots" the name of the people from whom he came; *unde dicitur* "Scotus" and "Scota."

19. So that the following is said of those matters—

---

18. [1] he E   [2] Foen- E Fein- P   [3] asrubramar E asrubartamar P [4] -nn E   [5] Cinciris P   [6] Egipt EP   [7] ar immed E ar imat P [9] ꝼessa E feassai *re-inked to* feaisai P   [10] eolusa E   [11] -lumma E -gh- P [12] dober V tuc P   [13] -ainn E -ann P   [14] ferand E feron (*changed by re-inker to* ferch-) P   [15] dobertha ꝩcE dobreth P   [16] ingin E   [17] *om.* .i. E: *ins.* do P   [18] Sgotai P   [19] *om.* ꝛ E   [20] combad E   [21] asbertha E atbertha P   [22] frie E *punctuated* fria arba. Sgot *by re-inker* P [23] Sgot P   [24] Sguit P   [25] -thi P   [26] raibe E raibhi P   [27] an P [28] -tt- E (*bis*): Sgota P
    19. [1] Conid E conadh P   [2] de E   [3] asbert P   [4] *om.* so E [5] *om.* siss EP

(*a*) i.e. at the Tower.

Athair cāich, Coimsid Nime . . .

Third Redaction.

(B 8 *a* 1 : M 264 *a* 1 : H 103 *a* 1 :
from ¶ 32; *β* 32.13 : *β*¹ 32.22 : *β*² 6.28.)

I.

The beginning of the Third Redaction is a translation into Irish of the first eleven chapters of the Book of Genesis. For the history of this translation, and of its connexion with the text, see ante, p. 6. In the following pages the Biblical text is printed in larger type (the verses being numbered);

BOOK OF GENESIS

CHAPTER I.

20. (1) *In* ¹*principio creauit Deus celum et terram* .i. ro ²thuissimh Dīa ³Neamh ꝛ ⁴talumh ⁵ar tūs.

y¹ ꝛ nī ⁶fuil tossach fair-⁷simh ⁸feisin, na foirceand.

y² Is amhlaidh ⁹dorighni Dīa na ¹⁰dūili : aroili dīb co ¹¹tosach ꝛ cen chrīch, amhail aingliu; ¹²araili dībh ¹³cu ¹⁴tossach ꝛ co ¹⁵forcend, amhail ¹⁶anmanda indlighthe ꝛ ¹⁷toirrthe in talman; ¹⁸araile dībh imorro co ¹⁹tossach ꝛ co ²⁰foircend ꝛ ²¹cen ²²foircend, amail ²³atait dāine, .i. ²⁴tossach for a ²⁵ngeinemain ²⁶corpardha ꝛ ²⁷forcend for a ²⁸corpthaib, ꝛ ²⁹gan ³⁰forcenn for a n-anmandaibh.

y³ Isin Domnach ³¹dorighni Dīa in mais ³²n-adhbul-mhōir ³³nemhcruthaigh ‡ .i. ³⁴adbhur na ndūl ³⁵corparda ‡′ .i. ³⁶tene ꝛ ³⁷āeor, ³⁸talam ꝛ usce ‖′, ‖ ‡ hi .xu. kallann ³⁹April dono do reir Ebraide ꝛ ⁴⁰Latinda, ‖ ‡′ cen co tucadh

---

20. *Variants from M unless otherwise stated. It may be said here, once for all, that the lenition of b, d, g, m, is almost invariably left unmarked in this MS.*   ¹ prindcipio   ² thuisim   ³ *ins.* .i. in tAthair Neamda   ⁴ talam   ⁵ *om.* ar tus: *ins.* isin tosach .i. isin Mac   ⁶ fuil tosach   ⁷ -seam   ⁸ na foirceand feisin B   ⁹ doroinde   ¹⁰ duile aroile   ¹¹ tosach   ¹² -oile   ¹³ co   ¹⁴ tosach   ¹⁵ foirceand M;

Poem no. V.

Third Redaction.

at the end of each chapter is a restoration of the text of the Latin MS. from which it was translated, with textual notes. The numerous glosses and interpolations are printed in smaller type, and all necessary annotations are given in the commentary at the end of this section of the entire work.

BOOK OF GENESIS

Chapter I.

20. (1) *In principio creauit Deus caelum et terram* i.e., God created Heaven and Earth at the first.

And He hath no beginning Himself, nor ending.

In this wise God made the creatures: some of them with beginning and without end, as Angels; some of them with beginning and with termination, as irrational beasts and fruits of the earth; some of them moreover with beginning and with termination and without termination, as are men—a beginning to their bodily birth and a termination to their bodies, and without termination to their souls.

On the Sunday God made the immense formless mass, [the materials of the corporeal creatures, fire and air, earth and water, upon the fifteenth of the kalends of April according to Hebrews and Latins, although no sun

---

a dot over c *erased* B   [16] -nna aindligthecha   [17] toirthi   [18] -oile
[19] tosach [20] -ceand   [21] cean   [22] -ceand   [23] itait na daine   [24] tosach
[25] -eam-   [26] chorparda   [27] foirceand   [28] *sic* M, corp B   [29] cen
[30] foirceand   [31] doridne   [32] -bal-moir   [33] -aich   [34] -bar   [35] *sic* M;
corpdha *changed by late corrector to* corpdhada B   [36] tened   [37] aeoir
[38] usqi ⁊ talam   [39] Aibril   [40] Laitinda

grīan [41]for rith co se ||'; is and [42]dorighni Dīa [43]tindscetal denma na ndūl.   Isin Lūan, ‡ hi .xiiii. kallann [44]April, |¦ dorighni Dīa Neam.   [45]Isand Mairt, [46]‡ hi .xiii. kallann [47]April, || [48]dorighni Dīa in talam, ⁊ [49]tug muir ina [50]timceall.   Isin [51]Cētāin, ‡ hi .xii. kallann [52]April, || [53]dorigni Dīa grīan ⁊ ēsca ⁊ [54]rēltanda ⁊ [55]renda nimhe. Isin Dardāin, ‡ .i. in .xi. kallann [56]April ||, dorigni Dīa na hanmanda [57]muiridhi ⁊ [58]eathaidi in [59]āeoir.   [60]Isan Āine imorro ‡ [61].i. hi .x. kallann [62]April, || [63]dorigni Dīa Adham ⁊ na huili anmanda talmaidi.   Ro [64]cumsain Dia imorro [65]isan [66]tSatharrnd ‡ .i. hi .ix. kallann [67]April |, .i. [68]ō [69]oipriugadh dūla nūa.

(2) Īar tuismeadh trā [70]nime ⁊ talman, is amhlaidh [71]bāi in talam, ⁊ sē dimain cen [72]torrti, ⁊ sē [73]fāss [74]falum cen [75]aitreabhaidhe.   Ocus no bīdis ‡ in tan sin || [76]dorchata [77]dlūithi for [78]dreich na [79]hāibhisi—

.i. [80]adbur [81]coitchend na ndūl—

⁊ [82]no fortairctha [83]Spīrut in [84]Comdedh for na [85]huiscib.

Ni [86]locdacht [87]trā rāiter [88]sund don [89]Spīrut Nāem, acht [90]dearrscaithi ⁊ miadhamlacht de, seacha dūilibh.

(3) Ocus ro rāidh Dīa ‡ .i. in tAthair Nemdha ||, Dēntar [91]in tsoillsi.   Ocus [92]dorignedh in tsoillsi. (4) Ro therba ⁊ ro [93]deiligh Dīa in [94]soillsi [s²M] ōna [95]dorchadaibh.   (5) Ocus dorad ainm ''Lāe'' don tsoillsi, ⁊ tuc ainm na [96]''Haidhchi'' do na [97]dorchaib. Ocus dorōnadh amlaidh sin [98]feascoir ⁊ [99]maiden .i. in [100]cēt lā.

---

[41] frith *stroke of abbreviation over f added sec. man.* B   [42] doroinde
[43] -eadal   [44] Aibril   [45] isin   [46] *ins.* dono   [47] Aipril   [48] doridne
[49] tuc   [50] thimchell   [51] chedain am, hi   [52] Aip-   [53] dorinde   [54] retlanda
[55] reanda   [56] Aip-   [57] -ide   [58] -ide   [59] *a point over the* e M   [60] isind
[61] *om.* .i.   [62] Aip-   [63] doroinde   [64] chumson   [65] isin   [66] -arnn
[67] Aib-   [68] *om.* o   [69] oibreadugad   [70] nimi   [71] *ins.* ro   [72] toirchi
[73] fas   [74] -am   [75] -ebaide   [76] -ada   [77] *the* 1 *written in rasura as*

was set upon its course as yet]; it is then that God made a beginning of fashioning the creatures. On the Monday, [on the fourteenth of the kalends of April,] God made Heaven. On the Tuesday, [on the thirteenth of the kalends of April,] God made the earth, and brought Sea around it. On the Wednesday, [on the twelfth of the kalends of April,] God made sun and moon and stars and heavenly bodies. On the Thursday, [on the eleventh of the kalends of April] God made the marine beasts and the birds of the air. On the Friday, moreover, [on the tenth of the kalends of April,] God made Adam and all the terrestrial beasts. Moreover God ceased on the Saturday, [the ninth of the kalends of April,] from the work of a new creation.

(2) Now, after the creation of Heaven and Earth, thus was the earth; fallow without fruit, bare and empty without indweller. And thick darknesses were at that time over the face of the abyss—

the common material of the creatures—

And the Spirit of the Lord was borne over the waters.

No wickedness is spoken here of the Holy Spirit, but excellence and honour of Him, beyond the creatures.

(3) and God [the Heavenly Father] said: Let the Light be made. And the light was made. (4) God separated and divided the light from the darknesses. (5) And He gave the name 'Day' to the light, and the name 'Night' to the darknesses. And thus were made evening and morning, the first day.

---

is also the eich of dreich B   [78] dreikh   [79] -beisi   [80] -bar. *A dot written over the* b, *afterwards scratched out, and later re-inserted,* B   [81] cheand   [82] no forchairthea   [83] -rud   [84] Choimdead   [85] hus-   [86] lochtach   [87] thra   [88] sunn   [89] -rit Naeim   [90] dears-   [91] in*n* *preceded by an erasure that would hold about 4 letters.*   [92] doridnead   [93] delidh   [94] thoillsi   [95] dorchaib   [96] -dche   [97] *sic* M -caib B   [98] -scor   [99] maidea*n* an .i. *with* in *written sec. man. above the* .i. M   [100] *om.* cet B

21. (6) Ro rāidh [1]dana : Dēntar [2]in ꝼirmamint a meadhōn na n-usci, [3]ꝛ fodlad na n-usci[3] ō na [4]huiscib. (7) Ocus [5]dorigni Dīa [6]in firmaimint, ꝛ ro fogail na usci ro [7]bātar fō Firmaimint ō na [8]huiscibh ro [9]bātar ōs Firmaimint : ꝛ [10]doirigneadh amlaidh sin. (8) Ocus [11]tug [12]Dīa ainm 'Nimhe' [13]do Firmaimint, ꝛ [14]dorighnedh [15]feascoir ꝛ [16]maiden, .i. [17]in lāā tānaise.

22. (9) Ro rāidh imorro Dīa : [1]Tinōilter na [2]husci atait fō Nimh [3]i n-ōen inadh, [4]ꝛ artraigeadh [5]in tirim : ꝛ dorigneadh amlaidh sin. (10) Ocus [6]is ē ainm [7]tug Dīa don [8]tirim, .i. [9]Talam : acus ro [10]gairmeastar Dīa [11]comthinōla na [12]n-uisci, [13]Muiridhi. Ocus [14]atconnairc Dīa cor bo maith. (11) Ocus [15]atbert Dīa : [16]Clandaigeadh [17]an talam fēr n-uraide, ꝛ fēr dogēna sīl ; ꝛ clannaigeadh[17] [18]crand toradh-[19]tairctheach, dodhēna toradh do rēir a [29]ceineōiḷ, ꝛ a mbia a sīl and féin for [21]talmuin. (12) Ocus ro lēig [22]in talum fēr n-uraide trīd, ꝛ fēr dognīdh [23]sīl do [24]rēir a [25]ceineōil ; ꝛ ro [26]lēc [27]crand dognīd torad, ꝛ no [28]thechtadh [29]gach sīl do rēir a [30]earnaili. Ocus [31]adconnairc Dīa sin, cor bho maith. (13) Ocus [22]dorighnedh [33]fescoir ꝛ [34]maiten, .i. [35]in tres lāā.

23. (14) Ro rāidh [1]imorro Dīa : Dēntar [2]lēspairedha solus-[3]thaitneamacha [4]i ꝼirmaimint [5]indimhi, [[s1]M] ꝛ [6]deilighead [7]lā ꝛ [8]aidhchi : ꝛ [9]bīt i [10]comartaibh ꝛ i [11]n-aimsiribh, i [12]l-lāithedhaibh ꝛ i [13]mbliadhnaibh, (15) co ro [14]taitneat i [15]firmaimint [16]ind nimi, ꝛ co ro

---

. **21.** [1] dono   [2] annirmaimint   [3-3] *om.* B.   [4] husc-   [5] -gne [6] annirmaimint   [7] badar   [8] husc-   [9] badar   [10] doridnead   [11] tuc [12] Di B   [13] donirmaimint   [14] -gnead   [15] -cor   [16] -dean   [17] *om.* in
    22. [1] -tear   [2] us-   [3] an en   [4] ꝛ ar- *dittographed owing to change of column* B   [5] an   [6] as   [7] tuc   [8] tal*main* B   [9] tirim (tirim acus *written* tir imacus) B : acus *here also in* M   [10] -estair   [11] coim-thinola (*a* g *written and erased after the second* o)   [12] n-usci [13] muirige   [14] adchonnairc   [15] adb-   [16] clannaigead   [17-17] *om.* B

21. (6) Further He said: Let the firmament be made in the midst of the waters, and let it divide the waters from the waters. (7) And God made the firmament, and divided the waters that were beneath Firmament from the waters that were above Firmament: and thus was it done. (8) And God gave the name of 'Heaven' to Firmament, and evening and morning were made, the second day.

22. (9) Moreover God said: Let the waters that are under Heaven be collected into one place, and let the Dry appear: and so was it done. (10) And this is the name which God gave to the Dry, 'Earth': and God called the assemblages of the waters, 'Seas.' And God saw that it was good. (11) And God said: Let the earth bring forth green grass, and grass that shall make seed; and let it bring forth the fruit-bearing tree that shall make fruit according to its kind, and that shall have its seed within itself upon earth. (12) And the earth put forth green grass, and grass that maketh seed according to its kind, and it put forth the tree that maketh fruit, and that hath every seed according to its species. And God saw that to be good. (13) And evening and morning were made, the third day.

23. (14) Moreover God said: Let brightly shining lights be made in the firmament of Heaven, and let them divide Day and Night: and let them be for signs and for times, for days and for years, (15) that they may shine in the firmament of Heaven, and

---

[18] crann   [19] thairceach   [20] a chel no a cenel   [21] -main   [22] an talam
[23] *ins.* a   [24] rel   [25] cheinel   [26] leig   [27] crann   [28] -eacht-
[29] gan B   [30] ernaile   [31] -chonn   [32] -gnead   [33] feascor : feascoir .i.
deireadh láe *written in top marg. in 18th cent. hand* B   [34] maidean
[35] an treas la

23. [1] Dia imorro   [2] -eada   [3] -tait-   [4] a fir-   [5] inime
[6] deligthear   [7] lae   [8] -dche   [9] bid   [10] -arthaib   [11] -sir-, *the* i
*yc*B   [12] -ead-   [13] mbliadain   [14] thaitnead   [15] -mam-   [16] indimi

[17]šoillsiget in [18]talam. Ocus [19]dorignedh amlaidh sin. (16) Ocus doróindi [20]Día dā [21]léaspaire [22]solus-móra : dorighni am in léspaire is mō ‡ .i. in [23]grēin ‖ co [24]ropdanaiged don lō, ⁊ in [25]léspaire is lughu isin [26]n-aidhci ‡ .i. [27]ind ēsca ‖. Ocus [28]dorigni rētlanda, (17) ⁊ ro [29]suigidh iat [30]i firmaimint [31]indimi, co ro [32]taitnidis for talmain, (18) [33]⁊ co ro aptainigdis [34]do lō ⁊ [34]do aidhchi, ⁊ co [35]ndeilightis [36]in [37]soillsi ō na dorchaibh. Ocus [38]atconnaic Día [39]sin, [40]cor bo maith. (19) Ocus [41]dorignedh [42]fescoir ⁊ [43]maitin, [44].i. in [45]cetramadh lāā.

24. (20) Ro rāidh [1]dana Día : [2]Turgbhat na [3]huisci [4]tondaitechu na hanma [5]beoaigheas, ⁊ [6]folūaimneachu fo firmaimint [7]indimi. Ocus [8]dorigned amlaidh sin. (21) Ocus ro [9]thuissim Día [10]bleidhmila móra ‡ muiridi ‖, ⁊ [11]ind uili n-anmand mbeōthach ⁊ [12]so-cumscaightheach ro [13]turgbatar na husci i n-a [14]n-ernailibh. Ocus ro [15]tuissimh Día [16]in uili [17]folūaimneachu do [18]rēr a [19]ceneōil, ⁊ [20]adconairc Día [21]cor bo maith sin. (22) Ocus ro, [22]bennai[ge]stear Día dōibh, ⁊ ro rāidh : Foirbridh ⁊ [23]barnimdaighter ⁊ līnaidh usci in mhara, ⁊ [24]imdaighthear na heōin for talmain. (23) Ocus [25]dorigned amlaidh sin [26]maiten ⁊ [27]fescoir, [28].i. in [29]cūicedh lā.

25. (24) Ro rāidh [1]dono Día, ‡ .i. [2]in Tuismeadh ‖ : [3]Turgbadh in [4]talmun (sic) na hanmanda [5]examla īar n-a [6]cenēl imchubhaidh, .i. iuminti ⁊ [7]tondaitechu, ⁊

---

[17] s-ged   [18] sic M, tal- B   [19] doridnead   [20] om. Dia   [21] lesbairi
[22] solusda mora   [23] grian   [24] rapdanaided   [25] -airi   [26] -chi
[27] int   [28] doridni   [29] suigig   [30] a   [31] indime   [32] thaitnidis
[33] ⁊ (obscured by a blot) con apdanigis   [34] don (bis)   [35] -gdis
[36] om.   [37] soll-   [38] adchondairc   [39] om.   [40] apparently go mbo
changed sec. man. to gor bo M   [41] -ead   [42] -cor   [43] -ten   [44] om. .i.
[45] ceathrumad la
24. [1] Dia dono   [2] turcbad   [3] husci   [4] tonnaichu   [5] -ges

may illuminate the earth. And thus was it done. (16) And God made two bright and great lights : He made the greater light [the sun] that it might rule over the day, and the lesser light in the night [the moon]. And He made stars, (17) and set them in the firmament of Heaven, that they might shine upon the earth, (18) and that they might rule over day and over night, and might divide the light from the darknesses. And God saw that to be good. (19) And evening and morning were made, the fourth day.

24. (20) God said further : Let the waters bring forth reptiles of the life that quickeneth, and birds under the firmament of Heaven. And so was it done. (21) And God created great [sea]-monsters, and every living and mobile beast which the waters brought forth in their species. And God created all the birds according to their kind, and God saw that to be good. (22) And God blessed them, and said : Increase and be ye multiplied, and fill the water of the sea, and let the birds be multiplied upon the land. (23) And thus were morning and evening made, the fifth day.

25. (24) Further God [the Creator] said : Let the earth bring forth the different animals after their fitting kind, cattle and reptiles, and the beasts of

---

[6] -echu   [7] -ime   [8] doridnead *changed by late corrector to* dorignead *in marg.* M   [9] tuisim   [10] -ili   [11] inn   [12] -caith-   [13] thurcbadar   [14] hern- B   [15] *written* c'ṗııi (*an abbreviation which would more naturally suggest* tursimh) B, c;ım M.   [16] inn   [17] -each   [18] reir   [19] cheniuil   [20] -chond-   [21] sin cor bo maith   [22] beandachais   [23] -gth-   [24] -gther   [25] dorignidh B doridnead M   [26] maiden   [27] -cor   [28] *om.* .i.   [29] -ead

25. [1] Dia dono   [2] *om.* in B: t;m. M. *So lower down in the* ¶, th;im.   [3] turcbad   [4] -muin   [5] ecs-   [6] -eol   [7] -aithechu

[8]bīasda in [9]talmun iar n-a n-earnailib imchuibhdibh;
⅂ [10]doridned amlaidh sin.   (26) Ocus do rāidh Dīa :
[11]Dēnum [12]in [13]Duini [14]for n-īmāigin ⅂ for [15]cosmhailus
fodēn, ⅂ remhapdanaighed do īascaib in mara, ⅂ do
[16]folūaimneaibh indimi, ⅂ do [17]bhīastaibh in uili
[18]talman.   (27) Ocus ro [19]thuissim Dīa in Duini [20]fō
īmāigin fodēn—

> Is amlaidh trā dorigni Dīa in duine, .i. a [21]corp do
> [22]talmain ‡', [23].i. a [24]chend a tīr Garad, a ucht ⅂ a bruindi
> a tīr [25]Arabia, a brū a [26]Lodain, a [27]cossa a tīr Agoiria, ‖' a
> ḟuil do usci ‡ in [28]āer ‖, a anāl do āeor, a [29]teas do [30]teinidh,
> a [31]anam do [32]tinfedh Dē.   Is amlaidh sin [33]atāt na [34]ceithre
> dūili [35]i ngach duine.

—ro thuisim [36]ēm fear ⅂ mnaī fo īmāigin Dē.   Ro
thuisim [37]iat (28) ⅂ ro [38]bennach dōibh ⅂ ro rāid:
Forbrid ⅂ dēntar bar n-imdugadh, ⅂ līnaidh in
[39]talmuin, ⅂ fomāmaigid dūibh hī, ⅂ [40]tigernaigid do
īascaibh in mara ⅂ do [41]eathaitibh inime ⅂ do na huilibh
anmandaibh [42]for talmain.   (29) Ocus [43]ro rāidh
Dīa : Doradus dāibh co follus in uili [44]ḟēar [45]tairgis
sīl for talmain, ⅂ na huili [46]crondu [47]techtait indtibh
fodēn | sīlni a [48]ceineōil |[(a)] [49]comchubhaid, ardāigh co
[50]mbēadh sin dāibh a mbiadh ⅂ a n-aileamain : (30) ⅂ do
uilibh anmandaibh in talman, ⅂ do uilibh [51]eathaitibh
in [52]nimi, ⅂ do na huilibh [53]da ḟil [54]cumscugadh i
talmain, ⅂ is [55]inntibh atā [56]ainim beoighes, co ro
[57]techat co tomultus.   Ocus [58]dorigned amlaidh sin.
(31) Ocus [59]adchondairc Dīa na huili [60]dorigni, ‡ ⅂
[61]do bhadar ‖, [62]comdar maithi co [63]hadhbul.   Ocus
[64]dorighnedh [65]fescoir ⅂ [66]maiten, in seiseadh lā.

---

[8] -sta   [9] -man   [10] dorigni B   [11] denaid   [12] om. in   [13] duine
[14] foim maigin (second word in rasura) B fornimaigin M   [15] cosmailis
[16] ḟoluaimneachaib innimi   [17] piastaib   [18] thal-   [19] tusim Dia in
Duine   [20] foi maigin B   [21] chorp   [22] thal-   [23] ⅂ for .i.
[24] cheand   [25] Araibia   [26] Lotain   [27] chosa   [28] aeoir   [29] theas
[30] thenid   [31] ainm B anim M   [32] thinfead   [33] itat   [34] -thri   [35] in
cach duine   [36] aen ḟear B   [37] ins. imorro: iad   [38] beandach

the earth after their fitting species; and so was it done. (25) [*This verse missing.*] (26) And God said: Let us make the Man under our own image and likeness, and let him have dominion over the fishes of the sea, and over the birds of Heaven, and over the beasts of the whole earth. (27) And God created the Man under His own image—

> Now in this wise did God make the Man: his body of earth [his head of the land of Garad, his breast and bosom of the land of Arabia, his belly of Lodain, his legs of the land of Agoiria], his blood of [the] water [of the air], his breath of air, his heat of fire, his soul of the breath of God. Thus it is that the four elements are in every man.

In truth He made man and woman under the image of God. He created them (28) and blessed them and said: Increase, and let your multiplication be accomplished, and fill the earth, and subdue it unto yourselves, and lord it over the fishes of the sea and the birds of the Heaven and all the beasts upon the earth. (29) And God said: See, I have given you all the grass that bringeth forth seed upon the earth, and all the trees that have the seed of their proper kind within themselves, that they may be for food and sustenance unto you: (30) and unto all the beasts of the earth, and unto all the birds of Heaven, and unto all that have motion upon the earth, and that have within them the soul that quickeneth, that they may have them for nourishment. And thus was it done. (31) And God saw all things that He had made [and that were], that they were wondrous good: and evening and morning were made, the sixth day.

---

[39] talam [40] tigernaidhi B [41] -dib [42] *ins.* fuilet [43] *om.* ro B [44] ̃fer [45] -rceas [46] chrunnu [47] -taid intib fodein silne [48] chen- [49] comcubhaib B [50] mbeith [51] -dib [52] nime [53] do fil [54] -gud [55] intib [56] ainm beoaiges [57] thechtad [58] -ghnidh B doridnead M [59] otconairc B [60] dorigne [61] ro badar [62] comdartha B [63] -dbal [64] -ridned [65] -cor [66] -den.

(a) These 3 words s^2 M.

20. (1)*(a)* In principio ¹creauit Deus caelum et terram.
(2) ²[Terra autem erat inanis et uacua] et ³tenebrae *⁴erant*
super faciem abyssi : et Spiritus ⁵*Domini* ferebatur super
aquas.   (3) Dixitque Deus : Fiat lux.   Et facta est lux.
(4) ⁶[Et uidit Deus lucem quod esset bona,] et ⁷diuisit ⁸*Deus*
lucem ⁹*a tenebris.*   (5) Appellauitque lucem 'Diem,' et
tenebras 'Noctem.' Factumque est ¹⁰<ita> uespere et mane,
dies ¹¹primus.

21. (6) Dixit quoque ¹[Deus] : Fiat firmamentum in
medio aquarum, et diuidat aquas ab aquis.   (7) Et fecit Deus
firmamentum, diuisitque aquas quae erant sub ²firmamento
³*ab aquis* quae erant super firmamentum : et factum est ita.
(8) Vocauitque Deus firmamentum 'Caelum,' et factum est
uespere et mane, dies secundus.

22. (9) Dixit uero Deus : Congregentur aquae quae sub
caelo sunt in locum unum, et appareat arida : factumque est
ita. (10) Et uocauit Deus aridam, Terram ; congregationesque
aquarum appellauit Maria.   Et uidit Deus quod esset bonum.
(11) Et ait ¹<Deus> : Germinet terra herbam uirentem et
²facientem semen, et lignum pomiferum faciens fructum iuxta
³genus suum, cuius semen in semetipso sit super terram.
⁴[Et factum est ita].   (12) Et protulit terra herbam uirentem
et ⁵*facientem* semen iuxta genus suum, lignumque faciens
fructum et habens unumquodque sementem secundum
speciem suam.   Et uidit Deus quod esset bonum.   (13) Factumque est uespere et mane, dies tertius.

23. (14) Dixit autem Deus : Fiant ¹luminaria in firmamento caeli, ²*et* dividant diem ac noctem, et sint in signa,
et tempora, ³[et] dies, et annos, (15) ut luceant in firmamento
caeli, et inluminent terram. Et factum est ita. (16) Fecitque
Deus duo magna luminaria : luminare maius ut praeesset
diei, et luminare minus ⁴[ut praeesset] nocti : et ⁵<fecit>
stellas, (17) et posuit eas in firmamento caeli, ut lucerent
super terram, (18) et praeessent diei ac nocti, et diuiderent

---

(*a*) *Italics* in the Latin text denote readings differing from that followed in
the Vatican *variorum* edition of the Vulgate (here called ST = Standard Text).
[Square] brackets mark words in the Latin not represented in the Irish translation.   <Angled> brackets denote words presupposed by the Irish translation,
but not represented in any of the MSS. of the Vulgate used in the Vatican edition.

lucem [6]*a tenebris.* Et uidit Deus quod esset bonum. (19) Et factum est uespere et mane, dies quartus.

24. (20) Dixit etiam Deus: Producant aquae [1]*reptilia* animae uiuentis, et [2]*uolatilia* [3][super terram] sub firmamento caeli: <Et factum est ita>. (21) Creauitque Deus cete grandia [4]<marina>, et omnem animam uiuentem atque [5]*motabilem* quam produxerunt aquae in species suas. Et [6]<creauit Deus> [7]omnia *uolatilia* secundum genus suum, et uidit Deus quod esset bonum. (22) Benedixitque eis [8]<Deus>, dicens: Crescite et multiplicamini, et replete aquas maris, auesque multiplicentur super terram. (23) Et factum est [9]<ita> uespere et mane, dies quintus.

25. (24) Dixit quoque Deus: Producat terra [1]*animalia diuersa* in genere suo, iumenta et reptilia, et bestias terrae secundum species suas; factumque est ita. (25) [2][*This verse missing.*] (26) Et ait [3]<Deus>: Faciamus hominem ad imaginem et similtudinem nostram, et praesit piscibus maris, et uolatilibus caeli, et bestiis universae[4][que] terrae [5][omnique reptili quod mouetur in terra]. (27) Et creauit Deus hominem ad imaginem suam. [6]Ad imaginem Dei creauit [illum] masculum et femĩam. Creauit eos, (28) Benedixitque illis [7][Deus] et ait: Crescite et multiplicamini, et replete terram, et subicite eam, et dominamini piscibus maris et uolatilibus caeli et uniuersis animantibus [8][quae mouentur] super terram. (29) Dixitque Deus [9]Ecce, dedi uobis omnem herbam adferentem semen super terram, et uniuersa ligna quae habent in semetipsis sementem generis sui, ut sint uobis [10]in escam: (30) et cunctis animantibus terrae [11]*omnisque uolucribus* caeli, et universis quae mouentur in terra, et in quibus est anima uiuens, ut habeant ad uescendum. Et factum est ita. (31) Viditque Deus cuncta quae fecit, et erant ualde bona: et factum est uespere et mane, dies sextus.

NOTES ON THE BIBLICAL TEXT, CHAPTER I.

The following abbreviations are used in these notes:—

Heb.—The original Hebrew text.
LXX.—The Greek rendering, commonly called the Septuagint.
OL.—The Old Latin version or versions.
Vulg.—The Vulgate.

ST—The Standard text, as set forth in the Vatican *variorum* edition
of the Vulgate. (For the *apparatus criticus* of the Latin
text, reference must be made to this comprehensive work.)
Δ—The MS. of the Vulgate used by the Irish translator.
Tr.—The Irish translator, or his translation.
R³, sR³—The Third Redaction of LG; a Scribe of the Third
Redaction.

¶ 20. [1]*creauit,* not *fecit,* as in R¹ R², showing at the outset
that we have now to deal with a Vulgate text. [2]The bracketed
words are paraphrased only in the text of Tr.: possibly by
sR³, who inserted some of the long interpolation just preceding, in order to complete its incorporation with the text.
It may be worth noting, as a coincidence, that the *sense* of
the paraphrase resembles the possible alternative reading of
the well-known syntactic ambiguity at the beginning of Heb.
(on which see any standard commentary, such as Driver's or
Skinner's). These opening words can be, and probably ought
to be, translated "In the beginning of God's creating . . .
the earth was without form . . ." To this version the sense
of the Irish text approximates. [3]The plural *dorchata,*
corresponding to the Latin *tenebrae,* is an illustration of
Tr.'s almost slavish literalness. On the other hand, he never
hesitates to strengthen his rendering by inserting synonyms
or adjectives (as here *dluithi*). [4]*Erant,* rejected in ST, but
contained in many MSS. *Nobidis* shows that it was found
in Δ. *In tan sin* corresponds to nothing in any MS., and is
presumably an incorporated gloss. [5]*Dei* in ST, *Domini* in
two MSS. only. [6]Either Tr. or sR³ has committed haplography. Possibly Tr.'s eye wandered unconsciously from
et uidit to *et diuisit.* [7]One of the commonest mannerisms
of Tr. is to render one Latin word by two synonyms, as here,
ro therba ⁊ ro deilig. [8]*Deus* rejected by ST, but supported
by a few MSS. as well as Heb. and LXX. [9]*Ac tenebras* ST:
but numerous MSS. have *a tenebris.* [10]No authority for
amlaid sin in any version or MS. [11]"One day" in all
versions and MSS.: "the first day" in Tr.

¶ 21. [1]*Deus* omitted, probably by a scribal error induced
by *dana* following. [2]Under the influence of the Latin text
Tr. has dropped the article before *firmamentum* in the later
verses of this ¶, as in the earlier redactions. [3]*Ab his* in ST.
Only one MS. (which also has the rare reading *Domini,*
¶ 20 note[5]) has *ab aquis.* The point is not of much critical

importance, as Irish idiom would almost require the repetition of the substantive.

¶ 22. [1]*Deus* not in any Vulg. MS. It is, however, found in LXX (καὶ εἶπεν ὁ θεός). [2]No authority for the repetition of *fer* in Tr., but it is practically required by Irish idiom. [3]*A chel no a cenel,* the variant reading in B, recalls the LXX κατὰ γένος καὶ καθ' ὁμοιότητα. [4]The bracketed words probably dropped by sR[3]. [5]*Adferentem* in ST *facientem* in OL, also found in a few Vulg. MSS.

¶ 23. [1]*Lēspaireda solus-taitnemacha* is a good illustration of the tendency to verbosity which Tr. displays, for all his literalness. [2]*Ut* in ST, but there is considerable·support for *et*. [3]No authority for the omission of *et*. [4]*Ut praeesset* omitted by one Vulg. MS. only. [5]No authority for *fecit* here. [6]*Ac tenebras* in ST. Two MSS. have *a tenebras,* and several *a tenebris.* One has *ac tenebris.*

¶ 24. [1]*Reptile* in ST: *reptilia* in a few MSS. and some quotations. The plural also in LXX. [2]*Volatile* in ST. Vulg. follows Heb. idiom in using a neuter singular collectively, and there is no Latin authority for the plural here. LXX, however, has the plural πετεινά. [3]Haplography by sR[3]: probably p̄ɔalm̄ lost before p̄maɪm̄. [4]No authority for *marina,* presupposed by the Irish *muiridi.* The latter is probably a gloss. [5]*Mutabilem* in ST, but *motabilem* has much support. [6]No authority for these words. [7]As before, the plural is used for singular collective. [8]*Deus* not in Vulg., but LXX has ὁ θεός. [9]Note ([10]) in ¶ 20 applies here also.

¶ 25. [1]*Animam uiuentem* in ST: nothing like rendering in Tr. in any version or MS.: possibly Tr. misread *uiuentem* as *diuersam.* [2]As verse (25) is almost literally identical with (24), it could easily have been passed over by a careless or lazy scribe. [3]*Deus* not in Vulg., but LXX has ὁ θεός. [4]There is some MS. authority for the omission of *que*. [5]This sentence lost, presumably on account of the repetition *terrae . . . terra,* or its Irish equivalent. [6]The punctuation of the Latin text presupposed by Tr. is different from that usually followed. [7]No authority for the omission of *Deus,* or [8]of *quae mouentur.* [9]*Co follus* or *is follus* is Tr.'s bad but invariable rendering for *ecce*. [10]*In escam* rendered by *a mbiad ⁊ a n-ailemain:* a good illustration of Tr.'s fondness for piling up synonyms. [11]*Omnique uolucri* in ST. No authority for the

CHAPTER II.

26. (1) Ro [1]foirbthighid didu na [2]Nimi ⁊ in [3]talam ⁊ [4]a n-uili cumdach.   (2) Ocus ro [5]comhslānaighstear Dīa isin [6]seisead lō in uili gnīm dorōindi; ⁊ ro cumsain Dīa isin [7]tsechtmadh lō ōn uili gnīm issed ōn ro [8]forbhthighthestar.   (3) Ocus ro [9]bennachas Dīa in seachtmadh lāā ⁊ ro [10]nāemastar hē, uair ro [11]cumsain ann ōn uili gnīm ro [12]tuissimh.

27. (4) Is iad so trā [1]tuismeadha in Nimi ⁊ in talman, in tan do [2]tuismit imalle, isin lō [3]a ndearnai [4]an Coimdi Dīa [4]Neam ⁊ [5]talum, (5) resīu na thurcbad in talam [6]uili [7]fualascaigh in [8]feraind, ⁊ resīu [9]ro clandaighedh in talam fēr in [10]feraind; ūair [11]nuchu dearna Dīa fearthain for talmain, ⁊ nī [12]ro bī and in tan sin [13]duini ro [14]oipredaigheadh in talam.   (6) Acht na freasgabad ōn talmuin [15]topar, ro [16]fliuchadh ⁊ ro bocadh [17]uili dreach in talman.   (7) Ro [18]crutaigh dono Dīa [19]duini [20]do criaidh in talmun coitchind, ⁊ ro [21]thinfeastar Dīa tinfeadh beathadh i n-a gnūis, ⁊ [22]dorignedh in [23]duine, i n-anmain na [24]beōaigheadh.

In tan [25]dorōnad duine ⁊ nach [26]raibi ainm fair, condebhairt Dīa re [27]cheatra hainglibh dul d'iarraidh anma dō. Ocus dochuaidh Michel dochum in airthir, ⁊ [28]adcondairce rētlaind .i. [29]Anatoile a ainm, ⁊ [30]dorat leis cēt litir [31]in n-anma sin. Ocus [32]docuaidh Raphel [33]fodhess, ⁊ atconnaic rētlaind [34]ann .i. [35]Dissis a hainm, ⁊ [30]dorat a cēt litir[36]. Ocus dochuaidh [37]Gaibriel [38]fotūaidh, ⁊ [39]atconnaic in [40]rētlaind [41]dianadh hainm Arethos, ⁊ [42]dorat

---

26. [1]-tigid   [2]Nime   [3]talman   [4]in uili MSS.   [5]chomslanaigestair   [6]sesed   [7]seachtmad . . . ised   [8]orbtigeastair   [9]bennachastair   [10]-astair   [11]cumsan and   [12]thusim
27. [1]t;meada indime   [2]thuismit M t;im M   [3]om. a ndearnai B   [←4]in Coimdiu .i. Dia nemda   [5]talam ⁊ resiu na thurgbad M: talam na turcbadh resiu B   [6]uile   [7]-caich   [8]feraind   [9]⁊ *instead of* ro (resiu ⁊ cland. *in rasura*) B   [10]feraind   [11]nocho   [12]roibi

CHAPTER II.

26 (1) So the Heavens and the earth and all their adornment were completed. (2) And God finished upon the sixth day all the work which He did; and God rested upon the seventh day from every work which He accomplished. (3) And God blessed the seventh day and hallowed it, for He rested in it from every work which He created.

27. (4) Now these are the generations of the Heaven and the earth, when they were created together, in the day when the Lord God made Heaven and earth, (5) before the earth was raising up all the plants of the field, and before the earth was producing the grass of the field; for God made not rain upon the earth, and there was not there, at that time, a man who should till the earth. (6) But from the earth would rise a spring, to moisten and to soften all the face of the earth. (7) So God created a man out of the clay of the common earth, and God breathed the breath of life into his face, and the Man was made, a soul that was quickened.

When Man was made and as he had no name, God said to four angels to go in search of a name for him. Michael went to the east, and saw a star, *Anatole* its name, and he brought with him the first letter of that name. Raphael went southward, and saw a star there, *Dusis* its name, and he brought its first letter. Gabriel went northward, and saw the star called *Arctos,* and brought with him the first letter of the name. Uriel went westward, and saw a star

---

[13] duine   [14] aitrebad   [15] tobar   [16] fliuchad   [17] *om.* uili : drech
[18] chruthaich   [19] ꝺuine   [20] don criaid in talman choitchind   [21] -tair
[22] doridnead   [23] dune   [24] mbeoaiged   [25] dorondad dune   [26] roibe
[27] ceithri   [28] atcondairc   [29] Anathole a hainm   [30] dorad (*bis*)
[31] an anma (*bis*)   [32] dochuaid   [33] -deas ⁊ adchonnairc   [34] *om.* ann
[35] Dessis   [36] *ins.* les   [37] Gabriel   [38] fothuaid   [39] adcondairc
[40] retla   [41] dianaid ainm   [42] dorad les

leis cēt litir [31]in n-anma sin. Dochuaidh [43]dana Uriel sīar,
꓿ [44]adconnaic [45]rētlaind isin [46]fuinedh [47]diana hainm
Mesimbria, ꓿ [48]tug leis in cēt litir. Ocus [49]adbert Dīa:
Legh, a [50]Uriel, na litri-sea. Ro rāidh [51]Uiriel: Adham.
Ocus adbert Dīa: Bīdh amlaidh[52].

28. (8) Ro [1]chlonasdar imorro Dīa Parrthus na
[2]Toili ‡ .i. [3]locc na n-airirdacht ‖ ōn [4]tossach, ꓿ is and
ro suighidh in duine ro [5]cruthaigistar, ‡ .i. Adham ‖.
(9) Ocus ro [6]thairg Dīa ꓿ ro tusim [7]don n-ūir in [8]uili
crand socraidh ālaind ō [9]feghadh, ꓿ in uili crand [10]āilgin
co [11]tomultus. Ro suidhigh [12]dana Dīa Crand
Bheathadh [13]a meadhon [14]Parrthuis, ꓿ [15]Crand [16]Feassa
Maithusa ꓿ Uilc. (10) Ocus no [17]thēigeadh sruth
[18]sechtair [19]a Parrtus, co [20]ceitri cennaib fair, do
[21]moethugadh ꓿ do [22]bocgucadh Parrduis, ꓿ in [23]talman
[24]uili co [25]coitcend.

y[1] Is [26]iat so imorro [27]anmanda na [28]ceitri [29]cend sin,
꓿ na [30]ceitri sruth [31]filit ‡ [32]sel ‖ [33]seachtar eistibh, fo
[34]ceitri airdibh in [35]domuin; .i. [36]Fisson ꓿ Geon, [37]Tigris ꓿
[38]Eofraiteis.

(11) Fisson imorro, ‡ [39]risinabar sruth nGaind, sair
[40]gach [41]ndīriuch [42]tēidside ‖—is ē in sruth sin
[43]timchellus uili [44]talmain [45]Euilath .i. inadh sin [46]a
ngeinidar ōr [47]lōgmur lān-ālaind; (12) ꓿ is andsin
fogabar [48]boellium, ꓿ in [49]leg lōgmar [50]eli [51]dianadh
ainm onichinus.

.i. cloch gabhus [52]inti delba na [53]mblāth. [54]Boellium
[55]imorro .i. [56]leg [57]lōgmar [58]lān-solusta, issī fogebh in

---

[43] dono   [44] atcondairc   [45] *ins.* in   [46] fuinead   [47] dianad *and om.*
hainm   [48] tuc les   [49] -beart   [50] Uiriel   [51] Urel   [52] *ins.* ol se
28 [1] clandustair   [2] Tole   [3] log   [4] tosach   [5] cruthaigestair
[6] thairc   [7] do nuir   [8] uile crand sochraid   [9] fegad   [10] ailgen
[11] -alt-   [12] Dia dono   [13] i   [14] -d;   [15] -ann   [16] fesa
[17] -ged   [18] seach-   [19] *om.* a Parrtus   [20] -thrib cend-   [21] maeth-
[22] bogugad   [23] tal- B, taiman *corrected prima manu to* talman M
[24] uile   [25] -cheand   [26] iad   [27] anmand   [28] -thri   [29] crand

in the sunset called *Mesembria,* and brought with him the first letter. God said: Uriel, read these letters. Uriel said: Adam. And God said: So be it.

28. (8) Moreover God planted a Paradise of Pleasure [*i.e.* the place of delights] from the beginning, and it is there that He set the man whom He had created[, Adam]. (9) And God prepared and created of the clay every tree pleasant and fair to see, and every tree sweet to taste. Also God set the Tree of Life in the midst of Paradise, and the Tree of Knowledge of Good and of Evil. (10) And a river would go past out of Paradise having four branches, to moisten and to soften Paradise, and the whole earth in general.

Now these are the names of those four branches, and of the four streams which are [a space] beyond, out of them, through the four quarters of the earth; Phison and Geon, Tigris and Euphrates.

(11) As for Phison, [which is called the river of Ganges, eastward straight it goeth]. It is that stream which surroundeth all the land of Euilath, that place where gold is generated, precious and most beautiful: (12) and there is found bdellium, and the other precious stone which is called onyx,

a stone which receiveth within itself the figures of flowers. Bdellium, moreover, is a precious, most brilliant stone,

---

cend, *the former word stroked through and expuncted* B   [30] cethri
[31] -lead   [32] *om.* sel   [33] sechtair   [34] cheithri h-   [35] -main
[36] Fison *hic et semper*   [37] *ins.* ⁊   [38] Eofraites   [39] frisin-   [40] cach
[41] -rech   [42] teitside   [43] -chillis   [44] thalmuin   [45] Euibath B
[46] angenend   [47] -mar   [48] bo eill-   [49] leag   [50] ele   [51] -naid
[52] innti   [53] *carelessly written so as to look like* niblath B
[54] bo ellium   [55] *om.* imorro   [56] leag   [57] *initial* l *in rasura*
extending back to g *of preceding word* B   [58] lan-ṡolusda isi

[59]mairgreit isin [60]ucht; ⁊ in baili [61]a ͭaghaibh hī, nī thēit seici, acht anadh [62]isin inat sin.

(13) Geon imorro, ‡ frisinabar Nilus, ‖ in sruth [63]tānaisse ‡ ⁊ [64]fothūaidh [65]thēitsidhe ‖ ⁊ is ē in sruth sin [66]timcellus ⁊ [67]tacmaigheas uili talmuin [68]na Heitheoibi. (14) In [69]tres sruth imorro .i. Tigris [70]‡ sīar [71]tēit-sidhe [72]gach [73]ndīriuch ‖ fri tīrib [74]Asardha. In [75]ceatramad sruth imorro .i. [76]Eufraiteis, ‡ [77]fodhess [78]gach [79]ndīriuch [80]thēidside, co roith[80] trē lār [81]mBabilōini. ‖

Tobar Parrduis, būan a blad ...

29. (15) [1]Rug īarom Dīa leis in [2]duine ‡ .i. Adham, ‖ ‡' īar n-a [3]dhēnum ⁊ īar n-a cruthugad[3], ‖' ⁊ ro suigidh hē i [4]Parrthus nà Toili, ardāigh co [5]n-oiprigeadh ‡ .i. co n-aireadh ⁊ co mbenadh, [6]gan allus [6]gan [7]torrsi ‖, ⁊ co [8]coimētadh, ‡ .i. co ro [9]selbadh [10]Parrthus [11]gan sārugadh [12]timna [13]⁊ aithni Dē ‖. (16) Ocus ro [14]athain Dīa do ar rāidis ris : Tomhail ⁊ caith [15]a [16]thorudh gach craind fil i [17]Parrthus, (17) Nī ro [18]chaithea do [19]toradh Craind Feassa Maithusa ⁊ Uilc imorro, uair [20]cibedh lā a caithfea nī do thoradh in [21]craind sin, [22]atbēla ō bhās.

y[1]   Ūair ro bo [23]chindti [24]demin [25]bāss dō, ōn lō ro chaithfeadh : is airi ro rāidhidh [26]so.

y[2]   Is airi ro [27]thoirmisc Dīa toradh in chraind sin do [28]chaiteam, co [29]feasad Adham a bheith fo cumachta ⁊ fo smacht in [30]Coimdhedh.

---

[59] -ret   [60] usin B (*a misreading of* uͬ)   [61] i fagaib   [62] isa ninat sin
[63] -usti   [64] bo-   [65] theid-   [66] -chillis   [67] tacmainges uili talmain
[68] na Theoipe B   [69] treas   [70] *ins.* ⁊   [71] theid   [72] cach
[73] -rech   [74] -rrda   [75] ceathrumad   [76] Eofraites   [77] fa B fo M :
deas M   [78] cach   [79] -reach   [80]-[80] *om.* B : thre   [81] mBaibiloine.
29. [1] ruc   [2] dune   [3]-[3] denam ... chru-   [4] -dus   [5] -ged

which findeth the pearl in its bosom : the place where it [the stone] findeth it [the pearl] it goeth no further, but abideth in that place.

(13) As for Geon, [the which is called Nilus], the second river, [northward it goeth] and it is that river which surroundeth and encompasseth the whole land of Ethiopia.   (14) As for the third river, Tigris, [westward it goeth straight] toward the Assyrian regions.   The fourth river, Eufrates, [southward it goeth straight, so that it floweth through the middle of Babylonia.]

Poem no. VI.

29. (15) Thereafter God took with Him the man [Adam, after he was fashioned and created] and set him in the Paradise of Pleasure, that he might till it [*i.e.* that he might plough and reap, without sweat and without weariness,] and keep it, [*i.e.* that he might possess Paradise without transgressing the covenant and commandment of God]. (16) And God commanded, having said to him : Partake and eat of the fruit of every tree that is in Paradise, (17) howbeit thou shalt not eat aught of the fruit of the Tree of Knowledge of Good and of Evil, for whatsoever day thou eatest aught of the fruit of that tree, thou shalt die the death.

For sure and certain was death for him, from the day in which he should eat : for that reason said He this.

The reason why God forbade the eating of the fruit of that tree, was that Adam might know that he was under the power and authority of the Lord.

---

[6] cen (*bis*)   [7] toirrse   [8] -edad   [9] aisebad   [10] -dus   [11] cen
[12] tinma B thimna M   [13] na haichne Dē   [14] aithin   [15] *om.* a
[16] torad cach   [17] -dus   [18] chaithi   [19] thorad chraind feasa
maithiusa   [20] ce la i caithfea   [21] chraind   [22] adb-   [23] chinti
[24] *written as though* deinin B   [25] bais   [26] seo   [27] thair-   [28] -thim
[29] feassam B   [30] Choimdead.

30. (18) Ro rāidh Dīa ¹dana : Nī maith duine do beith ²āenar. Dēnum desidhe dō ³fortachtaighidh bus ⁴cosmail fris.   (19) Ō ⁵ro cruthaighidh didu uili anmand in talman do criaidh, ⁊ uili ⁶folūaimhnigh in Nimi, tug Dīa ⁷leis iad co Hadhamh, co ⁸feghadh ⁊ co ⁹fessad ceti anmand ō ¹⁰ngairfidh Adham ¹¹iat. Ūair is ē ainm ¹²fil for ¹³gach ¹⁴anmand, in t-ainm ō ra ghair Adham hē ¹⁵annsin. (20) Ocus ro ¹⁶gairmeastair Adhamh ō ¹⁷n-anmandaibh ¹⁸fēin na huili anmanda ¹⁹sin, ⁊ ²⁰uile folūaimnechu Nime, ⁊ ²¹huili bhīasta in talman. ²²Nuchu n-agbadh Adhamh imorro in tan sin fortachtaigh dā chosmail ²³fēin. (21) ²⁴Ronfuid didhu Dīa sūan ²⁵sadhal sīr-codulta in Adam, ⁊ o ro ²⁶chodail Adhamh, ²⁷ro thōgaib Dīa ²⁸ōen asna ²⁹dā asnaibh, ⁊ ro līn o feōil a inadh.

Is ³⁰aire ro aslaigh Dia cotludh for Adamh, comad as ³¹aiti tuigsi na neichi spīradallta ⁊ ³²fiss na todochaide; ³³ar ro līn Dīa hē ō ³⁴spīrud ēagna ⁊ ³⁵fāistini ³⁶fōchētōir isin ³⁷cotludh sin.

(22) Ocus ro ³⁸cumdaig Dīa in t-asna dorad a Hadhamh, co mbo ³⁹bean ētrocht ⁴⁰lān-ālainn ⁴¹lān-dēnmach, ⁊ dorad leis co Hadham.   (23) Ocus ro rāidh Adamh : is follus ⁴²conid ī cnāim dom ⁴³cnāmaibh ⁴⁴⁊ ⁴⁵conidh feōil dom ⁴⁶feōil-sea ‡ is ī seo cēt ⁴⁷fāitsini dorighni Adamh ‖ ; ⁊ bidh ⁴⁸de a sloind-seo *uirago*, ūair is do fir ⁴⁹dorōnadh.

Is ī ⁵⁰so cēt coibhti ⁊ cēt ⁵¹fāistini dorigni Adamh, amail indistear isin ⁵²scriptuir dīadha .i. *Ecce* ⁵³*os de* ⁵⁴*ossibus meis, et caro de carne* ⁵⁵*mea.*

---

30. ¹ dono   ² aenur   ³ fortachtaidi   ⁴ chosmail   ⁵ ra chruthaid
⁶ foluaimneach inime tuc   ⁷ les   ⁸ fedad   ⁹ feasad   ¹⁰ ngairfead
¹¹ iad   ¹² fuil   ¹³ cach   ¹⁴ anmanna B   ¹⁵ and-   ¹⁶ -ist-
¹⁷ *om.* n-   ¹⁸ fen   ¹⁹ *om.* sin   ²⁰ uili foluaimneacha   ²¹ uili piasta
²² nocho   ²³ fen   ²⁴ ro find (*sic*) B   ²⁵ sadail sam-chotalta
²⁶ chotail   ²⁷ oen do thocaib (*sic*)   ²⁸ aen: in *written in marg. in late hand before* oen, *and then scratched out,* B   ²⁹ dia   ³⁰ airi ro

30. (18) God said further : It is not good for a man to be alone. Let us therefore make for him an helper that shall be like, unto him. (19) Now when every animal of the earth was formed of clay, and every bird of the Heaven, God brought them with Him to Adam, to see and know by what name Adam would call them. For this is the name that every animal hath, the name by which Adam called it at that time. (20) And Adam called all those animals by their own names, and all the birds of Heaven, and all the beasts of the Earth. But Adam could not at that time find an helper like to himself. (21) So God sent a quiet sleep of lasting slumber upon Adam, and as Adam slept, God took one of his ribs, and filled its place with flesh.

> This is why God enticed a sleep upon Adam, for it [sleep] is the chosen teacher of spiritual matters and of knowledge of the future : for God filled him forthwith with a spirit of wisdom and of prophecy in that sleep.

(22) And God fashioned the rib which He took out of Adam, so that it was a bright woman, perfect in comeliness and in shape, and He brought her with Him to Adam. (23) And Adam said : Lo, this is bone of my bones and flesh of my flesh [this is the first prophecy which Adam made]; and therefore let her name be *uirago,* seeing that it was of man that she was made.

> This is the first bride-gift and the first prophecy which Adam made, as it is related in the Holy Scripture, *Ecce os de ossibus meis, et caro de carne mea.*

---

foslaic   [31] aidi tuicsi na neichid spiritalta   [32] fis na togochaidi [33] aro   [34] -rait   [35] -tine   [36] -doir   [37] -tlad : *a dot with no significance over the* t, B   [38] -daid   [39] ben edrocht   [40] -aind [41] -tenm- B   [42] con i B, conid (*om. following* i) M   [43] chnamaib [44] *om.* ⁊ B   [45] conad   [46] feoil-sea so cet B : *om.* sea M   [47] faitsine dorigne   [48] he   [49] doronnad   [50] seo cet choibchi   [51] faitsine dorigne   [52] scribtuir   [53] oss B   [54] osibus M   [55] *om.* mea

(24) Is airi sin [56]fuicfis in duine [57]a athair ⁊ a māthair,
⁊ lenfas da śētigh, ⁊ [58]beidid dīas an āen cholaind,
‡ arāi grādha, no ar [59]tusmidh cloindi ||.   (25) Is
amlaid imorro baī [60]ceachtar de na [61]dēissi sin, ⁊ [62]siat
[63]nochta, .i. Adamh ⁊ a [64]sēitigh : ⁊ nīr bo [65]nār leo.

---

26. (1) Igitur perfecti sunt caeli et terra et omnis ornatus
eorum.   (2) Compleuitque Deus die [1] *sexto* opus [2]<omne>
[suum] quod fecerat; et requieuit [3]<Deus> die septimo ab
universo opere [4]<id> quod patrarat.   (3) Et benedixit <Deus>
diei septimo et sanctificauit illum, quia in ipso cessauerat ab
omni opere [suo] quod creauit [Deus ut faceret].

27. (4) Istae [1]*sunt* generationes caeli et terrae, quando
[2]<simul> creata sunt, in die quo fecit [3]Dominus Deus caelum
et terram.   (5) [4]Antequam oreretur in terra omne uirgultum
agri, et [5]*antequam* germinaret <terra> omnem herbam : non
enim pluerat [6]*Deus* super terram, et homo non erat qui
operaret terram.   (6) Sed fons ascendebat e terra, [7]inrigans
uniuersam superficiem terrae.   (7) Formauit igitur [Domi-
nus] Deus de limo terrae [8]<uulgaris>, et inspirauit in faciem
eius spiraculum uitae, et factus est homo, in animam uiuentem.

28. (8) Plantauerat autem [1][Dominus] Deus Paradisum
Voluptatis a principio, in quo posuit hominem quem forma-
uerat.   (9) Produxitque [Dominus] Deus de humo omne
lignum pulchrum uisu, et <omne lignum> ad uescendum
suaue.   Lignum etiam Vitae [2]<posuit Deus> in medio
Paradisi, Lignumque Scientiae Boni et Mali.   (10) Et
fluuius egrediebatur de [3]*Paradiso* ad inrigandum Paradisum
[qui inde diuiditur in] quattuor capita.   (11) [4][Nomen uni]

---

[56] fuicfeas   [57] a mathair ⁊ a athair   [58] biaitdit B   [59] t; mead

(24) Wherefore shall the man leave his father and his mother, and shall attach himself to his wife, and they shall be two persons in one flesh [for the sake of love, and for begetting of progeny.]. (25) Now in this wise were both of those twain, naked, to wit Adam and his wife : and they counted it no shame.

---

[5]Fison: ipse est qui circuit omnem terram Euilath, ubi nascitur aurum. [(12) et aurum terrae illius] optimum [est] : ibi inuenitur [6]bdellium et lapis onychinus. (13) [Et nomen] fluuio secundo, Geon: ipse est qui circuit omnem terram Aethiopiae. (14) [Nomen uero] fluminis tertii Tigris : ipse uadit contra Assyrios. Fluuius autem quartus, [ipsa est] Eufrates.

29. (15) Tulit ergo [Dominus] Deus hominem, et posuit eum in Paradiso Voluptatis, ut operaretur et custodiret illum. (16) Praecepitque ei [1]<Deus> dicens : Ex omni ligno Paradisi comede, (17) de Ligno autem Scientiae Boni et Mali ne comedas; in quocumque die comediris ex eo, [2]morte morieris.

30. (18) Dixit quoque [Dominus] Deus : Non est bonum esse hominem solum. Faciamus ei [1]<igitur> adiutorem similem sui. (19) Formatis igitur [Dominus] Deus de humo cunctis animantibus terrae, et uniuersis uolatilibus caeli, adduxit ea ad Adam ut uideret quid uocaret ea. Omne enim quod [2]<tunc> uocauit Adam animae uiuentis ipsum est nomen eius. (20) Appellauitque Adam nominibus suis cuncta animantia, et uniuersa uolatilia caeli, et omnes bestias terrae. Adam vero [3]<tum> non inueniebatur adiutor similis eius. (21) Inmisit ergo [Dominus] Deus [4]soporem in Adam; cumque obdormisset tulit unam de costis eius, et repleuit

---

[60] cecht-　　[61] desi　　[62] siad　　·[63] nocht　　[64] šet-　　[65] nair

carnem pro ea.   (22) Et aedificauit [Dominus] Deus costam
quam tulerat de Adam in mulierem, et adduxit eam ad Adam.
(23) Dixitque Adam: *Ecce* os ex ossibus meis, et caro de
carne mea; haec uocabitur Virago, quoniam de uiro *facta*
est.   (24) Quamobrem relinquet homo patrem suum et
matrem, et adhaerebit uxori suae, et erunt duo in carne uno.
(25) Erant autem uterque nudi, Adam scilicet et uxor eius,
et non erubescebant.

Notes on the Biblical Text, Chapter II.

¶ 26. [1]Septimo ST sexto OL. LXX, one Vulg. MS. *prima
manu* and one *secunda manu*.   [2]No authority for *omne*.
[3]*Deus* found in one MS. only: no other authority.   [4]No
authority for the emphatic form *issed ōn*.

¶ 27. [1]*Sunt* not in ST, but has fair support.   [2]No original
for *imalle* in any MS.   [3]*Dominus* rendered here, but not later:
see notes on this ¶.   In the Latin MSS., *Deus* is occasionally
omitted in the combination *Dominus Deus,* but not *Dominus.*
[4]The order of words in ST and all MSS. and Versions is *Et
omne uirgultum agri antequam oreretur in terra, omnemque
herbam regionis priusquam germinaret.*   [5]*Priusquam,* ST.
One MS. has *antequam,* which corresponds more closely to the
Irish repetition *resīu . . . resīu.*   But we can hardly lay any
critical stress upon this.   [6]*Dominus Deus* in ST and MSS.:
see note (³).   [7]*Inrigans* is represented in Tr. by two Irish
words, *ro fliuchad ⁊ ro bocad.*   This mannerism is so constant
in Tr. that it is hardly necessary to call further attention to it.
[8]*Coitchend,* which has no original in the Versions or MSS.,
is most likely an incorporated gloss.

¶ 28. [1]See note (³) in preceding ¶: no further note need
be taken of this point.   [2]No authority for these words.   [3]*De
loco uoluptatis* ST and all Vulg. MSS.: ἐξ Ἐδεμ LXX.   No

authority for *de Paradiso*. [4]This part of Tr. has suffered to such an extent from the intrusions of scribes and glossators that the Latin original cannot be restored with certainty. [5]Spelt *Phison* in ST, but several MSS. have the spelling with F. [6]The Irish *boellium* is the pardonable blunder of a copyist. The verbosity of the rendering of *et lapis onychinus* may be original, but is more probably a scribal modification, meant to make these hard words clearer.

¶ 29. [1]One MS. has *Dominus* here: κύριος ὁ θεός LXX, *Dominus Deus* O.L. [2]Literally rendered, *atbēla ō bās*.

¶ 30. [1]*Deside* in Tr.: no authority in Versions or MSS. [2]*Annsin*: no authority in Latin Vers., but conceivably Tr. looked up the Greek and misread ἐάν as ἔνθα. The rendering of this verse is less literal than usual. *Animae uiuentis* is treated simply as *animal,* and *omne* is transferred from the "names" to the "animals." [3]*In tan sin:* no authority in Versions or MSS. [4]Note the intrusive adjectives in Tr. here and after *ben* in the following verse. These may be due to the original Tr., but are more probably interpolated. See ¶ 31 note ([1]). [5]*Is follus,* as already said, represents an original *ecce. Ecce* also appears in the Latin quotation in the gloss, and it must have been familiar from some earlier version which also influenced R[2] (¶ 5 A). It is not found in any Vulg. MS. ST has *hoc nunc,* LXX τοῦτο νῦν. [6]*Sumpta* in ST and all authorities.

CHAPTER III.

31. (1) Ro bāi ‡ in tan sin ‖ nathair ba [1]celgachu ‡ ⁊ b'[2]amaindsiu ⁊ ba tūaichliu[1] ‖ ō uilib [3]anmandaibh in [4]talmun [5]dorōinde Dīa.

y[1] Ro [6]formthigh Lucifear fri Hadhamh, dearbh leis is ē dobert[h]a in Neam tar a [7]ēis, dia līnadh : [8]conidh airi sin dochuaidh [9]a ndeilb [10]naithreach, co ro [11]faslaigh [12]imurbus for [13]Eua, im thoradh in [14]craind ergartha do thomailt; co ro [15]faslaigh Eua for Adamh.

y[2] Is ī seo cēt [16]cheist ⁊ cēt [17]imcomarc [18]dorigni dīabul isin domun. *Cur precepit* etc.

Ocus ‡ is ī in athair sin ‖ ro rāidh [19]risin mnaī : Cid dīa [20]forcongair Dīa duibsi [21]gen nī do [22]chaitheamh do uili [23]crand [24]Parrthuis? (2) Ro [25]reagair in bhean [26]don nathraigh : [27]Caithmit ‡ ⁊ [28]no sāstar ‖ do thoradh na, crand [29]atat i [30]Parrthus; (3) ro [31]forchongair Dīa [32]dūin imorro na ro [33]chaithmis do thoradh in [34]craind atā [35]a meadōn [36]Parrthuis, ⁊ na [37]ro taidlimmis hē, [38]na [39]ro aiplium o thircur. (4) Ro rāidh imorro [40]in nathair [41]frisin mnaī : [42]Nuchu n-eipiltaisi etir ō bhās. (5) Do-[43]fuicfind Dīa imorro [44]secip lā chaithfithi-si do [45]toradh in craind sin, co [46]n-oslaicfiter bar ruisc ‡ .i. [47]im uilc ‖ .i. co mbeithi amail aingliu i tuicthi maiṫ ⁊ olc.

32. (6) [1]Atconnairc didu in bean cor bo maith in crand re [2]tomultus ⁊ re [3]chaithium, ⁊ [4]cor bo ṡocraidh

---

31. [1-1]cealgachu ⁊ fa hanmaindi ⁊ fa hamaindsiu ⁊ ba tuaithli [2] amaimsiu B   [3] *a dot over the* d *without significance* M   [4] -ɿnan [5] *ins.* do neoch; dorindi   [6] ̇foirmdig   [7] esi   [8] conad   [9] i [10] nathrach   [11] faslaich   [12] imarbuss   [13] Eba   [14] chraind [15] faslaid Eba   [16] chest M qist B   [17] -mch-   [18] -gne   [19] frisin [20] ro forch-   [21] cen   [22] chaithim   [23] chrand   [24] -d*uis* fesin : a bhaili *here written in marg. in late hand* B   [25] ̇frecair   [26] da

Chapter III.

31. (1) [At that time] there was a serpent, the wiliest[, the craftiest, and the subtlest] of all the beasts of the earth which God made.

> Lucifer was envious against Adam : he was assured that the Heaven would be given to him in his [own] room, to fill it. Wherefore he went in the form of a serpent, and enticed sin upon Eve, in the matter of eating of the forbidden tree; so Eve made enticement upon Adam.
>
> This is the first question and the first enquiry which a devil made in the world. *Cur praecepit* etc.

And [it is that serpent which] said unto the woman : For what reason hath God forbidden you to eat aught of every tree of Paradise? (2) The woman answered the serpent : We eat of [and are sated with] the fruit of the trees that are in Paradise; (3) but God hath commanded us not to eat of the fruit of the tree that is in the midst of Paradise, nor even to touch it, lest we die by a chance. (4) But the serpent said unto the woman : Ye shall not at all die the death. (5) But God knoweth that in whatsoever day ye shall eat of the fruit of that tree, that your eyes shall be opened [concerning evil]—that is, that ye shall be as angels, in good and evil fortune.

32. (6) So the woman saw that the tree was good for eating and for partaking, and that it was pleasant

---

nathair   [27] *an inserted* i *sprs. above* m *in late hand* B· caithmimait M [28] nar B   [29] itait   [30] -dus   [31] for-   [32] -nd   [33] caithis B [34] chraind   [35] i medon   [36] -dais ·   [37] ra thaidlimais   [38] *ins.* ꝺ [39] ra aibleam M: thirchur B   [40] an athair   [41] forsin   [42] nocho n-ebeltaisi itir   [43] fuicind   [44] seichip   [45] thorad in chraind   [46] -ther [47] in n-ulc

   32. [1] atchondairc M   [2] thomaltos M   [3] -eam M   [4] ro bo

so-airfiteach ō roscaibh ⁊ ō ⁵feghadh : ⁊ dorad ‡ in bean
|| nī do thoradh in ⁶craind dīa ⁷indsaigi, ⁊ ro
⁸chaitheastair, ⁊ ⁹dorat da fir ‡ .i. ¹⁰Adamh || ⁊ ro
¹¹chaiteastair.   (7) Ocus ro ¹²hoslaicit (a) | ruisc ‡
¹³meanman ⁊ ¹⁴aigenta || na ¹⁵deisi sin ‡ ¹⁶fri ¹⁷fios
⁊ ¹⁸eōlas in ¹⁹pecaich, ²⁰na ²¹dearnsiat ²²gos in ²³n-ūair
sin || ; ⁊ ō ²⁴ro tuicsedar a mbeith ²⁵nochta, ro ²⁶ṫuigsitar
²⁷duillinna na ²⁸fidhci ⁊ ²⁹dorinsetar ³⁰fūathrōga dōibh
‡ ³¹do na ³²duillinnaibh ||.   (8) Ocus adchualadar-somh
³³‡ .i. Adamh ⁊ Eua imorro || guth ³⁴an Choimhdia ‡
.i. Dē || ³⁵a n-imthigidh ‡ a ³⁶ndealbh ³⁷aingil || ³⁸a
bPairrthuis, ³⁹a bhfoghra gaoithi dearmhairi ⁴⁰īar
meodhōn lāi.   Ro ⁴¹ṫolaigh ⁴²hē ⁊ a ⁴³ṡetigh ⁴⁴a |
⁴⁵medhōn(b) chrainn Pairrthuis.

....

   33. (9) ¹Agas ro ²gairmeastair Dīa Adhamh ³‡ ō
guth aingleagda || ⁊ ro rāidh⁴ : A ⁵Adamh, cāit ataī?
     ....
(10) Ro ⁶frecair ⁷imorro ⁸Adhamh ⁊ ⁹ro rāidh :
                                     ....:...   ....
¹⁰Adchualadhus   do   ¹¹ghuth   ¹²a   bPairrthais,   ⁊
....
¹³romghabh ¹⁴eagla, ¹⁵ōr bham ¹⁶nocht, ⁊ ro ¹⁷foilgios
....
mē.   (11) Ro rāidh Dīa : Cia ¹⁸ro inndios ¹⁹dhuit do
       ....
bheith ²⁰nocht acht Mē fēin?   ²¹In ro ²²chaithis ²³torad
       ....

_____

sochraid M   ⁵ ṫegad·M   ⁶ chraind M   ⁷ hindsaigid M   ⁸ -ist- M
⁹ dorad M   ¹⁰ dAdam M   ¹¹ -thist- M   ¹² hoslaicid a M
¹³ menman Mβ²   ¹⁴ aicinta M aigennta β¹ -nntadh β²   ¹⁵ desin M
¹⁶ fria β¹²   ¹⁷ fis M   ⁻⁸ eolus β⁰²   ¹⁹ -aid M phecaidh β¹² (-ea- β²)
²⁰ nach β²   ²¹ dearnsad M dernsat β¹ ndern siad β²   ²² cus an M gus an β²
²³ om. n- Mβ¹²   ²⁴ ra thuicistair M ro tuigset ar β¹ ro tuigsat ar β²
²⁵ nocht M nochtadh β¹²   ²⁶ fuigseadar M fuigsiodar β¹²   ²⁷ duillinda
M duillionnadh β¹²   ²⁸ fice M fidhcidh β¹²   ²⁹ -rindsedar M rinnsetar β¹²
³⁰ fuathrogadh β¹² (-gh- β²)   ³¹ don na β¹²   ³² -eannaib M -enn- β¹²
³³ om. this gloss β¹²   ³⁴ in Choimded M in Choimhdia and om. .i. Dē β¹²
³⁵ na imthiged M .i. deanam thigidh β¹ ag denamh chucadh β²
³⁶ ndeilb M dealbh β²   ³⁷ swc M aingeal β aingila β¹ aingilia β²
³⁸ a Parrdus M om. β¹²   ³⁹ i fogur gaithi M, a bhfoghradh (g β²)
gaoithe dermhaire β¹²   ⁴⁰ iar meadon M iar mhedhoin (d β¹) β¹²

and agreeable to eyes and to sight : and [the woman]
took of the fruit of the tree to herself and she did
eat, and gave to her husband [Adam] and he did eat.
(7) And the eyes [of mind and understanding] of those
twain were opened [to a knowledge and perception of
sin, that they had not committed until that hour] ;
and as they realized that they were naked, they sewed
the leaves of the fig-tree and made them aprons [of
the leaves].   (8) And they [Adam and Eve] heard
the voice of the Lord [God] a-walking [in the form
of an angel] in Paradise in the sound of a violent
wind, after midday.   He and his wife hid them in the
midst of the tree-growth of Paradise.

33. (9) And God called Adam [making use of an
angelic voice], and said : Adam, where art thou?
(10) Howbeit Adam answered and said : I heard Thy
voice in Paradise, and fear laid hold on me, for I was
naked, and I hid me.   (11) God said : Who told thee
that thou wast naked, other than Myself?   Hast thou
eaten fruit of the Tree which I forbade thee?
(12) And Adam said : The woman whom Thou gavest

---

[41] falaid M folaidh β^{12} [42] Adhamh β^1 Adamh β^2 [43] seitigh β^{12}
[44] *ins.* iad β^{12} [45] i meadon chraind Parrduis M a medoin (dh β^2)
chrainn (cr- β^2) Pharrthais β^{12}: m(e)duin H (*throughout* H, *the lenition
of* b, d, g, *and* m *is rarely indicated*)
  33. [1] ⁊ M Ocus β^2 [2] -mist- M -mest- β^{12} [3] *this gloss in* M *only* :
there does not appear to be sufficient room for it in H   [4] *ins.* fris MH
[5] Adaim M   [6] freagair M fregair β^{12} [7] *om.* imorro β^{12} [8] Adam
H a Adhamh β [9] ra raid H   [10] -adus M -asadh β^{12} [11] guth-su M
[12] i Parrdus M *om.* β^{12} [13] romgob M gab H ro in ghabh β roghabh β^1
doghabh β^2 [14] egla H   [15] oir *for* ar *hic et semper* H, ar M,
oram β^{12} [16] anocht β^2 [17] foilg- M -ghas β^{12} [18] ro indis MH
(ra *for* ro *hic et semper* H) dinnis β^{12} [19] duit M β^1 duid H   [20] nocht.
Acht (*sic*) M nochtadh as β^{12} [21] ni ro M nior β nuar β^1 mar a β^2
[22] chaithios β -es β^{12} [23] torrad M β

(*a*) Text as printed from this point follows β, as a folio has been lost from B.
(*b*) H here begins.   Owing to the torn condition of the first leaf of H, only
words that are here underdotted remain in the opening lines.

[24]in [25]chrainn [26]do ro tairmioscios iomut?   (12) [27]Agas
do [28]rāidh Adhamh : [29]In bhean [30]doraitaisi damhsa
[31]in [32]āentaidh dorad [33]domh [34]do [35]chrann [36]ɔ ro
[37]chaithius.   (13) Ocus ro rāidh Dīa frisin [38]mnaī :
[39]Cia dīa ndernais anī so? Is [40]ead ro [41]freagraistair
[42]in bhean[43] : In [44]nathair nimhe ro [45]mheallastair mē,
ɔ [46]ro [47]chaithius.

34. (14) [1]Ocus ro rāidh in [2]Coimhdhi ris in
[3]nathair : Ūair [4]dorighni[s]-siu in nī [5]so, [6]isat
mallachta [7]eidir [8]uilibh anmandaibh ɔ [9]bīastaibh in
[10]talamh.[a] Bidh [11]ar do [12]bhruinni [13]imtigfea, ɔ bidh
talamh [14]caithfea ō [15]uilibh [16]lāethibh do [17]bheathadh.
(15) Ocus [18]suighidhfetsa [19]nāimhdenus [20]edrut ɔ in
[21]mnaī, ɔ [22]eadar [23]do śīl ɔ [24]sīol na mnā[23] : [25]tūairgfidh
[26]in bhen do [27]chenn, ɔ [28]intledaighfesu dīsi [29]i leith a
cosaibh. (16) Ro rāidh [30]dana don [31]mnaoi : [32]Imdaigh-

---

[24] an H β[12]   [25] -nd MH crann β[2]   [26] om. do: ro thairmisc
umut M: do ro thoirmisgis iomum β[12]   [27] ocus ro M: om. ɔ; ra H
[28] radh β[12]   [29] ins. fos β[12]: an ben da- H an bhean β[2]   [30] rad-
aisiu M -radaisidh β[1] -radaisi β[2]: dhamhsa β[12]   [31] im M
[32] oentaid H aon- β[12]   [33] dam MH damh β[12]   [34] don MH
do don β[12]   [35] crand H   [36] ins. in torad M   [37] chaithis
M -thes β[12]   [38] mnaoi β[2]   [39] cid dia ndearnais inni seo MH: anni β[12]
[40] edh β[12]   [41] raid M; freagair β[12]   [42] an ben, An athair H in bheinn
β in bhen β[12]   [43] ins. oga freagra M   [44] nathar β[12]: om. nimhe MH
[45] mellastair MH mheall β[12]   [46] om. ro β[1]   [47] chaithis torad in chraind
M: chaithes β[12].
    34. [1] om. ɔ M   [2] an for in M: Coimdiu fris in MH Choimdhe β[12]
(mh β[2])   [3] athraid M athair H nathar β[12]   [4] doridnis (om. siu) M
dorignis H rinnisigh β[1] rinnighsidh β[2]   [5] seo M   [6] ɔ isad mallachta M

me as companion gave me of a tree, and I ate.
(13) And God said unto the woman : Wherefore hast
thou done this thing? What the woman answered
was : The serpent deceived me, and I did eat.

34. (14) And the Lord said unto the serpent : In
that thou hast done this thing, thou art accursed
among all the animals and beasts of the earth. It
shall be upon thy breast that thou shalt go : it shall
be earth that thou shalt eat, for all the days of thy
life. (15) And I shall set enmity between thee and
the woman, and between thy seed and the seed of the
woman : the woman shall stamp upon thy head, and
thou shalt lurk aside from her, hiding from feet.
(16) Moreover He said unto the woman : I shall

---

isath β^{012} -chtadh β^1 -cht β^2 [7] itir MH idir β^{12} [8] uile
anamaibh β^{12} [9] piastaib M biastaib H   [10] talman M   [11] air β^2
[12] bruindi H -nne β^1 -ne β^2 [13] -mth- MH imtigfedh β^{12} [14] chaithfea MH
caithfedh β^{12} [15] uile β^1 [16] laithib M laoithibh β^{12} (-oth- β^1)
[17] -eth- β^{12} [18] suigid feadsa M suighfedsadh β^{12} [19] -deanus M
-denas β^1 [20] eadrud M edrud H   [21] mhnai β^1 [22] itir M idir β^1
edra β^2 [23-23] bhur siol β^{12} [24] síl MH   [25] tuaircfid MH -argfad β^{12}
[26] an ben H : an *also* β^2 [27] cheann M chend H cenn β^2 [28] intlaed-
faigfea-su M -fe-su H : dissi β : indleadaigh fesu disi β^{12} (fcs a β^2)
[29] i leath o chosaib M illeth o cossaib H i leit a cosuib β^2 [30] dono
Dia MH dan dia don mhnai β^{12} [31] mnai M mnai *om. y sprs. c* H
[32] -feadsa M -fetsa H iomadfadsa β^{12}

(*a*) The β MSS. treat *talamh* as indeclinable.

feadh-sa [33]t'athaisi, ⁊ [34]bidh [35]i ngalair ⁊ i [36]ngoirtius
tuismeadha do [37]chompiortha ⁊ do [38]chlanna ‡ .i.
[39]iomad [40]galar mīsda [41]dhuit ‖ ⁊ [42]bidh fo [43]chumhachta
(a)[44]ŧir [45]bia, ⁊ [46]biadh a [47]thighernus [48]ort.   (17) Ro
rāidh [49]imorro Dīa [50]go Hadhamh : [51]Ūair [52]atchuala-
dhus guth ⁊ aslach do [53]sētchi, ⁊ [54]an ūair ro [55]chaithis
don [56]chroinn ro [57]thoirmiosciusa [58]iomut, is [59]mallachda
in talamh [60]id'gnīmh : ⁊ [61]bidh a sāethraibh ⁊ a
snīmhaibh [62]chaithfea biadh [63]ō'n uilibh [64]lāethibh do
[65]bhethadh.   (18) Ocus [66]clannaighfidh [67]in talamh dit
spīne [68]gēra ⁊ [69]drisi [70]deilgneacha, (19) ⁊ [71]bidh in
allus do ghnūisi ‡ [72]⁊ i foghnamh do [73]chuirp ⁊ do
[74]cholla ‖ [75]caithfea [76]luibhi ⁊ [77]toirrthi [78]in [79]talamh,
⁊ [80]notsāsfar ō [81]bhiadhaibh : [82]cen cor athadchuir fon
[83]talmain d'indearna Dīa thū.   Ūair is do lūaithread
⁊ do[83] thalmain [84]dorōnadh, ⁊ is [85]fae [86]ragha.

35. (20) Ocus ro [1]ghairmeastair [2]Adhamh [3]ainm a
[4]sētchi .i. [5]Eua, [6]īar sin nī ro bhaī, [7]gor bho māthair

[33]thathaisi M tataisi β¹ daithaisi β²   [34]biadh β¹ biaidh β²
[35]ingalar M β¹² angalar H   [36]ngoirtes thuis- H -ort- β²:
tuismedh (ed β¹) do chomhphrechadh β¹²   [37]coimpearta M
-perta H   [38]clanda M clannadh (ch. β¹) β¹²   [39]imad galair MH
[40]ghalar miostadh β¹²   [41]duid MH   [42]biadh β¹ biaidh β²
[44]cumachta M cumhachtadh β¹² (comh- β²)   [44]tfir β¹²   [45]om. bia β¹²
[46]biaid MH biaïgh β¹ biaidh β²   [47]-earn- M tig- β² -as β¹   [48]fort MH
[49]om. imorro Dia β¹²   [50]co MH   [51]oir β¹²   [52]adchualadus M
adchualaidais (ais sprs yc) H -asadh β¹²   [53]seitchi H šeitche β¹²
[54]om. an MH   [55]chaithios β : do for preceding ro H   [56]chrund
MH chrann β¹ crann β²   [57]thairmis-ciusa M -cusa H -casadh β²¹
[58]ummut M umut H iomad β¹²   [59]-chta M -chtha H -achtadh β¹ -acht β²
[60]ad H it β : nim β nimh β¹²   [61]bid a saetraib H biodh a sethraibh β¹²
[62]caithfi H caitfedh β¹²   [63]o uilib MH on uile β²   [64]laithib MH

multiply thy shames, and it shall be in sickness and in distress that thou shalt bring forth thy offspring and thy progeny [i.e. thou shalt have many monthly sicknesses]. And under the power of a man shalt thou be, and his lordship shall be over thee. (17) Moreover God said to Adam: In that thou hast hearkened to the voice and incitement of thy wife, and in that thou hast eaten of the tree that I forbade thee, cursed is the earth in thy deed. It shall be in labours and in tribulations that thou shalt eat food, for all the days of thy life. (18) And the earth shall bring forth for thee sharp thorns, and spiny brushwood, (19) and it shall be in the sweat of thy face [and in the servitude of thy body and of thy frame] thou shalt eat of the plants and fruits of the earth and shalt be satisfied with victuals, till He shall have laid thee again under[(b)] the earth from which God made thee. For it is of dust and of earth that he was made, and under it shall he go.

35. (20) And Adam called the name of his wife Eua, by reason of the fact that she was mother of all living

---

[65] beathad M   [66] clandaigfead M clanaigfi H   [67] an H β^1 [68] geradh β^{12}
[69] drise M -sedh β^1 -sa β^2 [70] delglecha M -necha H -nechadh β^{12} [71] biadh β^{12}: an *for* in H   [72] ┐ a fodnum H ag fognamh β^{12} [73] choirp β^1 [74] colla β^2 [75] chaithfea M chaithfi H -feadh β^{12} [76] luibi H luibhibh β^{12} [77] toirthi MH toraibh β^{12} [78] an H na talmhan β^{12} [79] talman M   [80] notsastar M nodsastar H notfasfar β^{12} [81] bi- β^2 [82] cein MH gen go rathadhchuir β^{12} (*in* β^2 radh *corr. to* rath)   [83-83] *om.* β^{012} [84] -nnad M   [85] fai H   [86] radha β^2

35. [1] gairmistair M -m;t- H -ester β^{12} [2] a Adhamh β^{12} (Aadh. β^2)   [3] ainim β^{12} [4] seitchi MH (se- M) seitche β^{12} [5] Eabha β^{12} [6] iarsani H   [7] corbo MH gor ba β^{12}

(a) From this point the text of H is continuous till the end of the column.
(b) Following the reading of M.

na [8]n-uili [9]mbeō ‡ .i. na ndāine ‖.   (21) [10]Doroighni
[11]dana Dīa do [12]Adhamh [13]ꝛ da [14]sēithigh [15]tonochu ꝛ
inaru [16]croichnidhi (sic)[17], ꝛ ro [18]ēit iat.

36. (22) Ocus ro rāidh Dīa : Is follus [1]dorōnadh
Adhamh [2]amail [3]āen ūaine, go fios [4]maithiosa ꝛ uilc
[5]aigi—

[6]Mar [7]bhadh ed [8]adbēradh Dīa : Ni [9]uair Adhamh [10]an
nī rob āil [11]leis .i. bheith [12]amail [13]ōen [14]ūaine.   Ro [15]malairt
[16]imorro ꝛ ro [17]seachṁhaill in [18]maithius ꝛ in [19]glaine
mbunaid i ndernad hē.

[20]Dīchuiremh trā [21]anoissa [22]a [23]bPairthas, [24]na [25]ro
chaithea nī [26]do [27]Chrann [28]na [29]Beathadh, ꝛ [30]nara beō
hē trē [31]bhithadh.   (23) Ro [32]dhīchuir imorro Dīa
Adhamh [33]a Parrthus na Toile, ꝛ ro [34]suidhigh hē isin
[35]talmhuin coitchenn dīa [36]ndernadh [37]e.   (24) Ocus ro
[38]ordaigh Dīa [39]Hirufīn [40]a bhfiaghnuisi [41]Phairrtuis, ꝛ
[42]cloidheamh teinntighi [43]i n-a lāimh, do [44]choimhed
Parrthais ꝛ [45]slighidh Crainn [46]na [47]Beathadh.

---

[8] nuile M β[12]   [9] beo H in bheo β dhuine i and om. gloss β[12]
[10] doroindi M daroigni H dorighnedh β[12]   [11] dono MH om. β[12]
[13] Adamh β[1]   [13] is β[12]   [14] setig M seitchi H seitche β[12]
[15] donacha imaru β donacha ionnara β[12]   [16] croicind M croicend
changed by corrector to -eand H craicnedh β[12]   [17] ins. endatha H
[18] eid iad H.

    36. [1] dorondad M -ronn- H : dAdam H   [2] ainim aon uaine β[12]   [3] oen
uaindi co fis M aen uainni co fis H   [4] maithiusa M maithusa H -sa β[1]
[5] aici MH aigi β[12]   [6] ins. .i. MH   [7] bad M bud ead H badh β[12]
[8] -ered M -eiread H adbh- β[2]   [9] fuair H   [10] in ni MH β[12] indi ro
bail β   [11] ris β[12]   [12] amhuil β[1]   [13] eon M aen H aon β[1]
[14] uaindi M uainne H   [15]- lart M mhal- β[1]   [16] om. β[2]   [17] seachmall M
sechmall H sechmhail β[12]   [18] maithus H maithiosa β mhaithesadh β[12]

[i.e. of mankind]. (21) Moreover God made for Adam and for his wife tunics and mantles of hides, and clothed them.

36. (22) And God said : Lo, Adam hath been made as one of us, having a knowledge of good and of evil—

As though what God would say was : Adam obtained not the thing which he desired, to be as one of us. But he changed and neglected the goodness and the original purity in which he was made.

So let us drive him now forth from Paradise, lest he should eat aught of the Tree of Life, and lest he should be alive for ever. (23) Wherefore God drave Adam forth from the Paradise of Pleasure, and set him in the common earth of which he was made. (24) And God ordained a Seraph in the forefront of Paradise, with a fiery sword in his hand, to guard Paradise and the way of the Tree of Life.

---

[16] glaini H ghlainni mbuneadh indearnad M ghloine in buined inderna β^{12} (buinedh β^2) [20] -eam M -em H, diochuradh *and om.* tra β^{12} [21] anosa M anossa H anosadh β^{12} [22] *ins.* Adam MH [23] Parrdus M Parrtus H Parrtas β^{12} [24] no β^2 [25] ra chaithi H chaithedh β^{12} [26] don β [27] chrunn M crund H chrainn β . [28] *om.* na MH [29] bethadh β^{12} [30] nar ba M [31] bithu MH e tre bhiadhadh β^{12} [32] dhiochuir *and om.* imorro β^{12} [33] a Parrdus na Tole M Toili H Pharrthas natolia β^{12} [34] suigid M fuigid H suigh β^{12} [35] talam choitchind MH (-inn H); talamh β^{12} [36] -earn- M nderna β^1 ndernada β^2 [37] *om.* e MH [38] ordaid M -aidh β^1 [39] *om.* β^{12} [40] hi fiadnaisi M hi fiadnaissi H -fiadhnuise β^{12} [41] -d; M -th; H Pharrthais (-art β^2) β^{12} [42] claidem M claidim H -emh β^{12} tendtigi M tentigi H -ighe β^{12} [43] i laimh aingil β^{12} [44] choimet Parrduis M Pharrthus H *om.* Parrth. ⁊ β^{12} [45] sligheadh H slighe β^{12}: Chraind M Craind H Chrainn β^{12} (Cr. β^2) [46] *om.* na MH. [47] bhethadh β^1 betad β^2

31. (1) Sed et serpens erat [1]callidior cunctis animantibus terrae quae fecerat [Dominus] Deus; qui dixit ad mulierem : Cur praecepit Deus uobis ut non comederitis de omni ligno Paradisi? (2) Cui respondit mulier : De fructu lignorum quae sunt in Paradiso uescemur, (3) de fructu uero ligni quod est in medio Paradisi praecepit nobis Deus ne comederemus, et ne tangeremus illud, ne [2]forte moriamur. (4) Dixit autem serpens ad mulierem : Nequaquam morte moriemini, (5) scit enim Deus quod in quocunque die comederitis ex eo, aperientur oculi uestri, et eritis sicut [3]*angeli*, scientes bonum et malum.

32. (6) Vidit igitur mulier quod bonum esset lignum ad uescendum, et [1]pulchrum oculis, aspectuque delectabile; et tulit de fructu illius et comedit, deditque uiro suo qui comedit. (7) Et aperti sunt oculi amborum, cumque cognouissent esse se nudos, consuerunt folia ficus et fecerunt sibi perizomata. (8) Et [2]*audiuerunt* vocem Domini [3][Dei] deambulantis in Paradiso [4][ad auram] post meridiem. Abscondit se et uxor eius [5][a facie Domini Dei] in medio ligni Paradisi.

33. (9) Vocauitque [Dominus] Deus Adam et dixit : [1]<Adam> ubi es? (10) [2]*Respondit uero Adam dicens* : Vocem tuam audiui in Paradiso et timui, eo quod nudus essem, et abscondi me. (11) [Cui] dixit [3]<Deus> : Quis [enim] in-dicauit tibi quod nudus esses [4]nisi *egomet*? Ex ligno de quo tibi praeceperam ne comederes comedisti? (12) Dixitque Adam : Mulier quam dedisti sociam mihi dedit mihi de ligno, et comedi. (13) Et dixit [Dominus] Deus ad mulierem : Quare hoc fecisti? [5]*Hoc est quod respondit* mulier : Serpens decepit me, et comedi.

34. (14) Et ait Dominus [1][Deus] ad serpentem : Quia fecisti hoc, maledictus es inter omnia animantia et bestias terrae. Super pectus tuum gradieris, et terram comedis cunctis diebus uitae tuae. (15) [2][Et] inimicitias ponam inter te et mulierem, et [3][inter] semen tuum et semen illius. Ipsa conteret caput tuum, [4]et insidiaberis calcaneo eius. (16) Mulieri quoque dixit : Multiplicabo aerumnas tuas et

⁵conceptus tuos : in dolore paries filios, et sub uiri potestate eris, et ipse dominabitur tui. ‚(17) Ad Adam vero dixit ⁶[Deus] : Quia audisti ⁷uocem [et temptationem] uxoris tuae, et comedisti de ligno ex quo praeceperam tibi ne comederes, maledicta terra in opere tuo : in laboribus comedes ⁸e[sc]am cunctis diebus uitae tuae. (18) Spinas et tribulos germinabit tibi, et comedes herbas terrae, (19) in sudore uultus tui uesceris ⁹pane, donec reuertaris in terram de qua ¹⁰*fecit te Deus,* quia puluis es, et in puluerem reuerteris.

35. (20) Et uocauit Adam nomen uxoris suae ¹*Eua,* eo quod mater esset cunctorum uiuentium. (21) Fecit quoque [Dominus] Deus Adam et uxori eius tunicas pellicias, et induit eos.

36. (22) ¹Et ait ²<Deus> : Ecce Adam factus est quasi unus ex nobis, sciens bonum et malum : nunc ergo, ne ³[forte mittat manum suam et] sumat etiam de Ligno Vitae, et comedat et uiuat in aeternum, <emittamus eum de Paradiso>. (23) Emisit ⁵<ergo> eum [Dominus] Deus de Paradiso Voluptatis ⁶*et posuit eum in* terra de qua *factus* est. (24) ⁷[Eiecitque Adam] et collocauit <Deus> ante Paradisum [Voluptatis] Cherubin, et flammeum gladium ⁸[atque uersatilem] ad custodiendam uiam Ligni Vitae.

NOTES ON THE BIBLICAL TEXT, CHAPTER III.

¶ 31. ¹On the adjectives qualifying this word in Tr. and on the representation of the simple word *qui* by *is i in athair sin,* see the notes on this ¶. ²*O thircur,* which means "from a chance, accident," and in a good sense "from a windfall," suggests that the translator did not completely understand the Latin *forte.* I am indebted to Miss M. Joynt for some references to passages containing this word. ³*Dii* in ST and all MSS. θεοί LXX. The rendering "angels" is a piece of

Jewish exegesis, possibly conveyed to Tr. by some commentary. Skinner quotes Abraham ibn Ezra, † c. 1167.

¶ 32. [1]Tr. has missed the elegant chiasmus of the Latin.
[2]*Cum audissent* in ST and Vulg. MSS. Tr. here follows LXX
in making the clause independent (as in Heb.): καὶ ἤκουσαν
τὴν φωνήν κ.τ.λ. [3]By exception, *Domini* is here translated.
Only one Vulg. MS. omits *Dei*. [4]*Ad auram* has been curiously
misunderstood by Tr. [5]These words must have been lost from
the Irish text at an early date by some carelessness, which
in this case it is impossible to explain.

¶ 33. [1]LXX and a few Vulg. MSS. insert *Adam* here.
[2]Nearer to LXX (καὶ εἶπεν αὐτῷ) than to Vulg. (*qui ait*).
Adam may or may not be here an intrusive gloss. [3]*Deus*
rejected by ST, but found in several MSS. and ancient
quotations. [4]In Vulg., *quod nudus esses, nisi quod ex ligno*,
etc. (so in LXX, τὶς ἀνήγγειλέν σοι ... εἰ μὴ κ.τ.λ.) This must
have been the reading in Δ, but *quod* must have been
written in such a way that Tr. misread it as a contraction
for *egomet*, thus producing the nonsense *acht Mē fēin*, which,
naturally, has given some trouble to his copyists. He then
began a new sentence with *Ex ligno*, thus accidentally falling
into accord with the Hebrew punctuation. [5]Slightly closer
to LXX (καὶ εἶπεν ἡ γυνή) than to Vulg. (*quae respondit*).

¶ 34. [1]Only two MSS. omit *Deus*. [2]No authority in Vulg.
for inserting *et*, but LXX has καί. It also has (like Tr.)
ἔχθραν in the singular, unlike Vulg., in which *inimicitiam*
has very slender authority. [3]No authority for repetition of
inter in Vulg., but found in LXX. This point is of no
critical importance, however, as the repetition is practically
required by Irish idiom. [4]As suggested in the notes to
this ¶, Tr. does not seem to have completely understood this
passage: his rendering is rather free. [5]Tr. seems to have
regarded *conceptus tuos* as linked to the following words,
governed by *paries* rather than by *multiplicabo*, and to have
supplied in imagination *et* before *filios*. [6]No authority for
Deus here. [7]ᵀ *aslach* is possibly another instance of Tr.'s

fondness for duplication, but it may also be an intrusive gloss. *²eam* in Vulg., αὐτήν in LXX. Apparently Tr. took *eam* for a contraction of *escam*. ⁹A gloss has ousted the original translation of this simple word. ¹⁰*Sumptus eo*, Vulg. For a similar translation compare II. 23.

¶ 35. ¹*Hauam* in ST, but there is plenty of authority for *Eua*, as well as some for *Aeua, Aeuam,* and *Euam.*

¶ 36. ¹This ¶ has suffered considerably in translation or transmission. ²No Latin authority for *Deus*, but LXX has κύριος ὁ θεός. ³The equivalent of these words was lost early, presumably because two consecutive sentences began with *na ro.* ⁴There is an effective rhetorical aposiopesis in the text here, in all versions from Heb. downwards. But Tr., assuming that something had dropped from the text, has made an attempt at filling the gap! ⁵No authority for *imorro*, but LXX and a few Vulg. MSS. have καί, *et.* ⁶*Ut operaretur terram de qua sumptus est* in ST. Tr. has here gone altogether off the rails. We have already seen reason to suspect (¶ 33 note (⁴) above) that the handwriting of Δ was not perfectly clear to him, and it is conceivable that *ut operaretur* was so written as to be read carelessly as *et posuit eum in.* Once more we see *sumptus* translated as though it were *factus* (cf. II 23, III 19). ⁷Possibly Tr. or one of his copyists thought these words superfluous after *ro dhīchuir*, just before. ⁸*I n-a lāimh* appears to be a gloss that has ousted the Latin *atque uersatilem.*

CHAPTER IV.

37. [1]Is follus [2]as so, [3]inn airt [4]ro bhadar [5]a bPairrthus [6]corptar [7]oca.

(1) Ro [8]etargnaigh imorro [9]Adhamh[6] [10]Eua a [11]seitigh.[a] Ro [12]choimpir sī, ꝗ ro [13]thuisimh Cāin [14]dō.

Chāin [14, 15]*poseissio* no [16]*lamentacio* [17]*interpretatur*, .i. is ē [18]mīnughadh ꝗ cīall fil isin [19]bhfocail sin, [20].i. Cāin .i. [21]sealbh: ꝗ [22]is do [23]foillsighadh na [24]cēilli sin ro rāidh Adhamh [25]Caneithi .i.—

ro [26]sealbhus duine trē [27]Dīa. (2) [28]Ocus ro [29]thuissimh [30]dana Eua [31]dorighissi mac [32]eile, .i. Abēl. Is [33]amhlaidh [34]imorro [35]bhaoi [36]Abēil, [37]na [38]āoeghairi caoirach [39]hē, ꝗ Cāin .i. [40]tīrfreacuirti ēiside. (3) [41]Dorighnidh imorro īar [42]lāithedaibh [43]imdaibh [44]con n-edhbradh Cāin [45]māini do [46]thortibh in [47]talamh do Dhīa: (4) [48]dorighni dono [49]Abēl [50]iodhbartha do [51]phrīomhgheinibh [52]derrscaidhthechaibh a [53]treōit do Dhīa. Ocus ro [54]fēgastair [55]in [56]Coimhdhia [57]co [58]Habēl ꝗ [59]go maoinibh, (5) nī ro [60]fēgastar [61]imorro [62]go Cāin [63]no [64]go [65]maoinibh.

Is as ro [66]thuigestar Cāin [67]gor tholtnachset maoini Abēl do Dhīa, [68]nī ro [69]toltnaighsetar [70]imorro [71]a maoini fēin,

<hr>

37. [1] as β[12]   [2] aso M ais so β   [3] inairet M indaired H as follus as so ar (air β[2]) a ndibirt β[12]   [4] ra badar H   [5] i Parrdus M a Parrthus H i Pharthas β[12]   [6-6] gur torrchadh (torrchad β[2]) i dergnaidh Adhamh ꝗ β[12]   [7] occa H   [8] etargnaid M eadargnaid H   [9] Adam H   [10] *ins.* agus: Eabha β[12]   [11] a setig M, a. seitig H, *om.* a seitigh ro choimpir si β[12] (*but not* β)   [12] comper M   [13] tuismedh β[12]   [14-14] do Cain M a (fa β[2]) chialluighes (ci- β[2]) β[12]   [15] posesio M possesio β[12]   [16] -tio M β[2]   [17] *om.* β[12] (*b*)   [18] mineagud M ciall ꝗ miniughadh β[12]   [19] focol M bhfocal β[12]   [20] is M β *om.* β[12]   [21] selb M seilbh β[12]   [22] *om.* β[12]   [23] foillseagad M sealbhughadh β[12]   [24] -le β[12]   [25] canei β canai me β[12]   [26] selbus M -as β[12]   [27] Dhia β[12]   [28] agas β[12]   [29] tusim M (*the* im *sprs. s* M): toismidh β[12]   [30] *om.* M   [31] doridise M *om.* β[12]   [32] aile .i. Aibel M   [33] amhladh β[12]   [34] *om.* β[12] (*this word almost invariably om. by the* β MSS.)   [35] bai M bhi β[12]   [36] Aibel M Abel β[12]   [37] *om.* na β   [38] aegairi chaerach M aoidhire β[1] aoidhre β[2]: caorach β[12]   [39] *om.* β[12]   [40] tirfrecnairc frechuirthig esige (*a* d *sprs over the* g) M: tir-freacuirthe eisidhe β[12]   [41] -ridned M

CHAPTER IV.

37. It is evident from this that so long as they were in Paradise, they were virgins.

(1) Now Adam knew Eua his wife.   She conceived and brought forth Cain to him.

> Cain, *possessio* or *lamentatio interpretatur*, i.e. this is the explanation and meaning which is in that word, "Cain"; i.e. "possession." And to set forth that meaning Adam said "Caneithi," i.e.

I have acquired a man through God.   **(2)** And Eua brought forth again another son, Abel.   Thus was Abel, a shepherd of sheep, and Cain, an husbandman was he.   **(3)** It came to pass, moreover, after many days, that Cain would offer gifts of the fruits of the earth to God : **(4)** but Abel made offerings of the choice firstlings of his flock to God.   And the Lord looked upon Abel and upon his gifts, **(5)** but He looked not upon Cain and upon his gifts.

> Thus did Cain understand that the gifts of Abel were acceptable to God, but that his own gifts were not accept-

---

-nedh *and om.* imorro β^{12} [42] laitheadaib M laidhidaibh β laidhidegh β^{12} (-eg β^2)   [43] iomdh- β^{12} [44] conedbrad (the d y sbs c) M go n-iodhbaradh *and om.* Cain β^{12} [45] maine M maoine β^{12} [46] thoirthaib M thoraibh β^{12} [47] talman M   [48] doridni M do (*om.* righni dono) β^{12} [49] Aibel M Abeal β^1 [50] edbarta M -barthadh β^{12} (-arr- β^1)   [51] primgenib M priomhghinibh β^{12} [52] dearrscaitheachaibh M derscaidh-thechaibh β^{12} [53] threoit M -oid β^{12} [54] *a very faint dot over the* f M   [55] an β^{12} [56] Coimdi M   [57] go β^{12} [58] Haibel M   [59] co a mainib M da m. β^{12} [60] fegastair M   [61] *om.* β^{12} [62] *om.* M, do β^{12}.   [63] na M   [64] da β^{12} [65] mainib M mhaoin- β^{12} [66] thuigistair M   [67] cor tholtnaigsead maine M gur tholtnach siad maoinibh β^{12} [68] nior ro β^{12} [69] tholtnaigsedar M toltnach siad β^{12} [70] *om.* β^{12} [71] a yc M:

(*a*) Here a lacuna in H begins.

(*b*) Not *om.* in β, but a corrector who thought it ought to be there but did not notice it inserted it in marg.   It is written as an abbreviation (an *i* and a p crossed) and probably was so written in B, in such a way that it could easily be overlooked.

[72]ar [73]ticeth [74]teine do [75]Nimh [76]for [77]eadhbartaib Abēl, [78]nī [79]tigedh imorro [76]for [80]iodhbairtaibh [81]Cāin.

Ocus ro [82]fergaidh Cāin [83]go [84]dearmhāir, ꞁ [85]dorochair a [86]ghnūis ‡ a [87]t-toirsi ꞁ [88]in dubha ‖.

38. (6) [1]Ocus ro rāidh [2]in [3]Coimhdhia [4]go Cāin : [5]Cidh ar [6]ar [7]feargaighais, ꞁ [5]cidh ara [8]torchair do ghnūis [9]‡ i t-toirrsi ‖?   (7) [10]Cidh ōn, ar Dīa, nach [11]fuidbheasu a [12]comāin madh maith [13]doghneis? [14]Madh olc [15]dono [13]dogneis, bidh [16]fogus a [17]indeochadh [18]fort. (8) Ocus [19]adubhairt Cāin [20]co [21]Habēl, go a bhrāthair : Tīagham amach isin [22]bhfearann.   [23]Īar [24]tochtain [25]dāibh [26]isin [27]bhferonn ro [28]comhēirigh Cāin [29]an aghaidh [30]Aibeōil [31]a bhrāthar, ꞁ ro [32]mairb hē—

y[1]   [33].i· isin [34]cathraigh [35]danadh ainm Damascus.

y[2]   [36]Abēl dono, cēd marb in domain, ꞁ rob ē Aibēl [37]in cēt [38]mairtir(a) ro [39]bāi arīam, ꞁ [40]ba(b) toltanach ro adaimh a martra[40].

(9) (c)Ocus ro rāidh Dīa [41]go Cāin : [42]Cāit a [43]bhfuil [44]Abēl do bhrāthair? Ro [45]fregair Cāin : Nī [46]feidar; cidh ōn, ‡ [47]ar Cāin ‖, in [48]missi [49]is [50]coimhēdaigh dom' bhrāthair[50]?

---

maine M mhaoiue β[12]   [72] ꞁ β[12]   [73] teigead (ge *in rasura*) M tigedh β[12]   [74] tene M   [73] neimh β[12]   [70] fo M (*bis*) [77] iobarrthaibh β[1] iodhbarthaibh β[2]   [78] *ins.* ꞁ M   [79] thiced M [80] idbartaib M iodhbarraibh β[12]   [81] Chain β   [82] feargaidead M fergadh β[12]   [83] co M   [84] dermhar β[12]   [85] ro chuir β[12] (*om.* do-) [86] gnuisi M   [87] toirrsi M ttuirsedh β[12]   [88] andubha β[12]
  38. [1] *This word spelt* agus, agas *indifferently* β[12]   [2] an β[12] [3] Coimdi M -mhdia β[2]   [4] co M   [5] cia β[12] (*bis*)   [6] *om.* β[12] [7] fergaidis *y sprs. s* M fergais β[12]   [8] ttor- β[2]   [9] *an interrogation-mark ins. here* β[2] : i toirrsi M attuirsed β[2]   [10] ced M cia β[12] [11] -bhesa β[12]   [12] chomain M -aoin β[12]   [13] dognes M doghnidhis β[12] (*bis*) [14] ma β[12]   [15] *om.* M β[12]   [16] focus M   [17] ineochad β[12] [18] *om.* M fert β[12]   [19] adurbairt M   [20] go β[12]   [21] Haibel co M : *om.* go β[12] [22] ferann M bhfer- β[12]   [23] *om.* β[12]   [24] tiachtain M   [25] *ins.* imorro,

able—in that fire would come from Heaven upon the offerings of Abel, but would not come upon the offerings of Cain.

and Cain was exceeding wroth, and his countenance fell ‡ in distress and in gloom. ||

38. (6) And the Lord said unto Cain : Wherefore wast thou wroth, and wherefore hath thy countenance fallen [in distress]? (7) How now, said God, shalt thou not obtain its equivalent if thou doest well? But if it be evil that thou doest, vengeance for it shall be nigh unto thee. (8) And Cain said unto Abel his brother : Let us go out into the field. After they had gone into the field, Cain rose up against Abel his brother and slew him,

In the city which is called Damascus.
Now Abel was the first dead man of the world, and he was the first martyr that ever was; and with good will he made confession in martyrdom.

(9) And God said unto Cain: Where is Abel thy brother? Cain answered: I know not. How now, [said Cain], is it I who am custodian for my brother?

---

doib M: doibh β^{12} ^{26} ins. amach M ^{27} fearann M bfer- β^2 -ann β^{12}
^{28} choimerig M coimh- β^1 -rghe β^{12} ^{29} in M ^{30} Abel β^{12}
^{31} a brathair β om. β^{12} ^{32} ins. iad a da laim fo bragait cor ba M:
marb M; mharbh e β^{12} ² ^{33} om. .i. M ^{34} chathraid M chathraigh β^2
^{35} dianad M darab ainim β^{12} ^{36} sic M: om. cet marb . . . Aibel β.
Abel (din sic, bracketed in both MSS.) an ched mairbh ꝋ marthar bha
[ba β^2] ariamh ꝋ ba [badh β^2] toltanach [toil- β^2] ro H-Adhamh a
mhartra [martra β^2] β^{12} ^{37} an β ^{38} mairtir M ^{39} bhaoi ariamh β
$^{40-40}$ do tholtanaich ꝋ ro adaim a martra M ^{41} co M ^{42} cia hait β^{12}
^{43} fuil M bfuil β^{12} ^{44} do derbhrathair [dh β^2] Abel β^{12} ^{45} frecair M
fregair β^{12} ^{46} feadar M fedair β^1 ^{47} om. ar Cain: an β^{12}
^{48} misi M β^{12} ^{49} bhas β^1 bus β^2 $^{50-50}$ comhedaid do β^{12}

(a) s² M.   (b) H here resumes.   (c) s¹ M.

y³ Is ī ⁵¹so ⁵²in ⁵³dara ⁵⁴cēd bhrēg, .i. ⁵⁵an ⁵⁶dīabhul ar ⁵⁷ttūs, ⁵⁸Cāin īartain. ....

(10) Ocus ro rāidh Dīa ⁵⁹go Cāin : ⁶⁰Cid dorōinnais⁶⁰? ⁶¹Nūallaigh ⁊ ⁶²ēigidh ⁶³chugum don ⁶⁴talmhunn guth ⁊ foghar ⁶⁵fola do ⁶⁶brāthar.

y⁴ Trī ⁶⁶nūalla ⁶⁷ro saghat dochum Dē ⁶⁸gan ⁶⁹fuireach : .i. ⁷⁰nūall fola ⁷¹finnghaili, ⁷²amhuil ⁷³nūaill fola ⁷⁴Abēil īar n-a dortadh ⁷⁵do Chāin, ⁷⁶da bhrāthair; ⊦ ⁷⁷nūall ⁷⁸pheacaidh ⁷⁹indirigh, amhuil ⁸⁰nuall ⁸¹pheacadh na ⁸²Sodamdha : ⊦ ⁸³nūall ⊦ gair na mbocht īar mbreith ⁸⁴ūaithibh a n-⁸⁵ionmhais ⊦ ⁸⁶īar n-a ⁸⁷slat.

39. (11) ¹Biadh-sa ²dono ⊦ tū ³mallachdha for ⁴talmhain ‡ ⊦ ⁵budh ⁶mallachta dono ⁷in talamh ‖ ⁸ro foslaic a bēal ⊦ ⁹ro ghabh fuil do ¹⁰brāthar ‡ ¹¹īar n-a ¹²dortadh ‖ ¹³dot lāimh.

y¹ ¹⁴Ūair āirmid na staraigeda dīada co rob do řid chnāma camaill ro marb Cāin a brāthair og ingairi chāerach.

(12) ¹⁵Agus ¹⁶in tan ¹⁷oibridfeasu ¹⁸in ¹⁹talamh sin, ni⁽ᵃ⁾ ....

---

⁵¹ seo M ⁵² an β¹² ⁵³ daradh breg β¹ ⁵⁴ cet breath (*sic*) M ⁵⁵ *om.* an M ⁵⁶ diabal MH β¹² ⁵⁷ tus MH β¹² ⁵⁸ *ins.* ⊦ M ⁵⁹ co M ⁶⁰⁻⁶⁰ doronnais pecad ⊦ gnim n-adbal M cia doroinnis β¹² ⁶¹ nuallaid MH ⁶² egid M eigid H eighidh β¹² ⁶³ chucum M chugam β¹² ⁶⁴ talmain M tálamh β¹² ⁶⁵ foladh β¹² ⁶⁶ bhrathair β : bh- *also* β¹² ⁶⁶ nuala M nuaillaidh β¹² ⁶⁷ do H : saiged M, sagaid H ⁶⁸ cen M ⁶⁹ fuireach M fhuirech β¹² ⁷⁰ nuaill β¹² ⁷¹ fingaile M fingaili H fionghaile β¹² ⁷² amail MH ⁷³ nuall fola MH n. foladh β¹ ⁷⁴ Aibel M Abel β¹ ⁷⁵ dha β¹² ⁷⁶ dia H, *om.* da bhr. β¹² ⁷⁷ nuaill β¹² ⁷⁸ pecaid MH pecaidh β¹² ⁷⁹ *om.* M ⁸⁰ nuaill β¹² ⁸¹ pecaid M pecadh β¹² ⁸² Sodoma H Sodomaitibh β¹² ⁸³ nuaill β¹

This is one of the first two lies—the devil first and Cain afterwards.

(10) And God ,said unto Cain: What hast thou done? The voice and cry of thy brother's blood maketh complaint and call unto me from the earth.

There are three cries which made their way to God without delay: the cry of the blood of kin-murder, as the cry of the blood of Abel after it was shed by Cain his brother: the cry of iniquitous sin, as the cry of the sin of the Sodomites: and the cry and lamentation of the poor, when their goods have been taken from them and when they have been slaughtered.

39. (11) Thou also shalt be accursed upon the earth [and the earth also shall be accursed] which hath opened her mouth and received the blood of thy brother [after it had been shed] at thy hand.

For the sacred historians consider that it was with a shank of a camel-bone that Cain slew his brother, as he tended sheep.

(12) And when thou shalt till the earth, she shall not

---

[84] uadhadh β^{12} [85] indmais MH ionmhus β^{12} [86] ar β^1 om. β^2 [87] slad M β^{12}

39. [1] biasu MH   [2] om. dono ⁊ tu β^{12}: om. ⁊ H, but yc [3] -chta M -uighe β^{12} [4] tall- β^2 -mhuin β^{12} [5] bid M bu β^{12} [6] -chda M mallach dana β, mallaighthe β^1 -uighe β^2: om. dono β^{12} [7] an H [8] ro (ra H): sluig (sl- M) Abel MH: fosglaic a beul β^{12} [9] rogob M ragab H   [10] bhrathair β (bh- also β^{12})   [11] ar M β^1 [12] dhor- β^1 [13] dod H β^{12} [14] y^1 in M only   [15] ocus M   [16] an M β^{12} [17] oibrigfeadfa-su M oibrigfessu H oipd oibrid feasu β^1 cuspd oibrid corr. in marg. to oipd β^2 [18] an H   [19] talmain M

(a) H is preserved continuously from this point to the next lacuna.

[20]thibradh a [21]toirtha dhuit : ⁊ [22]biasu [23]faelnedach ⁊ [24]teitheach ‡ a [25]hinud i n-inud ‖ for [26]talmhain. (13) Ocus ro rāidh Cāin [27]go Dīa : Is mō ⁊ is [28]fuilliu [29]m'indirghi [30]inās mar [31]dlighim loghadh.

y[2] [32]Dearchāiniudh [33]dono [34]dorighni Cāin [35]sund [36]in tan [37]ro rāid na brīathra-sa : Nī [38]gheabha-sa a [39]Dē, ⁊ nī [40]thibrea [41]damh loghadh [42]ce dagneor [43]aithrighi. Ocus [44]egnach Dē dō-[45]som sin.

(14) Is follus, ar Cāin, [46]dichraighsiu misi [47]andiu ō [48]dhreach in [49]talamh, ⁊ [50]namfoilgeabhthar ōd' ghnūis. [51]Bam [52]teichtheach [53]faelnedach-sa for [54]talmhuin, ⁊ [55]muirfidh ⁊ [56]nīmhcheagela [57]neach mē. (15) Agas ro rāidh Dīa [58]go Cāin : Nī [59]ba [60]hamhlaidh sin [61]doghentar, acht [62]pīanfaithair a [63]secht [64]cudruima [65]gach aon [66]do [67]mhuirfeas Cāin—

y[3] .i. Nī hē [68]leighios [69]peacaidh [70]fogheabha bās [71]oband amhuil [72]saili, acht [73]mera [74]go [75]fada [76]gorab [77]mōidi do [78]phīan ⁊ do [79]dīoghail.

Ro [80]suidhidh Dīa Cāin [81]i [82]comhartha [83]conach marbhadh [84]nach [85]duine hē.

y[4] .i. [86]cnocc ina [87]ēadan [88]‡ ⁊ cnoc ceachtar a dā grūad ⁊ cnoc for cach cois ⁊ for cach lāim ‖[88], ⁊ a bheith [89]ghan [90]ulcha, [91]no a bheith [92]teiththeach.

---

[20] thibra MH -bhr- β tiubhradh β[12]   [21] thoirthi MH thoradh β[12]   [22] biadhsa β[12]   [23] -neadach M faoil- β[1]   [24] techech M teithibh β[12]   [25] a hinad aninad M anin *with* ad *above* H hionad, ionad β[12]   [26] -an β[1]   [27] co MH [28] fuilli MH   [29] minndirgi H in inmirge β[1] inneirge β[2]   [30] na H [31] dhl- β[12]   [32] der- MH -nead M -nid H -aoinedh β[12]   [33] *om.* β[12] [34] -dne M -gni H dorinigh β[12]   [35] sunn β[12]   [36] antan H β[1]   [37] so β[12] : *om.* ro raid na briathra-sa β[012] : na briathra-sa *in* M *only*   [38] geba-su MH gheabadh (*om.* -sa) β[12]   [39] Dhe β[1]   [40] tibra M thibri H thibredh β[1] thiubhredh β[2]   [41] dhamh β[12] : logad dam MH   [42] ge dogneor M ge do ner H ced agnair β[12]   [43] -ide M -igi H -ighthe β[12]   [44] ecnach MH [45] dosam sin H do san am sin β[012]   [46] dichuirid-siu M diacuirisi H diachragh *and om.* -siu β[12]   [47] aniug MH aniu β[12]   [48] dreich MH -ech β[12]   [49] -lman M an tal- H   [50] nomfoilgebthar MH -gebhar β[12] (gh- β[2])   [51] bain β[12]   [52] teicheach M -teach H teichthech β[12] (-teith β[2])   [53] -nead- M faoil- β[12]   [54] -lmain M   [55] murf. H muirbhfedh β[12]

yield her fruits unto thee : and thou shalt be a wanderer and a fugitive [from place to place] upon the earth. (13) And Cain said unto God : Greater and huger is my iniquity than that I deserve forgiveness.

It was despair that Cain expressed there when he said these words : Thou, O God, shalt not receive, and shalt not give me forgiveness, though I should work repentance. That was a blasphemy of God on his part.

(14) Lo, said Cain, Thou hast driven me today from the face of the earth, and I shall be hidden from Thy face. I shall be a fugitive and a wanderer upon the earth, and anyone shall slay me, and shall not spare me. (15) And God said unto Cain : Not thus shall it be done : but everyone who shall slay Cain shall be punished sevenfold.

i.e. Sudden death is not the remedy for sin that thou shalt obtain as thou thinkest : but thou shalt live long, so that thy punishment may be the greater.

God set Cain in a sign, so that no man should slay him—

a lump upon his forehead [and a lump (on) each of his cheeks, and a lump on each foot and on each hand] and his being beardless, and being a fugitive.

---

[56] nimcoicela MH (-gela H) -chealgadh β^{12} [57] nech MH β^{12} [58] co MH [53] bu β^2 [60] -ladh β^{12} [61] do-dhentar β^{12} [62]-faidear M -faigter H -fuighther β^{12} [63] seacht M ś- β^{12} [64] cuduma MH chodrumadh β^{12} (cod- β^2) [65] cach oen M cach aen H : gac β^1 [66] om. do MH   [67] muirfes MH marbhas tú β^{12} (mh- β^2)   [68] -ges M -g; H   [69] pecaid MH pecadh β^{12} [70] fogeba MH fogheabhadh β^{12} [71] opand M obann H β^2 [72] śaile M śaili H saoile β^{12} [73] mairradh β maredh β^{12} (mair- β^1) [74] co MH   [75] fata M fadadh β^{12} [76] corob M corop H gurab β^{12} [77] moide M β^{12} [78] pian M   [79] digal MH dh- β^{12} [80] śuigid MH (ś- M) suighe β^{12} [81] hi H   [82] -thadh β^{12} [83] connach H gonach β^{12} [84] om. nach β^{12} [85] duine nduine β [86] cnoc M cnoc ionna β^{12} [87] hedan H etan M edan β [88-88] in M only   [89] cen M can H gan β^{12} [90] ulchain M ulchadh β^{12} [91] ┐ M   [92] teitheadach M teichteach H (the ch yc), teitheach β^2

40. (16) [1]Ro scibh Cāin [2]imorro o [3]freagnarcus in [4]Coimhdhedh, ⁊ ro [5]aitreabhaidh, [6]is sē [7]teitheach [8]dāsachtach, i rind [9]airtheraigh [10]an feroinn dar ainm[10] [11]Eden—

.i. [12]ferand sin fil [13]inn airthear na [14]Haissia.

(17) Ro [15]etairgnaidh Cāin a [16]sēitigh ⁊ ro [17]coimparastar [18]sī [19]mac .i. [20]Enōch, ⁊ ro [21]cumhdaigh-sium [22]cathraigh, ⁊ [23]tug [24]ainm dī ō [25]ainm a [26]mic[27], .i. Enōch. (18) Ro [28]thusim [29]imorro Enōch [30]Iaradh, [31]⁊ [32]ro ᵛthuisimh [33]Iaradh [34]Mauiabel. [35]Ro thuisimh [36]Mauiabel Matusael. [37]Ro [38]tusimh [39]Matusael Laimhīach ‡ [40]dīamus .i. ōn dā mnāi ‖.

41. (19) [1]Dorad [2]imorro [3]in [4]Lamhīach [5]sin dā [6]sēitigh, [7]Adda ⁊ [8]Sella a [9]n-anmanda-sidhe. (20) [10]Agas [11]ro thusimh Adda [12]Iabal; is [13]ēisidhe [14]ba hathair ‡ [15]⁊ [16]ba [17]taoisech ‖ [18]na n-āgairi ⁊ nanī [19]no aitreabhdais |[(a)] a [20]bpuiblibh ‡ [15]⁊ [21]a bhfāissaighibh ‖. (21) Iubal imorro [22]ainm a [23]bhrāthar; is ēsidhe [24]ro bha athair ‡ ⁊ [25]rob aireach ‖ [26]nanī ro [27]chlechtaitis cruit ⁊ [28]orgain. (22) Ro [29]tusmestair [30]dana [31]Sealla [32]mac [33]don [34]Laimhīach [35]cēadhna .i. [36]Tupalcān [37]a

---

40. [1] ra scib H   [2] om. β[12]   [3] freacnarcus MH (frec-H) fergnarcus β[2]   [4] Coimdead M an Choimdead H Choimhdhe β[12] [5] aitreb MH (-eab M)   [6] ⁊ M ise H om. is β[12] re for se β[2]   [7] teichtheach H [8] dhasachtach [blank space that would hold four letters] fuind β : dh. i bhfuinn β[12]   [9] iartharaid M iartharaig H airerthaigh β[12]   [10-10] om. β[12]: in (an H) fearaind (f. M fer- H) MH: dianaid M dianad H   [11] Etan M Eadon no Eden H Edin β[1] Eoin β[2]   [12] om. ferand sin fil β[12]: fearann M fuil H   [13] an iarthar M an oirrther H   [14] Haisia M Asia (om. na) β[12]   [15] eadargnaid (edar- H) MH: edar- β[12]   [16] setig M seidid H   [17] choimpristair MH -peir- β[12]   [18] om. si MH   [19] imac β[2] [20] Eanoch β[1] Eanoc β[2]   [21] cumdaigsim H chum- β[12] -siom β[12] [22] cathraid M   [23] tuc MH   [24] ainim β[12]   [25] anmuin MH ainmuin β ainim β[12]   [26] mhic β[12]   [27] ins. primgenid M   [28] tuisim M ra thuis. H thuisiumh β[12]   [29] om. β[12]   [30] ins. mac .i. M: Iarad M Iaareth H Iaret β[12] [31] om. ⁊ M   [32] M ra tuisim H om. β[12]   [33] ins. imorro MH: Iareth Manuel H Iarec β[1] Iaret β[2]   [34] ins. mac .i. M; Mauibel M   [35] ro (not ra) thuisim H om. β[12]   [36] Maubel mac .i. Maithiusael M; Manuel Mathasael H Mauabel Matusaoil β[2]   [37] ra H: om. ro tusimh, ins. ⁊ β[12]   [38] thusim M

40. (16) Then Cain departed from the presence of the Lord, and dwelt, a wild fugitive, in the eastern border of the land called Eden—

The land which is in the east of Asia.

(17) Cain knew his wife, and she conceived a son, Enoch; and he founded a city and gave it a name from the name of his son, Enoch. (18) And Enoch begat Irad, and Irad begat Maviahel, Maviahel begat Mathusahel. Mathusahel begat Lamech [the bigamist, i.e. (so called) from the two wives].

41. (19) Now that Lamech took two wives, Ada and Sella their names. (20) And Ada bore Iabel; he it is who was father [and chief] of shepherds and of those who used to dwell in tents [and in desert places]. (21) Iubal, moreover, was the name of his brother : he it is who was father [and leader] of those who would handle harps and organs. (22) And Sella bore a son to the same Lamech, Tubalcain his name. He,

---

thuisim H   [39] Mathasáel mac .i. Laimiach M Mathusael Laimiach H *om.* Matusael β^2 [40] *this g. in* M *only.*

41. [1] darad H   [2] *om.* β^{12} [3] an H *om.* β^{12} [4] Laimiach MH Lamiach β^{12} (-iac β^1)   [5] hi sin .i. β^{012} [6] seitig M seitid H [7] *ins.* .i. MH   [8] Sealla H β^{12} [9] -and-side MH (-sidi H) *om.* a nanmanda β^{12} [10] ocus M   [11] ra H thuisim Ada (*foll. by full stop*) H : thuisiumh β^1 -iomh β^2 [12] *ins.* mac do Laimiach .i. M   [13] eside M eissidi H csidhe β^{12} [14] bu hathar β^{12} [15] *probably* .i. *to be read for* ⁊ (*bis*) *all* MSS.   [16] bu β^2 [17] taiseach M toissich H   [18] do, *with* na *sprs.* ys M : na naegairi H nagari β^{12} haegairib M   [19] ra aitreabadais H -trebd- M noch aitreabhas β^{12} [20] puiblib M   [21] i fásaidib M a bfasaibh β^{12} [22] ainim β^{12} [23] brathar M brathair β^{02} [24] rob athair M ro ba β^1 [25] ro badh β^2 [26] *looks like* nam *in* β^1, *but may be given benefit of doubt: certainly* nam β^2 [27] clechtaidis M lechtatis β leachtadaois β^{12} [32] organ M   [29] thuismedar β^{12} [30] dono M *om.* β^{12} [31] Sella M   [32] mac *dittographed* β^1 [33] do β^{012} [24] -ech β^1 [35] cetna M cedna β^{12} [36] Tubalchain M Tubalcon β^{12} [37] -dhe β *om.* a

(a) H lacuna begins.

εinm-side. ³⁸Rob ēside ³⁹imorro ⁴⁰an ⁴¹chēd ⁴²cheard
⁴³ᴉ ⁴⁰an ⁴⁴cēad gabha ᴉ ⁴⁵in chēad ⁴⁶ŝāer. Ocus ⁴⁷rug
⁴⁸Sella inghen īarsin, .i. ⁴⁹Nema siur ⁵⁰Tubalcāin.

⁵¹Ba hī ⁵²sin in ⁵³chēad druineach ᴉ is ī ro ⁵⁴chēad-chum
ēdach re cāch ar ⁵⁵ttūs.

42. (23) ¹Agas ro rāidh ²Laimhīach re ³ŝēitchibh .i.
re ⁴Hada ᴉ re ⁵Sella : ⁶A ŝēitchi Laimhīach⁶, ⁷ēistidh
mo ⁸guth⁹, oighidh ᴉ ¹⁰tuigidh mo ¹¹bhrīathair. ¹²Ūair
ro ¹³mharbhus ¹⁴fer amuigh ¹⁵aniu, ᴉ is ¹⁶inund fodhēn
ro ¹⁷chreachnaideas ¹⁸annsin. ¹⁹Uairistar ²⁰form, ᴉ
²¹tri ²²formad ro ²³mhairbhus in ²⁴māeth-ōglach ²⁵sein.

²⁶ᴉ ²⁷ba gnīomh comhāidhmhi lesiumh sin, ²⁸ūair is tria
²⁹dhīomus ᴉ ³⁰in dōcbhāil ro rāidh.

(24) ³¹In tī ³²trāā ³³muirfeas Cāin, ³⁴indechfaidhair
in ³⁵tseachtoll ᵗfair : ³¹in tī ³²imorro ³³mhuirfes
³⁴Laimhīach, ³⁵pīanfaidhair hē a ³⁶secht ³⁷cudrama fa
seachtmhoghait.

43. (25) Ro ¹etargnaidh ²dana Adhamh ³dorighisi
‡ .i. |⁽ᵃ⁾ ⁴Eua ||, ᴉ ⁵ro ⁶thusimh sī mac dō, ⁷ᴉ do ro

---

ainm-side β¹² ³⁸ ro ba hisidhe β² ³⁹ *om.* imorro M β¹² ⁴⁰ in M β² (*bis*)
⁴¹ cet M (*ter*) ced β² ⁴² cerd β² goba . . . cherd . . . ŝaer M ⁴³ *om.* ᴉ
β¹² ⁴⁴ ched-ghabhadh β¹² (gabh- β²) ⁴⁵ an β¹² ⁴⁶ ŝaor β² ⁴⁷ ruc M
⁴⁸ Sealla β¹ Seall β² ⁴⁹ Neama β¹ ⁵⁰ Thubalchain M ⁵¹ fa M
⁵² sidhe β¹² ⁵³ ched ruinech M ced dr. β² ⁵⁴ chet M ced cumedach
β⁰¹² ⁵⁵ tus M β¹²
42. ¹ ocus M β² ² Lamiac β¹ Laimiach M β² ³ heitchib M ⁴ Hadda M
β¹² ⁵ Sealla β¹² ⁶⁻⁶ da ŝeitig Laimiach (*attached to preceding*) M *om.* β¹²
⁷ estig M ⁸ ghuth β¹² ⁹ *ins.* ol se M ¹⁰ tuicid M tugadh β²,
an attempt made afterwards to insert an i *before the* g ¹¹ briathra M
-thar β¹ ¹² *om.* β¹² ¹³ mbhairbhus β² ¹⁴ fear M ¹⁵ aniug M
¹⁶ inand M ann β¹² ¹⁷ chrechtnaideas M cheachtnaighius β cechtnaighes
β¹² ¹⁸ *om.* β¹ ¹⁹ oir (uair β⁰) is tar (tair β²) ᵗform (f. β⁰) β⁰¹²
²⁰ formad M ²¹ tria M ²² ᵗfor- β² ²³ marbas M mharbhas β¹²

moreover, was the first wright, the first smith, and the first carpenter. And Sella bore a daughter thereafter, Noemma, sister of Tubalcain.

She was the first weaver, and the first who fashioned raiment for everyone in the beginning.

42. (23) And Lamech said to his wives, Ada and Sella : Ye wives of Lamech, hear my voice, heed and understand my word. For I have slain a man without, today, and it is the very same thing that I wounded (him) there. He injured me, and through jealousy I slew that tender youth.

And he thought it a deed for boasting, for it was through his haughtiness and in vainglory that he spoke.

(24) He then who shall slay Cain, it shall be revenged upon him sevenfold : but he who shall slay Lamech, shall be punished seventy and seven times the equivalent.

43. (25) Then Adam knew again <his wife>, [to wit Eua] and she bore a son to him, and Adam called that

---

[24] maoth- β^{12} (*In β^2 owing to change of page dittographed thus:* in maethog | an maethoglach) [25] sen M sin β^{12} [26] .i. β^0 [27] fa gnim comaidme lesim in gnim sin M 'go maidhmi leasiumh β^{12} [28] oir β^2 [29] dimus M -mas β^1 [30] ind tocbail M in docbal β^2 [31] an β^{12} (*bis*) [32] thra M *om.* β^{12} [33] murfeas M ro mharbhas β^{12} [34] indeachfaidear M -faigher β^1 -faisgar (s *expuncted*) β^2 [35] seacht ollfair M secht oll fair β techt ollfair β^{12} [32] *om.* β^{12} [33] muirfeas M muirbhthas β^{12} [34] Lamiac β^1 [35] -dear M dher β^{12} [36] seacht M secht β^{12} [37] cutruma fo seachtmogat M cudrumadh (cad- β^1) fo seachtmhoghadh (s- β^1) β^{12}

43. [1] eadar- M eadargnadh β^2 [2] dono M dion β^1 dionn β^2 [3] -disi M dorighsi β [4] Eabha β^{12} [5] *om.* ro β^2 [6] thuisim M tuisiomh β^{12} [7] *om.* β^{12} (*not β*); *om.* do ro M, -easd- M Adam M

(a) s^2 M.

gairmeastair Adhaimh in mac sin[7] .i. [8]Seth : ⁊ [9]is edh
ro rāidh : [10]Dorat [11]Dīa [12]dhamh, ‡ air Adhamh ||
[13]"ar" .i. sīol [14]sāmh [15]saineamhail aile, tar [16]a ēisi
[17]Abeōil ro mhairbh Cāin. (26) [18]Ro ghenair |(a) mac do
[19]Seith .i. Enos [20]a ainm-side. Is [21]ē an tEnos sin ro
[22]thionnsgain ar [23]ttūs ariam in [24]gairm ⁊ [25]atach anma
[26]an Coimhdhia.(b)

β.	β[12].
43a. Mac dh'Enos Cáin-ean. Mac do-sidēn Male-leth. Mac do-sidēn Iáreth. Mac do-sēn Enoc. Mac do-sidēn Matasaliam. Mac do-sēn Laimhiach. Mac do sidhēn Nōe.	Ghein Enos Canaan. Gein Canaan Malaleel. [1]G h e i n Malaleel Iaret. Gein Iaret Enoc. [2]Gein Enoc Matusalem. [2]Gein Matusalem Lamiac, ⁊ mac dosin Nōe.

---

37. (1) Adam vero cognouit [1]Euam uxorem suam, quae
concepit et peperit Cain, [dicens] Possedi hominem per
Deum.   (2) Rursusque peperit [2]*filium alium,* Abel : fuit
autem Abel pastor ouium, et Cain agricola.   (3) Factum est
autem post multos dies ut offerret Cain de fructibus terrae
munera [3]*Deo,* (4) Abel quoque obtulit <Deo> de primogenitis
gregis sui, et de adipibus eorum.   Et respexit Dominus ad
Abel et ad munera eius, (5) ad Cain uero et ad munera eius
non respexit.   Iratusque est Cain uehementer et concidit
uultus eius.

38. (6) Dixitque Dominus ad Cain : Quare mestus es, et
cur concidit facies tua?   (7) [1]Nonne si bene egeris recipies?
Sin autem male, statim in foribus peccatum aderit; [sed
sub te erit appetitus eius, et tu dominaberis illius].

---

[8] Set β[2]   [9] is seadh ro raidh β ro radh (*om.* is edh) β[12]   [10] tug β[12]
[11] *om.* Dīa M   [12] dam ar M *om.* dhamh . . . ar .i. β[12]   [13] *om.* ar M
[14] saimh β[2]   [15] seanamhuil eile β[12]   [16] *om.* a M β[12] : eis β[12]
[17] Aibeoil ro marb M Abel do mharbhadh (*om.* Cain) β[12]   [18] ⁊ ro

son Seth; and thus he spake : God hath given me [said Adam] "ar" that is, other gentle excellent seed, in the room of Abel, whom Cain slew. (26) A son was born to Seth, Enos his name. It is that Enos who began at the very first to call upon and to invoke the name of the Lord.

β.	β^{12}.
43a. A son to Enos, Cainan. A son to him, Malalehel. A son to him, Iared. A son to him, Enoch. A son to him, Mathusalam. A son to him, Lamech. A son to him. Noe.	Enos begat Cainan. Cainan begat Malalehel. Malalehel begat Iared. Iared begat Enoch. Enoch begat Mathusalam. Mathusalam begat Lamech, and Noe was son to him.

---

(8) Dixitque Cain ad Abel fratrem suum : Egrediamur ²*in agrum*. Cumque essent in agro, consurrexit Cain aduersus Abel fratrem suum et interfecit eum. (9) Et ait ³*Deus* ad Cain : Vbi est Abel frater tuus? Qui respondit : Nescio; num custos fratris mei sum? (10) Dixitque ⁴<Deus> ad ⁵*Cain* : Quid fecisti? Vox sanguinis fratris tui clamat ad me de terra.

39. (11) Nunc igitur maledictus eris super terram, quae aperuit os suum et suscepit sanguinem fratris tui de manu tua. (12) <Et> cum operatus fueris eam, non dabit tibi fructus suos : uagus et profugus eris super terram. (13) Dixitque Cain ad *Deum* : Maior est iniquitas mea quam ut ueniam merear. (14) Ecce eicis me hodie a facie terrae et a facie tua abscondar. [Et] ero uagus et profugus in terra, omnis ¹[igitur qui inuenerit me] occidet me.

---

geinther β^{12} ¹⁹Șeth M β^{12} ²⁰ *om.* a ainm-side *ins.* ⅂ β^{12} ²¹ he in M ²² thinscain M thion sguin β^{12} ²³ tus riam M : -amh β^{1} mgh- β^{2} ²⁵ atath M aatach β^{12} ²⁶ in Choimdead M, on Choimhdhia β^{12}
43a. ¹ gein β^{2} ² gen β^{2} (*bis*)

(*a*) *s*¹ M.
(*b*) B lacuna begins. The ¶ here numbered 43a attempts, on the part of the late copies, to supply connecting matter between the two sides of the gap.

(15) Dixitque ei *Deus* : Nequaquam ita fiet, sed omnis qui occiderit Cain septuplum punietur. Posuit[que] *Deus* Cain ²<in> signum, ut non eum interficeret omnis ³[qui inuenisset eum].

40. (16) Egressusque Cain a facie Domini habitauit in terra, profugus, ad orientalem plagam Eden. (17) Cognouit autem Cain uxorem suam, quae concepit ¹[et peperit] ²<filium nomine> Enoch : et aedificauit ciuitatem, uocauitque nomen eius ex nomine filii sui Enoch. (18) Porro Enoch genuit Irad, et Irad genuit Mauiahel, et Mauiahel genuit Mathusahel, et Mathusahel genuit Lamech.

41. (19) Qui accepit uxores duas, nomen uni ¹Ada, et nomen alteri Sella. (20) Genuitque Ada Iabel, qui fuit pater habitantum in tentoriis atque pastorum : (21) et nomen fratris eius Iubal, ipse fuit pater canentium cithara et organo. (22) Sella quoque genuit ²Tubalcain, qui fuit malleator et faber in cuncta opera aeris et ferri. ³Soror vero Tubalcain Noemma.

42. (23) Dixitque Lamech uxoribus suis ¹Ádae et Sellae : Audite uocem meam, uxores Lamech, auscultate sermonem meum, quoniam occidi uirum in uulnus meum, et adulescentulum in liuorem meum. (24) Septuplum ultio dabitur de Cain, de Lamech uero septuagies septies.

43. (25) Cognouit quoque adhuc Adam ¹[uxorem suam], et peperit filium, uocauitque ²nomen eius Seth, dicens : Posuit mihi semen aliud pro Abel, quem occidit Cain. (26) Sed et Seth natus est filius, quem uocauit Enos : isti coepit inuocare nomen Domini.

Notes on the Biblical Text, Chapter IV.

¶ 37. *Hauam* in ST, but as before *Euam* has much support. ²*Fratrem eius* in ST and all Versions and mss. ³*Domino* in ST and all Versions and mss.

¶ 38. [1]This verse, of which the best commentators can make but little, is baldly paraphrased by Tr., who has omitted the unintelligible last clause altogether. [2]The Irish is closer to LXX (διέλθωμεν εἰς τὸ πεδίον). The original is lost from the Massoretic Hebrew text, but must be supplied (the English Revised Version makeshift "and Cain told Abel his brother" is inadmissible). [3]*Dominus* in ST, but ὁ θεός in LXX. [4]*Deus* omitted in Vulg., but ὁ θεός in LXX. One Vulg. MS. has *Dominus*. [5]*Eum* ST and all MSS. No equivalent in LXX.

¶ 39. [1,][3]These two similar passages are necessary to the sense, and presumably were in the original text of Tr. It is a curious coincidence that they should both have disappeared. [2]*In* omitted by ST, but there is authority for it, as for *in Cain signum* and *in signum Cain*.

¶ 40. [1]7 *ro thuisim* was probably in the text originally, but dropped out early. [2]*Filium nomine* found in four MSS., but ST omits.

¶ 41. [1]This name is spelt with one *d* in all Versions and MSS. [2]The interpolated *mac don Lāimhiach cēadna* doubtless was originally a gloss explaining the personality of Tupalcān (Tubalcain). There is no authority behind the statement in Tr. that he was the *first* craftsman in his trades. [3]There is no authority for the verbose Irish *ocus rug Sella ingen īar sin*.

¶ 42. [1]Tr. here follows Vulg. against other Versions in transferring the names of the wives from the beginning of the song (where the poetical structure requires them) to the prose introductory matter. The translation of the song is corrupt, and as it stands is partly unintelligible. See the notes to this ¶.

¶ 43. [1]*A sēitig* has been extruded from the text by the gloss .i. *Eua*. [2]The speaker was certainly Eve, not Adam. The latter name, for which there is no authority whatever, is doubtless an interpolation.

CHAPTER V.

44. (1) As [1]ē so thrā leabar ‡[(a)] .i. in Genis, no canōin pedarlaigi ‖ tuismeada Adaim.   Isin lō in ra [2]thuisim Dīa in duine fo chosmailis fodēin, (2) ro thuisim fear ᚋ mnāi, ᚋ ro beandach dōib, ᚋ tuc in n-ainm as *Adam* ‡[(a)] .i. duni ‖ dōib isin lō in ro thuismit.

y[1] Āirmit eōlaig na sdairi dīada nā ro beannaig Dīa do Adam ō daridni in pecad.

y[2] Ī cind sē n-ūair co leith do lō doridni Adam ᚋ Eba in pecad, .i. torad Chraind na hAithni do ch[(b)]aithem, trē aslach na nathrach.

(3) Tricha bliadan ar cēt ro bo slān do Adam in tan rucad Seth dō (4) ᚋ doridned lāitheada Adaim īar tuismed [3]Seth dō .i. ocht cēt bliadan, ᚋ ro thuisim maccu ᚋ ingena.   (5) Ocus [4]doridnead [5]uile sāegal [6]Adaim .i. [7]tricha ar [8]nōib cētaib bliadan, ᚋ adbath Adam [9]īar sin.

y[3] [10]Ocus ro hadnaiced sin chathraid dīanad ainm Ṡabrōn, co roibi a chorp sa baili sin co tānic in dīli tar in domun: cor scarsad tonna na dīlenn a chorp ᚋ a cheand re chēle, co rucsad leo na tonna in cenn o Ṡabrōn co Golgotha, cor thoiris an Golgotha co chrochad Crīst.   Co rob trē chend Adaim tarla cend na croichi: co ndeachaid fuil in Choimdead fo agaid Adaim, conad mar sin do baistead Adam ar tūs, do rēir eōlach na sdairi dīada[10].

45. (6) Cūic bliadna ar cēt imorro [1]fa slān do Seth in tan rucad [2]Enos dō.   (7) Seacht [3]mbliadna ar cūic cētaib īar tuismead Enos fa hē sāegal [4]Seth, ᚋ ro

---

44. [1] se seo M   [2] *spelt* th;im *wherever it occurs* M   [3] Seith H

CHAPTER V.

44. (1) Now this is the book [of Genesis, or of the Old Testament canon] of the creation of Adam. In the day in which God created Man under His own likeness (2) He created man and woman, and blessed them, and gave them the name from *Adam* [i.e. *man*] in the day wherein they were created.

y[1] Those skilled in sacred history consider that God gave no blessing to Adam after he committed the sin.

y[2] At the end of six hours and a half of the day did Adam and Eve commit the sin, namely the eating of the Tree of Knowledge, by the incitement of the serpent.

(3) An hundred and thirty years had Adam complete when Seth was born to him, (4) and the days of Adam after the birth of Seth to him were made eight hundred years, and he begat sons and daughters. (5) And all the life of Adam was made nine hundred and thirty years, and Adam died thereafter.

And he was buried in the city which is called Hebron, so that his body was in that place till the Flood came over the world: and the waves of the Flood sundered his body and his head each from the other, and the waves carried the head with them from Hebron to Golgotha. It abode in Golgotha till the Crucifixion of Christ. And it was through the head of Adam that the end of the Cross came: and the blood of the Lord fell over the face of Adam, and thus was Adam baptized for the first time, according to men skilled in sacred history.

45. (6) An hundred and five years were complete for Seth, when Enos was born to him. (7) Five hundred and seven years was the life of Seth after

---

[4] -ned H   [5] uili H   [6] Adam M   [7] *spelt* triK *in* M   [8] nae M
[9] iartain H   [10-10] *in* M *only*
45. [1] ba H   [2] Enoss H   [3] bliadna *yc* H   [4] Seith H

(*a*) These glosses interlined.   (*b*) H resumes.

thuisim ⁵maccu ⁊ ingena.   (8) Dā bliadain dēc ar sē
⁶chētaib ⁷fa hē uili ⁸sāegail Seth, ⁊ adbath Seth īar sin.

46. (9) Nōcha ar chēd bliadan ‡ .i. deich mbliadan
ar ¹nāe ²fichtib bliadan ‖ is ead fa slān do Enos ³in tan
rucad Cainen dō.   (10) Īar tuismed imorro(ᵃ) ⁴Chainen
dō, fa beō hē fri rē chūic mbliadan ⁵dēc ar secht cētaib,
⁊ ro thuisim maccu ⁊ ingena.   (11) Ocus ⁶doridnead
uili lāitheada Enos .i. cūic bliadna ar nāi cētaib, ⁊
adbath īarsin.

47. (12) Seachtmoga ar chēt bliadan ¹‡ .i. deich
mbliadan ⁊ ocht fichit bliadan ‖ is ed ²fa slān do
³Chainean ⁴in tan ro thuisim Malalel.   (13) Ceathracha
ar seacht cētaib bliadan imorro is ed ⁵fa beō Cainen
īar ⁶tuismed Malalel ⁷dō, ⁊ ro ⁸thuismistair maccu ⁊
ingena.   (14) Ocus ⁹dorignit uili ¹⁰lāitheada ¹¹Chainean
.i. deich mbliadan ar nāi cētaib bliadan, ⁊ adbath
¹²īarsin.

48. (15) ¹Cūic bliadna ²sescad ar chēd is ed ³fa slān
do Malalel ⁴in tan ro thuisim ⁵Iareth.   (16) Tricha ar
seacht cētaib bliadan imorro ba beō hē īar ⁶tuismed
Iareth, ⁊ ro thuisim maccu ⁊ ingena.   (17) Ocus
⁷doridnit uili lāitheada Malalel ⁸cūic bliadna nōchat
ar ocht cētaib, ⁊ adbath ⁹īarsin.

49. (18) Dā bliadain seascad ar chēd ¹fa slān do
²Iareth ³in tan ro thuisim ⁵Enōc.   (19) Ocht cēd bliadan

---

⁵ macu *hic et semper* H   ⁶ chedaib M   ⁷ ba H   ⁸ saegal Seith H
   46. ¹ nai H   ² *sic* H, fichit M   ³ an tan rugad H   ⁴ Chainein,
do bo beo H   ⁵ deg H   ⁶ dorigned uili laitheda Enóss H
   47. ¹ *ins.* dono H   ² ba H   ³ -nén H   ⁴ an H   ⁵ ba H
⁶ tus (*om.* -med) H   ⁷ *om.* dō H   ⁸ thuisimstair H   ⁹ dorigned H

the birth of Enos, and he begat sons and daughters. (8) Six hundred and twelve years was the whole of the life of Seth, and Seth died thereafter.

46. (9) An hundred and ninety years, [that is, nine score and ten years] were complete to Enos when Cainan was born to him. (10) Now after the birth of Cainan·to him, he was alive for a space of seven hundred and fifteen years, and begat sons and daughters. (11) And all the days of Enos were made nine hundred and five years, and he died thereafter.

47. (12) An hundred and seventy years [that is, eight score and ten years] were complete for Cainan when he begat Malalehel. (13) Seven hundred and forty years moreover was Cainan alive after Malalehel was born to him, and he begat sons and daughters. (14) And all the days of Cainan were made nine hundred and ten years, and he died thereafter.

48. (15) An hundred sixty and five years were complete for Malalehel when he begat Iared. (16) Seven hundred and thirty years was he alive, moreover, after the birth of Iared, and he begat sons and daughters. (17) And all the days of Malalehel were made eight hundred ninety and five years, and he died thereafter.

49. (18) An hundred sixty and two years were complete for Iared when he begat Enoch. (19) Eight

---

[10] laitheda H   [11] -nén H   [12] Cainén iartain H
    48. [1] Cuig H   [2] lxx. H   [3] ba H   [4] an H   [5] Iaareth H
[6] -edh H *hic et semper*   [7] dorignid uili laithedha H   [8] *ins.* .i.; cuig H   [9] Malalel iartain H.
    49. [1] ba H   [2] Iaareth H   [3] an tan ra thuisim Enoch H

(a) H preserved continuously from here.

imorro ro baī ⁴ina beathaig īar tuismed ⁵Enōc, ⁊ ro
thuisim maccu ⁊ ingena.   (20) Ocus ⁶doridnead uili
lāitheada ⁷Iareth .i. dā bliadain sescad ar nāi cētaib, ⁊
adbath ⁷Iareth īarsin.

50. (21) Cūic bliadna sescad ar chēt ¹fa slān do
²Enōc ³in tan ro thuisim ⁴Mathasalem.   (22) Ocus is
do ⁵rēr Dē ro imthig Enōc : dā chēd bliadan imorro
dō   ⁶i mbeathaid choitchind chāich īar tuismed
⁷Mathusalam, ⊤ ro thuisim maccu ⊤ ingena.   (23) Ocus
⁸dorignaid uili ⁹lāitheada Enōc .i. cōic bliadna sescat
ar trī cētaib, (24) ⊤ ¹⁰ro imthig ¹¹do rēr ¹²thoile Dē,

⊤ ¹³fa ¹⁴in inadaib diamraib ¹⁵dīthrubdaib, ō beathaid
choitchind chāich, no aitrebad ¹⁶in fer ¹⁷sin cēin,

no co ¹⁸ruc Dīa leis hē,¹⁹

⊤²⁰ ro co ṡuigid hē ²¹i Parrdus ūasal Adaim. Ocus is ē
²²in t-Enōc sin, ²³.i. mac ²⁴Iareth, ro airic na dēcc
²⁵n-anmand airegda Ebraidi, ō ro ²⁶cēt-gairmead Dīa ar
tūs(a), o anmandaib ēcsamlaib na nEabraide.

51. (25) ¹Ro thuisim dono Mathasalem Laimiach,
isin sechtmad bliadain ochtmogat ar ched a aisi.
(26) Da bliadain ar ochtmogaid ar secht cetaib fa beo
Mathasalem iar tuismed Laimiach do, ⊤ ro thuisim
maccu ⊤ ingena.   (27) Ocus doridnit uili laitheda
²Mathasaelim, .i. noi mbliadna ceathrachad ar noe
cedaib, ⊤ fuair bas iartain.

---

⁴ ana beathaid H   ⁵ Enóch H (*bis*)   ⁶ dorigned a uili laitheda H
⁷ Iaareth H (*bis*)
     50. ¹ ba H   ² Enoch H   ³ an H   ⁴ Mathasailem H
⁵ reir Dia ra himig Enóch H   ⁶ a mbethaid H   ⁷ Mathasailem H
⁸ dognidh H   ⁹ laitheda H   ¹⁰ ra imid   ¹¹ do reir H
¹² thoili H   ¹³ bá H   ¹⁴ *om*. in H   ¹⁵ dithrubaib H   ¹⁶ an H

hundred years, moreover, was he in his life after the birth of Enoch, and he begat sons and daughters. (20) And all the days of Iared were made nine hundred sixty and two years, and Iared died thereafter.

50. (21) An hundred sixty and five years were complete for Enoch when he begat Mathusalam. (22) And it is in God's way that Enoch walked: two hundred years had he in the common life of every man after the birth of Mathusalam, and he begat sons and daughters. (23) And all the days of Enoch were made three hundred sixty and five years, (24) and he walked according to the will of God,

And it was in waste and desert places, away from the common life of every man, that that man was living for a season,

till God took him with Himself,

and set him in the noble Paradise of Adam. Now this is that Enoch son of Iared, who invented the ten excellent Hebrew names, by which God was first called, out of the different names of the Hebrews.

51. (25) Now Mathusalam begat Lamech, in the hundred eighty and seventh year of his age. (26) Seven hundred eighty and two years was Mathusalam alive after the birth of Lamech to him, and he begat sons and daughters. (27) And all the days of Mathusalam were made nine hundred forty and nine years, and he died thereafter.

---

[17] sain H   [18] rug H   [19] *ins.* a Parrdhus H   [20] cur śuigid H   [21] a H   [22] an H   [23] *om.* .i. H   [24] Iaareth H   [25] n-anmanda aireada Eabraidi H   [26] -meadh H

51. [1] The marks of prolongation are here omitted in accordance with p. xxvi   [2] Written Mathasaeli in VM. Not understanding this, sM wrote Mathasael-i

52. (28) Ro thuisim imorro Laimiach Noe, isin dara bliadain ar ochtmogat ar chet a aisi.

Is hē dono eitercheart ⁊ mīnugad cīallaidi in anma, ¹.i. Nōe, .i. *requies* .i. cumsanad.

(29) Uair is ed ro raid Laimiach iar tuismed Nae: Bid he in mac-sa ²coimdidnaphas ⁊ saerfas sind o gnimaib ⁊ o gnimaib ar lam isin talmain mallachtnaich mirathmair, ro eascain Dia,

ar pecad Adaim ⁊ Eua ⁊ Cāin chlāin, chosnomaich, chelgaig, cona chloind.

(30) Coic bliadna nochad ar coic cetaib ba he saegal Laimiach iar tuismed Noe do, ⁊ ro thuisim maccu ⁊ ingena.   (31) Ocus dorignit uile laitheada Laimiach .i. seacht mbliadna sechtmogat ar ³secht cetaib, ⁊ fuair bas iarsin(*a*) . . . .

-----

44. (1) Hic est liber generationis Adam.   In die qua creauit Deus hominem ad similitudinem ¹*suam,* (2) masculum et feminam creauit eos, et benedixit illos, et uocauit nomen eorum "Adam," in die qua creati sunt.   (3) Vixit autem Adam centum triginta annis et genuit ²[ad similitudinem et imaginem suam, uocauitque nomen eius] Seth : (4) et facti sunt dies Adam postquam genuit Seth octingenti anni, genuitque filios et filias.   (5) Et factum est omne tempus quod vixit Adam, anni nonaginti triginta, et mortuus est.

45–49. It is unnecessary to transcribe the Latin of these formal paragraphs, but some important details with regard to the ages of the Patriarchs are set forth in the notes at the end of the chapter.

-----

52. ¹ is *for* .i. M   ² coimdid naphas M   ³ sē M

(*a*) M lacuna begins.

52. (28) Moreover Lamech begat Noe, in the hundred eighty and second year of his age.

This is the interpretation, and the significant sense of the name Noe; *requies,* or "rest."

(29) For thus did Lamech speak after the birth of Noe : this boy shall be he who shall comfort and deliver us from labours, from the labours of our hands in the accursed ill-fated earth, which God cursed,

for the sin of Adam and Eve, and Cain, the iniquitous, contentious, and deceiving, with his progeny.

(30) Five hundred ninety and five years was the life of Lamech after the birth of Noe to him, and he begat sons and daughters. (31) And all the days of Lamech were made seven hundred seventy and seven years, and he died thereafter . . . .

---

50. (21) ¹Porro Enoch uixit sexaginta quinque annis et genuit Mathusalam.   (22) Et ambulauit Enoch cum Deo postquam genuit Mathusalam *ducentis* annis, et genuit filios et filias.   (23) Et facti sunt dies Enoch trecenti sexaginta quinque anni, (24) ambulauitque cum Deo [et non apparuit] quia tulit eum Deus.

51. (This paragraph partakes of the formal nature of most of the chapter.)

52. (28) Vixit autem Lamech centum octoginta duobus annis, et genuit [filium (29) uocauitque nomen eius] Noe, dicens : Iste consolabitur nos ab operibus et laboribus manuum nostrarum in terra, cui maledixit Dominus.   (30) Vixitque Lamech postquam genuit Noe quingentos nonaginta quinque annos, et genuit filios et filias (31) et facti sunt omnes dies Lamech septingenti septuaginta septem anni, et mortuus est² . . .

Notes on the Biblical Text, Chapter V.

¶ 44. [1]The punctuation, doubtless by accident, follows the OL. But there is no authority for the substitution of *suam* for *Dei*. [2]This passage was perhaps dropped from Tr. owing to an eye-confusion induced by the similar passage in the preceding verse.

¶ 45–49. In the ages of the Patriarchs Tr. follows the authority of LXX (and Isidore) as against Vulg. This is shown in the following table. (A = age of each patriarch at birth of firstborn, B = years lived after firstborn, C = total age.)

	Septuagint.			Vulgate.			Irish Translation.		
	A	B	C	A	B	C	A	B	C
Seth ...	205	707	912	105	807	912	105	507	612
Enos ...	190	715	905	90	815	905	190	715	905
Kenan ...	170	740	910	70	840	910	170	740	910
Mahalalel	165	730	895	65	830	895	165	730	895
Jared ...	162	800	962	162	800	962	162	800	962
Enoch ...	165	200	365	65	300	365	165	200	365
Methu-selah	167	802	969	187	782	969	187	782	945 (sic)
Lamech	188	565	753	182	595	777	182	595	677 (sic)

In the Irish text .xl. has been miswritten for .lx. in the age of Methuselah, and in the age of Lamech a "c" has been omitted. The 677 years of Lamech's age is a mere copyist's mistake which has here been corrected in the text, .dc. having been written instead of .dcc. The reduction of the age of Seth by 300 years has no authority.

¶ 50. [1]This paragraph has been much worked over by the interpolation and assimilation of details from the apocrypha of Enoch. It has almost parted company with the Latin original.

¶ 52. [1]There is here a hint that Tr. is for the moment becoming weary of his work. He does not show his usual care in finding different words for *operibus et laboribus* : contrast verses 4, 5 of this chapter, where he has duly observed the difference of *dies* and *tempus* (*lāitheada, sāegal*). The rendering (or more probably the transmission) of the paragraph is rather too free for any certain establishment of the Latin text. [2]It is uncertain whether *iarsin*, the last word before the lacuna, belongs to v. 31 (where the Latin does not call for it) or begins the lost v. 32, which enumerated the sons of Noah.

Chapter VI.

53. . . . (*a*)Ro forcongair Dīa] for chlannaib Se[th na
ro chummascdais cairde]s fri clannaib Cain, ꞇ na ra [clann-
aigdis friu ꞇ na tucdais] mna dib.   Arai sin tra, odchond-
[cadar clanna Seth iad, tucsat ingena] airedha clainn Cain.
Tangadar tar [in forcital, ꞇ ro clannaigset] friu tar sarugad
nDe.   Conad airi sin [ro geinsit fomoraig ꞇ] lupraganaig
ꞇ cach egosc dodea[lbda torothorda ra bai] for dainib an
domuin ria ndilind.

A[tberat araile nach dib-sidi] iarricht imorro;   is do śil
Chaim.

54. (3) Ocus ra [raid Dia : Ni anfaid nios] fada
mo Spirad isin duine ‡ .i. ana [17] . . . . .] duine ∥,
conaid coland ‡ .i. ar a ro-med d[15] . . . . ∥ ꞇ]
forbabtar laithedha in duini i cind fichet [bliadan ar
cet.   (4) Do badar] imorro for talmain ar tan sin
giganteis, ‡ .i. cora[id o macaib] mileata ꞇ ó
hingenaib colacha Cain ∥.

55. (5) Ot[chondairc Dia] imorro—

techt tar timna dóib ‡ a feirg, a feill, a f[10 . . . .]rad, a
n-úaill, a n-ecrabad ∥, ra chindustair na hui[li daini] do
dibadh ꞇ do dilgend.

—Conad iarom ra raid Dia : (7) [Sgrios]fed, ar Se,
an duini ra thuisim o dreich an talman, ‡ [8conid tucad]
dono dilgenn for uilib anmandaib an talman, ꞇ for
enaib an aeoir ∥ uair tanig aithrechus dam a ndenma.
(8) Fuair Náe imorro airmidin ꞇ onoir a fiadnaisi De—

---

54. [1] The small number prefixed to this and such similar lacunae as
cannot be certainly filled up indicates the approximate number of
characters that have been lost: the number of lost *letters* may have

CHAPTER VI.

53. . . . God forbade the descendants of Seth to mingle friendship with those of Cain, or to beget children by them, or to take wives from them. In spite of that, however, when the descendants of Seth saw them, they took the beautiful daughters of the descendants of Cain. They transgressed the commandment, and had children by them in despite of God. Wherefore there were born giants and dwarfs and every unshapely monstrous being that was among the people of the world before the Flood.

> Others say however that it is not of them that they were found: it is of the seed of Ham.

54. (3) And God said: My Spirit shall not remain longer in man [i.e. in . . . . . man] for he is flesh [i.e. for the exceeding greatness of his (sins? . . .)] : and the days of man shall be brought to a close at the end of an hundred and twenty years. (4) Now there were *gigantes.* upon the earth at that time, [i.e. champions of the warlike sons and the fleshly daughters of Cain.]

55. (5) Now when God saw—

that they were transgressing the covenant [in wrath, in treachery, in . . . ., in pride, in impiety], He determined to annihilate and to destroy all men.

Wherefore God said: (7) I shall root out, said He, Man, whom I have created, from the face of the earth, [(so there was brought) destruction upon all the beasts of the earth and upon the birds of the air] for repentance for having made them hath come on Me. (8) But Noe found favour and honour before God.

---

been greater, for allowance must be made for possible compendia, contractions, and suspensions.

(a) A few letters of the previous line left (. . . `sadt . a . . .), which will not fit in with anything.

Air is e Náe aenfer firen forbthe frith do chlannaib sainemla Seith, na ra cumaisc fri clannaib claena Cain.

56. (11) Ra truaillned ⁊ ra línad tra an talam o ulc ‡ ⁊ indirgi na ndaini ‖; (12) ⁊ ód chondairc Dia ani sin (13) ra raid fri Náe : Tanig, ar Se, crich ⁊ forba na huili cholla am fiadnaissi. Millfed ⁊ malartfad uili aitrebaidi an talman, ‡ otá min co mór ‖.

57. ‡ Ra raid Dia dono fri Náe ‖ (14) Dena-sa, ar Se, duit feisin airc lethain luchtmair lan-fáirsing, o crandaib snaigthi slemnaigthi—

y¹ nach dernad ⁊ nach dingentar long bus samail di ar med, ar daingne, ar disli, ar deig-dénum.

y² Ocus is amlaid dorindead ⁊ ceitri slesa furri.

Déna-sa dono inti aideda imda ecsamla, ⁊ slemnaig-fedsa in aircc ar medón ⁊ dia n-echtair o bidamain.

y³ (a) Is é imorro aigned fil isin bidamain, nach milleadh cruimi na gaetha na uisce na tes ngreine, na cranda do curter inti.

(15) Ocus dena-su tri cet cubad hi ḟad na hairci, ⁊ caoga cubad in a ¹leithedh, ⁊ tricha cubad ina hairdi. (16) Ocus déna seinistir isa n-aircc, ⁊ aen chubad ana tigi.

y³ (b) Atiad a hadbair, .i. glae iuda ⁊ ²bidamain ⁊ cré, ‡ .i. úir thiri Siría ‖. Bui Dia Anarlaoite ra chumaisc na hadbair sin tré na cheli, tré forgeall Dé fair : brathair do Eibifenius do ṡaer na hairci. Uair do mac do [¹⁰· . . .] ³nus iad araen. Aitreb a comuir cach cineil [ainmide i]nti, Nir cuiread aen ⁴tairrngi uma na iaraind inti. [Is re

---

57. ¹ *The final* d *is a little doubtful*   ² *The scribe began to*

For this Noe is the one righteous perfect man who was found, of the excellent children of Seth, who had not mingled with the iniquitous children of Cain.

56. (11) Now the earth was corrupted and filled with evil [and with the iniquity of men], (12) and when God saw that, (13) He said unto Noe : The end and termination of all flesh hath come before Me. I shall destroy and confound all the inhabitants of the earth [both small and great].

57. [Moreover God said to Noe :] (14) Make thou, said He, for thyself a broad capacious roomy ark of timbers chipped and smoothed—

so that never was made nor shall be made a ship like unto it in size, in firmness, in trustworthiness, and in good craftsmanship.
And thus was it made, with four sides to it.

Make also within it many various chambers, and let the ark be smooth inside and out with pitch.

Now this is the nature that pitch possesses, that no worms, nor winds, nor water, nor sun-heat destroys the timbers that have been placed in it.

(15) And make three hundred cubits in the length of the ark, and fifty cubits in its breadth, and thirty cubits in its height. (16) And make a window in the ark, and one cubit in its thickness.

These are its materials, glue and pitch and clay, [that is, mould of the land of Syria]. It was Dia Anarlaoite who mixed these materials together, by the revelation of God. He was brother to Epiphenius, the wright of the ark, for they were the two sons of (—)nus. There was a dwelling in preparation for every sort of

---

write cré here, but realised and corrected his mistake after writing the r
[3] *The first half of this* u *torn away*   [4] *the* g *sprs.* c H

bida]main do chomdluthugad a clar ré cheili.   Secht
la [amain] sul do ꝼer tosach na dilenn, ꞁ is amlaid bai Náe
cona [macai]b, ꞁ a leth-gluini dessa fúithib, ꞁ siad ag
edarguidi Dé im [f]oirithin d'fadbail.

Da raid Dia co Náe : Dena-su imorro [d]orus na hairci
ara slis, ꞁ dena cendacuili inti co ꝼeicib deiligtecha
eaturru.

58. (17) Daber-sa co fóllus ‡ ar Dia ‖ uisci na
dilenn for talmain, do marbad hina huili cholla hi
ꝼuil ¹spirad bethad fo nim, ꞁ biaid forba ꞁ crich for na
huilib itát a talmain.   (18) Ocus doden caradrad rit,
ꞁ raga-su ²isa n-aircc ꞁ do ṡeidig ‡ .i. Coba ingen
Laimiach, do ṡiur-sin ‖, ꞁ do micc ꞁ seitchi do mac
imailli ritsiu, ‡ ꞁ is úaid do geinsid diblinaib ‖.
(19) Ocus bera leat isa n-airc caraid cacha hanmanda
in ecoisc chechtarda fil for talmain, ardáig a mbethad
do choiméd ‡ ꞁ silta uaithib iar ndilinn ‖.   (21) Bera
dono let isi n-áircc biad cubaid comadais ‡ do cach
anmanda, *et reliqua,* dligtheach ꞁ indligthech ‖, ꞁ bid
biad duidse ꞁ doib-sim sin do chaithim.   (22) Daroini
tra Náe na huili neithi ro forchongair Dia dó.

54. ¹(3) Dixitque Deus : Non permanebit Spiritus meus in
homine ²*diutius,* quia caro est, ³eruntque dies illius centum
uiginti annorum.   (4) Gigantes autem erant super terram in
diebus illis⁴ . . .

---

58. ¹ *the a sbs.*   ² *first written* ifa *and afterwards corrected.*

animal within it.   Not a nail of bronze or of iron was put into it: with pitch was its timber secured together. There were only seven days before the first of the Flood poured down, and thus were Noe and his sons, with their right knees bent under them, interceding with God to obtain succour.

God said unto Noe : Make, moreover, the door of the ark in its side, and make chambers within it, with separating roof-beams between them.

58. (17) Lo [said God] I shall bring the water of the Flood over the earth, to slay altogether flesh in which is a spirit of life beneath the heaven, and there shall be termination and end upon all that are in the earth.   (18) And I shall make a compact with thee : and thou shalt go into the ark, thou and thy wife [Coba, daughter of Lamech, thy sister] and thy sons and the wives of thy sons together with thee [and of thee were they born on both sides].   (19) And thou shalt take with thee into the ark a pair of every animal, in each shape that is on the earth, in order to preserve their life [and for seeding from them after the Flood].   (21) Thou shalt take also with thee into ark food, meet and fitting [for every animal, *et reliqua*, lawful and unlawful] and it shall be food for thee and for them, to eat thereof.   (22) So Noe did all the things which God commanded him.

---

55. (5) Videns autem Deus[1] . . ... (7) Delebo, inquit, hominem quem creaui a facie terrae, [2]ab homine usque ad animantia, a reptili usque ad uolucres caeli, paenitet enim me fecisse eos.   (8) Noe vero inuenit gratiam coram [3]Deo

56. . . . . [1](11) Corrupta est autem terra [coram Deo] et repleta est iniquitate.   (12) Cumque uidisset Deus [2]. . . . (13) Dixit ad Noe : Finis uniuersae carnis uenit coram me [3]. . . . Ego disperdam eos cum terra.

57. (14) [1]Fac tibi arcam de lignis leuigatis.   Mansiunculas in arca facies, et bitumine linies intrinsecus et extrinsecus. (15) Et sic facies eam : trecentorum cubitorum erit longitudo arcae, quinquaginta cubitorum latitudo, et triginta cubitorum altitudo illius.   (16) Fenestram in arca facies, et in <uno> cubito consummabis summitatem.   Ostium autem arcae pones ex latere deorsum : cenacula et tristega facies in ea.

58. (17) Ego ergo adducam diluuii aquas super terram, ut interficiam omnem carnem in qua spiritus uitae est subter caelum, uniuersa quae in terra sunt consumentur. (18) Ponamque foedus meum tecum, et ingredieris arcam, tu et filii tui, uxor tua et uxores filiorum tuorum tecum (19) et ex cunctis animantibus uniuersae carnis bina induces in arcam [1]. . . . (20) . . . . ut possint uiuere.   (21) Tolles igitur tecum ex omnibus escis quae mandi possunt, et comportabis apud te, et erunt tam tibi quam illis in cibum. (22) Fecit ergo Noe omnia quae praeceperat illi Deus.

NOTES ON THE BIBLICAL TEXT, CHAPTER VI.

¶ 54. [1]Verses 1, 2, lost. [2]*In aeternum*, Vulg. [3]This obscure and probably corrupt passage, usually (though not always) taken by commentators to indicate a limitation of the life of the human individual, is understood by Tr. in the alternative sense—a term upon the duration of the human race.   [4]The remainder of this verse dropped out.

¶ 55. [1]Remainder of this verse and verse 6 dropped out. [2](*Conid tucad*) *dílgenn* is obviously a marginal comment which has entered the text, and probably necessitated some subsequent modification of the context to modify the nonsense which it produced. [3]*Domino* in ST., but *Deo* has some support.

¶ 56. [1]Verses 9, 10 omitted or lost. [2,3]These passages possibly discarded by Tr. or by a copyist because they repeat matter set forth immediately before.

¶ 57. [1]This ¶ has been rendered with tolerable literalness; only in one place does Tr. stray from the text—where he, renders the corrupt and unintelligible *in cubito consummabis summitatem* as though it meant that the walls of the ark should be a cubit thick. This is also the theory of the author of the poem no. V: but the text cannot bear this meaning. The rendering of *tristega*, "storey," by *feice*, "roof-beam," is noteworthy. The paragraph is so farced with glosses that it is difficult to keep on the track of the biblical narrative.

¶ 58. [1]The long passage here omitted enumerated the birds, cattle, reptiles, etc. It must have been in Tr. originally, for it is presupposed by the *et reliqua* of the gloss following. Probably some impatient scribe dropped them as being irrelevant to the main purpose of the present text.

Chapter VII.

59. (1) Ocus da raid Día ré Náe : Imthig-siu isin aircc ⁊ do muintir uili mailli rit, ar as tú aen-firén fuaras isin chinead-sa. (2) Béra leat dono isin aircc na sechta ⁊ na sechta ona huilib anmandaib glanaib, .i. mascul ⁊ femen. Bera lett dono a dó ⁊ a dó ona hanmunnaib inglanaib, .i. mascul ⁊ femen. (3) Bera dono let na sechta ⁊ na sechta o ethaidib glanaib inimi(a) .i. mascul ⁊ femen. Bera dono let na deda ⁊ na ¹deada do na foluaimnechaib inglanaib .i. mascul ⁊ femen. (4) Daber-sa dono, ar Día re ²Nae, a forba an ʂechtmad laithi oniu, fleochad silteach saidbir for talmain, ri re cethrachat laa ⁊ cethrachat aidchi. Ocus dilegfad ⁊ dicurfet o dreich an talman in uili fó-thairisim dorignus. (5) Darone tra Nae na huili ra athin Día dó.

60. (6) Sé cet bliadan dono ba ʂlán do Náe an tan tanig an dile tar in talmain, (7) ⁊ dochuaid Náe, cona macaib ⁊ cona seitchib imailli ris, isa n-aircc for uisci na dilenn, (8) ⁊ rug leis na huili anmanna glana ⁊ inglana (9) amail ro forchongair Día dó.

61. (10) O ra comlanaiged tra secht laithi na sechtmaini, ra iltóndaid ⁊ ra imdaig uisci na dilenn for talmain (11) ⁊ ra brisit uili thopur na haibeisi mori—

ra brucht ⁊ ro ʂceustar an talam súas ina huili thoipri diamra díchelta ra badar and.

Ra foslaigid dono cámfithisi ‡ ⁊ seinistir ‖ nimi anúas (12) ⁊ ra ʂilʂedar andsin cetha trena troim-¹fleachaid for talmain fri ré ²cetracha laa ⁊ cethracha aidchi :

---

59. ¹ *the* a *sbs.*   ² *sprs.* c H
61. ¹ *The first* a *yc* H   ² *thus written in full, not* -chat

Chapter VII.

59. (1) And God said unto Noe : Go into the ark, and all thy people with thee, for thou art the only righteous man that I have found in this generation. (2) Thou shalt take with thee into the ark sets of seven of all the clean animals, male and female. Thou shalt take with thee sets of two of the unclean animals, male and female. (3) Thou shalt take with thee more-over sets of seven of the clean birds of heaven, male and female. Thou shalt take with thee sets of two of the unclean fowls, male and female. (4) I shall bring, said God unto Noe, the end upon the seventh day from today, a strong showering deluge upon the earth, for the space of forty days and forty nights. And I shall extinguish and remove from the face of the earth every substance which I have made. · (5) So Noe did all that God commanded him.

60. (6) Now six hundred years were complete for Noe when the Flood came over the earth, (7) and Noe, with his sons and with their wives along with him, went into the ark upon the waters of the Flood, (8) and he took with him all the animals clean and unclean (9) as God commanded him.

61. (10) Now when the seven days of the week were completed, the waters of the Flood swelled mightily and increased upon the earth, (11) and every spring of the great deep burst open—

the earth opened up and vomited altogether the hidden secret springs that were in it.

Moreover the sluices [and windows] of heaven were opened from above, (12) and then strong heavy-wetting showers poured upon the earth for a space of forty days and forty nights :

(a) First written *glaiab inmi* and then corrected.

⁊ caoga ar cet laa imorro ra bai can tragadh.   I seachtmad
³loo deg an mís tanusti ‡ .i. an mís Mai ‖, ra thinscain an
dili fertain: isin ló sin ‡ .i. hi sechtmad decc in mis
tanaisi ‖, luid Náe a muintir ochtair isa n-airc.

(13) In airtical dono ‡ .i. a tosach ‖ an lái in ra
thinoilit na huili anmanda tria chetugad ⁊ cumachta
Dé dochum na hairci dia hinotacht, ‡ is andsin sanradh
do linadh ‖ ra lainecradh in airc druim-lethan domain.

Bá gnim saethair suad-lama, o chlarud chaem-cumachta.

62. (15) Iar ndul trá do Náe ina aircc cona muintir
ochtair, ⁊ iar ¹tinol na n-uili ²anmidi ⁊ na n-uili anmand
n-ilarda n-examla inti (16) cos na huilib neichib
taiscithib ra athin Dia do Náe, ra íad Día dia n-echtair
an airc (17) ⁊ doradad for talmain fri re cethrachat laa
⁊ cethrachat aidchi.   Ocus ra imdaigid na huisci ⁊ ro
thogbadar na huisci súas an airdi o talmain in aircc
(18) úas tondaib na dilenn.

Ocus ra bai an aircc ar snam a hinad a n-inad.

63. (19) Ra forbair ⁊ ra imtaid an t-uisci for
talmain (20) co ruacht coic cubaid deg úas cach sleib
is airdiu ra bai ¹fó n-uili nim.   (21) Ocus tucad dilcend
⁊ comarba [*lege* commarbad] coitcend for na huilib
dainib (22) ⁊ for na huili a raibi spirad bethad for
talmain—

ar a n-íumus ⁊ ar a n-anumuloid do Dia.

(23) Ba marthanach imorro Náe a aenur, ⁊ cach áen
ra bai amaille ris isin aircc; (24) ⁊ ra bai an diuli for
dreich an talmain ri ré ²caoga ar cet laa,

can esbaid can digbáil forri.

---

³*first written* loog; *the* de *y sprs.* c H
   62. ¹*Doubtful mark here ins.* c H   ²anmidi ⁊ *y sprs.* c H

and it was an hundred and fifty days without drying up. On the seventeenth day of the second month [the month of May] the Flood began to pour : on that day [i.e. on the seventeenth of the second month,] Noe, his company of eight persons, went into the ark.

(13) In the article, [that is, in the beginning] of the da, in which all the animals assembled, by the command and power of God, to the ark to enter it, [it is then exactly that it was filled] the broad-keeled deep ark was fully ordered.

It was the product of the labour of skilled craftsmen, with boarding of beauty and strength.

62. (15) Now after Noe went into his ark, with his company of eight persons, and when all the creatures and all the manifold various beasts were assembled within it, (16) with all the things in store, which God had commanded Noe, God shut the ark from the outside, (17) and there was a downpour upon the earth for a space of forty days and forty nights. And the waters increased, and the waters bore the ark aloft from off the earth (18) upon the waves of the Flood.

And the ark was swimming from place to place.

63. (19) The water increased and augmented upon the earth (20) till it reached fifteen cubits above every highest hill that was under the whole heaven. (21) And destruction and a general common death was brought upon all men, (22) and upon all that had a spirit of life upon the earth,

for their haughtiness and lack of humility toward God.

(23) But Noe alone endured, and all that were with him in the ark; (24) and the Flood was over the face of the earth for a space of an hundred and fifty days,

without diminution or decreasing.

---

63. [1] fo yc **H**   [2] *written* .l.a.

59. (1) Dixitque *Deus* ad ¹*Noe* : Ingredere, tu et omnis domus tua, arcam; te enim uidi iustum [coram me] in generatione hoc. (2) Ex omnibus animantibus mundis tolles septena septena, masculum et feminam. De animantibus uero non mundis, duo duo, masculum et feminam. (3) [Sed et] de uolatilibus caeli <mundis, tolles> septena septena, masculum et feminam. <De uolucribus non mundis tolles duo duo, masculum et feminam>, ³[ut saluetur semen super faciem uniuersae terrae]. (4) Adhuc enim ego pluam super terram quadraginta diebus et quadraginta noctibus, et delebo omnem substantiam quam feci de superficie terrae. (5) Fecit ergo Noe omnia quae mandauerat ei *Deus*.

60. (6) Eratque ¹<Noe> sescentorum annorum quando ²diluuii aquae inundauerunt super terram, (7) et ingressus est Noe et filii eius ³*et uxores eorum* cum eo in arcam ⁴propter aquas diluuii. (8) De animantibus quoque mundis et immundis . . . . . (9) sicut praeceperat Deus ⁵*eo·*

61. (10) Cumque transissent septem dies aquae diluuii inundauerunt super terram (11) ¹· . . . <et> rupti sunt omnes fortes abyssi magnae et ²cataractae caeli apertae sunt (12) et facta est pluuia super terram quadraginta diebus et quadraginta noctibus. (13) In articulo diei illius ingressus ³ . . . .

62. (15, 16) *These verses paraphrased only* . . . . sicut praeceperat ei Deus, [et] inclusit ¹*arcam Deus* deforis. (17) Factumque est diluuium quadraginta diebus ²<et quadraginta noctibus> super terram. Et multiplicatae sunt aquae, et eleuauerunt arcam in sublimine a terrae. (18) . . . . super aquas <diluuii>.

63. (19) Et aquae praeualuerunt nimis super terram . . . . (20) quindecim cubitis altior fuit aqua super montes ¹*sub uniuerso caelo.* (21) ²· . . . uniuersi homines (22) et cuncta in quibus spiraculum uitae est in terra mortua sunt. (23) . . . . remansit autem solus Noe et qui cum eo erant in arca. (24) Obtinueruntque aquae terras centum quinquaginta diebus.

Notes on the Biblical Text, Chapter VII.

¶ 59. ¹*ad eum* (in some MSS. *ad illum*) Vulg. : but πρὸς Νῶε in LXX. There is no authority in any of the Versions or

MSS. for the emphasis laid upon Noah being the *one* just man of his generation.   ²The distinction between unclean and clean birds is lost not only from Vulg., but even from the current text of Heb.   It is, however, preserved in LXX, which is clearly the authority here followed by Tr.: καὶ ἀπὸ τῶν πετεινῶν τοῦ οὐρανοῦ τῶν καθαρῶν ἑπτὰ ἑπτὰ, ἄρσεν καὶ θῆλυ; καὶ ἀπὸ [πάντων] τῶν πετεινῶν τῶν μὴ καθαρῶν δύο δύο, ἄρσεν καὶ θῆλυ.   The word πάντων, not rendered by Tr., is absent from some important MSS.   ³The equivalent of these words were dropped out from "∫H and were reinstated in the margin, most likely by the copyist himself on discovering his mistake.   They have crept back into the text in the wrong place (gloss after vi. 19).

¶ 60. ¹Nῶε in LXX, not in Vulg.   ²*An dile* is closer to ὁ καταλυκσμός (LXX) than to *diluuii aquae* (Vulg.): contrast *aquas diluuii* in the following verse (in LXX, τὸ ὕδωρ τοῦ κατακλυσμοῦ), duly rendered *uisci na dilenn* by Tr.   ³The abbreviation of the verbal exuberance of the original text is probably due to weary scribes; compare the abbreviation of the repeated catalogue of the animals in v. 8.   ⁴*Propter aquas = for uisci:* has Tr. misread *super* for *propter*?   ⁵*Noe,* Vulg.

¶ 61. ¹A passage omitted here, presumably because it merely repeats what has gone before.   ²*Cataractae* (LXX καταράκται) which may here be translated "sluices," represents the Heb. *'ĕrubōth*, literally "windows" (so in English Auth. and Revised versions).   A glossator seems to have discovered this meaning from some source of information, and to have interlined .i. *seinistir*.   When this ᵹ became *g*, the .i. as usual slipped into ꞇ.   ³From this point to the beginning of ¶ 62 the passage has been written in an abridged or paraphrased form, and deserts the Latin original.

¶ 62. ¹Τὴν κιβωτόν in LXX: but *arcam* not in any Vulg. MS.   ²Not in ST, but found in numerous Vulg. MSS., and also in LXX.

¶ 63. ¹*Sub uniuerso caelo* is out of place; it belongs to the clause at the end of v. 19, which is here omitted.   Two clauses have here been abbreviated and combined into one.   ²Here, and also in v. 23, a long catalogue of the creatures which perished is again omitted.

CHAPTER VIII.

64. (1) Ra ¹chuimnig imorro Dia ‡ ⁊ ra airchis ‖ ani Naei ⁊ na n-uili anmandaib ⁊ na n-uili úmenti ra badar amailli fri Nae ina airc. Ocus dorad Dia gáeth ‡ do ṡugad na n-uisci ‖ ⁊ ²ro digbaid na huisci. (2) Ocus ra hiadaid topur na haibéisi ⁊ camfithisi nime, ⁊ ra thairmiṡcid na fleochadha do nim.   (3) Ocus ra thathcursedar na huisci don talmain is na hinadaib as a tancadar, ⁊ ra digbaid na huisce a cind caoga ar cet laithi.   (4) Seacht laithi sechtmogad ⁊ secht mís don aircc o thuind do thuind, corgab airisim a sleib Armeinia.   (5) Ra ṡergaid na huisci cosin deccmad mís. Isin cet ló don deccmad mís adces mullaidi na sliab.

65. (6) I cind cethracha laa iarsin ra ¹ḟoslaic Náe seinistir na haircce ⁊ rusléig an fiach amach, (7) ⁊ ní thanig doridisi.   (8) ‡ An sechtmad lá iar sin ‖ do leig-sin an colam amach—

⁊ ra dún an airc andiaid an choluim ar omun na ngaeth—

(9) Ocus tanic an colum ²ar culu, air ni ḟuair baili a tairisfed—

⁊ do thairind ar an airc, o nach ḟuair ḟoslaicthi hi, ⁊ gabais glés dá gulbuin forsan clár—

⁊ do sin Náe a laim amach ar cend an choluim ⁊ tuc leis asdeach hé isa n-airc.   (10) Ra léig dono dorigisi a cind secht laa amach an colum, (11) ⁊ tanig a ḟescur ‡ an lai cetna ‖ ⁊ gesca olacraind cona duillennaib úraidi ina belaib.

Ocus do béndach Náe eisim de sin ⁊ ra mallach an fiach,

Chapter VIII.

64. (1) But God was mindful of [and had compassion upon] the said Noe, and all the animals and all the cattle that were with Noe in his ark.   And God sent a wind [to suck up the water], and the water decreased.   (2) And the well-spring of the deep and the sluices of Heaven were closed, and the showers from Heaven were withheld.   (3) And the waters were restored to the earth into the places whence they had come, and the waters decreased at the end of an hundred and fifty days.   (4) Seventy and seven days and seven months was the ark from wave to wave, till it took rest in a mountain of Armenia.   (5) The waters were drying up till the tenth month.   Upon the first day of the tenth month the tops of the mountains appeared.

65. (6) At the end of forty days thereafter Noe opened the window of the ark and let out the raven (7) and it came not again.   (8) [On the seventh day thereafter] he let out the dove—

and closed the ark after the dove, for fear of the winds—

(9) And the dove came back, for it found no place where it should stand,

and descended upon the ark, as it found it not opened, and made a working with its beak upon the board—

and Noe stretched his hand forth for the dove and brought it with him into the ark.   (10) Then he let the dove out again at the end of the seven days, (11) and it came in the evening [of the same day] with a twig of an olive-tree having its fresh leaves in its beak.

And Noe blessed it, and cursed the raven; and for that,

---

65. [1] s *y sprs. c* H   [2] r *y sprs. c* H

⁊ tuc ³Dia de sin a dath-sain forsan ⁻fiach ⁊ taitnem an
⁴fiaich fair-sim ar anumlacht in ⁵fiaich.

Ra thuig Náe cor digbaid na huisci.   (12) Ocus aráidh
ra ernaid secht laa aili an tan ra leig ⁶amach an colum
an tres feacht, ⁊ ni thanig dorigisi,

uair ni rangadar a les.

66. (13) An cet la don cet bliadain ‡ iar ¹ndilind ‖
ar sugad na n-uisci, do ²scail Náe dorus na hairci, ⁊
do dech sé an doman ana thimchell.   (14) Isin sechtmad
laa fichit don cet mí tanig Dia do labairt fris, (15) ⁊
is ed ra raid Dia co Náé : (16) Eirig asa n-airc, ar Se,
⁊ do šeidid ⁊ do ³mic ⁊ seitchi do mac, (17) ⁊ beir lat na
huili ⁴anmanna filed isa n-airc ⁊ incheimnig for
talmain.   Forbrid ⁊ ⁵dobarnimdaighther for talmain.
(18) Dachuaid diu Nae asa n-airc—

hi sechtmad fichit ‡ ésca Mai imorro | an mís tanaisi :

.i. an mís Mai atharrach isin cet bliadain.

Sé cet bliadan do 'bo šlan do Náe an tan sin.   Sé bliadna
caoga ⁊ se cet ⁊ mili bliadan o cruthugad Adaim co sin, *ut
dixit,*

Cēt aimser in bethad bind . . .

Dachuaid imorro seidig Náe, ⁊ dochuadar a mic ⁊
⁶dochuadar seitchi a mac (19) ⁊ na huili ainimidi
rabadar isa n-airc eisti.

Isin sechtmad fichit an mís cetna atharraig tanic eisti,
an ⁷Aine imorro a laithi sechtmaine.   Conad se deg ⁊

---

³ Dia *y sprs. c* H   ⁴ f *y sprs. c* H   ⁵ *second* i *y sbs. c* H
                     ⁶ amach *y sbs. c* H

God gave the colour of the former to the raven, and the sheen of the raven to the other, for the insubordination of the raven.

Noe understood that the waters were decreased. (12) Howbeit, he waited other seven days and then let out the dove for the third time, and it came not again—

for there was no need.

66. (13) On the first day of the first year [after the Flood], upon the sucking-up of the waters, Noe loosened the door of the ark and looked on the earth round about him. (14) On the twenty-seventh day of the first month God came to speak with him, (15) and thus God spake unto Noe : (16) Rise from out the ark, said He, thou and thy wife and thy sons and the wives of thy sons, (17) and take with thee all the beasts that are in the ark, and step forth upon the earth. Increase and be ye multiplied upon the earth. (18) So Noe went out of the ark,

in the twenty-seventh day [of the moon of May] of the second month :

that is, the secondary month of May in the first year.

Six hundred years were complete for Noe at that time. One thousand six hundred fifty and six years from the creation of Adam till then, *ut dixit,*

Poem no. VII.

—and further the wife of Noe went, and his sons and the wives of his sons (19) and all the beasts that were in the ark went out of it.

On the twenty-seventh day of the same secondary month, he came out of it : as regards the day of the week, on

---

66. [1] d *y sprs. c* H   [2] l *yc* H   [3] i *y sbs. c* H   [4] *written* aña
[5] *written* do bar nim daighther   [6] the u *sprs. s* H   [7] *written* Aen mi H

bliadain deiside ra bai Náe isa n-airce.   An sechtmad deg
don mis cetna, ‡ .i. in mís Mai ||, ra thinscain an dili
fertain : an dechmad uathad ésca ‡ in mís tanaisi ǁ an mí
doluid Náe isa n-airc, ⁊ a muintir ochtair, cos na huilib
anmandaib ⁊ anmigib rug leis inti : .i. cupla do cach
ꝼiadach neoch do beth re sílad .i. ceitri lanumna do dainib,
⁊ ceitri lanumna deg do énaib, ⁊ secht lánumnu do chinelaib
eisc, ⁊ lanomain do cach cinel egsamail o sin amach bai isa
n-airc.   Dia Haini didine arai laithi sechtmaini dochuaid
Náe isa n-airc, ⁊ Dia Mairt dolodar aisti iartain, *ut dicitur,*

Dia Haine docúas inti . . ..

·67· O thucad dana an dili tar an doman, ra baided na
huili dainé (*sic*) acht Náe cona tri macaib ⁊ cona ceitri
mnáib, amail ra raidsimar romaind.   Ar is é Náe an tAdam
tanaisti, cosa mberar fir domain; ⁊ Énócc an tAdam saér
(*sic*) : Crist imorro an tAdam deidenach, trés ar sáerad sil
an trir remraite do raidsimar romaind, an a tuc hé féin a
croich césta tar cend an trir sin dá n-eissi, ⁊ dorad an
mbroid a Hiffern dar saerad lucht na coic n-aimsir ar aen
sligi.

68. Sé cet bliadan do ba ṡlán do Náe an tan tanig an dili
tar an doman : caoga ⁊ tri cet bliadan ra bai Nae a mbethaid
iar ndilinn : conad caoga ⁊ noi cet bliadan sin uili.   Uair is
e Náe an ceatramad duine do sil [1]Adaim as[s]ia saegal
indisis cánoin, .i. Adam ⁊ Iareth ⁊ Mathasáilem ⁊ Náe.
Tricha ⁊ noi cet bliadan saegal Adaim.   Dá bliadain sescat
⁊ noi cet saegal Iareth.   Noi mbliadna sescat ⁊ noi cet
saegal Mathasailem.   Caoga ⁊ noi cet bliadan saegal Náe :
amail adbearar andso—

Ceatra as [s]ia saegal slán . . . .

---

68. [1] y *sprs.* s H

Friday.   So that thence Noe was a year and sixteen
<days> in the ark. On the seventeenth day of the same
month, [that is, the month of May], the Flood began to
shower : on the tenth of the moon [of the second month]
of the month, Noe went into the ark with his company of
eight persons, and with all the animals and beasts that he
took with him into it. These were, a couple of every wild
creature, whatsoever should be for seeding; to wit four
human pairs, fourteen pairs of birds, seven pairs of species
of fish and a pair of every different kind from that
onwards, that were in the ark. As regards the day of the
week, it was a Friday that Noe went into the ark, and
Tuesday they came out of it afterwards, *ut dicitur,*

Poem no. VIII.

67. Now when the Flood was brought over the world, all
men were drowned save Noe and his three sons and their
four wives, as we have said above. For Noe is the second
Adam, to whom the men of the world are traced : and
Enoch is the innocent (?) Adam : but Christ is the last
Adam, by whom the seed of the aforesaid three, already
mentioned, were saved, when He gave Himself on the cross
of suffering instead of those three, after their time, and
brought the harrowing over Hell by which the people of
the five Ages all at once were saved.

68. Six hundred years were complete for Noe when the
Flood came over the world : three hundred and fifty years
was Noe in life after the Flood : so all that makes nine
hundred and fifty years. For Noe is one of the four men
of the seed of Adam, of whom the Canon telleth that had
longest life—namely Adam, Iared, Mathusalam, and Noe.
Nine hundred and thirty years was the life of Adam.
Nine hundred sixty and two years the life of Iared. Nine
hundred sixty and nine years the life of Mathusalam. Nine
hundred and fifty years the life of Noe : as is said here—

Poem no. IX.

64. (1) Recordatus est autem Deus Noe, cunctorumque animantium et omnium iumentorum quae erant cum eo in arca.   ¹<Et> adduxit ²<Deus> spiritum super terram, et inminutae sunt aquae.   (2) Et clausi sunt ³fontes abyssi et cataractae caeli, et prohibitae sunt pluuiae de caeli. (3) ⁴Reuersaeque aquae de terra euntes et redeuntes, et ceperunt minui post centum quinquaginta dies, (4) Requie- uitque arca mense ⁵septime uicesima septima die mensis super ⁶montem Armeniae.   (5) At uero aquae ibant et decrescebant usque ad decimum mensem.   Decimo enim mense prima die mensis apparuerunt cacumina montium.

65. (6) Cumque transissent quadraginta dies, aperiens Noe fenestram arcae [quam fecerat] dimisit coruum, (7) qui . . . ¹<non> reuertebatur . . .   (8) Emisit quoque columbam . . . (9) quae cum non inuenisset ubi requiesceret [pes eius], reuersa est . . . extenditque manum et adpraehensam intulit in arcam.   (10) Expectatis autem ultra septem diebus [aliis] rursum dimisit columbam [ex arca] (11) at illa uenit [ad eum] ad uesperam, portans ramum oliuae uirentibus foliis in ore suo.   Intellexit ergo Noe quod cessassent aquae [super terram].   (12) Expectauitque nihilominus septem alios dies, et emisit columbam, quae non est reversa ultra ²[ad eum].

66. (13) ¹[Igitur sescentesimo] primo anno, [primo mense], primo die [mensis] <post> inminutae sunt aquae [super terram], et aperiens Noe tectum arcae aspexit ²· . . . (14) Mense ³primo septima et uicesima die mensis ⁴· . . . (15) locutus est autem Deus ad Noe, dicens: (16) Egredere de arca, tu et uxor tua, filii tui et uxores filiorum tuorum [tecum] : (17) cuncta ⁵<que> animantia quae sunt apud te . . . educ tecum, et ingredimini super terram.   Crescite et multiplicamini super terram.   (18) ⁶Egressus est ergo Noe et filii eius, uxor illius et uxores filiorum eius cum eo, (19) sed et omnia animantia . . . .

NOTES ON THE BIBLICAL TEXT, CHAPTER VIII.

¶ 64. ¹*Et* in only two Vulg. MSS., but καί in LXX.   ²*Deus* not in any Vulg. MS., but ὁ θεός in LXX.   ³Plural in Vulg.

and LXX, but singular in Tr. [4]The rendering of this verse seems a little closer to LXX : καὶ ενεδίδου τὸ ὕδωρ πορευόμενον ἀπὸ τῆς γῆς· ἐνεδίδου τὸ ὕδωρ καὶ ἠλαττονοῦτο κ.τ.λ. [5]These numbers have become corrupted : evidently .uii lá .xx. has degenerated into .uii. lxx. [6]Plural in Vulg. and LXX, but sing. in Tr.

¶ 65. [1]*Non* not in ST, but in numerous MSS. (in nearly half, however ins. *sec. man.*). Also in LXX. [2]The biblical text has suffered severely by glossarial encroachment and substitution in this paragraph.

¶ 66. [1]Tr. in its present form corrupt and imperfect. *Iar ndilind* must be removed as glossarial : perhaps *ar sugad* has somehow developed out of *ar sē cētaib.* Confusion of a scribe's eye has caused the loss of *primo mense.* [2]The words filling this gap have no biblical warrant : they are a gloss, which has ousted the original text. [3]*Don cēt mī* is a mistake : all Versions agree on "the *second* month." [4]Here again a gloss has expelled the original sentence. [5]-*que* not in ST, but in several MSS. : also καί in LXX. [6]This verse is interrupted by a chronological interpolation in the middle of a sentence. The mention of Noah's wife before his sons is in accordance with LXX : but it may be a mere translator's inadvertence.

¶ 67, 68. These paragraphs are interpolations, and are no part of the Biblical Text.

Chapter XI.

69. (10) Ced bliadan ba slan do Ṡem an tan ra thuisim Arifaxad, a cind dá bliadain iar ndilinn. (11) Cuig cet bliadan imorro bai iar tuismedh Arafaxad, ꝛ ra thuisim macu ꝛ ingena.

70. (12) Cúig bliadna trichat ba slán do Airifaxad an tan ra thuisim Saile.   (13) Tri bliadna ar tri cetaib bá beó Arafaxad iar tuismedh Ṡaili dó, ꝛ ra thuisim macu ꝛ ingena.

71. (14) Tricha bliadan do bo ṡlan do Ṡaili an tan ra thuisim Éber.   (15) Tri bliadna ar ceithri cetaib imorro bá beo hé iar tusmedh Eber dó, ꝛ ra thuisimh macu ꝛ ingena.

72. (16) Ceitri bliadna trichad imorro bá slan do Eber an tan ra thusim Faillech.   (17) Ocus tricha ar cet bliadan bá beo he iar tusmedh Ḟaillech do, ꝛ da thusim macu ꝛ ingena.

73. (18) Tricha bliadna ba slan do Ḟaillech an tan thusim Réú.   (19) Noi mbliadna ar dib cetaib imorro ba beo he iar thusmedh Réu dó, ꝛ ro tuisim macu ꝛ ingena.

74. (20) Cuig bliadna trichat ba slan do Réú an tan ra thuisim Sarúch dó.   (21) Cetheora bliadna ar dib cetaib imorro bá beó hé an tan ‡(a) no iar ‖ ra tusmedh Sarúch do, ꝛ ra tuisim macu ꝛ ingena.

75. (22) Tricha bliadna imorro ba slan do Ṡaruch an tan ra thusim Náchor.   (23) Da cet bliadan imorro bá beó hé an tan ra tusmedh Nachór dó, ꝛ ra tuisim macu ꝛ ingena.

(a) This gloss interlined above.

Chapter XI.

69. (10) Sem had an hundred years complete when he begat Arfaxad, at the end of two years after the Flood. (11) Five hundred years was he, further, after the birth of Arfaxad, and he begat sons and daughters.

70. (12) Thirty-five years were complete for Arfaxad when he begat Sale. (13) Three hundred and three years was Arfaxad alive after the birth of Sale to him, and he begat sons and daughters.

71. (14) Thirty years were complete for Sale when he begat Eber. (15) Four hundred and three years was he alive further, after the birth of Eber to him, and he begat sons and daughters.

72. (16) Thirty-four years moreover were complete for Eber when he begat Faleg. (17) An hundred and thirty years was he alive after the birth of Faleg to him, and he begat sons and daughters.

73. (18) Thirty years were complete for Faleg when he begat Reu. (19) Two hundred and nine years moreover was he alive after the birth of Reu to him, and he begat sons and daughters.

74. (20) Thirty-five years were complete for Reu when he begat Saruch. (21) Two hundred and four years moreover was he alive when [or, after] Saruch was born to him, and he begat sons and daughters.

75. (22) Thirty years moreover were complete for Saruch when he begat Nachor. (23) Two hundred years moreover was he alive when Nachor was born to him, and he begat sons and daughters.

76. (24) Noi mbliadna fichit dono ba slan do Nachór an tan ra thuisim Taré.   (25) Noi bliadna deg imorro ar cét ba beo hé iar tusmedh Tharé dó, ⁊ ra tuisim macu ⁊ ingena iartain.

77. (26) Sechtmoga bliadan ba slan do Tharre an tan ra thusim Abram ⁊ Nachór ⁊ Aram.   (32) Acus ba hé uili saegail Tharre coic bliadna ar dib cetaib, ⁊ adbath a Carrán a tir Chandán iartain.

Ocus is é an tAbram sin cendadart an tres aimser an domain : da bliadain ar nochat ar noi cetaib ó dilinn co gein Abraim a tír Chailldiorum.

NOTES ON THE BIBLICAL TEXT, CHAPTER XI.

On the displacement of this passage see p. 11 *ff·* It is not necessary to print the Latin original here : Tr. adheres to Vulg., and ignores LXX, which inserts an additional generation (Καινάν. between Arfaxad and Sale), and has several differences in the numerical statements of the ages. The only deviations in Tr. from ST are the age of Eber (130 instead of 430) and of Reu (35 before son's birth, 204 after as against Vulg. 32–207).   There is some very slight

---

CHAPTER VIII (resumed).

78. (20) Ra chumdaig Náe altoir don Choimdid ‡ iar ndilinn ‖ ⁊ doroini idbarta toltanacha forthi do Dia ona huilib cethraib ‡ ⁊ óna huilib énaib ‖ ⁊ eathaidib glanaib—

⁊ is i sin cet ¹altoir ra cumdaiged ²sa domain.

---

78. ¹ *y sprs. s* H   ² *scribe wrote* ⁊ *and then wrote* s *with a sbs. over it*

76. (24) Twenty nine years were complete for Nachor when he begat Thare. (25) An hundred and nineteen years moreover was he alive after the birth of Thare to him, and he begat sons and daughters thereafter.

77. (26) Seventy years were complete for Thare when he begat Abram and Nachor and Aram. (32) And all the life of Thare was two hundred and five years, and he died in Haran in the land of Canaan thereafter.

And that Abram is the head-rest of the Third Age of the world : nine hundred ninety and two years from the Flood to the birth of Abram in the land of the Chaldeans.

---

support for the Irish figures, but most likely they originated in copyists' errors : it is easy to confuse xxxii with xxxu and ccciiii with ccuii. In H, our only MS. for this portion, the word *cuig* in the Reu passage is written in full, so that the error, if it be an error, goes back to "/**H**. The spellings Saruch (ver. 20) Nachor (vers. 22, 26) Aram (v. 26) as against the ST Sarug, Nahor, Aran, are to be noted.

---

78. (20) Noe built an altar unto the Lord [after the Flood] and made acceptable offerings upon it unto God, of all the clean four-footed beasts [and of all birds] and clean fowls.

That was the first altar that was built in the world.

(21) Ocus bá so-airigthi ailgen lá Dia an edbairt sin;
ocus adbert Dia fri Náe, Nocha mallachab ‡ .i. nocha
tibar dilind || don doman doridisi ardaig na ndaine,
ar is aibrisc a n-aicned ⁊ is tairberta trascartha
airiugad ⁊ imragad in cridi dáennae dochum uilc do
dénum.   Nocha muirbeb dono o so ³amach in n-uili
n-anmain mbi amail doronus.   (22) Acht beidit ó na
huilib láthib don talmuin .i. earrach ⁊ samrad ⁊ fodmar
⁴[⁊ gemred cen cumsanad].

---

78. (20) Aedificauit autem Noe altare Domino, et tollens
de cunctis pecoribus et uolucribus mundis obtulit holocausta
super altare.   (21) Odoratusque est *Deus* odorem suauitatis
et ait ad eum: Nequaquam ultra maledicam terrae propter
homines, sensus enim et cogitatio humani cordis in malum
prona sunt [ab adulescentia sua].   Non igitur ultra percutiam
omnem animantem sicut feci.   (22) Cunctis diebus terrae,

Chapter IX.

79. (1) Ra bendach Dia Nae cona macaib, ⁊ adbert
friu: Foirbr[id ⁊ dobar]nimdaigther ⁊ linaid an
talmain, (2) ⁊ bid ſar smacht ⁊ far [n-uamain for
uil]ib anmundaib an talman, ⁊ for uilib énaib an aeoir
[archena—

⁊ ro] thidnaicc doib uili domain,

iascc an mara (3) ⁊ cach an[mide der]scaigther ⁊ a
ſuil betha : ⁊ caithfigthisi na huili sin amail uile úraidi,

---

³ am *sprs. c* H   ⁴ *these words torn away*

(21) And God considered that offering to be worthy
of acceptation and pleasant. And God said unto Noe :
I shall not curse [i.e. I shall not bring a Flood upon]
the world again by reason of men, for fragile is their
nature, and the perception and imagination of the
human heart are given over and subdued to work
wickedness. I shall not slay, moreover, from hence-
forth every living soul as I have done. (22) But all
the days of the earth there shall be spring and summer
and autumn and winter without cessation.

[sementis et messis], frigus et aestus, aestas et hiemps, [nox
et dies], non requiescent.

NOTE ON THE BIBLICAL TEXT, CHAPTER VIII.

¶ 78. This paragraph represents the text of ST with
tolerable literalness : but whether with intention or not, the
strong anthropomorphism of verse 21 is softened.

CHAPTER IX.

79. (1) God blessed Noe and his sons, and said unto
them : Increase and be ye multiplied and fill the earth
(2) and your authority and terror shall be over all
the beasts of the earth and all the birds of the air
together—

and He gave the whole world to them,

fish of the sea (3) and every beast that moveth and
that hath life in itself : and ye shall eat of those all,

(4) cénmótha aen ni namá, .i. can feoil cona fuil do chaithem.   (5) Ár sirfeadsa ⁊ toibeochad bar ſuili-si cna huilib phiastaib ⁊ ona huilib dainib, ⁊ sirfead anmain cach duine o cach áen muirfes hé.   (6) Ar cach áen doirtfes in ſuil ndaena, doirtfigter a ſuil aris : fó imaigin ⁊ cosmailus De dorigned an duine. (7) Sibsi imorro, ar Dia fri Náe cona macaib, forbrig ⁓ dobarnimdaigter ⁊ linaid an talmain.

80. (8) Asbert dono Dia fri Nae cona macaib, (9) Ordaigfedsa ⁊ biaid mo charadradh imailli frib ⁊ for bar claind do bar n-eissi (10) ⁊ fris na huilib tangadar asin airc.   (11) ⁊ ni thibar dilinn tar an Domun doridisi,

cénmothá an tan dofas crich coitchend chaich i l-loo bratha.

(13) Dabér imorro comartha mo charadraig daib isin <n>em, ⁊ cein adcifigter an comartha sin o nim (15) ni bia crich na comarba coitcend for na dainib.   Is e so in comartha, .i. mo boga ina sduaig isin nim.

Conad do sin ata an sduag nime .i. a tabairt do chomartha caradraig do chlannaïb Nae iar ndilinn, .i. co mbia Dia an áentaid friu, aireid ¹adcistear an sduag nime.   Is follus imorro asso cona roibhibh an sduag nime ria ndilind,

⁊ nocha bia coic bliadna dég ria mbrath.

(19) O na tri macaib-si tra Náe, .i. Sém, ⁊ Cám ⁊ Iaféth, ra ſilsad ⁊ ro thuismit an t-uili chinead dáena iar ndilinn.

80. ¹ second a sbs.

as of every green thing, (4) except only one thing : ye shall not eat of flesh with the blood thereof.   (5) For I shall demand and require your blood of all beasts and of all men, and I shall demand the life of every man from every one who shall slay him.   (6) For everyone that shall shed man's blood, his blood shall be shed in turn : under the image and likeness of God was man made.   (7) But ye, said God to Noe and his sons, increase and be ye multiplied and fill the earth.

80. (8) Moreover God said unto Noe and his sons, (9) I shall ordain, and there shall be, My friendship with you and upon your progeny after you (10) and with all that came out of the Ark.   (11) And I shall not bring a Flood over the world again,

> except when the common end of every man shall come about in the Day of Judgement.

(13) Moreover, I shall put a sign of My friendship to you in the Heaven, and so long as that sign shall be seen from Heaven (15) there shall be no end nor common death upon men.   This is the sign, My bow arching in the Heaven.

> Therefore for that purpose is the rainbow, given for a sign of friendship to the progeny of Noe after the Flood, that God shall be united with them so long as the rainbow is seen.   Howbeit it is clear from this that the rainbow did not exist before the Flood,
>
> > and that it shall not have being for fifteen years before the Judgement.

(19) From those three sons of Noe, Sem, Ham, and Iafeth, was the whole human race after the Flood begotten and born.

81. (20) Ra thindscain dono Náe tirfrecar do denum,
ɼ ra clannastar finemain.   (21) Ocus luid fechtus Náe
in a diaid sin i n-a theipernácuili do ól ɼina.   Rangab
¹meisci, ɼ do thuit a chodlad fair, ɼ do rochair a edach
de, co mbai nocht ina theiparnacal.   (22) Iar sin doluid
Cám .i. athair Chandain, anadóchum, ɼ adchondairc
bullu imnara a athar iar n-a nochtad, co ndernaid
gairi uime.   Luid amach iarsin ɼ adɼed dia braitrib, ‡
.i. do Iaféd ɼ do Sém ‖ amail ra bai a n-athair ɼ sé
nocht.   (23) Dalodur imorro Sém ɼ Iáfeth isin
tebernacuili, ɼ is amlaid imorro dochuadar ɼ a culu
rempu, árdáig co nach faichtis feli a n-athar : ɼ
doradsad a édach ²thairis ɼ ra ɼagsad ana codlad hé, ɼ
lodar uad iarsin.   (24) An tan imorro ra eirig Nae as
a chodlad, do faillsiged dó gnimartha na mac sin;
conad andsin ra mallach a athair Cám, ɼ is ed ra ráid :
(25) Is mallachda ɼ is coirpthi, ɼ biaid Cám coma mogh
moghad dá braithrib.   (26) Ocus isbert Nae : Ra
bendacha an Coimdi ani an Sém, ɼ bid Cam a ɼognam
dó; (27) Ocus ra lethnaidi Dia Iáfeth, ɼ aitrebad a
teibarnácuilib Sem, ɼ bid Cam ag fognam do Iafeth.

Conad hé Cam cet duine ra mallaigedh iar ndilinn,

conad iarsin ra 'geinidar lupracanaig ɼ fomoraig ɼ gaburchind
ɼ cach egasg do-delba archena fil for dainib—

Iarsin tucad gid dilgend ar Chandandaib, ɼ tucad a ferand
do macaib Israel a comartha na mallacht cedna sin.   Uair
ro bo do síl Chaim Candandai, ɼ is tresin mallachtain cedna
dilgend clann Dardain ɼ Ioiph, cor marb cach a cheli dib.

—conad hé sin bunad na torathar.

81. ¹c *sprs. s* **H**   ²is *sprs. s* **H**

81. (20) Now Noe began to work husbandry, and planted a vineyard. (21) And on a time, after those things, Noe went into his tent to drink wine. Drunkenness seized hold on him, and his sleep fell on him, and his raiment slipped down from him, so that he was naked in his tent. (22) Thereafter came Ham father of Canaan, in to him, and saw the shameful members of his father which had become uncovered, and he made a mock of him. Then he went out; and he tells his brethren [Iafeth and Sem] how that their father was naked. (23) So Sem and Iafeth came into the tent; and in this manner they went, with their backs forward, that they should not see the nakedness of their father: and they put his raiment over him and left him asleep, and came again away from him. (24) Now when Noe arose from his sleep, the doings of those sons were revealed to him; and then his father cursed Ham, and thus he spake: (25) Cursed and corrupt is Ham, and he shall be as it were a slave of slaves for his brethren. (26) And Noe said: Let the Lord bless the aforesaid Sem, and let Ham be in service to him; (27) and let God enlarge Iafeth, and let him dwell in the tents of Sem, and let Ham be in service to Iafeth.

So that this Ham is the first man who was cursed after the Flood:

and thereafter there were born dwarfs and giants and horse-heads and every unshapely form in general that there is among men—

Thereafter there was brought [as it were] [a] destruction upon the Canaanites, and their land was given to the sons of Israel, in token of those same curses. For the Canaanites were of the seed of Ham, and it is through that same curse that there was the destruction of the children of Dardan and Ioph, so that each of them slew his fellow.

—so that that was the origin of the monsters.

[a] See the note on this paragraph.

79. (1) Benedixitque Deus Noe et filiis eius, et dixit ad eos : Crescite et multiplicamini et implete terram (2) et terror uester ac tremor sit super cuncta animalia terrae et super omnes uolucres caeli [1]. . . . . (3) Et omne quod mouetur et uiuit erit uobis in cibum quasi holera uiuentia . . . . (4) excepto quod carnem cum sanguine non comedetis. (5) Sanguinem enim animarum uestrarum requiram de manu cunctarum bestiarum et de manu hominis, de manu uiri [et fratris eius] requiram animam hominis, (6) Quicumque effuderit humanum sanguinem, fundetur sanguis illius : ad imaginem quippe Dei factus est homo. (7) Vos autem crescite et multiplicamini et . . . . . implete terram.

80. (8) Haec quoque dixit Deus ad Noe et ad filios eius cum eo, (9) [Ecce] ego statuam pactum meum uobiscum et cum semine uestro post uos (10) et . . . cunctis quae egressa sunt de arca . . . . (11) . . . . nequaquam . . . . erit deinceps diluuium dissipans terram . . . . (12) . . . . hoc signum foederis . . . . (13) ponam in nubibus . . . . (19) [1]Tres . . . . filii Noe, ab his disseminatum est omne humanum genus . . . .

81. (20) Coepitque Noe uir agricola exercere terram et plantauit uineam. (21) [1]. . . . . . . inebriatus est, et nudatus est in tabernaculo suo. (22) Quod cum uidisset Ham pater Chanaan, uerenda scilicet patris sui esse nuda . . . . . . nuntiauit duobus fratribus suis foras. (23) At uero Sem et Iafeth . . . . incidentes retrorsum . . . patris sui uirilia non uiderant. (24) Evigilans autem Noe ex uino, cum didicisset quae fecera<n>t fili<i> su<i> . . . (25) ait : Maledictus [2]*Cham*, servus seruorum erit fratribus suis. (26) Dixitque <Noe> : Benedictus Dominus <Deus> Sem, sit *Cham* servus eius. (27) Dilatet Deus Iafeth, et habitet in tabernaculis Sem, sitque *Cham* seruus eius.

NOTES ON THE BIBLICAL TEXT, CHAPTER IX.

¶ 79. [1]This part of the verse has probably been lost owing to confusion caused by the repetition of the equivalents of *mouentur . . . mouetur*. A glossator, observing the omission of the reference to fishes, inserted it in *oratio obliqua*, which betrays the intrusion.

¶ 80. [1]As in previous passages, glossarial interpolations borrowed from *Sex Aetates Mundi* have here ousted the biblical lemmata; and though the framework of the Latin original is preserved, the words of the text cannot be completely recovered.

¶ 81. [1]The remarks on the preceding paragraph are applicable here, if anything, to yet greater extent. [2]There is slight support in the MSS. of both LXX and Vulg., for the substitution of *Cham* for Chanaan (or Chandan): but (a) such an obvious, if inaccurate, change could have been made at any stage independently, and (b) it must have been made in the H tradition subsequently to the incorporation of the interpolated passages.

The following notes, which should follow ¶ 85 (pp. 142–3), are printed here for typographical convenience :—

82. (32) Haec familiae Noe iuxta populos et nationes suas: ab his divisae sunt gentes in terra post diluuium.

83· (1) Erat autem terra labii unius et sermonum eorundem . . . . .

84. (2) . . . . . (3) Dixitque alter ad proximum suum: Venite faciamus lateres, et coquamus eos igni. Habuerantque lateres pro saxis et bitumen pro cemento. (4) Et dixerunt: Venite faciamus nobis ciuitatem et turrem cuius culmen pertingat ad caelum, et celebremus nomen nostrum, antequam diuidamur in universas terras.

85. (5) Descendit autem *Deus* ut uideret ciuitatem et turrem quam aedificabant filii Adam : (6) Et dixit Deus, Ecce, unus est populus et unum labium omnibus: coeperuntque hoc facere, nec desistent a cogitationibus suis donec eas opere compleant. (7) [Venite igitur] descendamus et confundamus ibi linguam eorum, ut non audiat unusquisque uocem proximi sui. (8) Atque ita diuisit eos Dominus ex illo loco in universas terras, et cessauerunt aedificare ciuitatem. (9) Ed idcirco uocatum est nomen eius Babel, quia ibi confusum est labium uniuersae terrae, et inde dispersit eos *Deus* super faciem cunctarum regionum.

¶ 82. This, the only surviving portion of the "Table of Nations," is very freely paraphrased in Tr.

The rendering of Chapter XI, 1–9, is useless for critical purposes: the story has been practically re-written; inflated (after the manner of the later romances) with cumbrous accumulations of adjectives; and rendered partly unintelligible, especially in verses 4 and 6, by intrusive glosses.

Chapter X.

(*Vers.* 1–31 *desunt.*)

82. (32) Ra silsad imorro clanna Nae, ⁊ ro imdaigsead for talmain amail adbert Dia friú : ⁊ ra roinnsed ⁊ ra fogailsead an talmain eturru iar ndilinn.

Chapter XI.

83. (1) Is amlaid imorro bai an talam an tan sin, ⁊ áen berla inand ag na huilib dainib ra batar fair,

⁊ Goirthigern a ainm, .i. an berla Ebraidhi,

no cor scailed na berlada ag an Tur.   Is amlaid so adcaemnacair sin dia ndernad gnim n-ingnad(*a*) n-indligteach isin domun an tan sin dorisi.

84. [¹⁷ . . . .] difuluing fir an domain an tan sin [¹⁵. . . . .] btha amor thoraid in talmain toir c[⁹. . . . . . .]htuig a rabadar.   (3) Ocus adbert cach dib ri araile [⁹. . . . . .] co tirmaigem an criaid ro-ruaid, ro-rigin [⁵. . . . . .]id, taidlig, tesaidi, curab caidigter cairrgi cruaide, [⁵. . . . . .] garba.   Dentar dono lind an bidamain blaith bith[⁴· . . .]in : ara n-ael n-alaind n-aendatha.   (4) Ocus dono ráidsed beos : [⁴. . . . . .] ⁊ dentar lind cathair chaem-¹cumdaigthi ⁊ dun daingen [bi]th-²foduigthe.   Dentar lind dono tor ro-mór, ro-remar, rigda, ro-ard, ro-fada, co ria ‡ co feici fir ‖ nime ‡ no uas aeor ard uasnadach ‖ cleithi cendmullaig an tuir sin.   Ocus dono mortar ⁊ medaigter ar n-ainm anós ar irdarcus, riasiu ronscailter ⁊ ronscapthar hi crichaib ciana comaigthi.   Ocus dorigned uili leosam an gnim sin.

---

84. ¹ cum *sprs. s* H   ² *the* MS. *reads* bith-foghlaidhi, *which cannot be right.*

(*a*) Not clearly written : ngnað apparently covering over something else (indecipherable) that had been written in error.

Chapter X.

82. (32) So the children of Noe increased and multiplied upon the earth as God said unto them : and they divided and parted the earth between them after the Flood.

Chapter XI.

83. (1) Now the earth was in this wise at that time, all men that were upon it having one and the same language,

and Gorthigern was its name, i.e. the Hebrew language,

until the languages were separated at the Tower, That came to pass in this manner, when a wonderful lawless deed was done in the world at that time once again.

84. [An] intolerable [famine ? ? seized the] men of the world at that time [and there could not be fo]und a trough (?) of the fruit of the [. . . . .] earth in the east where they were.   (3) And each said to the other [go to,] that we may dry the very red, very stiff . . . bright heated clay, that it may be as solid as hard . . . . rough rocks.   Let there also be made by us the smooth ever-[stiff?] pitch : for their beautiful lime of uniform colour.   (4) Moreover they said further : . . . . and let there be made by us a fair-erected castle, and a strong everlastingly founded fortress.   Let there be also made by us a very great, wide, royal, lofty, tall, tower, that the ridgepole of the summit of that tower may reach [that men may see] the heavens, [or above the high upper air].   And thus let our name be magnified and enlarged from on high in glory, before we be divided and scattered through lands distant and strange.   And this deed was wholly done by them.

85. (5) Ra thainustar imorro Dia do [fech]ad na catrach ⁊ an tuir ro cumdaigsed maic Adaim—

.i. maic an duini thruaid thalmaidi phecaid ⁊ oiltua sin isin [1]scribtuir diada .i. maic Adaim do rád dib.

(6) Ocus adbert Dia: Is follus ataid na huili dáini conad aen phopul iad, conad aen berla fuil acu: [2]‡ ⁊ nocha n-uil ‖ ⁊ nocha n-anfad ona [3]n-imraitib ra thinscansadar, nocha chomlánaiged iad [2]‡ o gnimaib ‖. (7) Comḟuiscem iarom ⁊ bruigem a mberla blaith, builid, binn, conna ra thuigi neach dib guth araili. (8) Ra mescaid dono, rá medraid, rá meraigid an lucht sin ré hilar na mberla [4]n-anaich<ne> n-examail : ⁊ is amlaid sin ra ansadar óna gnimuib ra thinscansadar dono do denum. (9) Ocus is airi sin ra gairmead ainm an inaid sin Babel, .i. cumasc : ar is and ra cumuscid uili berla an talman, .i. na da berla sechtmogat, o tri macaib Náe. Ra scáil Dia na cineada sin isin n-uili talmain.

Here the Extract from the Book of Genesis ends.

86. Ra raind Náe an doman a tri itir a macaib, .i. Sém an Aissia, Cam an Afraicc, Iafeth an Eóraip. Ocus adbath cach fer dib ana rand bodeisin: .i. marb tra Sém a mullaig Sleibi Radruip do thes ngreine, marb Iafeth a mullach Sleibi Formeinia, adbath (a)Cam a mulla (sic) Sleibi Rafán. Conad ar an fath sin adrubrad an duan-sa,

(b)*Athair cāich, Coimsid Nime* . . . . .

87. [1]Ar sin [2]trā [3]ro [4]ḟeallsat clanda Adaim for ūaill ⁊ for [5]dīmos ⁊ for imarbus ⁊ for fingail, .i. Cāin mac Adaim [6]in sindser ro [7]marb-sidēn a [8]dearbrāthair .i. Abēl, tria

---

85. (5) Now God descended to see the city and the tower which the sons of Adam were building—

i.e. the sons of the wretched, earthy, man of sin: that is a reproach in the divine scripture, to call them 'sons of Adam.'

(6) And God said: Lo, all men are as it were one people, and they have one language; and they will not cease from the purposes which they have begun, till they have fulfilled them.   (7) Let us therefore confuse and crush their smooth, gentle, tuneful speech, that none of them may understand the voice of another. (8) So that people was confused, maddened, and caused to err, with the multitude of the different unknown languages: and thus they left off from their deeds which they had begun to do.   (9) Wherefore the name of that place was called "Babel," i.e. "confusion": for there all the languages of the world were confused, to wit the seventy-two languages, from the three sons of Noe.   God scattered those nations into the whole earth.

---

86. Noe divided the world into three parts among his sons: Sem in Asia, Ham in Africa, Iafeth in Europe.   And each of them died in his own division.   Sem died on the summit of Sliab Radruip of the heat of the sun, Iafeth died on the summit of Sliab Armenia, Ham died on the summit of Sliab Rafan.   So that the following song was said of that matter—

Poem no. V.

87. Thereafter the children of Adam played false, in pride, in haughtiness, in sin, and in kin-murder: Cain son of Adam, the elder, he slew his brother Abel through his

---

deeds.''   *The second* i *of* gnimaib *sbs. and blotted.*   [3] h-im. MS.
[4] *bracketed letters not in* MS.

87. (*variae lectiones from* H, *text from* M) [1] iar   [2] thra   [3] ra (*ut semper*)   [4] feallsad   [5] dimus   [6] an seindser   [7] marbsigein
[8] derb-

(*a*) Cain MS.   (*b*) M here resumes.

[9]saint ⁊ tria [10]formot, do ḟid chnāma [11]chamaill; conad airi sin [12]dorad Dīa [13]dīlind [14]tars in n-uili doman.

[15]Ocus nīr gein mac a cind a bliadna ō athair [16]acht Adam namā, ūair is fīr nar [17]slān acht āen bliadain [18]Adaim, [19]madab imslān, in ūair [20]ro [21]compread Cāin.

88. Seth mac [1]Adam imorro, [2]in treas mac [3]aireada [4]ro bai [5]ac Adam, [6]⁊ is ūad [7]atāt fir domain uili, ‡ .i. Nāe mac Laimīach meic [8]Mathasalem meic Enōc meic Iareth meic Malaleth meic Cainen meic [9]Enos meic [10]Seth meic Adaim. ||[(a)] [11]Is hē thrā Nae [12]in [13]tAdam [14]tānusti, [15]cosa [16]mberar fir [17]domain uili. [18]Ūair ro [19]bāid [20]in [21]dīli [22]sīl [23]Adaim, [24]acht [25]Nāe cona trī macaib .i. [26]Sem, [27]Cam, [28]Iathfed, ⁊ a [29]ceithri mnā [30].i. Coba [31]⁊ Olla [32]⁊ [33]Oliua ⁊ [34]Olīuana.

[35]Imroimadair [36]‡ dosfaidead || [37]clanna [38]Adaim, [39]co tard [40]Dīa [41]dīlind [42]tarsin [43]uili [44]doman, [45]conach tērno [46]nech beō [47]eisti acht lucht na [48]hairci .i. [49]Nāe [50]cona [51]trī macaib .i. Sem, [52]Cam, Iathfed cona [53]ceithri mnāib .i. Coba ⁊ Olla [54]⁊ Oliba ⁊ Olībana,[53]

[50]amail asbert[50]—

Slūag nād chlōe cūa-chel . . . . .

---

[9] ṡaint   [10] formad   [11] camuill   [12] darad   [13] an dile
[14] tarsa nuili   [15] *om.* ⁊   [16] ach o Adam   [17] ṡlan   [18] Adhaim
[19] madob imlan an   [20] do   [21] -pred
88. [1] Adaim and *om.* imorro H   [2] an tres H   [3] aireda H
[4] *om.* ro H   [5] ag H   [6] *om.* ⁊ H   [7] ataid H   [8] -sail- H
[9] Enois H   [10] Seith H   [11] orú is é Nae H oir is e an (in β²) Noe
sin β⁰¹²   [12] an H   [13] tAdhamh β¹²   [14] tanaisti H tanasti β
tainaiste β¹²   [15] gusa β⁰¹²   [16] mairedh β¹ mared β²   [17] *ins.* an
and om. uili β⁰¹²: uili *also om.* H: domh- β¹²   [18] oir β¹²: do H   [19] bhaith
β bhaidh β¹²   [20] an H β   [21] diliudh β¹²   [22] siol β⁰¹²
[23] nAdhaimh uili β Adhamh uile β¹²   [24] ach H   [25] Noe gona tri
macaibh β: Naoi gona thri macaibh β¹²   [26] Semh β   [27] Caim β
[28] *ins.* ⁊ β¹²: Iafeth H β Iaphet β¹²   [29] ceitri H gceithre mnaibh β¹ᵘ

envy and jealousy, with a shaft of a camel-bone. Wherefore God brought a Flood over the whole earth.

Now never was son born of father at the end of a year save [from] Adam only: for it is true that one year of Adam was not complete, if indeed it was quite complete, when Cain was conceived.

88. As for Seth, son of Adam, one of the three eminent sons which Adam had, from him are the men of the whole earth. [Noe s. Lamech s. Mathusalam s. Enoch s. Iared s. Malalehel s. Cainan s. Enos s. Seth s. Adam]. Now Noe is the second Adam, to whom are traced the men of the whole earth. For the Flood drowned the seed of Adam save Noe and his three sons, Sem, Ham, Iafeth, and their four wives Coba, Olla, Oliva, Olivana.

The progeny of Adam sinned [fell]; so God brought a Flood over the whole earth, so that not one escaped from it alive except the people of the ark, to wit Noe and his three sons, Sem, Ham, Iafeth, with their four wives Coba, Olla, Oliva, and Olivana.

As one said—

Poem no. I.

---

cceitre mnaibh β^2 ³⁰ *om.* .i. β^2 ³¹ *om.* ꓶ β^{12} ³² *om.* ꓶ β^{12} ³³ Oliu M Oliva β^1 *om.* β^2 ³⁴ Olibana M Olivana β^1 ³⁵ *this y om.* H: im ro imair β imromhair β^{12} ³⁶ *om.* β^{012} ³⁷ *ins.* a suidiu β: clann β^{02} clainn β^1 ³⁸ Adhaimh β Adhamh β^{12} ³⁹ co darat β co tarat β^{12} ⁴⁰ *om.* β^{12} ⁴¹ an dillinn β in diliu β^{12} ⁴² tarsan β^{012} ⁴³ uile β^{012} ⁴⁴ dhomainn β domhainn β^1 domhaann β^2 ⁴⁵ gonach β^{12} ⁴⁶ *om.* M neach β^{12} ⁴⁷ *om.* β^{012} ⁴⁸ haïrcedh β^{12} ⁴⁹ Noe β^{012} ⁵⁰⁻⁵⁰ a chlann ꓶ a mnaibh do reir an file β^{12} ⁵¹ thri β^0 ₅′ Cham ꓶ Iafeth β^0 ⁵³⁻⁵³ ceathra mnaibh .i. Cobha Olla Oliua Oliuana ⁵⁴ ꓶ Oliba *om.* M *and sprs. but miswritten* ꓶ Olibana ⁵⁵ amail adbert an fili H amail asbeart an filidh β

(a) Text of B here resumes, but is still preserved in the transcripts only.

89. Ō [1]Adam [2]co dīlind [3]in chēt āis. [4]Is ē seo [5]am [6]in līn [7]bliadan fil innti [8]cheadus,[4] .i. sē [9]bliadna [10]cāecad [11]ar sē [12]chēdaib [13]ar [14]mīle, [15]amail asbert [16]in file—[15]

Cēt aimsir in bethad bind . . . .

[17]Is [18]iad [19]seo [20]airich [21]na cēt āisi sin [22]cona [23]sāeglaib, īar Seth [24]cheadas[22]—

[25]Adam	dccccxxx bl.		[27]Cainen	dccccx bl.
[26]Seth	dcxii bl.		[28]Malaleth	dccc bl.
Enos	dccccu bl.		[29]Iareth	dcccclxu bl.

[30]Enoc	ccclxu bl.
[31]Mathasalem	dccccclxix bl.
[32]Laimiach	[33]dcclxxuii bl.

[34]Sem [35]dono rogob i nAisia, Cam [36]i nAfraic, [37]Iathfed [38]a nEoraip, [39]amail asbert in fili,

Sēm rogab i n-Aisia n-ait . . . .

90. Ra thuismid ⁊ ra chlannaigsed tra na tri meic-sin Nae, .i. Sem, Cam, Iafeth, cineada ⁊ clanda imda ilarda examla, .i. da chinel sechtmogat ‡ .i. da chined dég ar tri fichtib ‖.   Is amlaid seo imorro ra tusmid ⁊ ra scailit na cinela sin, .i. secht cinela fichit dib o Sém, tricha imorro o Cham, a cuig dég o Iafeth, conad da chinél sechtmogat sin uili.   Ocus conad dá berla sechtmogat tucad doib iar tairmesc an Tuir Nemruaid; conad a cind decc mbliadain iarsin do tebustair Feinius Farrsaid berla na nGaeidel as na dib sechtmogat, co rustaisealb dia dalta, .i. do mac Adnomuin, .i. do Gaeidel.

No comad a cind decc mbliadan iar scailead don scoil for cach leth dorébi Feinius Farsaid(a) ‡ .i. in sai ‖ berla na nGaeidel as na dib berlaib sechtmogat, ⁊ dorad iarsin do Niul, dia mac bodeisin.

Darad-sidi do Gaeidil Glas mac Niuil ⁊ dia macaib-sein bodeisin, conad uada-sidi ainmnigter in berla sin.

---

89. [1] Adhamh β^{012} [2] go dilionn β go dilinn β^{12} [3] an ched ais H in ced aois β ced aois an domhuin β^{12} (-ain β^2)   [4-4] *om.* β^{12} as H   [5] *om.* am H β [6] an H *om.* β [7] bliadhna β [8] ceadus β inti *and om.* cheadus H   [9] -dhna β^{012} [10] caogad β^{012} [11] re β^{12} [12] chead β ched β^{12} [13] air β^2 [14] mili H mhili β mhile β^1 [15-15] *om.* β^{12}: amhuil β [16] inso H in fili β^1 [17] *ins.* ⁊ H β^{012}: as β^{012} [18] iat β [19] so H β^{12} [20] airid H airigh β athrachadh β^{12} [21] na cet aissi H na haoisi β na haoise β^{12} [22-22] marlle ris an rae do mhair siad β^{12} [23] saeghlaib H

89. From Adam to the Flood is the First Age. This is the tally of years that are in it first, one thousand six hundred fifty and six years, as the poet said,

Poem no. VII.

These are the leaders of that First Age, with their lives, after Seth first of all—

Adam	930 years		Cainan	910 years
Seth	612 „		Malalehel	800 „
Enos	905 „		Iared	965

Enoch	365 years
Mathusalam	969 „
Lamech	777 „

So Seth settled in Asia, Ham in Africa, Iafeth in Europe, as the poet said,

Poem no. II.

90. Now those three sons of Noe, Sem, Ham, Iafeth, begat and fathered many numerous and various nations and progenies, to wit, seventy-two peoples [i.e. three score and twelve peoples]. Now thus were these peoples born and scattered : twenty-seven of them from Sem, thirty from Ham, fifteen from Iafeth, which makes in all seventy-two peoples. And there were seventy-two languages given to them after the confusion of Nemrod's Tower : so that in the end of ten years after that, Feinius Farsaid extracted the speech of the Gaedil out of the seventy-two languages, and set it forth to his fosterling, the son of Agnomain, Gaedil.

> Or perhaps it was at the end of ten years after the scattering of the school on every side that Feinius Farsaid [the sage] extracted the speech of the Gaedil out of the seventy-two languages, and gave it afterwards to Nel, his own son.

> He gave it to Gaedil Glas son of Nel, and to *his* sons; so that from them is the language named.

saoghlaibh β   [24] chedus H cheatas   [25] Adhamh β[012]   [26] Set β[12]
[27] Cainan β Canaan β[12]   [28] Malalel β Malaleal β[12]   [29] Iarat β[12]   [30] dcclxu
β[012]   [31] Mathasailem H Methusalem β[12]   [32] Lamhiach β Lamiac β[12]
[33] dcclxuii M dcclxxuiii β[12]   [34] ins. do Naoi ⁊ a thriar mac .i. β[12]
[35] om. dono: dogab imorro an Aissia H: dana roghabh in nAissia β gab
Sem an Asia Cam an Aifric ⁊ Iafeth (Iaphet β²) Europ β[12]   [36] a nAfraicc
H in nAfraic β   [37] Iafeth H   [38] in nEoraip β   [39] amail inso
H amhail asbert infili β om. β[12]

(*a*) interlined.

91. Ra imdaig tra uimir na ⸢inel sin [sech n-uimir na mberla; ar] ataid isa nAffraicc il-chinela [im oen-berla, cen (?)] atharrach tengad accu. Is ed fodera sa(n), na rab[atar] ach da chinel sechtmogat thall acon Tur, an tan ra sg[ailed na] berladha : ⁊ cé ra himdaigead na cinela, na ro im[daiged (?) i] n-airim chinel n-examail iad, acht a leigiud a fo-tasgor na cinel [ba] nesa doib. Conad lia na cinela iar tothacht an[date na berlae, cian] cob lia iar n-uimir.

92. ¹Conad ō na trī macaib sin Nāe ro ²geneadar ³na dā ⁴chenel ⁵sechtmoġat īar ⁶n-dīlind, ⁷cona dib berlaib sechtmogat ⁸tucad dōib ⁹īarsin, ac ¹⁰tairmesc ¹¹in Tuir ¹²Nemrūaid. ¹³Conad i cind ¹⁴decc ¹⁵mbliadan ¹⁶īarsin ro ¹⁷thebistair ¹⁸Feinius Farrsaich ¹⁹bērla na ²⁰nGāedeal ²¹as na ²²dīb bērlaib ²³sechtmogat.¹

²⁴Tricha ¹‡ no .uii.xx ‖ mac ²⁵badar ²⁶ag ²⁷Sem, ²⁸um ²⁹Airifacsad, ²⁸um ³⁰Assur, ²⁸um ³¹Peirsius.

> ³²Ocus is ³³dia ³⁴sīl-sidi na ³⁵Hebraidi. ³⁶Is iad so na ³⁷cōic ³⁸meic ³⁹ō ra sīlad aigi, .i. ⁴⁰Alam, ⁴¹Assur, ⁴²Airifacsad, ⁴³Luid, is Aram : ⁊ cia ⁴⁴ainmnigter ⁴⁵cōic meic ⁴⁶ag Sem, ni ⁴⁷tabar a ⁴⁸n-āirim ⁴⁹acht ⁵⁰cinead dā mac dīb.

⁵¹Tricha ⁵²mac imorro badar oc Cham, im ⁵³Chuss, im ⁵⁴Mesram, im ⁵⁵F̄uth im ⁵⁶Chandán,

> Ocus ⁵⁷cia ⁵⁸ainmigter ⁵⁹tricha mac ⁶⁰oc Cam, ni ⁶¹tabar a n-āirem ⁶²acht cinead ⁶³dā mac dīb.

---

92. ¹⁻¹ *om.* H : conadh o thri macaib-siden Noe β (*these words om.* β¹² ² gheinseadar β⁰¹² (g- β², -edar β¹ -edair β²) ³ *om.* na β¹² ⁴ cheineil β⁰¹² (-el β¹²) ⁵ deag is tri fithchiod β⁰¹² (deg . . fithcit β¹²) ⁶ -inn β⁰¹² ⁷ *ins.* o chlannaib Naoi β¹² : conadh da bhearla β, gonadh da bherladh β¹² ⁸ tugadh doibh β⁰¹² ⁹ iarsoin β⁰¹² (-soin β¹ iair- β²) ¹⁰ toirmeasg β toirmiosg β¹² ¹¹ an β² ¹² Neamhruaidh β Nemrodh β¹² (-mh- β²) ¹³ conadh a ccend β ⁊ a gcenn β¹² ¹⁴ deich β¹² ¹⁵ bliadhna β⁰¹² ¹⁶ -ṡoin β ¹⁷ teipestair β⁰¹² (-ar β²) ¹⁸ Fionnus Farsaigh β¹² F. Fairsaidh β ¹⁹ berladh β¹² ²⁰ nGaoidheal β⁰¹² (-dhel β¹²) ²¹ *ins.* ⁊ β¹ ²² di bherlaibh β da bherladh β¹² ²³ sechtmhodh β¹² ²⁴ *text from here printed as in* H : *interlined* ⁊ *in* H only ²⁵ *ins.* ro M do β¹² : bhadair β bhadar β¹² ²⁶ ac M a β¹² ²⁷ *ins.* mac Nae β¹² ²⁸ im M β (*bis*) ²⁹ Airifaxat β Arfacsat β¹² ³⁰ Asur M ³¹ Persius M β⁰¹² ³² uair M : *om.* is β⁰² ³³ da sil-side M ³⁴ síol-sen β ; síol (*om.* sen) β¹² ³⁵ Heabraidi M Heabhraidhe β⁰¹²

91. Now the number of those peoples increased beyond the numbers of the languages; for there are in Africa many peoples having one language, and no change of tongue. This is the reason thereof, that there were only seventy-two peoples yonder at the Tower, when the languages were separated: and though the peoples were multiplied, they were not multiplied in the computation of different peoples, but were left as a subordinate company of the peoples nearest to them.   So that the nations are greater in substance than the languages, though they are not greater in number.

92. So that it is from those three sons of Noe that the seventy-two peoples were born after the Flood, with their seventy-two languages that were given to them thereafter, at the confusion of Nemrod's Tower.   And it was at the end of ten years thereafter that Feinius Farsaid extracted the language of the Gaedil out of the seventy-two languages.

Sem had thirty [or twenty seven] sons, including Arfaxad, Assur, Persius—

and it is of his seed that the Hebrews come.   These are the five sons from whom he had descendants, Elam, Assur, Arfaxad, Lud, and Aram: and though five sons of Sem are named, I do not give in enumeration the descent of more than two of them.

Ham had thirty sons, including Chus, Mesraim, Fut, Chanaan,

and though thirty sons of Ham are named, I do not give in enumeration the descent of more than two of them.

(-aidh β^{12})   [36] no comad iad so M no gomadh iat so β ⁊ is iad so β^{12}
[37] cuig β coig β^{12} [38] maic β^{12} [39] oir síoladh aige β da (do β^2) cloinn ar bhfagham (air bhfh- β^2) sliocht β^{12}: aici M   [40] Alamh β^2
[41] Asur M   [42] Arafaxat M Arifaxat β Arfacsad β^{12} [43] Luidi Saram MH Ludi Sarain β Ludi Saram β^{12} [44] ghth- β^{12} -thear M   [45] coig β na coig β^{12}
[46] ac M aig Semh β sin Seim β^{12} [47] tabhair β^{012} [48] airem M aireamh β airemh β^{13} [49] ach H   [50] cinneamh en dá mhac dibh β ceinemh in da mhac dhiobh β^{12} [51] Triothchad (Triochad β^2) mac bhadh ag Cam mhac Naoi um Cus um Esrom um Futh um Canaan β^{12} [52] mac aile oc Cam M mac eile o Cham β [53] Chus M Cus β [54] Esram H Easrom β [55] Futh β [56] Cannain β [57] gia β [58] -gthear M -ghthear β -ghther an β^{12} [59] triotchad β^1 triothchadh β^2 [60] ag Cam β sin *and om.* oc Cam β^{12} [61] tabhair β tabhar β^1 toabhar β^2
[62] diobh acht cinneadh da mac β^{012} (dhiobh, cinedh, mhac β^{12})   [63] *ins.* a H

A [64]cūig dēg [65]imorro [66]ag Iafeth.

<table>
<tr><td>M :</td><td>H</td></tr>
</table>

[67]im [68]Danai, [39]im [70]Grēgus, [65]im [71]Espanus [69] im [72]Goimerus : [73]no [74]is [75]morṡeser ar fichit do macaib badar aici ⁊ .i. oc Sem ‖.

no [76]cumad iad so anmanda [77]na mac sin Iathfeth, .i. [78]Gomer, [78]Magoc, Magia, Iaban, Tubal, [79]Masoth, [80]Tirus, [81]Maisechda.

⁊ ni tabar a n-āirim ach cinedh tri mac dib. Ni hamlaid ra badar na meic aili can geinemhain uaidhib; acht ri ro geinir uaidib ni ar bu dingmala ainm ceineoil da tabairt forro.

Is [82]amlaid [83]sin [84]imorro [85]do [86]ṡīlsad na [87]cinela sin, [88].i. a [89]secht fichit dīb ō Ṡem, [90]tricha imorro ō Cham, [91]cūic [92]cenela dēg o [93]Iafeth,[88] [94]*ut dicitur*

Tricha mac mīn, monar ngle . . . . .

93. Iathféth dono mac Náe, [1]is úad tuaiscert-leth na Haissia ⁊ lucht na Heorpa uili. Sém imorro for medon Aissia, ó Sruth Éofrait co tracht airthir an betha. Cam dono ragab-sidi an Affraicc, ⁊ deiscert-leth na Haissia.

94. [1]Iáfed [2]dono[3], is iad a [4]chlann-sidi [5]lenfamaid [6]anossa. [7]Is [8]úad [9]tūaiscert-[10]leath [11]na [12]Haissia [15]uili, .i. [14]Aissia Beg [15]⁊ [16]Airmein [17]⁊ fir na Sceithīa

---

[64] cuic dec M   [65] *om.* β   [66] oc Iathfed M ag Iaphet β
[67] in β um β[12]   [68] -nn- β[012]   [69] um β[12] (*ter*)   [70] Greagus β[12]
[71] Easp- β[012]   [72] Gomerus β Gomerius β[1] Gomeretis β[2]   [73-73] o seisear dhiobh (dhiobh β[2]) mar ata β[12]   [74] *om.* is β   [75] morseisiur air fichit do mhacaibh bhadar ag Semh β   [76] gomadh β, *possibly* cumad iad so cert-anmanda *in* M: *the writing here partly effaced by a blot badly rubbed out, and there is room for a letter or two more than is printed in the text*   [77] mac Iafeth   [78] Maghach (Magach β[1] -och β[2]) Madia Iuban β[12]   [79] Massoth β[12] Massoc β   [80] Tiras β[012]
[81] Maisecdha β Maisectadh β[12]   [82] amhladh β amhlaidh β[12]   [83] seo

Iafeth had fifteen,

including Danai, Gregus, Espanus, Gomerus: or [Sem] had twenty-seven sons.

And I do not give in enumeration the descent of more than three of them. It is not the case that the other sons had no descendants: but none were born from them worthy of being called "a people."

Or perhaps these are the names of the sons of Iafeth—Gomer, Magog, Madai, Iavan, Tubal, Mosoch, Tiras, Maisechda.

Thus it is that those peoples were descended, twenty-seven from Sem, thirty from Ham, fifteen from Iafeth, *ut dicitur*

Poem no. III.

93. Iafeth son of Noe, of him is the northern side of Asia and the people of all Europe. Sem over the middle of. Asia, from the river Euphrates to the eastern region of the world. Ham settled in Africa and on the southern side of Asia.

94. As for Iafeth, it is his progeny which we shall follow now. From him is the northern side of all Asia, namely Asia Minor, and Armenia, and the people of

---

M β so β^{12} [84] *om.* β^{12} [85] ro M β^{012} [86] silad M sioladh β^{012} (ṡ β^2)   [87] cenela M cineala β cinedhaibh β^1 cinethchaibh β^2 [88-88] *om.* β^{12} [89] seacht xxit diobh o Seimh triocha β^{12} [90] *ins.* ⁊ M   [91] *ins.* ⁊ M : a cuig deg β [92] cinela H   [93] Iathfed M   [94] amail asbert in teolach seo M amail isbert an filidh β do reir an fhile β^{12}

93. [1] *sprs. s* H

94. [1] Iathfed M Iaphet β^{12} [2] tra M β *om.* β^{12} [3] *ins.* mac Nae M mhac Naoi β^{12} mac Nai mac Laimhiach β [4] cland-sen M chlan β^1: *om.* side β^{012} [5] lean- β -aoid β^{12} [6] *om.* M β^{012} [7] *ins.* ⁊ β [8] uadh β uaidh β^{12} [9] tuaitsciort β^{12} (-th- β^2)   [10] leithi M   [11] na *dittographed* β^1 [12] Haisia M β^{012} [13] *om.* M β^{012} [14] Aisia M Aissia β^{12} [15] .i. *for* ⁊ β^{12} [16] Airmen M Armein β^{12} [17-17] *om.* β

[15]┐ is [19]ūad [20]an Grēg Beg ┐ an Grēg Mōr [17]┐ Grēg na
[21]Halax*andria*.[18]   [22]Ocus is ūad [20]lucht na Heorpa [23]uili.

[24]Ocus dono is dīa cloind cach gabāil dogab Ērinn, cenmothā
Cessair namā.[22][24]

95. (A) Do chlannaib Iafed andso bodesta.   Iafeth dono
mac Náe ┐ Oliuana a bean, ro thechtsad ocht maccu, .i.
Gomer, Magóg, Maigia, Iabal ‡ no Eónae ‖ ‡ .i. an
seindser ‖, Tubal, Masoch, Tirus, Maisegda.

(B) Gomer imorro, is uada ataid Galladagdai, ┐ is inann
iadside ┐ Gailli.   Ainm aili dóib Gailligregi.

> Cid día n-abur Gailligregi ré síl Gomeir meic Iafeth?   Ninsa.
> Gailli iad do bunad adbeir Asuidhir, ┐ dorad rigi an feraind
> dianad ainm Bétania don Gregdo-sidi irandus dia thir ar chongnam
> fris.   Ra ansad aigi an agaid a braithrech; ┐ is airi sin adberar
> Gailligregi riu, ar a mbeith itir Greg ┐ Gaillia do bunad, ┐ ni
> heir comad mac do Goimer Gregus.

(C) Teasallus mac Grēguis ra cumdaig an catraig diana
ainm Tesalónica, ┐ is inti ro follamnaigsed a flaithus.   Is
uad ainmnigter in Tesaill iar firind, ┐ o <a> athair
ainmnigter an Greg.

(D) Ceitri meic la Goimeir, .i. Ripad Scot o taid Scuit;
┐ dob eisein Ibath mac Goimeir, senathar Feiniusa
Farrsaid ‡ .i. Feinius Farrsaid mac Baaith meic Ibaith
meic Goimeir meic Iafeth ‖.

> Cid dia n-abar Greg Sceithegda re Gaeidealaib, ar ní do šil
> Neimid meic Adnomain iad do bunad?   Is do lucht na Sceithia
> dóib, uair is do šil Feiniusa Farrsaid doib cá raibi flaithus na
> Sceithia.   Acht ceana ni raibi rigi na Sceithia aigi acht a flaithus,
> ┐ ar a mbeith do chlannaib Goimer adberar Greg re Gaeidelaib;
> ┐ as decair lind a (a)scartain ré Goimér da reir sin.

(E) Na tri meic aili Goimeir, .i. Asceinex, otaid Reigine,
Erifam-o taid Páplagoine, Togarm o tait Frigia ┐ Ilia.

[18-18] *om.* M   [19] uaidh β^1 uatha β^2 [20-20] *om.* β^{12} [21] -dreach β
[22-22] *om.* β [23] uile β^{12} [24-24] *om.* M β^{12}

Scythia; and from him are Graecia Parva, and Graecia Magna, and Alexandrian Greece.   Of him also are the people of all Europe.

Moreover it is of his progeny that is every Taking which took Ireland, save only Cessair.

95. (A) Of the children of Iafeth here now.   Iafeth son of Noe and Olivana his wife, they had eight sons, Gomer, Magog, Madai, Iabal or Iavan, [the eldest], Tubal, Mosoch, Thiras, Maisegda.

(B) As for Gomer, of him are the Galladagdae [= Galatae], and they are the same as the Galli.   Another name for them is Gallograeci.

> Why is the seed of Gomer son of Iafeth called ''Gallograeci''?
> They were fundamentally Galli, says Isidorus: and the ruler of
> the land called Bithynia gave to the Greeks a portion of his land
> for giving him help.   They stayed with him to oppose his
> brethren; and for that reason they are called Gallograeci, because
> they were fundamentally in part Greeks, in part Galli; and it
> will not arise that Gregus was a son of Gomer.

(C) Thessalus son of Gregus built the city called Thessalonica, and therein he ruled his kingdom.   From him is Thessaly named authentically, and Greece is named from his father.

(D) Gomer had four sons, Rifath Scot from whom are the Scots; now he was Ibath son of Gomer, the grandfather of Feinius Farsaid [Feinius Farsaid s. Baath s. Ibath s. Gomer s. Iafeth].

> Why are the Gaedil called Greeks of Scythia, seeing that
> fundamentally they are not of the seed of Nemed son of
> Agnomain?   They are of the people of Scythia, for they are of
> the seed of Feinius Farrsaid, who had the princedom of Scythia.
> However, he had not the kingdom of Scythia, but its princedom:
> and as they are of the progeny of Gomer, the Gaedil are called
> Greeks.   We find it hard to disconnect them from Gomer on that
> account.

(E) The three other sons of Gomer were Aschenez, of whom are the Rhegini, Rifath of whom are the Paphlagonians, Thogorma of whom are Phrygia and Ilia.

(a) MS. -thair, clumsily corrected sec. man.

(F) Maigia no Meda mac Iafed, *a quo* Meda; ⁊ ragabsa ı ochtar o Meadaib rigi an domain.

(G) Ionán mac Iafeth, is uaidib-séin ataid Iondaid, ⁊ is uad rasgeinseadar Eoldaid. Ocus ainm aili do, Greg mac Iafeth. [Is uad] ainmnigter an cuiged berla na Gregi, .i. an berla Eol[da, ⁊ is ua]d ainmnigter Gregaig iar firind. Uair is co Gregus mac [Iafeth ber]ar genelach Alaxandair meic Philip rig Greg, ⁊ is uad Gregaig [⁴· . . .]cain. Ocus is uad adberar an Muir Eonda.

(H) Coig meic aigi-sidi, .i. Elisa, Tairsis, Seithim, Dodáinim, Gregus. Elissa *a quo* Eigila, .i. geinilach Sicimórum. Tairsis, is uad Tairsis ⁊ Cillegda. Seithim *a quo* Ioif mac Saduirn, amail adbeir leabar Augustin o Chathair De, ⁊ uada Ceitheagdai. Is uaidib-sein ainm-nigther cathair na Cipricai, .i. Ceithunt.

(I) Dodainim, is uadha-sidi Rodai. Is uaidib-sein ra foglad indseda Mara Toirrian, cona cinelaib examlaib, .i. Inis Roid, ⁊ Inis Coirbdith, ⁊ Inis Sicil, ⁊ Inis Creid, ⁊ Inis Ceithiria, ⁊ Inis Rodain, ⁊ oiléna eirimda ele, ineóch na ra thuirmsemar súnd, árdaig mi-chuimni. Gregus *a quo* Gregaig.

(K) Tubal, is uada atáid Iberdaid ⁊ Espandai; ‡ no comad mac d'Iaféd Easpanus o táid Espandai ||, ⁊ Celtiberdai, ⁊ Édaldai. Uair Eiperus, do śil Tubail do chinel Iafeth, a quo Eipiritarum, ⁊ ór gein Ianus rí na Heiperda. Is é cet ri da gab Románchu, ⁊ is úad ainm-nigter mí Ienuair, ⁊ is úad Coirinti.

(L) Massoch, is uada ataid Capadusdai.⁽ᵃ⁾ Tiruss, is uada ataid Tragdai. Maissegda, dibaid-sein.

(M) Magóg, is uada ataid fir na Sceithia ⁊ na Gaith, .i. Gaidil. Cuig meic lá Magóg, .i. Baath, ⁊ Ibath, ⁊ Barachan, ⁊ Emoth, ⁊ Aithechta. Baath dono, mac dó-sein Feinius Farrsaid, athair na Sceithegda. Feinius Farrsaid dono,

---

(a) *Capaddai* written and ᵹ changed clumsily to ⅁ ; (= dus), *sec. man.*

(F) Madai or Meda, son of Iafeth, *a quo* the Medes; and eight men of the Medes took the kingship of the world.

(G) Ionan son of Iafeth, from them (*sic*) are the Ionians, and from him were the Aeolians born. He has another name, Gregus son of Iafeth. From him is named one of the five languages of the Greeks, the Aeolic, and from him the Greeks are named authentically. For the genealogy of Alexander son of Philip, king of Greece, is traced to Gregus son of Iafeth and from him are the . . . (?) Greeks. Also, the Ionian Sea is named after him.

(H) He had five sons, Elissa, Tharsis, Cetthim, Dodanim, Gregus. Elissa *a quo* Aetolia, the pedigree-stem of the Siculi. Tharsis, from him are Tarsus and the Cilicians. Cetthim, *a quo* is Iuppiter son of Saturn, as the book of Augustine *De Ciuitate Dei* saith, and of whom are the Citii. From them is named the city of the Cyprii, namely Citium.

(I) Dodanim, from him are the Rhodii. By these people the islands of the Torrian Sea, with their various inhabitants, were appropriated, to wit Rhodes, and Carpathos, and Sicily, and Crete, and Cytherea, and the Balearic Islands, and very many other islands which we have not enumerated here, owing to failure of memory. Gregus, *a quo* the Greeks.

(K) Tubal, from him are the Iberi and the Hispani [or perhaps Easpanus was a son to Iafeth, and from him are the Hispani] and the Celtiberi and the Itali. For [it is] Eperus, of the seed of Tubal of the race of Iafeth, *a quo* the Epirotae, and from whom sprang Ianus, king of the Epirotae. He is the first king who took over the Romans. From him is named the month of January, and from him are the Quirites.

(L) Mosoch, of him are the Cappadoces. Thiras, of him are the Thraces. Maisegda is missing.

(M) Magog, of him are the men of Scythia and the Goths, that is, the Gaedil. Magog had five sons, Baath, Ibath, Barachan, Emoth, Aithechta. As for Baath, his son was Feinius Farrsaid, father of the Scythians. As for Feinius

mac Baaith meic Magóg meic Iafeth.   Adberaid araile imorro is Feinius Farrsaid mac Baaith meic Ibáith meic Goimeir meic Iafeth.

(N) Ibath dono, an mac aili do Magóg, mac dosaidi Alainius.   Tri meic aigi-sidi, .i. Airmein, Negua, Isicón. Coic meic ag Armón (*sic*), .i. Gotus, Uiligotus, Cebitus, Brugandus (*sic*), Longbardus.   Negúa dono, ceitre[a] meic lais, .i. Uandalus, Saxus, Bogardus, Longbardus.   Isicon imorro, an tres mac Elainius, ceitri meic lais, .i. Frangcus, Romanus, Albanus *a quo* Albania an Aisia Big, ⁊ Albanactus mac Britan meic Siluius meic Ascain meic Aeniasa meic Anicis a quo Alba Iartair : ⁊ Britus, o raiter Indsi Bretan.

(O) Is andsin do randad an doman a tri randaib, .i. Eóraip ⁊ Afraicc ⁊ Assia.   Secht mbliadna decc ré scailead na mberlad tanig an ced fer do śil Iáfeth is an Eóraip, .i. Alainius mac Ibaith meic Magog meic Iafeth meic Náe. Alainius, is uada atáid Fraingc ⁊ Romanaig; ⁊ is amlaid thanig a tri meic laiss, .i. Airmein, Neagua, Issicon : conad a fus ra clannaigsed na macu adchualumar.

(P) Saxus mac Negúa meic Alainius meic Ibaith meic Magóc meic Iafeth Meic Náe, is úad Saxain.   Emoth mac Magóc, is úad fine thuaiscert an domuin.   Barachán, *a quo* Gaeidel, mac Eitheoir meic Bai meic Tai meic Barachain meic Magoch.   Aitheachtaig mac Magóch, is dia chloind-sein na thuatha thangadar an Erinn ria nGaidelaib, .i. Parrthalón mac Sera meic Sru meic Esrú meic Praimint meic Aithechtaig meic meic (*sic*) Magóch meic Iafeth meic Náe : ⁊ Neimid mac Adnomain meic Paim meic Thait meic Sera meic Srú.   Ocus adberaid aroili do lebraib corab ar slicht an meic do fagaib Parrthalon thair[b] do Neimead, .i. ar slicht Adla meic Parrthaloin.   Ocus clanda Neimid, .i. Gaileoin ⁊ Fir Bolg ⁊ Fir Domnánd ⁊ Tuaith Dé Danund. As dóib-sin do chan an file.

Magog mac an Iafeth . . . .

(a) At first written ꝓ (i.e., *tri* three) : afterwards c-e was written flanking the i, to turn the word into *ceitre* four.
(b) The *h*-dot doubtful.

Farrsaid, he was son of Baath s. Magog s. Iafeth.   Others say however that Feinius Farrsaid was s. of Baath s. Ibath s. Gomer s. Iafeth.

(N) As for Ibath, one of the two sons of Magog, his son was Alainius.   He had three sons, Airmen, Negua, Isicon. Airmen had five sons, Gotus, Uiligotus, Cebitus, Burgandus, Longbardus.   Negua had four sons, Vandalus, Saxus, Bogardus, Longbardus.   Isicon, the third son of Alainius, had four sons, Francus, Romanus, Albanus, *a quo* Albania in Asia Minor, and Albanactus s. Britan s. Silvius s. Ascanius s. Aeneas s. Anchises, *a quo* western Alba, and Britus, from whom are called the Islands of Britain.

(O) Then was the world divided into three divisions, Europe, Africa, Asia.   Seventeen years before the scattering of the languages there came the first man of the seed of Iafeth into Europe, Alainius s. Ibath s. Magog s. Iafeth s. Noe.   Alainius, of him are the Franks and the Romans.   And his three sons came with him, Armen, Negua, Isicon: so that on the hither side they begat those sons of whom we have heard.

(P) Saxus s. Negua s. Alainius s. Ibath s. Magog s. Iafeth s. Noe, of him are the Saxons.   Emoth s. Magog, of him is the people of the north of the world.   Barachan, *a quo* the Gaedil, s. Etheor s. Bai s. Tai s. Barachan s. Magog. Aithechtaig s. Magog, of his progeny are the peoples who came into Ireland before the Gaedil—Parthalon s. Sera s. Sru s. Esru s. Praiment s. Aithechtaig s.(a) Magog s. Iafeth s. Noe: and Nemed s. Agnomain s. Paim s. Tat s. Sera s. Sru.   Others of the books say that Nemed was of the family of the son whom Parthalon left in the east, Adla s. Parthalon.   Also the children of Nemed, the Gaileoin and Fir Bolg and Fir Domnann and Tuatha De Danann.   Of those the poet sang,

Poem no. IV.

(a) Disregarding the dittography in the text.

(Q) Is iad tra na cineada sin .i. clanda Iafeth, ra gabsad ferandus ⁊ flaithus na ·Heorpa uili, ⁊ tuaiscert-leithi na Haissia : ⁊ is iad sin cuig prim-chinéla deg chlainni Iafeth cona ḟo-chinelaib : ⁊ ra ṡealbsadar feranda imda isan n-Aissia, .i. o Ṡliab Mai ⁊ o Ṡliab Tur a tuaid co Sruth Danai ⁊ coruigi an Sceithia tuaiscertaig : ⁊ ra ṡelbsad an Eoraip uili, coruigi an aigen muiridi fuineada Insi Bretan ⁊ conuigi an Espain treuillig budeas, .i. Tuillṡlicht.   Da chlannaib Iafeth meic Náe conuigi sin, cona prim-chinelaib ⁊ cona fo-chinelaib, ⁊ cona ngabalaib ⁊ cona ferandaib, itir Aissia ⁊ Eóraiph.

96. Na tri meic-si tra Náe ra thuirmsemar romaind .i. Sém ⁊ Cam ⁊ Iafeth : ria ndilinn ruġtha an triur sin. Ocus adberaid araili co rugad mac do Nae iar ndilinn, .i. Eoinitus : ⁊ Éthán an rand feraind do gab, ⁊ as na tri randaib aili ra teibead a ferand. Ocus rob estrolagda maith he, iar n-a ḟoglaim o athair, o Náe.

97. Coba bean Nae, is i ra ḟig édach ré cách iar ndilinn.

Eua ben Adaim, is i ra ḟig tonag di féin ⁊ do Adam ar tus, an tress la iar teacht a sruth Tibir diaid a n-aitrigi, iar n-a ḟorchongar do Dia fuirri.

Catafola a n-ingen, rugad araen ré Cain, seitchi Phendain meic Adaim, is i ra ḟigh édach ria chách. Is uimpi doronad an t-ed.

Iafeth mac Nae, is e ra ṡeind cruit ⁊ organ ar tus íar ndilinn.

(a) Sem mac Náe, an cet goba ⁊ an cet cherd ⁊ an cet ṡaer iar ndilinn.

Nae imorro, ra thindscain tirfrecar do denum, an cet bliadain iar ndilinn : .i. dorigni ar ⁊ búain, ⁊ do chlandustair fineamain.

Cam mac Nae imorro ranig snam ⁊ aircheadal ⁊ filidecht ar tus.

Ora airiġ tra Cam iarsin co ticfad an dili, ⁊ na faidi cá thirchartain co ticfa dílgend chlainni Adaim, tria ḟingail Chain for a braithrib, do rindi tri colamna ceithir-(b)ṡlis, .i.

(a) The initial S is of an extravagant ·shape; it looks as though the scribe thought that it was a ꝺ·

(Q) Now these are those peoples, to wit the progeny of
Iafeth, who took the territory and princedom of all Europe
and of the northern side of Asia; and those are the fifteen
chief people of the progeny of Iafeth, with their subordinate
people.   And they possessed many territories in Asia,
namely from Mount Amanus and Mount Taurus northward
to the river Don, and to Northern Scythia : and they
possessed all Europe to the ocean of sea in the west of the
island of Britain, and to three-cornered Spain in the south,
i.e. the Astures. (?)   Of the progeny of Iafeth son of Noe
down to this, with their chief peoples and their subordinate
peoples, their takings and their territories, both in Asia and
in Europe.

> 96. As for the three sons of Noe that we have reckoned above,
> Sem, Ham, Iafeth: before the Flood were those three persons
> born. Others say that a son was born to Noe after the Flood,
> named Ionitus. Ethan was the portion of territory which he
> received: out of the other three portions was his portion selected.
> He was a good astrologer, having learnt it from his father Noe.

97. Coba, wife of Noe, she it is who wove raiment for
every one after the Flood.

Eua wife of Adam, she it is who first wove an apron
for herself and for Adam, on the third day after coming
from the river Tiber (*sic*: *lege* Tigris) after their penance,
when God had commanded it to her.

Catafola their daughter, who was born along with Cain,
wife of Pendan son of Adam, she it is who wove raiment
before anyone else : about her was the jealousy excited.

Iafeth son of Noe, it is he who first sounded a harp and
an organ after the Flood.

> Sem, son of Noe, the first smith, the first wright, the first
> carpenter after the Flood.
> As for Noe, he began to work husbandry in the first year after
> the Flood. He made ploughing and reaping, and planted a
> vineyard.
> Ham, son of Noe, first attained to swimming and poetry and
> bardism.
> Now when Ham understood thereafter that the Flood should
> come, and the prophets were foretelling that a destruction of
> the progeny of Adam should come, by reason of Cain's kin-

columan d'ael, ⁊ colaman do criaid, ⁊ colaman do chiaraig.
Ocus do sgrib intu scela na haimsiri cora mairdis iar ndilinn.
Ra millead an colaman ᴁeil ⁊ an colaman criadh, ⁊ ra mair
an colaman ciarach. Conad he ra indis scela na haimsiri ria
ndilinn; ⁊ mairid iartain.

Olibana a ben-sidi, ⁊ is i ra cet-cum edach iar ndilinn.

98. ¹Grēcus mac Iathfeth, is ²ūad in Grēg ³Mōr ⁊ in
Grēg ⁴Beg ⁊ Grēg na ⁵Halaxandria.   Espānus mac
⁶Iathfeth, ō tait ⁷Espāndai. Gomerus mac ⁸Iathfeth,¹
dā ⁹mac ¹⁰lais, .i. ¹¹Emoth ⁊ Ibath.   ¹²Emoth, is ¹³ūad
fine thūaiscert in domain.¹³   ¹⁴Ibath, dā ¹⁵mac ¹⁶lais,
.i. ¹⁷Bodb ⁊ Baath.   ¹⁸Bodb, ¹⁹diar bo mac ²⁰Dohe.
Elenus ²¹mac ²²Dohe, trī ²³meic ²⁴lais, .i. ²⁵Airmen,
Negūa, Isicon.   ²⁶Airmen ²⁷imorro, ²⁸cōic meic ²⁹lais,
³⁰.i. ³¹Gutus, ³²Cibidus, ³³Uiligothus, ³⁴Burgandus,
³⁵Longbardus. ³⁶Neagūa ³⁷imorro, trī ³⁸meic ³⁹leis, ⁴⁰.i.
⁴¹Saxus, ⁴²Boarus, Uandalus.   Hisicon ⁴³imorro, ⁴⁴in
⁴⁵treas mac ⁴⁶Elenuis, ⁴⁷ceithri ⁴⁸meic ⁴⁹lais, ⁵⁰.i.
Romanus, Frangcus, ⁵¹Britus, Albanus. · Is ⁵²hē in
tAlbanus sin ⁵³rogab ⁵⁴Albain ⁵⁵ar ⁵⁶tūs ⁵⁷cona ⁵⁸chloind,
⁊ is ⁵⁹ūad ⁶⁰ainmnigther ⁶¹Albu : ⁶²co ro indarb ⁶³a
⁶⁴brāthair ⁶⁵tar Muir ⁶⁶nIcht, ⁶⁷conad ūad Albanaich
leatha Hoidia.·

99. ¹Magoc ²mac ³Iathfed, ·is ⁴dia ⁵chloind-⁶sen na
⁷tūatha ⁸tāncadar ⁹in ¹⁰Ērinn ¹¹‡ ar tūs ‖ ¹²rīa
¹³nGāeidelaib, .i. ¹⁴Parrthalōn mac Sera meic Srū meic

---

98. ¹⁻¹ om. β¹² : Greacus m. Iafet, &c., β   ² uadh β   ³ mhoir β
⁴ bheg β   ⁵ Halaxandreach β   ⁶ Iafeth β   ⁷ Easpain β
⁸ Iafeth β   ⁹ mhac β⁰¹²   ¹⁰ leis β¹²   ¹¹ Eamot β¹²   ¹² om. β¹²
¹³⁻¹³ uadh finidh thuaisciort in domhain β uatha fine tuaitsciort (-ths- β²)
in domhuin β¹²   ¹⁴ Iobat β¹²   ¹⁵ mhac β⁰¹²   ¹⁶ leis β¹²
¹⁷ Boidhbh β⁰¹²   ¹⁸ om. M Boidhbh β⁰¹²   ¹⁹ dar β¹²   ²⁰ Dothe β
Tote β¹²   ²¹ mhac β¹²   ²² Dothe β Dote β¹²   ²³ mic β¹²
²⁴ leis β¹   ²⁵ Armen β⁰¹²   ²⁶ Armen M β¹²   ²⁷ dono β om. β¹²
²⁸ cuïg mic β¹²   ²⁹ leis β¹   ³⁰ om. .i. β¹²   ³¹ Gotus β⁰¹²   ³² om. M
³³ -gotus M β⁰¹²   ³⁴ -ntus M β⁰¹²   ³⁵ -bh- β Longabairdus β¹²
³⁶ Negua β⁰¹²   ³⁷ om. β⁰¹²   ³⁸ mic β¹²   ³⁹ lais β⁰²   ⁴⁰ om· .i. β⁰¹
⁴¹ Sacsus β¹²   ⁴² Boairus β¹²   ⁴³ om. β¹²   ⁴⁴ in yc M: an β¹²

murder against his brethren, he made three four-sided columns, one of lime, one of clay, and one of wax. And he wrote upon them the histories of the [antediluvian] age, so that they should endure after the Flood. The columns of lime and of clay were destroyed, and the column of wax remained: and this it was that related the histories of the Age before the Flood, and it survives thereafter.

Oliuana his [Iafeth's] wife, it is she who first fashioned raiment after the Flood.

98. Grecus s. Iafeth, of him is Graecia Magna and Graecia Parva and Alexandrian Greece.   Espanus s. Iafeth, from whom are the Hispani.   Gomer s. Iafeth had two sons, Emoth and Ibath.   Emoth, of him is the northern people of the world.   Ibath had two sons, Bodb and Baath.   Bodb, who had a son Dohe.   Elenus s. Dohe had three sons, Airmen, Negua, Isicon.   As for Airmen, he had five sons, Gutus, Cebidus, Uiligothus, Burgundus, Longbardus.   Negua moreover had three sons, Saxus, Boarus, Uandalus. Isicon moreover, one of the three sons of Elenus, had four sons, Romanus, Francus, Britus, Albanus.   This is that Albanus who first took Alban, he and his children, and of him is Alba named: so he drove his brother across the sea of Icht, and from him are the Albanians of Latium of Italy.

99. Magog son of Iafeth, of his children are the peoples who came into Ireland at first before the Gaedil, namely Partholon s. Sera s. Sru s. Esru s.

---

⁴⁵ tres β thres β¹²   ⁴⁶ Heloni β⁰¹²   ⁴⁷ cethri β⁰ ceithre β¹²
⁴⁸ mic β¹²   ⁴⁹ leis β   ⁵⁰ om. β⁰¹²   ⁵¹ Briotus β¹²   ⁵² e an β⁰¹²
⁵³ roghabh β⁰¹²   ⁵⁴ -uin β¹²   ⁵⁵ air β¹²   ⁵⁶ ttus β   ⁵⁷ gonadh β¹²
⁵⁸ cloind M chloinn β⁰¹²   ⁵⁹ uadha β uadh β¹²   ⁶⁰ -ghthair β
-ghther β¹²   ⁶¹ Alba β¹²   ⁶² gor iondairb β gur hionarbadh β¹²
(-airb- β²)   ⁶³ ins. Britus β Briotus β¹²   ⁶⁴ bhr- β⁰¹²   ⁶⁵ tair β²
⁶⁶ nIocht β²   ⁶⁷ gonadh uaidh Albanaigh β⁰¹² (conadh β⁰)

99. ¹ Magoth β Magog β¹²   ² mhac β¹²   ³ Iafeth β Iaphet β¹²
⁴ da β¹²   ⁵ chloinn β⁰¹²   ⁶ sin β¹²   ⁷ tuathadh β¹²   ⁸ thangadair β
tangadar β¹²   ⁹ an β⁰¹²   ¹⁰ Eirinn β¹²   ¹¹ om. β⁰¹²
¹² re β¹³   ¹³ nGaedhealaibh β nGaoidhil β¹²   ¹⁴⁻¹⁴ om. β⁰¹²

[19]Easrū meic Gāeidil Glais meic Niūil meic Fēiniusa Farrsaig meic Bathatha meic Magog meic Iathfeth meic Nae : no[14] [15]Parrthalon mac [16]Sera [17]meic [18]Srū meic [19]Easrū meic [20]Pramint meic [21]Aitheachda meic [22]Magoth meic [23]Iathfeth[24, 25]. Ocus [26]Neimead mac [27]Adnoimin meic [28]Phaim meic Thait meic [29]Seara meic Srū [30]meic Easrū, ⁊rl.[30]. [31]Ocus Clanda Nemid, [32].i. [33]Galeōin ⁊ Fir [34]Bolc ⁊ Fir [35]Domnand ⁊ [36]Tūatha Dē Danand.

[37]Ocus fineada Cloindi Beothaig meic Iarmuineōil Fatha meic Neimid, .i. Tūatha Taiden ⁊ Domnannaig dia roibi Conall Cruachain, ⁊ Clanda Umoir, ⁊ Cruithnich na Cruachna, ⁊ aicmeada Slebi Uiri, dia rabadar na riga, .i. Tindi mac Conrach ⁊ Mac Cecht ⁊ Fir Chraibi, dia roibi Tindi mac Conrach, ⁊ Eochaid Dala. Ocus airmid eolaig corob d'iarsma na fineadach sin Clanna Morna ⁊ sentuatha Condacht olchena.[37]

100. [1]Conad do na gabāil sin Parrthalōin ⁊ Nemid, ⁊ do genelaigib na tūath sin olchena[1], do chanad so—

Magog mac an Iafeth . . . .

[2]Scuirem do chlannaib Nāe ⁊ dia n-imthechtaib. Adfēdsam do chlannaib Gāeidil bodesta ⁊ dia n-imtechtaib ⁊ dia ngabhālaib.[2]

Miniugad Gabal nErenn.

These two paragraphs are all that represents § I in Min.

μΛ 25 γ 40   μR 90 δ 14

101. Mīniugudh Gabal nĒrenn, ⁊ a [1]senchais, ⁊ a rēmend [2]rīgraidi, annso sīs, [3]⁊ ethre i mbēolo aissneisen, ⁊ labra ōg [4]dondni remunn, ō [5]thosuch [6]in libair [7]anūas co tici [8]so, *ut [9]dicit historia.* Hybernia

---

[15] Partholon β Pairrthalon β[12]: mhac β[12]   [16] Searra β Serra β[12]
[17] mhic β[12] (*hic et semper*)   [18] Sruth β[12]   [19] Esru β[012]   [20] Braimint β Framint β[12]   [21]Eachachta β[012]   [22] Magog β[12]   [23] Iafeth β Iaphet β[12]   [24] mc Seara mc Sru *ins. and erased* β   [25] *ins.* mic Naoi β[1] mic Noe β[12]   [26] Neimheadh β is uaid (uadh β[2]) Neimhedh mhac β[12]   [27] Aghnomain β[012] (mh β[12])   [28] Paimm. Tait β[012]   [29] Sera β[12]   [30-30] *om.* β[012]   [31] ⁊ Clann Neimeadh β ⁊ is o Neimedh β[12]   [32] ⁊ M

Gaidel Glas s. Nel s. Feinius Farsaid s. Bathath s. Magog s. Iafeth s. Noe : or Partholon s. Sera s. Sru s. Esru s. Brament s. Aithechda s. Magog s. Iafeth. And Nemed s. Agnomain s. Pamp s. Tat s. Sera s. Sru s. Esru &c.   And the progeny of Nemed, to wit the Galeoin, the Fir Bolg, the Fir Domnann, and the Tuatha De Danann.

And the families of the progeny of Bethach s. Iarbonel *Fáith* s. Nemed, i.e. the Tuatha Taiden and the Domnannaig, of whom was Conall of Cruachu, and the progeny of Umor, and the Cruithne of Cruacha, and septs of Sliab Fuirri of whom were the kings i.e. Tinde s. Conri, and Mac Cecht, and the Fir Chraibi, of whom was Tinde s. Conri and Eochu Dula.   And learned men reckon that of the relics of these families were the Clanna Morna and the old populations of Connachta in general.

100. So that of the said Takings of Partholon and of Nemed, and of the genealogies of those peoples in general, was this sung—

Poem no. IV.

We shall leave off from the progeny of Noe and their adventures.   We shall tell now of the progeny of Gaeidel and of their adventures and their Takings.

----

101. An explanation of the Takings of Ireland, and of her history, and of her royal roll, here below; and a recapitulation of the narratives, and a clear statement of the matter before us, from the beginning

om. β[12]   [33] Gaileoin β   [34] Bolg β Bholg β[12]   [35] Domhnaind β Domhuann β[12]   [36] Tuat β[2]   [37-37] *om.* β[012]

100. [1-1] *om.* β[012] amhuil asbeart in fili β, do reir in ḟile β[12]   [2-2] *not in* M

101. *This and the following matter down to the poem* Gāedel Glas ōtait Gāedil *missing from* μV. *The text of the missing portion printed from* μ[A], *with variations from* μR *unless otherwise stated.*   [1] séanchas   [2] -raide innso   [3] ⁊ ethre *om.* μ[A]: ambeolu aisneisin μR   [4] duinn remund μ[A]   [5] -ach   [6] ind   [7] *om.*   [8] indso   [9] dicunt

insola [10]possita est in occidente; sicut [11]Ade Paradisus
in australi plaga orientis [12]poissitus est, ita Hibernia
in [13]septimprionali parte, apud [14]occasum sita est.
Sic similes [15]sunt natura humi[16], sicut similes sunt
ambo locis in orbe: quoniam sicut absque bestia
Paradisus est, ita periti Hiberniam non habere
serpentem uel leonem uel ranam uel murem nocentem
uel draconem uel [17]scorpium uel [18]unum noxium
animal nisi [19]lupum tantum testantur. Hibernia ergo
dicitur 'insola [20]occasus.' 'Hyberoc' Grece, 'occasum'
[21]dicitur Latine; 'nia' autem uel [22]'nyon' Grece,
[23]'insola' Latine dicitur. ‡ [24]Hybernia autem proxima
[25]Britanie insola: [26]spacone[a] terrarum angustior, sed
[27]situ fecundior. Hoc[b] ab Affrico in Boriam
porrigitur, cuius partes priores in Hiberniam,[c] ‡' id
est in [28]Espaniam ||' et Cantabricum Occianum
intendunt; unde et Hibernia dicta. Scotia[d] autem
dicta, quia a Scotorum gentibus colitur. Illic nulla
[29]anguis, auis rara, apes[e] nulla: adeo, ‡' non sic in
hoc tempore ||', ut aduectos inde [30]pulueris[f] [31]seu
lapillos, si quis alibi sparserit inter apiaria,[g]
examina fauos deserunt ||. ‡ Scoti autem [32]a Scota,
filia regis [33]Egipti Pharaonis, sunt dicti, que [34]fuit
[55]Nelii uxor. ‡' [36]Phoeni autem a Foenio [37]Fariseo
dicuntur ||'. [38]Scoti autem idem et Picti, a picto
[39]corpore, ‡' quasi [40]scissi ||', eo quod [41]aculeis ferreis
cum atramento variarum figurarum [42]stigmate
adnotentur ||. [43]Heriu [44]dono ab [45]heroibus nominata
est. [46]‡ Sudet qui legit ‡.

historici   [10]poisita   [11]Adae   [12]poisitus   [13]septim trionaili
[14]occassum, the first c sprs. yc μR   [15]om.   [16]ins. sunt   [17]scorpiam:
-puim corrected later μ∧   [18]unam   [19]lupam   [20]occassus   [21]dicunt
[22]nyaon   [23]innsola (Latine sprs. yc μR)   [24]Hibernia   [25]Britaniae,
the t sprs. yc μR   [26]spacō μ∧ spatio μR   [27]sutu   [28]Hispaniam
[29]angis   [30]pulueres   [31]seuo lapilos μ∧   [32]nearly a whole line
of writing, probably written in error, erased here.   [33]Aegipti Faraonis
[34]fuit sprs. yc μR   [35]Neli ux(or sprs. yc. μR)   [36]Foeni   [37]Faisiseo μ∧
[38]Scotiorum μ∧   [39]corpoire   [40]scisi   [41]acules ferres μ∧ aculeis
feraeis μR   [42]stimate   [43]Heri μ∧ Hereo μR   [44]dana   [45]h-ioribus μ∧

of the foregoing book down to this, *ut dicit historia.*
The island of Ireland is situated in the west; as the
Paradise of Adam is situated on the southern coast of
the east, so Ireland is in the northern portion, toward
the west.   Those lands are as similar by nature, as
they are similar by their positions on the earth: for
as Paradise hath no noxious beast, so the learned
testify that Ireland hath no serpent, lion, toad,
injurious rat, dragon, scorpion, nor any hurtful beast,
save only the wolf.   And so Ireland is called "the
island of the west": "Hyberoc"[h] in Greek is called
"occasum" in Latin; 'nia' or 'nyon' in Greek is
called "insula" in Latin.   [Now Hibernia is next to
the island of Britannia: in extent of territory it is
narrower, but in soil it is more fertile.   This stretches
northward from Africa, and its foremost parts tend
toward Iberia, { that is, Spain } and the Bay of
Biscay; whence also Hibernia takes its name.   It is
called Scotia also, because it is inhabited by the nations
of the Scots.   Within it is no serpent, rare bird,
nor bees; to such an extent—{ not at this time } —
that if anyone were to scatter in any place amongst
beehives dust or gravel carried from thence, the
swarms would desert the honeycombs.]   [The Scoti
are named from Scota, daughter of Pharao King of
Egypt, who was wife of Nelius : { They are called Feni
from Fenius Farsaid {.   The Scots are the same as
the Picts, so called from their painted body, { as
though *scissi{*, inasmuch as they are marked with an
impression of a variety of devices by means of iron
needles and ink.]   Moreover the country is called
Ēriu from the heroes.   [Let him who readeth
perspire !]

---

⁴⁶ this is a gloss, marginal in μ∧ *expressed by initials* s.q.l. *in* μR, s.q¹.
l;. *in* μ∧

(a) Read *spatio.*   (b) Read *haec.*
(c) Read *Hiberiam,* and omit the preceding *in.*
(d) Read *Scotia autem, quia ab Scotorum gentibus colitur, appellata.*
(e) Read *apis.*   (f) Read *pulueres.*   (g) Read *aluearia.*
(h) The final *c* must be read as a Greek *sigma*: 'hyberoc' is meant for
ἕσπεοος. as 'n on' for νῆσον, accusative of νῆσος.

102. Ō [1]thrib macaib [2]Nōi trā ro līnait trī [3]ranna in talman, .i. Eorpa, [4]Affricca, Assia. Sem mac, [5]Nōe dana rogab [6]ind Aissia, ꝛ secht cenēla fichit [7]ūad innti. Cam in [8]Affraicc ꝛ tricha [9]cenēl ūadh [10]inte. [11]Iafeth [12]mac Nōi [13]ind Eoraip ꝛ [14]in tūaiscert Aissia, [15]ꝛ cōic [16]cenēla dēc [17]ūad intib : *de quibus hoc* [18]*carmen,*

Sem rogab i n-Aisia n-ait . . .
Tricha mac mīn monar nglē . . .

O Iafeth dana in t-airter-[19]thūascert [20].i. Scithecda ꝛ Armenndai, ꝛ lucht na [21]Hassia Bicce ꝛ ergabāla ꝛ [22]ciniuda nEorpa uile, co lucht na [23]n-indsi atāit frie aness ꝛ atūaidh ꝛ anīar, [24]ꝛ ōthā Slēibe [25]Riphi atūaidh co [26]trāigh na Hespāine. Ocht meic [27]trā la Iafeth, [28].i. Magoth—ba sē [29]in t-ochtmadh mac. Dā mac [30]dono la [31]Magoch .i. [32]Ibadh ꝛ Baath. Ō [33]Ibadh īarom rīg Romān. Mac dono [34]do Baadh, Fēnius [35]Farrsaid ō [36]fuilet Scithecda, ꝛ [37]dia sīl Gāidil. Ō Ibad [38]Fraincc, Romāin, Saxain, ꝛ Brettain ꝛ Albandai. Ō Magoch mac Iafeth [39]didiu, na tūatha rogabsat Ērinn rīa [40]nGāidelaib, .i. [41]Parthalōn mac [42]Sera meic Srū meic Esru meic [43]Briamin meic Fathecht meic [44]Baaidh meic [45]Magoch meic Iafeth meic Nōe : Nemed mac [46]Adhnomain dana meic Phaim meic Thait meic [47]Sera meic Srū : ꝛ clanna [48]Nemhid, .i. Gaileōin ꝛ Fir [49]Bolgc ꝛ Fir Domnann. *De quibus* [50]Finntan *cecinit,*

Magog mac an Iafeth.

---

102. [1] tri   [2] Noe   [3] randa an   [4] ꝛ Africa ꝛ Assia   [5] Nae tra [6] in Assia   [7] uada innte   [8] Affraic   [9] gēn uada   [10] *om.*   [11] Iafedh μᴧ [12] *om.* mac Noi   [13] in Eoraip   [14] *om.* in   [15] *om.* ꝛ   [16] gn̄ *in* both MSS.   [17] uada inntib   [18] cairmen   [19] tuaisc-   [20] *om.* .i. : Scithecdai ꝛ Armendai   [21] Haisia Bice   [22] cineda na Heorpa uili : ciniuda *miswritten* cinuida μᴧ, *and a dash put over the first stroke of the u to correct the error*   [23] ninnsi tainait fria anes ꝛ atuaith

102. Now of the three sons of Noe were filled the three divisions of the earth, Europe, Africa, Asia. Sem s. Noe settled in Asia, and twenty-seven nations were descended from him therein. Ham in Africa, and thirty nations from him therein. Iafeth s. Noe in Europe and in the north of Asia, and fifteen nations from him therein: *de quibus hoc carmen,*

Poem no. II.
Poem no. III.

From Iafeth is the north east, Scythians, Armenians, and the people of Asia Minor, and the colonists and nations of all Europe, with the people of the islands that are over against it from the south, north, and west, and from the Riphean Mountain out of the north to the shore of Spain. Iafeth had eight sons, one of whom was Magog: he was the eighth son. Magog had two sons, Ibath and Baath. From Ibath afterwards came the rulers of the Romans. Baath had a son Fenius Farsaid, from whom are the Scythians: of his seed is Gaedil. From Ibath are the Franks, Romans, Saxons, Britons, and Albanians. From Magog son of Iafeth are the peoples who took Ireland before the Gaedil, Partholon s. Sera s. Sru s. Esru s. Braiment s. Aithech s. Baath s. Magog s. Iafeth s. Noe: Nemed s. Agnomain s. Paim s. Tait s. Sera s. Sru: and the progeny of Nemed, the Gaileoin, the Fir Bolg, and the Fir Domnann. *De quibus* Finntan *cecinit,*

Poem no. IV.

---

[24] *om.* ꝛ   [25] Ripe atuaid   [26] traig (g *sprs. yc* μR) na Haespaine   [27] *om.* tra la   [28] ꝛ Magoch   [29] an tochtmad (*om.* mac)   [30] *om.* dono   [31] Bmagoc   [32] Baad ꝛ Ibad   [33] Ibad   [34] da Baad   [35] Farsaich   [36] fuil   [37] *ins.* is   [38] Frainc ꝛ Romain ꝛ S. ꝛ Bretain ꝛ Albanda   [39] *om.* didiu   [40] nGaidil- *and om.* .i.: nGail- μ∧   [41] Partol-   [42] Soera   [43] Bramin   [44] Baaid   [45] Magoich   [46] Agnomain m. Paim m. Tait   [47] Sera m. Stera m. Stru   [48] Nemid   [49] Bolc   [50] hoc carmen dicitur Finntan *the last two words in marg.*

THE VERSE TEXTS OF SECTION I.

I.

R¹ ¶ 7 (L 1 β 8 : F 1 β 28).   R² ¶ 15 (V 1 γ 23 : E 1 β 38 :
P 1 β 32).   R³ ¶ 88 (β 34, 14 : β¹ 34 . 30 : β² 10 . 15 :
M 267 γ 47 : H 102 α 30).

1.   ¹Slūag nād ²chlōe ³cūa-chel,
⁴Nōe ⁵nīr ⁶bo ⁷niath-lēn,
⁸scēl ⁹co ¹⁰ngrāin ¹¹ro glēad gēr—
¹²Sēm, Cam ocus ¹³Iäfēth.

2.   ¹Mnā ²cen ³mīdend, ⁴mōr-ŕeba,   5
ōs dīlind ⁵cen ⁶dībada;
⁷Coba, ⁸brīgda ⁹in ¹⁰bāin-ela,
¹¹Olla, ¹²Oliua, Olīuana.

1. ¹ sluaig FR³ H sluagh V sluac̄c̄ P   ² claoi EP chle β⁰¹² clae MH
³ gua-chel LR² ecnad chel F conad chel M conadachel H   ⁴ *ins.*
ac M, ag H: Naoi E Nai P Nae MH   ⁵ níor β⁰¹²   ⁶ ba L bu V
bho β bhodh β¹²   ⁷ miad-len LR³ midathlen F niath-nel VE matha-ncl
P niadh-lén β⁰¹²   ⁸ sgel FE sc̄c̄ P sceal β⁰¹²   ⁹ ˙gan β¹²   ¹⁰ ngradh
VE ngrad P ghrádh β⁰¹²   ¹¹ ro gleaid F rongleath gen V ro˙glē gen
E rongleadh ˙gen P ro gleodhagh *and om.* ger β⁰¹²   ¹² S. is C. is I. F

II.

R¹ ¶ 8 (L 1 β 14 : F 1 γ 2).   Min ¶ 102 (μΛ 25 δ 23;
μ. R 91 α 23).   R³ ¶ 89 (β 34 . 29 : β¹ 34 . 47 : β² 10 . 29 :
M 267 δ 15 : H 102 α 39).

¹Sem ²rogab ³i ⁴n-Aisia n-ait;
⁵Cam ⁶cona ⁷chlaind ⁸sin ⁹Afraic;   10
¹⁰Iafeth uasal ¹¹is a ¹²maic,
¹³'siat rogabsat ¹⁴i n-Eoraip.

¹ Semh β   ² do˙gab F μΛ H rogab *dittographed* μR roghabh β⁰¹²
² rogob M   ³ ind μΛ an β H inn β¹²   ⁴ n-Assia L Aissia F μΛ β H
Asia μR β¹²   ⁵ Camh β   ⁶ gonadh β¹ .i. β²   ⁷ claind L clainn μR
cl- μΛ H cloinn β chloinn β¹ clann β² cloind M   ⁸ in μΛ μR san

THE VERSE TEXTS OF SECTION I.

I.

1. A host that a wintry death would not subdue,
   Noe, there was no hero's weakness,
   a story with horror has been made clear with
          keenness—
   Sem, Ham, and Iafeth.

2. Women without evil colour, great excellences,
   above the Flood without extinctions,
   Coba, vigorous was the white swan,
   Olla, Oliva, Olivana.

β⁰¹² H ¹³ Iafedh V Semh Camh (⅂ *yc*) Iatafen E Iaphet β¹² (*not* β) Iathfeth M

2. ¹mnaa L ²ccŏmtin̄ P, gen β gan β¹² can H ³mideng F midhen β mhidhen β¹² mīcing H ⁴moreua F morf̄eba V morf̄eabha E morfephai, P mór Ebha β níor Ebha β¹ nior obha β² moreba M moireaba H ⁵gan EP β⁰¹² can H ⁶diġbada VH dibhada β diobhadha β¹² ⁷Cobba L Cobha E β⁰¹² ⁸brighdha VP brigha β brioghdha β¹² brig H ⁹an H ¹⁰baneala FE banela V mbaineala E banealai P baneala β ben aladh β¹² ¹¹Ola *changed by re-inker to* Ollai, P ¹²Oliba Olibana L Olliua Oilibana E Olipa Olipā P Oliua Oliuana β Olliva Olivana β¹ Oilliua Olivana β² Oliba Olibana M Oliu Olibana H

II.

Sem settled in pleasant Asia;
Ham with his progeny in Africa;
noble Iafeth and his sons,
it is they who settled in Europe.

β⁰¹ H ann β² sa nAfraic M ⁹Affraicc L μ∧ Adffraic F Aifraic β¹ Aifric β² Afraicc H ¹⁰Iafiath F Iafedh μ∧ Iaphet β⁰¹ Iathfed M ¹¹*om.* is μR ¹²mc F, mcc μ∧ meic μR M mhac β⁰¹² ¹³is iad dogab sin F hite rotrebsat μ∧ ite rotrebsat μR is iad roghabhsat Eoraip β⁰¹² (roghabh in Euroip β⁰¹) is iad rogob an MH (doġab an H) ¹⁴sin Eoraip F: *om.* in μ∧

III.

R¹ ¶8 (*not traceable in* L : F 1 γ 10). Min ¶102 (μΛ 25 δ 25 ; μ R 91 a 25). R³ ¶ 92 (β 34 . 43 : β¹ 35 . 14 : β² 11 . 11 : M 267 δ 38 : H 102 β 19).

¹Tricha ²mac ³mīn, ⁴monar² ng̣lē,
⁵cinsit ō ⁶Cham ⁷mac ⁸Naē,
a ⁹secht ¹⁰fichit ¹¹fil ō ¹²Sēm,   15
¹³is a ¹⁴cōic dēc ō ¹⁵Iafēth.

¹ Triocha β triothchat β¹² (-ad β²)   ²⁻² cenel comul μΛ chenel
comol μR   ³ mind F   ⁴ is rad MH   ⁵ cinnsit F cinset μR β¹²

IV.

R¹ ¶ 10 (L *first two and half quatrains frayed away* 1 β 47 : F 1 δ 8). Min ¶ 102 (μΛ 25 δ 42 : μR 91 β 10). R³ ¶ 95, 100 (β 35 . 14 : β¹ 35 . 30 : β² 11 . 31 : M 268 a 35 : H 99 a 50).

1.   ¹Magog ²mac ’an ³Iafeth,
       ⁴atā cinnti a ⁵chland :
      ⁶dīb ⁷Parthalōn ⁸Banba,
      ⁹ro bo ¹⁰chadla a ¹¹band.   20

2.   Ba ¹dīb ²Nemed ³nōithech,
       mac ⁴Agnomain ⁵ōen :
      ⁶ba dīb ⁷Gand, ⁸dīb ⁹Genand,
      ¹⁰Sēngand, ¹¹Slāine ¹²sōer.

3.   ¹Cland ²Eladan ³imda,   25
      ⁴fa dīb ⁵Bres, ⁶can brēig :
      mac ⁷Eladan ⁸arm-gāith,
      ⁹meic ¹⁰Delbāith ¹¹meic ¹²Nēit.

1. ¹ Magoth LF Magoch Min Magoc MH   ² mhac β²
³ Iaphet β¹² Iathfeth MH (in ¶ 100)   ⁴ ata cinti F atascinnte μΛ
ataichinte μR ataithchinte β atait chinte β¹ tait cinte β² ad aithindti
M adaithinti H   ⁵ chlann F Min β¹ clann β⁰²   ⁶ *ins.* ropa μR :
dibh β diobh β¹²   ⁷ Parrtolonn F Parrthalon μΛ β¹² MH Partolon μR
Partaloin β   ⁸ Bannbha β Banbha β¹²   ⁹ do bo F ro po μΛ ro
ba μR do bu β⁰¹² do ba H   ¹⁰ chalma μΛ cadla μR acadla β¹²   ¹¹ bann
F Min bhand β bhann β¹²

2. ¹ dhibh β diobh β¹²   ² Nemid F μR H Nemedh μΛ Neimheadh
β⁰¹² Nemead M   ³ naethach F naitech μΛ noethech μR naetheach β⁰¹²
(-ach β¹²) noitheach M naideach H   ⁴ Agnumaid F Adnomain μΛ H

III.

Thirty sleek sons, a brilliant fact,
they sprang from Ham son of Noe,
twenty-seven who are from Sem,
and fifteen from Iafeth.

chinsiat β cinsed M cinnsed H 　　^{6} Cam μR 　　^{7} mcc $\mu_\wedge$ 　　^{8} Noe
$\mu_\wedge\mu$R β^{012} Naee H 　　^{9} ocht $\mu_\wedge\mu$R seacht H 　　^{10} fidhchet β^1 fidhet β^2
^{11} ar sin F uad o Sem $\mu_\wedge\mu$R (uadh $\mu_\wedge$) fuil β^{012} dib H 　　^{12} Sem β^{01} $\mu_\wedge$ M
^{13} om. is F $\mu_\wedge$ M in β^{012} H 　　^{14} .u. deg F dó déc μR cuig deag β cuig
deg β^{12} H cuic decc M 　　^{15} Iafedh $\mu_\wedge$ Iaphet β^1 Japhet β^2 Iatfedh M

IV.

1. 　　Magog son of Iafeth,
   there is certainty of his progeny :
   of them was Parthalon of Banba—
   decorous was his achievement.

2. 　　Of them was noble Nemed
   son of Agnomain, unique ;
   of them were Gand and Genand,
   Sengand, free Slaine.

3. 　　The numerous progeny of Elada,
   of them was Bres, no untruth :
   son of Elada expert in arms,
   son of Delbaeth son of Net.

Agnomhain β^{12} Agnomen M 　　^{5} aen F $\mu_\wedge$ ain β^{012} aein H 　　^{6} om. ba
dib μR : ba dhibh β ba diobh β^{12} 　　^{7} Gann F μR β^{12} 　　^{8} is $\mu_\wedge$ dibh β
diobh β^{12} 　　^{9} Genan F Genann $\mu_\wedge$ Gaenann μR Ganann β^{12} 　　^{10} Seangann
$\mu_\wedge$ Sengann μR M Seangand β H Sengan β^{12} 　　^{11} Slaigne β^1 Slaingne
β^2 Slaene M Slane H 　　^{12} saer F $\mu_\wedge$ MH saor β^{012}
　　3. ^{1} clann F β^{012} clanna μR clanda H 　　^{2} Eladhan F Ealadain
$\mu_\wedge$ β^1 M Elatha μR Ealadhain β^{02} 　　^{3} imdha $\mu_\wedge$ β iomdha β^{12} : om. μR
^{4} ba Min β^{012} H 　　^{5} Bress Min Breas β M 　　^{6} gan breicc $\mu_\wedge$ cen
breic μR gan bhreig β^{012} (br- β^2) cen breg M 　　^{7} Eladain $\mu_\wedge$ M
Elathain μR Eladhain β Ealadhain β^{12} 　　^{8} felgaith $\mu_\wedge$ -ghaith β^{12}
^{9} mhic β^{12} 　　^{10} Delbaeith μR Dealbhaidh β^{01} Dealbaith β^2 MH (-dh β^2)
^{11} mic β^{012} (mh- β^1) Neid FH β 　　^{12} Neitt $\mu_\wedge$

4.   ¹Meic ²Indai ³meic ⁴Alldai—
          ⁵Allda ⁶ba ⁷mac ⁸Tait,   30
        ⁹meic ¹⁰Thabuirn ¹¹meic ¹²Eno,
          ¹¹meic ¹³Baith, ¹⁴Ebaith ¹⁵ait.

5.   ¹Meic ²Bethaig, ³meic ⁴Iardain,
          ⁵meic ⁶Nemid ⁷hūi ⁸Phāim:
        ⁹Pāimp ¹⁰meic ¹¹Thait ¹²meic ¹³Sera   35
          ¹⁴meic ¹⁵Srū, ¹⁶Braimin ¹⁷bāin.¹⁵

6.   ¹Braimin ²meic ³Aithechta
          ⁴meic ⁵Magog, ⁶mōr ⁷blad,
        ⁸ro-bās a n-a ⁹n-aimsir
          ¹⁰comthaidbsin ¹¹ri ¹²Mag.   40

4. ¹ mac β⁰¹² ² Innui L Indui μ∧ Inndui μR India β¹² ³ mac β
mic β¹² ⁴ Alldui L μR Allai F μ∧ MH Alla β⁰¹² ⁵ Alldui L Min
Alli F Allai β MH Allaidh β¹² ⁶ fa MH ⁷ mc̄c̄ μ∧ ⁸ Taitt L μ∧
Taid β ⁹ mic β⁰¹² ¹⁰ Thabairnn F Tabuirn μ∧ Tabuirnn μR
Tabairn β⁰¹² Thabairn M ¹¹ mic β mhic β¹² (bis) ¹² sic LF
Ceno Min, Enna β H Eanna β¹² Enda M ¹³ Baath L β¹² Baaith μ∧ β
MH Baaid μR ¹⁴ ins. meic L Min MH, mic β mhic β¹²: Ebath L
Ebaid F Ibaith μ∧ Magoich μR Ebhaith β Eabhaith β¹² ¹⁵ aitt L
μ∧ H Baaith μR

5. ¹ om. meic Min; mac β mhic β¹² ² Beothaig FM Bethach Min,
Beothaigh β⁰² Beothagh β¹ ³ ins. ba Min; mac Min mic β⁰¹²
⁴ Iarbaneoil μ∧ Iarboneol μR Iarbhoneoil β Iarbonel β² -boneil M
-boinel H ⁵ mic β⁰¹² (mh- β¹) ⁶ Neimid FM Neimhidh β
Neimhed β¹ -mhedh β² ⁷ hó L o F hua μ∧ ua βⁿ¹² hu M ⁸ Paimp
LF Paim μR M Phaimp β Poimp β¹² ⁹ Paim L (yc in marg.), also
μ∧ MH Paimp β Poimp β¹² ¹⁰ mac β⁰¹² (mh- β¹) ¹¹ Thaitt L

V.

R² ¶ 19 (V 1 δ 9 : E 1 γ 21 : P 2 a 13 : D *from quatrain*
10, 3 a 1). R³ ¶ 86 (M 267 a 1 : H 101 a 36). *Also collated,*
copy in Book of Ui Maine (U) 38 a 24.

1.   ¹Athair ²cāich, ³Coimsid ⁴Nime,
          ⁵in Rī ⁶ūasal ⁷ainglige,
        ār ⁸Cuingid, ār ⁹Coimde, ār ¹⁰Cend
          ¹¹cen ¹²tūs, cen crīch, cen ¹³forcend.

1. ¹ atair U ² chaich M caith U ³ coimsidh (*the second* i
and the dot of the d *due to re-inker*) P coimsich M coimsig H ⁴ nimi

4.   S. Inda, s. Allda—
      Allda who was s. Tat,
      s. Tabarn s. Enda,
      s. Baath, [son of] pleasant Ibath.

5.   S. Bethach s. Iardan
      s. Nemed grandson of Paimp:
      Pamp s. Tat s. Sera
      s. Sru s. white Braiment.

6.   Of Braiment s. Aithecht,
      s. Magog, great in renown:
      there happened in their time
      a joint appearance against a Plain.

Tait F μR β^{12} H Taitt $\mu_\wedge$ Taid β $\qquad$ ^{12} mic β^{012} $\qquad$ ^{13} Sera M
Seara β H Serra β^{12} $\qquad$ ^{14} om. meic $\mu_\wedge$: mac β mic β^{12} $\qquad$ $^{15\text{-}15}$ Easru
ain β^2 $\qquad$ ^{16} ins. meic L μR M H, mac β: Bimbfind F Esru Min H
Easra β Easru M $\qquad$ ^{17} briaim $\mu_\wedge$ ain MH.

6. ^{1} ins. mac β mic β^{12} meic MH: Braimid F Briamin $\mu_\wedge$ Briamain
μR Braimint β Fraimint β^1 Froimint β^2 Praimint MH $\qquad$ ^{2} ins. ba
F Min: mac F Min β, mic β^{12}: ba mac dittographed, μR $\qquad$ ^{3} Fattecht
L Aithichta F Fathecht $\mu_\wedge$ Baaith μR Eachachda β^{012} (-dha β) Eachada M
^{4} mac β mhic β^1 mic β^2 $\qquad$ ^{5} Magoth LF β Magoch Min Magoc MH
^{6} ins. ba L: moir β $\qquad$ ^{7} ins. a β^{012}: bladh $\mu_\wedge$ β^{02} blath β^1 $\qquad$ ^{8} robasa
nanamsir L ro bassa riana [i expuncted] naimsir μR ro pass ria naimsir
$\mu_\wedge$ ro ba sona a naimsir β^{012} (sona in naimsear β); do FM, da bas ina
H ina also M $\qquad$ ^{9} om. n- FM (amsir F) $\qquad$ ^{10} comthadbsin L comthaibsin
F co taidhbsin ria mag $\mu_\wedge$ oca taibsin dar mag μR com thaibhsen β gon
dubh sin a reimed β^{12} comthaibsib M comtaib (with sin sprs. yc) H
^{11} re F R^3 $\qquad$ ^{12} Magh β

V.

1.   Father of all, Master of Heaven,
      the noble angelic King,
      our Champion, our Lord, our Head,
      without beginning, end, or termination.

HU $\qquad$ ^{5} mac maith Muire ingine M an ri H $\qquad$ ^{6} uassal E $\qquad$ ^{7} -de E
-ghe P -dhi H -ghi U $\qquad$ ^{8} cuindigh V, cuinnidh E cuinge (written over
and defacing another word) P cuingidh U $\qquad$ ^{9} coimdhi V, -dhe E
-gi M -di H coimsid U $\qquad$ ^{10} cenn M ceand U $\qquad$ ^{11} gan PU, can H
(throughout the line) $\qquad$ ^{12} tuis E $\qquad$ ^{13} foircenn P foircenn M
forceand U

2.　¹Ferr nā ²cach rī ³in ⁴Rī ⁵raith　　　　45
　　　⁶lasndernad ⁷in ⁸maiss mōr-maith,
　　　⁹grāda ¹⁰Nime, ¹¹cāem in cloth,
　　　¹²arāen ¹³issin ¹⁴cēt Domnoch.

3.　¹Delbais secht ²nime ³sin Lūan,
　　　sin Mairt muir, ⁴talum ⁵tond-būan ;　　50
　　　⁶sin ⁷Chētain, ⁸esca is ⁹grēin ¹⁰nglē ;
　　　¹¹neōil ¹²is eōin ¹³Dia ¹⁴Dardāine.

4.　Duine ¹ro ²delbad īarsin,
　　　³debrad ! ⁴isin ⁵n-Āenditin,—
　　　⁶tucad, ⁷etir ⁸chois is ⁹cend,　　　55
　　　¹⁰assin ¹¹doman ¹²cāem ¹³coitchend.

5.　　　¹Gniomrad in ²tseisedh ³laoi lāin,
　　　　　⁴aisneidfed dūibh sin ⁵deg-dāil,
　　　　　anmann' in talman, thīar tair,
　　　　　an deilb ⁶n-ill-dathaig 'nAdhaim.　　60

6.　¹Cend ²Adaim ³airdirc co ⁴hōg
　　　⁵tucad a tir maith Malōn :
　　　⁶is ⁷tairis ⁸tēgaid amach
　　　⁹srotha ¹⁰Parrduis ¹¹co ¹²bladach.

7.　¹Bruinde ²ind ³īir ⁴Harōin ⁵aird,　　65
　　　⁶a ⁷bru a ⁸Baibiloin ⁹bith-gairg,
　　　a ¹⁰chossa a ¹¹Labain ¹²lēr-blā,
　　　a ¹³sliasta ¹⁴a tīr ¹⁵Gogoma.

2. ¹maraid dogres MU (-raigh U), fear H　　²gach EP　　³an P
⁴rig MU　　⁵rath U　　⁶lassnernadh V lasndernadh E lasandernad
PU (written over another word P) lasnderna MH (-san- M)　　⁷an H
⁸mais EPM om. U　　⁹gradha VPU　　¹⁰nimi EU　　¹¹coemda cloth
VEP (caemda E caomdha P), caem a cloth HU　　¹²maraen EMHU
araon P　　¹³isin E isin PHU isa M　　¹⁴chet E cedomnach H
domnach PU
　　3. ¹dealbais PMH　　²nimi HU　　³sind VE isin P san H
⁴talom E, -am MH　　⁵tonn- VEPH　　⁶sa VH san P　　⁷cet- PU
chedain M　　⁸escca P　　⁹griam VEPMHU　　¹⁰n- om. VEHU
¹¹neoill MH niuil EU. In U written over something else, apparently
nuiil　　¹² ┐ M　　¹³om. dia MU　　¹⁴-aeine E -aoine P diard- MU
　　4. ¹ra H　　²dealbad EMH dhealbadh P　　³debradh EP dearbad
M deadbrad U　　⁴isind E isa M isan H　　⁵aoindidin E n-aoine didin
P aendidin HU naindidin M　　⁶tucadh V tugadh EU tuccad P
⁷itir EMH　　⁸cois EPU　　⁹cheand M chend H ceand U　　¹⁰asin
E (the a yc E) isin PMU issin H　　¹¹domhan E domun MH
¹²chaem VMH caom EP (-mh P) caem U　　¹³coitchenn VEP choitchenn
H choitchend M choitceand U

2.   Better than every King is the King of Grace
          by whom was made the great excellent world-stuff,
          the orders of Heaven, fair the fame,
          together on the first Sunday.

3.   He formed the seven heavens on the Monday,
          on the Tuesday sea, earth with enduring surface;
          on the Wednesday, moon and bright sun;
          clouds and birds on Thursday.

4.   Man, who was formed thereafter,
          Debrad! on the Friday,—
          he was taken, from foot to head,
          out of the fair common earth.

5. The works of the full sixth day
   I shall relate to you in (this) good company;
   [I shall tell of] the beasts of the earth, west and east,
   of the form of Adam, rich in colour.

6.   The head of renowned Adam perfectly
          was taken from the good land of Malon:
          through which go forth
          the rivers of Paradise famously.

7.   The breast of the man from lofty Aron,
          his belly from ever-fierce Babylon,
          his legs from Laban, a conspicuous land,
          his thighs from the country of Gogoma.

5. *this quatrain in* EP *only*: *printed as in* E, *these variants from*
P: [1]gnimrad   [2]-sed   [3]lai   [4]aisneidhfit   [5]deghaill
[6]nillath-   [7]nAdhuim

6. [1]tucad (tugudh U) cend (ceand U) Adaim co hog ‖ a fearand
(-und U) molfach (molbthach U) Malon (Molon U) MU: ceand H
[2]Adhaim E, Aduim P   [3]oirdaircc V airrdeirc E airrdirc P airrdhirc
H (*the mark of lenition scratched out*)   [4]hogh PH   [5]tucadh P
[6]om. U   [7]*the is sprs. yc* E   [8]tec(ad) V tecaid MH tegait U
[9]srotha V (*the a yc* V) srota P   [10]Parrthais V Parduis E Partais P
Parrthuis H Parrthais U   [11]go E   [12]bhladhach P blatach U

7. [1]bruinne E bruindi PHMU   [2]an MH in U   [3]fir EPU
[4]Haron EH Haraib M Hardon U   [5]ard EU *also* H, *but an i sbs.*
yc H   [6]a *sbs. yc* E   [7]pru P   [8]Biblon E Lotain M Babilon U
[9]-garg EU lan-gairg M   [10]cosa E lama MU   [11]Laban EMHU
[12]leir mbla E leir bla H erbla U   [13]sliasda E: chosa M, lama H
cosa U   [14]i U   [15]Goghoma V Gagoma E Gogomah- (no Gomaa
sec. man. in marg.) P Gomaa M Gouma H Gogama U

8.   Trī ¹trāth ²d'Adum ³cen ⁴anmain
        ⁵īar n-a ⁶chruthugud ⁷do ⁸talmain;   70
        ⁹ardāig ¹⁰Fir ¹¹do ¹²baī trī trāth
        ¹³cen ¹⁴anmain n̄-a ¹⁵churp ¹⁶chāem-gnāth.

9.   ¹Triar ²ro ³chruthaig a ⁴chorp ⁵cāin
        ⁶īar ⁷n-ērge dō n-a ⁸bethaid,
        ⁹allus ¹⁰d'usce, ¹¹ba dia deōin,¹¹   75´
        ¹²tess ¹³tened, ¹⁴tinfed ¹⁵āeoir.

10.   ¹Adaig ²Adaim fīal ³in ⁴feth
        sair ⁵ar ⁶slēib ⁷Parrduis ⁸Partech;
        ⁹ro ¹⁰altuig ¹¹ḟaicsin ¹²grēine
        ¹³tar(a) mullach ¹⁴in mōr-¹⁵sleibe.   80

11.   ¹Adraim, adraim ²thusa, a ³Dē!—
        ⁴is ē ⁵cēt-guth ⁶do ⁷rāid ⁸sē:
        ⁹ac ḟaicsin ¹⁰Eua ¹¹āine,
        ¹²and ¹³dorigne ¹⁴a ¹⁵chet-gāire.

12.   ¹A chēt-imthecht, ²cāine guis   85
        ³co ⁴tobar ⁵Pairtech ⁶Parrduis:
        a ⁷chēt-rith, ⁸rem ⁹co ndaithe,
        do ¹⁰dechsain na ¹¹hēnlaithe.

8. ¹ thrath VMH tra U   ² d'Adamh E d'Adam M d'Adham U
³ gan EPU   ⁴ anmuin H   ⁵ ar U   ⁶ cruth E chruthad P
cruthadh U chruthugud M: *other* MSS. *have* cruth-   ⁷ don M ar HU
⁸ *ins.* trom EP: thal- E talmhuin P   ⁹ -igh EPU   ¹⁰ fir PU
¹¹ ro VEP da U   ¹² baoi E boi P bhi U   ¹³ gan EPU can H
¹⁴ anmuin PH   ¹⁵ corp E chorp H   ¹⁶ caomhgnath E caomgnath P
chaemnar M chaemngnath H comgnath U
    9. ¹ ceathrar M   ² *om.* ro M; do H dar U   ³ cruth- E
cruthaidchi M cruthaidh H cruthad U   ⁴ corp EPU chuirp M
⁵ choin M   ⁶ ar U   ⁷ n-erghi V neirge dho E neirge do P
nergi M neirgi HU   ⁸ bethaigh V beathoid M bhethaid HU
⁹ *ins.* a U   ¹⁰ dusqi E duisqe P is uisqi M duisqi H   ¹¹⁻¹¹ fodein
M badeoid U   ¹² tes VEMH teass P teas U   ¹³ tenidh V teinfedh E
tineth P tinedh H tenead U   ¹⁴ tinfedh V teinfedh E tinfeadh U
¹⁵ aieoir P aiger M: *the* e *written over another letter* H
    10. ¹ aiged EH acc P aidheadh U   ² Adhaim EU Adaimh P
³ a EHU   ⁴ feith P   ⁵ fri VEPH   ⁶ Sliab VEP (bh EP)
MHU   ⁷ -dhuis E -tais P -dais M -thuis H dhais U   ⁸ pairtech E
ftach P partiach U   ⁹ ra H   ¹⁰ atlaig E alt- P altaig MH
failtigh U .   ¹¹ *ins.* ag EP: aigsin E aicsin P faisci U   ¹² grene

8.	Three days had Adam without life
	after his formation from earth;
	because of a Man who was three days
	without life in His ever-fair body.

9.	There were Three Persons who formed his fair
		body
	after he arose alive;
	sweat from water, it was with his good will,
	heat of fire, breath of air.

10.	The night of Adam, generous the repose,
	eastward upon Pairtech Mountain of Paradise;
	he welcomed the sight of the sun
	over the top of the great mountain.

11.	I adore, I adore Thee, O God!—
	this was the first word that he uttered:
	When he saw noble Eve,
	then he made his first laugh.

12.	His first walk—beauty of strength—
	to the Spring of Partech of Paradise:
	his first race, a course with swiftness, ·
	to see the birds.

VMH greini P in ngreni U　　　　[13] dar VEDUH do M　　　[14] an EPH
[15] sleibhe E slebe DM sleiphe P slebi H sleibi U

11. [1] adram adraim E adhrum adhrum U　　　[2] tu VEPMU tusa D
thusu H　　　[3] Dhe, *lenition mark faded* D　　　[4] hiss̄ V iss̄ ED hise P
is H　　　[5] toisech VEPD ced guth M toiseach H　　　[6] ro DU　　　[7] raidh EU
[8] še E　　　[9] hic aiscin VD ic aisgin E ac faicsin PM hic aicsin H ig
faigsin U　　　[10] Ebha E Eba M　　　[11] ane V ainee E aille M ailli HU
[12] ann DH　　　[13] dorinde E dorindi M dorine H dorighni U　　　[14] in D
[15] ced EDH ched PM: gairi H

12. [1] chetna V ched EM ced P: imtecht EP imdhecht U　　　[2] caine
guiss V cain aguis M caini uiss H lith gan geis U　　　[3] go DU
[4] topur VE top- PDH tobor U　　　[5] prech PD -each V paitrech EH
pairtiach M parrtiach U　 ＼　　　[6] partuis V parrdais E pairtais P
parduis D parrthuis H parrthais U　　　[7] ced E cheit D ched PM
[8] rem VDM reim EP ceim U　　　[9] condaithi D co ndaite P conaichi M
conaithi H condhaithe U　　·　　　[10] descain E dechsinn P descuin D
decain U　　　[11] haenlaithe P -laithi D henlaithi MH

(a) Here D begins.

13. ¹Cōic ²lā ³dēc, ⁴nī ⁵lūad ⁶sāeb,
d'⁷Adam is d'⁸Eua ⁹marāen,   90
co ¹⁰toracht ¹¹demon ¹²donīm
¹³dia ¹⁴saigid ¹⁵i ¹⁶nĀenditin.

14. ¹Delb ²nathrach, corp ³āeoir ⁴sēim
⁵tuc ⁶leis ⁷diabul ⁸sin ⁹droich-rēim :
¹⁰litri ¹¹trias ¹²ro chan, nī ¹³as līach,   95
¹⁴Iae, Uau, Iae ꝛ Īath.

15. ¹Atā ²sund ³in ⁴fāth—⁵rofess—
ar a n-⁶apar : Clē ⁷sech ⁸dess :
⁹ar ¹⁰is ī ¹¹in ¹²lām ¹³chlē chrom
¹⁴ro ¹⁵riged ¹⁶cosin ¹⁷uboll.   100

16. Īar ¹n-imarbus ²dōib—nīr ³dlecht—
⁴ro ⁵laite ⁶i tīr ⁷n-aird ⁸nĒgept :
⁹remes ¹⁰trī ¹¹mīs ¹²īarsin maidm
¹³rusbiath ¹⁴rusēit ¹⁵ind āen-phailm.

17. ¹Ro ²coimpred ³Cāin, ⁴nīr chīan ;   105
⁵ro ⁶coimpred, ⁷rucad ⁸Abīal ;
do Chāin ⁹chrīn ¹⁰in ¹¹cachta,
¹²ro len ¹³gnīm na ¹⁴mallachta.

13. ¹ coig EP cuig H   ² laithe VE laithi PDH   ³ deg EHU
⁴ nocho M; *ins.* is U   ⁵ luadh EP luag M slicht U   ⁶ saobh E
saob P saebh U   ⁷ Adum VH Adhum EU   ⁸ Ebha E Eba PD
Eu H   ⁹ -aon EP -oen D   ¹⁰ torracht EP tanic U   ¹¹ demun VH
deaman E demhan P deman M   ¹² do nimh E do nim *other* MSS.
Perhaps to be read do[g]nīm   ¹³ da mellad MU   ¹⁴ saighid V
saicc P soig D : *om.* MU   ¹⁵ ind D san MH isin U   ¹⁶ aondidin E
aoinedittin P oendidin D aindidin M aendidin HU
14. ¹ dealb EPH dealbh U   ² natr- EPH   ³ aer U   ⁴ eim
VH śeim ED seimh P em M emh U   ⁵ tug E   ⁶ les D
⁷ demin M diabal H demon U   ⁸ co MH tre U   ⁹ droch-reim VE
drochmen P droichrem D ndrochmen M ndrochmein H drochmein U
¹⁰ littri V   ¹¹ tria ro can E triarrochan D trias archan M resar
chan U   ¹² ra H   ¹³ is MU   ¹⁴ Ia Ae Uau ꝛ Aiath MSS.; *except*
Ainath P, ia uau ꝛ en iach M iae, uau, iaiath U
15. ¹ is he sin MU (e U)   ² sunn EPD   ³ an H   ⁴ fat U
⁵ ro-fes ED ro-feass P ro feas M ra-fess H rotfeas U   ⁶ apur V
abartar E apartar P abar MU   ⁷ seach MUH   ⁸ des EHU deas
PM thes D   ⁹ air P ardaig MHU (-gh U)   ¹⁰ issi VP as i E is hi M
¹¹ an EPH   ¹² lamh EP laam D   ¹³ chle crom VH : cle chrom E

13.   Fifteen days, it is no idle tale,
had Adam and Eve together,
till a demon of misdeeds (?)
reached them, on a Friday.

14.   The form of a serpent, a body of thin air,
the devil took to himself on the evil course:
the letters through which he made incantation—a
wretched affair—
were *He, Vav, He,* and *Yodh.*

15.   There is the reason—it is familiar—
why men say "Left beyond right":
because it is the crooked left hand
that was stretched to the apple.

16.   After they had sinned—it was not lawful—
they were cast into the lofty land of Egypt:
A space of three months after the transgression
the one palm-tree fed and clothed them.

17.   Cain was conceived, it was not long;
Abel was conceived and brought to birth;
to withered Cain of the shackle
the deed of the curse adhered.

cle crom PU (crum P) chrom chle *written first and then corrected* D
[14] do MH da U   [15] righed P righeadh U [11]   [16] cossin V cosind E
gusin PU cosa nuball H   [17] ubhall E nup, *expanded in marg. in
later hand* nubhuill P ubaoll D uball M ubull U
16. [1] ninarbus U   [2] do P doibh U: *two letters (apparently* do)
erased after this word H   [3] drecht H   [4] ra H   [5] laithi VD
laiti P late M laitea U   [6] a MH   [7] nairdd V nard EHU
[8] nEighept V nEigept EH nEigep (*sic*) P Egeptt D   [9] remiss V
remis E reimeas P remess D   [10] tri miss *om. in text and ins. by
late corrector in marg.* V   [11] mhis U   [12] triasin V re sin H
[13] rossbiath V rosbiath EU   [14] roset E rosneit V rusneith P
rusneid H roseith *the mark of lenition erased* U   [15] in VEMU an
PH aon pailm E aonpa *with* ilm *added by corr. in marg.* P oen pailm
D naen-pailm M aen-phailm H aen-pailm UE
17. [1] ra H   [2] choimp- D coimpread M coimbread U   [3] Chain D
[4] nir cian D ni chel M ni cel U   [5] rucad ro coimpread M: ra H:
7 ru coimbread Abel U   [6] coimpredh V com- E   [7] rucadh VE ruccad P
rugad D   [8] Aibial D Aibel M Abel U   [9] crin EPHU crich M
[10] an H   [11] cachtai P chachta DMH   [12] roglen ED dolen M ralen
H ronlen U   [13] gnimh E   [14] mallachtai D

18.   [1]Lotar d'[2]id([a])pairt dā [3]reithe
        [4]Abēl, Cāin [5]nīr [6]chleithe;   110
        [7]nochor indraic [8]leis in Rīg
        [9]in [10]idpairt [11]ruc [12]leis [13]Cāin.

19.   [1]Tāinic rath [2]ruithne [3]Rīg [4]grīan
        [5]forsin [6]idpairt [7]ruc [8]Aibīal :
        [9]dē ro [10]līn [11]formad [12]is [13]ferg   115
        Cāin colach na [14]clāen-cherd.

20.   ([b])[1]Rogaib [2]Cāin n-a [3]lāim [4]luind
        [5]lecain [6]cintaig [7]in [8]chamuill :
        [9]co Haibēl [10]lēim [11]co [12]luindi,
        [13]conid [14]ro [15]marb [16]d'āen-[17]builli.   120

21.   [1]Tuc [2]Seth a [3]lāim re [4]lecain
        [5]ac faicsin fola [6]in [7]phecaid :
        [8]'sē ṡin [9]in fer [10]cen [11]urchra
        arar [12]fās in [13]chēt-ulcha.

22.   [1]Adberait [2]rind na [3]heōlaig,   125
        lucht [4]in [5]ēcnai il-[6]cheōlaig,
        nach [7]īāsait ṇa [8]clocha ō [9]chēin—
        [10]ō'n lō [11]rosfer fuil [12]Aibēil.

---

18. [1] Lodar HU   [2] idbairt E edbairt U   [3] rethe D reithi H
[4] Aibeil MH Anel U   [5] ni MH gam U   [6] chlethe D cleite E
chleithi P cleithi H clethe U   [7] nocho ro gab ri na rig DE (gaib D)
nochar gab ri na rig P noar gab ri na rig M nochor indraicc lasin ri H
nocho rogab in rig rel U   [8] lassin V   [9] ind VE inn P   [10] idpart
E idbairt PD eadbairt U   [11] rucc P rug M   [12] leiss V lais P
[13] Caen U
    19. [1] tanic VU tanuig D tanig H   [2] ruithni VPDH ruitni E
ruithin M ruithen U   [3] righ VE ri H rigrian U   [4] nel M   [5] for
ind VDM forand E forin P foran H ar an U   [6] edpairt VDH iopairt
(sic) E inpairt P idbairt U : reithi M   [7] rug ED   [8] Abial VPDH
Aibel M Abel U   [9] om. de M   [10] lion E   [11] formud V format PU
[12] ┐ M   [13] fearg VMU ferrcc P   [14] claen-redhg V claon-cerd E
-redhg (no claoin-cerd in marg.) P -redg D -cheard M -cealg U
    20. [1] -gabh PU -gob M ragab H   [2] Caidin P   [3] laimh EP
[4] luinn E : luind om. and sprs. cD   [5] leca M lecca U   [6] cintaich VD
-taigh E chinntach P chintach M chintaig H   [7] an PH   [8] chamhaill
E camaill P chamuill H camhaill U   [9] co Habial VEH co Hab. P

18. They went to offer two rams,
Abel, Cain who was not noble;
the King did not consider worthy
the offering which Cain brought with him.

19. There came the grace of the brilliance of the
King of Suns
upon the offering which Abel brought:
thence did envy and anger fill
sinful Cain of the crooked crafts.

20. Cain took in his savage hand
the guilty jaw-bone of the camel;
to Abel he leapt with violence,
so that he slew him with a blow.

21. Seth set his hand to the jaw-bone,
on seeing the blood of the sin:
he is the man without deficiency
upon whom the first beard grew.

22. The learned tell us,
the people of wisdom of manifold melody,
that from a long time the stones grow not—,
from the day when Abel's blood suffused them.

go Haibial D go Habial H co Hauel U   [10] lem DHU   [11] go DU
[12] luinde VEP luinne D luindhi U   [13] conadh EP -ad MHU   [14] ra H
[15] mharb EH marbh PU   [16] do en V d'aon E d'en PH d'oen D
[17] buille VED bhuilli P bulle U

21. *This quatrain is here in* EP, *follows no.* 32 *in* M, *and is absent
from all the other* MSS.   [1] tig E   [2] Seith EP   [3] lamh EP lam M
[4] *ins.* a E   [5] ar bfaigsin E ag faigsin P   [6] an P   [7] pec. E pecaig M
[8] sin fen (fein P) in fer (fear M) PM   [9] an E   [10] gan E can M:
in P *another word has been re-inked into* can   [11] urcra MSS.   [12] fas P
[13] ced-ulcai E cet-ulchai P

22. [1] atberait VU adberad E atberuit D adbearaid MH   [2] rinn PD
[3] -aigh VU   [4] ind VD an EPH na MU   [5] egna E egno (*written* egl-)
P ecna DH heagna M hegna U   [6] ceolaigh E ceol- P.hil-cheolaich D
-cheolaich M -checlaigh U   [7] hassait V na hasad E asait P assuitt
D nach fasaid M hassaid H fasait U   [8] cloca U   [9] cein P chen
M chein, *the* i *expuncted* U   [10] o rusben riu M o da ben riu U
[11] rosben ED   [12] Abel VU Abeil PH

(a) *s*[2] M here.   (b) *s*[1] M here resumes.

23. ¹Rogabsat ²secht ³ccnuic ⁴īar sain
     ⁵for ⁶Cāin, ⁷īarsin ⁸fingail;   130
     ⁹cnoc ¹⁰cechtar a ¹¹dā ¹²chos ¹³cain,
     ¹⁴is dā ¹⁵chnoc ¹⁶for a ¹⁷lāmaib.

24. ¹Cnoc ²ina ³ētan, ⁴mo nūar,
     is ⁵cnoc ⁶cechtar a dā ⁷grūad :
     ⁸tar ⁹chnoc ¹⁰a ētain, ¹¹ro-¹²līach,   135
     ¹²in ¹³t-uball ¹⁴tarlaic ¹⁵Laimiach.

25. ¹Laimīach ²dīgamus ³cen ⁴gāi
     is ⁵ē cēt-ḟer ⁶thuc ⁷dā ⁸mnāi :
     ⁹leis ¹⁰dorochair ¹¹Cāin ¹²crom
     ¹³dia ¹⁴tarlaic ¹⁵fair in ¹⁶uboll.   140

26. Dā mac ¹Laimīach, ²lāechda a ³mbrīg,
     Iubal ⁴is ⁵Tubalchāin :
     Iubal fuair ⁶cruit in ⁷cara,
     ⁸Tubalchāin ⁹in cēt-¹⁰goba.

27. ¹Edpairt ²Abēil, mar ³adclos   145
     ⁴rucad ⁵dia ⁶ēis ⁷i ⁸Parrdos;
     ⁹is ē ¹⁰sin ¹¹in ¹²rethe ¹³rān
     ¹⁴tucad ¹⁵dar ¹⁶cenn mac ¹⁷nApram.

23. ¹-sad VEMH ragab- H   ² seacht M   ³ cnuicc V cnuic
EPDMH cnuich U   ⁴ -sin EMPU -soin D   ⁵ ar MU   ⁶ Chain VMH
Caidhin P   ⁷ isin EH iarsan P tresin U   ⁸ iarsindinguil,
with ḟ *yc above the* d D bhfingail P ḟingail H fingal U   ⁹ cnocc VH
¹⁰ chechtar M cecthar U   ¹¹ dha VEU   ¹² choss V chos E cos PU
¹³ choin M chain H   ¹⁴ ⁊ EDMU   ¹⁵ cnoc EPU   ¹⁶ na EDM
ar a U   ¹⁷ lamhaibh VE lamhaiph P
     24. ¹ cnocc VH   ² ara M   ³ edan EMHU   ⁴ munuar V ·
monnuar E manuar UM   ⁵ cnocc H   ⁶ ceachtar M   ⁷ gruadh VEPU
⁸ dar VEPH ar U   ⁹ cnoc VEDUM chnocc P cnocc H   ¹⁰ an edain E
ind etuin D in edain M a ēdain HU   ¹¹ ra H   ¹² liadh E liad D
¹² a E an H   ¹³ tubull V tubhall EP turchur U   ¹⁴ tarluic D ro
thelg M ra thilg H ro theilg U   ¹⁵ Laimhḟiach E Laimfiach P *marg.*
Lamiach DU
     25. ¹ Lamiach VEU Laimfiach P   ² dighamuiss D diamus M
bigamus U   ³ gan PD can H: co mbrig U   ⁴ goe E gaoi P
⁵ he cet fer V cet fer *also* E: fear M   ⁶ tuc VPU tucc E tug D thug H
⁷ dia E   ⁸ mnaoi P   ⁹ lais VEPH les U   ¹⁰ adrochair M

23. After that seven wens took hold
upon Cain, after the kin-murder :
a wen [upon] each of his fair feet,
and two wens upon his hands.

24. A wen in his forehead, alas,
and a wen [upon] each of his cheeks :
through the wen of his forehead, very
wretched !
[went] the apple which Lamech cast.

25. Lamech the two-spoused, without falsehood,
he is the first man who took two wives :
by him did crooked Cain fall,
after he cast the apple upon him.

26. The two sons of Lamech, valiant their
strength,
Iubal and Tubalcain :
Iubal invented harps of music (?),
Tubalcain was the first smith.

27. The offering of Abel, as it hath been heard,
was taken after him into Paradise ;
that is the very splendid ram
which was given in place of the sons (*sic*)
of Abram.

adrocair U   [11] Caidhin P   [12] cromm E crum P   [13] ar arde
arlaig in tubull U   [14] tarlaicc E -luig D -laig H   [15] aire D
[16] ind ubull E ubhull P tuboll D tuball M dub. H

26. [1] Lamiach EU Laimh- P   [2] laocdha P loechda D laech co
mbrig M laechdha U   [3] mbrigh VEPDU   [4] *sic* EU, ⁊ *all other* MSS.
[5] Tupcai P (*bis*) Tubalchoein D Tubalcain U   [6] chruit D   [7] charae
E carui P   [8] Tubalcain (*a stroke through the stem of the* b) U
[9] *om.* E, an HP   [10] gaba VDHU gabae E gabhadh P

27. [1] hedp- E eadhp- P hedb- PD edb- M eadb- U   [2] Aibeil DH
Aibel M Abhel U   [3] atcloss V adcloss E atclos PD daclos M doclos HU
[4] rucadn V ruccad E rucad P rugad DU   [5] da MU .   [6] hes V ess
D es U   [7] hi VEPD a HU   [8] Pardos VD Pardoss E Parrtos H
Parrtus HU   [9] *ins.* ⁊ U : is hessin V isse P hise D : hessin (*om.* is) H
[10] *om.* sin U   [11] an PH   [12] reithe EP reithi MH   [13] rain H
[14] tucadh V tuccad EP tugad D   [15] ar M tar HU   [16] cend EHU
[17] nAbram VDPM Abram (*om.* n-) EU, nApraim H

28. ¹Crocenn ²ind ³rethe sin rīam
     ⁴riacht ⁵d'Abrām īar ⁶nAbīal: 150
     ⁷itches ⁸im Crīst ⁹cen ¹⁰chinaid,
     ¹¹ic ¹²fosaic ¹³dīa ¹⁴desciplaib.

29. Daisia fa sead ainm ¹in chroind
     co ²torad n-imda n-āloind,
     ³a Muig Aron a ⁴Parrdus—   155
     dīa ⁵ndernad ⁶in ⁷t-imarbus.

30. ¹A hocht cethrachat ²nōi cēt
     is ³mīle, nī ⁴himarbrēcc,
     ō rē ⁵ind ⁶Adaim ⁷chētna ⁸cain
     ⁹co ¹⁰Haprām, ¹¹cossin ¹²n-athair.   160

31. ¹Tricha ²nōi cēt ³bliadan ⁴mbān
     ⁵sāegal ⁶Adaim ⁷ria imrād:
     deich ⁸mbliadan, ⁹risin ¹⁰uile,
     ¹¹sāegal ¹²a mnā ¹³mong-buide.

32. ¹Sāegal ²Seith ³is eōl ⁴dam ⁵sin   165
     a ⁶cūig dēc ar ⁷nōi ⁸cētaibh:
     ⁹cūig bliadna ¹⁰nōi cēt ro ¹¹clos
     no ¹²co ¹³rug ¹⁴in ¹⁵t-ēc ¹⁶Enos.

28. ¹crocand V croccann E croicenn PM crocann D crocend H
croicend U   ² in EMU an PH   ³ reithe V reithi EMHP rethi D
rithi U   ⁴ doriacht VEPDH do ruacht M aructh U   ⁵ om. d' U
⁶ nAip- P nAibeil M nAbhel U   ⁷ atches VPU itchess EM hitchess D
atces P itcheas M adces H   ⁸ an P am MH   ⁹ gan P cin D can
MH om. U   ¹⁰ cinaid D dar cabair U   ¹¹ hic osaicc, with f sprs.
cD ig P do M   ¹² fossaicc E asaic M asaigh U   ¹³ da U
¹⁴ deisciplaib E disgiplaib (in marg. absdalab) P apsdalaib M deiscep. H
aptalaib U

29. this quatrain om. VEDHU   ¹ an croinn P   ² dtor. nimdha P
³ amuigh P   ⁴ Parrtos P   ⁵ -adh P   ⁶ am P   ⁷ -bhas, in
marg. timarbus P

30. ¹ a hocht ceathrachad cem [cein?] glan, | mili ar noe cedaib
bliadan, | o re Abraim chedna chain, | co Hadam, cus in athair M
² noe V nai ced H   ³ mili HU   ⁴ -breg D himirbreg HU   ⁵ inn P
an H in U   ⁶ Adhaim VEU Adaimh P Adauim D   ⁷ cetna VH

28. The hide formerly of that ram
    came to Abram after Abel :
    it was seen about Christ without fault
    as He washed for His disciples.

29. Daisia, that was the name of the tree
    with much and beautiful fruit,
    in the Plain of Aron in Paradise—
    for which the sin was committed.

30. Eight and forty, nine hundreds
    and a thousand, it is no fiction,
    from the time of that same fair Adam
    to Abram, to the father.

31. Thirty and nine hundred clear years
    was the life of Adam with its fame;
    ten years, with all of those,
    was the life of his yellow-haired wife.

32. The life of Seth, I have that knowledge,
    fifteen over nine hundreds :
    five years and nine hundred, it was heard,
    until death took Enos.

---

chetnai E cedna P   ⁸ chain ED ˙   ⁹ go D gu U   ¹⁰ Habram EU
¹¹ cós in EP gussin D cusan H gusin U   ¹² om. n- EDUH : athair E
athauir D

31. ¹ trica U   ² noe M nai U   ³ -ain P mbliadan U   ⁴ om. m-
MH   ⁵ saogh⁼ P saedhal (no g written sec. man. above the d)
D soegul U   ⁶ Aduim D Adhaim U   ⁷ ria imradh EP re imrad
MH re imrath U   ⁸ -dh- H   ⁹ riss sin V rissin EDH iarsin U
¹⁰ huile D mile H ule H uili U   ¹¹ saogh- P soegal D saegul U
¹² Eua U   ¹³ buidhe VE budi H bhuidhe U

32. ¹ saocc- P soegul U   ² Seth EDMU   ³ as H   ⁴ damh VP
⁵ sain V soin ˙D   ⁶ do MU   ⁷ se DM   ⁸ cettaib E cetaip P
cetauibh D   ⁹ cuic VM se EP   ¹⁰ nochad V nochat ED .lxxxx. at P
noe cet M   ¹¹ closs VP chloss E : ra clos H   ¹² go DU cho H
¹³ ruc VMHU   ¹⁴ an PH   ¹⁵ teg VEPDMH tec U   ¹⁶ Enoss VE

33.·   Deich ¹mbliadan ²nōi cēt, ³cen crāid,
        ⁴āes meic ⁵Enosa, ⁶Caināin :   170
        ⁷nōi ⁸cēt ⁹acht ¹⁰a cūic, ¹¹co ¹²mblaid,
        ¹³sāegal ¹⁴Malaleith mōr-¹⁵glain.

34.   ¹Cūic ²bliadna ³sescat, ⁴nōi ⁵cēt
        ⁶do Iareth ⁷rīa ⁸ndul ⁹i n-ēc :.
        ¹⁰trī ¹¹chēt sescat ¹²a ¹³cūic ro ¹⁴clos   175
        d'¹⁵Enōc ¹⁶rīa ¹⁷ndul ¹⁸i ¹⁹Parrtos.

35.   ¹Ochtmoga ²bliadan ³co mblaid
        ocus ⁴nōi ⁵cēt do ⁶bliadnaib—
        ⁷is ē sin ⁸in ⁹sāegal ¹⁰seng
        ¹¹tucad do ¹²Mathasalem.   180

36.   ¹Sāegal ²Laimīach, ³lūaiter ⁴lat,
        ⁵secht cēt ⁶a ⁷cūic ⁸sechtmogat :
        ⁹sāegal ¹⁰Nōe, ¹¹nōeb a ¹²blad,
        ¹³caeca ar ¹⁴nōi ¹⁵cētaib ¹⁶bliadan.

37.   Trī meic ¹d'Adam ²ca mbāi ³cland—   185
        Seth, ⁴Sile, Cāin ⁵clāen-cam :
        a ⁶teora mnā, ⁷būadach ⁸brīg !
        Olla, ⁹Pip, ⅂ ¹⁰Pithīp.

---

33. *This quatrain om.* U   ¹ mbliadna P   ² lxxxxat c̄c̄ cradh P nai
cet M nochat *other MSS.*   ³ cen crad VEDH (*in* E *an open* a
resembling u) co ngrain M.   ⁴ *ins.* a V : aess VED aois P   ⁵ Enois
VP Enos ED   ⁶ Chainean V Cain ean P Cainan D Cainean (*the* i *and
second* a *sbscr. apparently in a slightly different ink*) H   ⁷ nai M
⁸ cett E   ⁹ ach H   ¹⁰ *om.* a MH   ¹¹ *ins.* bliadna MH : ar *for*
co MH   ¹² mblaidh V bloid M blaid H   ¹³ saoghal P   ¹⁴ Malaleth
VED Malaleit P Malalel M   ¹⁵ gloin D

34. ¹ coic VED coig P da M decc U   ² mbl. U   ³ sesca M
⁴ *ins.* is : nai M   ⁵ cett E   ⁶ d'Iareth U   ⁷ re MHU   ⁸ dul P
ndol D nul H   ⁹ adecc V a dh- P adec ineg D a dec M a deg H
aneg U   ¹⁰ sesca tri cet U   ¹¹ cet VM   ¹² *om.* a E   ¹³ coic VD
coicc E coig P *om. and* cuig *ins. in bad hand in marg.* U   ¹⁴ closs VE
¹⁵ Enocc ED Enogh P Enog H   ¹⁶ re MHU   ¹⁷ ndol D   ¹⁸ hi VPD a H
¹⁹ Parrthoss V Pardoss ED Parrthos P Parrdus M Parrthus H Parrtus U

35. ¹ -gha EP sechtmogha MU   ² -ain P   ³ *com* mblaid V : co
mblaidh U   ⁴ noe V   ⁵ cett E   ⁶ -aip P   ⁷ is he sin E hisse

33.   Ten years and nine hundred, without vexation
the age of the son of Enos, Cainan;
nine hundred save five, with renown,
the life of Malaleth great and pure.

34.   Sixty five years, nine hundred
to Iareth before going to death:
three hundred sixty and five was it heard
to Enoch before going into Paradise.

35.   Eighty years with fame
and nine hundreds of years—
that is the stately life
which was given to Mathusalem.

36.   The life of Lamech, to you is it mentioned,
seven hundred, five and seventy:
the life of Noe, holy his renown,
fifty over nine hundreds of years.

37.   Adam had three sons who had progeny—
Seth, Sile, Cain perverse and crooked:
their three wives, victorious strength!
were Olla, Pip and Pithip.

---

sin D ^{8} an H ^{9} saog- P -gul U ^{10} seang U ^{11} tuccadh E
tugad PD tugadh U ^{12} Mathasaileam VH Matha Salem EP (*the
second* m *dotted sec. man.* P) Mathusalem D

36. ^{1} saoghal P saeghal U ^{2} Lamiach VU Lamech ED ^{3} luater U
^{4} latt P leat U ^{5} seacht M ^{6} seacht mbliadna caecad M secht
mbliadna trichat U(*a*) ^{7} coic VED coig H ^{8} -moghad V -moghat E
-mogad H ^{9} saoghal P soegul P ^{10} Naoi P Naee MH ^{11} naeb V
naobdha P niamda MHU (-dha U) ^{12} bladh VDU ^{13} coica D
^{14} nai M ^{15} cettuip E cetuib D cetaibh U ^{16} -dhan P

37. ^{1} *om.* d' MU: Adum VH Adham E Adaum D Adaim M
Adhaimb U ^{2} coa mbae E ga mbaoi P coamboi D ga mbi U
^{3} clann D ^{4} Sili H ^{5} claon P cloen D: cham VDU chamm E
^{6} dteor P tri MHU ^{7} buadhach VU ^{8} brigh VPD a mbrigh
EU a mbrig MH ^{9} Pib U ^{10} Pithib EDMU Pitib P

(*a*) *In marg. of* U: seacht moghat seacht ccet is e so airemh is firianigh do
reir an biobla.

38.   Trī meic ¹Nōe nair ²cech ³neirt,
⁴Sem, ⁵Cam, ⁶Iafet ⁷aurdairc :   190
is ⁸re ⁹C'am, ¹⁰calad ¹¹cīape,
¹²ro ¹³scarad ¹⁴ind ¹⁵airdrīge.

39.   ¹Cata ²Rechta ³ba ben ⁴Sem,
Cata ⁵Chasta ben ⁶Iafeth,
Cata ⁷Flauia, ⁸co ⁹ngrād ¹⁰ngrinn,   195
ainm mnā ¹¹Caim, ¹²nocho ¹³celim.

40.   ¹Cam ²ro gab ³i ⁴nAffraicc n-ait,
⁵Iafeth ⁶rogab ⁷i ⁸nEoraip ;
nī ⁹chelar ¹⁰duinne, dar Dīa !—
Sem ¹¹rogab ¹²uile ¹³i ¹⁴nAisīa.   200

41.   ¹Tricha ²cined, ³rād ⁴nglan nglē
⁵cinsit ⁶ō Cham mac Noē :
a ⁷secht fichit, fuil ⁸ō ⁹Sem,
¹⁰a cūic dēc ō Iafeth.

42.   ¹I ²Slēib ³Radruip ⁴aided ⁵Sēim ;   205
⁶bās ⁷Iafeth ⁸i ⁹Slēib ¹⁰Armēin ;
¹¹i ¹²Slēib ¹³Raphan, ¹⁴rād ¹⁵nglan nglē,
¹⁶ro-thatham Cam ¹⁷meic ¹⁸Noē.

38. *This quatrain om.* M   ¹ Nai P Nae HU   ² gach PU cē D cen H
³ nert U   ⁴ Seim·P Semh U   ⁵ Cham ED Camh PU   ⁶ *ins.* is U :
Iafeth PU   ⁷ aurd'airce E oirrdirc P airdirc HU   ⁸ is ria
VPH his ro Cam ED   ⁹ Camh· U   ¹⁰ caladh VEU   ¹¹ ciabe EH cipe P
cebe U   ¹² do H   ¹³ scaradh VU sgarad P   ¹⁴ int D an H in U
¹⁵ ardrighe E n-airdrighe P ard- D
    39. ¹ Catirasta U   ² Reacht H   ³ fa bean M   ⁴ tSem V
tSeim P tSeim H Semh U   ⁵ Casta EDHU Gasta P   ⁶ Iafedh V
Iafet P Iathfed M   ⁷ Flaia M Flagia H   ⁸ go U   ⁹ ngradh VPU
ngrain M   ¹⁰ ngrind VPHU grind E   ¹¹ Cam P   ¹² nocha PDH
¹³ ceilimm E chelim D ceilim PU
    40. ¹ Camh P   ² ragab H rogabh U   ³ ind VP inn E an H
⁴ *om.* n VP : Affraic P Athfraic M Affraich U   ⁵ Iathfed M   ⁶ dogab H
rogabh U   ⁷ inn V ind P an H   ⁸ nEoruiph E   ⁹ cel ar P chel ar
duine D chel arduin U   ¹⁰ duini H duine *all other* MSS. *except* U
¹¹ rogob M ragab H   ¹² huile D uili MHU   ¹³ inn VE an H
¹⁴ Aissia VH Assia EDU
    41. This quatrain *om.* VDU ; follows quatrain 21 in E.   In M the
quatrains in this part of the poem are in the following order :—37, 40,

38.   Three sons of noble Noe, of every [kind of]
        strength
    Sem, Ham, glorious Iafeth:
    from Ham, for all his firmness,
    the high-kingship was sundered.

39.   Cata Rechta, she was the wife of Sem,
    Cata Casta, the wife of Iafeth,
    Cata Flavia, with pleasant love,
    was the name of Ham's wife, I conceal it not.

40.   Ham settled in pleasant Africa,
    Iaphet settled in Europe;
    it is not hidden from us, before God!—
    Sem settled altogether in Asia.

41.   Thirty races, a pure, clear saying,
    sprang from Ham son of Noe:
    twenty seven, which are from Sem,
    fifteen from Iafeth.

42.   In the mountain of Radrap the fate of Sem;
    the death of Iafeth in a mountain of Armenia;
    in the mountain of Rafann, a pure, clear
        saying,
    the great sleep of Ham son of Noe.

41, 39, 42, omitting 38. [1] Fichi M   [2] cinedh E cineth P cinead M
[3] radh E   [4] glan gle EPM   [5] cinsed E -set P -sead M   [6] Cham m.
Naoie E; Naoie *also in* P, Naei M   [7] coic dec badar PM   [8] og PM
[9] Seimh EP   [10] a cuig deg o Iathfeth E Is a cuig dec ag
Iathafeit P is a undec at Iathfeth M. *The version of this quatrain in* H
is as follows:—
    Tricha cinedh Chaim colaig   cinnsed on fir can olaid,
    . a secht fichit fuil o Sem   a cuig deg ac Iatafet.

    42. [1] hi VEPD a MH   [2] sleip P sleb MU   [3] Radhruip P Rathuiris
M Radraip H Rathuir chain U   [4] aiged VH aidedh E aighed P
bas MU   [5] Sem EDMU Seimh P Ŝeim H   [6] bass E   [7] Iathfed M
[8] hi. P a H   [9] sleb EM sleab U   [10] Armen VM Armein U
[11] hi EPH   [12] sleb M sliab U   [13] Rapan V Rafan MH Rafin U
[14] radh VP   [15] raglan gle U glan gle VPMH glam ngle E   [16] ro hatham
V ro athtam ED (*in* D *changed sec. man. by writing* th *sprs. and
expuncting the 2nd* t) ro attham P ro ratham do ratham (*in rasura*) H
ro hathim U   [17] mc V mc E mac U   [18] *written* ixe P: Naei M Naee H

43.   ¹Airde ²hairce, ³baile ⁴itā
       ⁵tricha ⁶cubat ⁷cutroma ;   210
       trī chēt ⁸cubat ⁹i n-a ¹⁰fat ;
       ¹¹n-a lethet ¹²cōica ¹³cubat.

44.   ¹Ōen-²chubat ³'n-a ⁴tigi ⁵thair,
       ⁶itir ⁷fid ⁸is ⁹bidumain :
       ¹⁰bidumain ¹¹uimpi ¹²cen brōn,   215
       ¹³dīa 'muig ¹⁴ꓶ ¹⁵dīa ¹⁶medōn.

45.   A doras ¹assan ²sliss ³sōer,
       ⁴amail ⁵ro ordaig ⁶Noē ⁷nōem ;
       ⁸dāig ⁹ro oslaiced ¹⁰a tōeb ¹¹thair
       ¹²ār Crīst, ār ¹³Cenn, ār n-Athair.   220

46.   Trī ¹cōecait ²mīle co ³mbūaid
       ⁴airde ⁵Thuir ⁶noithig ⁷Nemrūaid,
       cāeca ⁸mīle ⁹tar ¹⁰cech ¹¹leth
       ¹²rogab ¹³in Tor ¹⁴trēn ¹⁵rīgthech.

47.   ¹Trī ²cethrair ³trī fichit, ⁴fīr,   225
       ⁵āirem ⁶thoisech ⁷is trēn-⁸rīg
       ⁹lasandernad ¹⁰thoir ¹¹in Tor,
       im ¹²Nemrūad, im ¹³Nabcodon.

43. ¹ airdi PMH arde na hairce fir trath U   ² *ins.* na M (*also in* H, *but erased*): aircce VE airce P airci D hairci MH   ³ baili ED bail H i fail tra M   ⁴ itha V itta P ta DH (*before the* t *an a faintly sbs.* cH   ⁵ caeca M   ⁶ cubad MH cubhat U   ⁷ cutruma VE cudruma PH cutramma ·D cudrama U   ⁸ cubad VM   ⁹ inna D ana H   ¹⁰ fad EMH   ¹¹ na leithe V leithed EPM na llethe D lethat U   ¹² coeca V coicca D caeca M   ¹³ cubad VM cubatat E cubaat (*sic* √D, *but in* D *copied like* cubattt) D

44. ¹ aon P aen HU   ² chubad M cubhat U   ³ ina natigi U (*the dittography caused by a change of line*)   ⁴ tighi VP tighe EP tige D   ⁵ tair PU thoir M   ⁶ etir V eitir EP   ⁷ fidh VP ïid EMH bi U   ⁸ ꓶ U   ⁹ bittummain E bidamuin MH bidomain U   ¹⁰ uitumain VP bittummain E bitumain D bidamain M bidomain U   ¹¹ impe E impi PM immpi D umpi U   ¹² gan EPU can H   ¹³ diamuigh VP diamuich ED imaig M immaigh U   ¹⁴ occus P   ¹⁵ ar MU   ¹⁶ medhon VU meton P.

45. ¹ ara PMH asa D ar U   ² slis EMHU slios PH   ³ saer VDMH saor P   ⁴ is amlaid E samlaid DHU   ⁵ ro ordaigh VE ro orduighl D rosordaigh U ra *for* ro *as usual in* H   ⁶ *om.* Noe ED (*ins. sec. man.* D) Naoi P Nae MH Nai U   ⁷ naem VMHU noeb ED naom P   ⁸ daigh VEP (*also perhaps* D, *but the mark of lenition*

43. The height of the ark, a place in which are
thirty balanced cubits;
three hundred cubits in its length;
in its breadth, fifty cubits.

44. One cubit in its thickness eastward,
what with wood and pitch:
pitch about it without regret (?),
outside and inside.

45. Its door out of its free side,
as holy Noe ordained;
for He would open its side eastward,
our Christ, our Head, our Father.

46. Thrice fifty miles with victory
was the height of the famous Tower of Nemrod;
fifty miles over every side
did the strong royal Tower contain.

47. Thrice four men and three score, truly,
the reckoning of leaders and strong kings
by whom the Tower was made in the East,
including Nemrod and Nabcodon.

faded) ardaigh U: co ros foslaic a taeb thair M   ⁹ roslaicedh V
roslaiced ED hosluiced P foscail H oslaicthi (om. ro) U   ¹⁰ om. a
VEP: taeb VD taobh P thaeb H taib U   ¹¹ tair HU   ¹² ar Crist
chaem ar ar n-athair M ar Cris (sic) uais ar innathair U   ¹³ cend EH

46. ¹ coecat V choicat E lᵃ P choica (with a d apparently following,
but erased) D chaecaid M   ² cubat EP mili U   ³ -dh EPU
⁴ ins. fa he M, ba he U: arddi E airdi MH   ⁵ tuir E in tuir MU
⁶ noithich VE noitᶜ P om. MU naithid H   ⁷ -dh E Neamruaid M
Neamrudid with attempt sec. man. to turn the first d to an a U   ⁸ mili
MH   ⁹ dar E for HU   ¹⁰ gach VEPDU cach MH   ¹¹ leath M
¹² rogob M dogab H -bh U   ¹³ an PH   ¹⁴ trenuilleach M   ¹⁵ rigtheach V
-tech PH righeach U

47. ¹ om. M   ² chetrair E cethruir P ceathrar M ceathrair HU
³ ar fichit instead of tri f. M: tri .xx. ficit fir (sic) U   ⁴ co M
⁵ dairim V dairem P airim EU   ⁶ tuissech V taoisech P toissech D
thaiseach M toisech H taiseach U   ⁷ in M   ⁸ ri E righ PU
⁹ lassandernadh V -adh also E -earn- M lasadngadh U   ¹⁰ tair VP
thoir (the lenition mark faded) D thair HU   ¹¹ an PH   ¹² -adh U
¹² Nabgadon VPDU -gaton P Nabhgodon U

48.　　　¹Im ²Assur, im ³Ibad ⁴n-ard,
　　　　　　im ⁵Laitin is ⁶im ⁷Longbard,　　　　　　　230
　　　　　　im ⁸Grēcus, ⁹im Gomer nglē
　　　　　　im ¹⁰Ēber mōr mac ¹¹Saile.

49.　　　¹Im ²Boidb, im ³Britus ⁴cen brath,
　　　　　　⁵im ⁶German is ⁷im ⁸Garad,
　　　　　　⁹im ¹⁰Scithus, im ¹¹Gothus nglan,　　　　235
　　　　　　im ¹²Dardan, Sardan solam.

50.　　　¹Rī na ²talman is na tor
　　　　　　³in Rī ⁴sīnes ⁵cach ⁶sāegol,
　　　　　　⁷būanaided mo ⁸chruth, mo chlī
　　　　　　cid ⁹ōen in ¹⁰t-abb sa' t-airdrī.　　　　　240

51.　　　Ro ¹scāilti na ²bērla ³dōib
　　　　　　do ⁴trāetad ⁵Nemrūaid nert-mōir;
　　　　　　⁊ ro ⁶trascrad ⁷in Tor,
　　　　　　⁸comad ⁹īsligthe ¹⁰a n-ūabor.

52.　　　¹Cōic ²bliadna cethrachat cain,　　　　　245
　　　　　　³mīle secht cēt do ⁴bliadnaib,
　　　　　　ō ⁵thosach ⁶domain co ⁷n-ūaill,
　　　　　　⁸no co ⁹torchair ¹⁰Tor ¹¹Nemrūaid.

---

48. ¹ Amasur Amabad M　　²Asir P Asur HU　　³Baad D Baadh
(written like ƀaττ⋄) E Ibath H Ibhadh U　⁴ *om.* n- VPH　⁵ Latin E
Laidin HU　⁶ am H　⁷ -bhard U　⁸ Gregus MH　⁹ mac Gomer
gle M　¹⁰ Emir V Eimer P Emer MH　¹¹ Sale U

49. ¹ am MH: Imodbh U　　² Bodb VH Boid EPDM　　³ Boritus
(*the* o *expuncted*) V Brittus E　⁴ gan brath P co mblad MU (-dh U)
⁵ um P　⁶ Gomer H　⁷ am H　⁸ Garadh V Gharadh U　⁹ um P
¹⁰ Garath M Scotus H Scithius U　¹¹ Scotus H Gothius U　¹² Dardarn
(*but the second compendium perhaps to be read* ai) D

50. *This quatrain om.* VED, *in this place in* PM, *and in* HU *at the
end of the poem, where it is more appropriate so far as the sense is
concerned: the version of the last line in* H *is probably correct, as it
ends with the word* athair.　¹ Rig U　² talmhan U　³ an H

48.   Including Assur and lofty Ibad,
Latinus and Longbardus,
Grecus and brilliant Gomer,
great Eber son of Sale.

49.   Including Bodb and Britus without deception,
Germanus and Garad,
Scithus and pure Gothus,
Dardan and swift Sardan.

50.   King of the earth and of the lords,
the King who prolongeth every life,
may He make enduring my form, my body
though the abbot and the high king be alike.

51.   The languages were dispersed for them,
for the subjection of Nemrod, great in strength;
and the Tower was overturned,
so that their pride was humiliated.

52.   Five years and forty fair,
a thousand seven hundreds of years,
from the superb beginning of the world,
till the Tower of Nemrod fell.

[4] sineas MU sinus H   [5] gach PU   [6] saoghal P saegal H saeghul U
[7] buanaiged mo cruth can cair, is é ar n-ab is ar n-athair H, buaidnaidh-
eadha dom chorp cain co tuga in tab sin tathair U   [8] cruth mo clí P
[9] aon P   [10] tab M in tadm (?) sa tairdrigh P

51. [1] sgaoilti P sgailti D scailtea MU   [2] berlae E   [3] doip P
doibh U   [4] traethad VEDH traothad P thraedad (t sprs. over first d
yc) M thraethad U   [5] -oid M   [6] thascrad E -grad PD -cairtea U
[7] an P   [8] comud V combad E gumad U   [9] isslitte V isliti E islide PD
islidi MHU   [10] annuabar PU (first n expuncted P) anuabur D
anuabar PH

52. This quatrain om. VMH.   [1] Coig P   [2] mile P   [3] mili DU
[4] -aiph P -uib D   [5] tosach P -eac U   [6] -uin E   [7] mbuaidh U
[8] om. no P: no go D   [9] torcair P ndorcair U   [10] ins. in P   [11] -ruad
D -ruaidh U

53. ¹I m-Maig ²Senair, ³īarsin Tor,
     ⁴ro ⁵tinōlad ⁶in ⁷chōem-scol,   250
     ⁸sin ⁹chathraig ¹⁰Ibitēna,
     ¹¹do ¹²foglaim na ¹³n-il-bērla.

54. ¹Eōlaig na ²mbērla, ³is ⁴blad ⁵bind
     ar ⁶a n-ērgna ⁷nostuirmim,
     im ⁸Fēinius ⁹Farsaid ¹⁰co ¹¹rath,   255
     ⁊ im ¹²Chai ¹³cain-brethach.

55. ¹Hiruath, ²Nenual brāthair Niūil,
     ³⁊ ⁴Gāedel mac ⁵Ethiūir,
     ⁶Dauid ⁊ Loth ⁷na land,
     ⁸Saliath, ⁹Nabgadon, Forand,   260

56. ¹Talemon, ²Cainan, ³nī ⁴chel,
     ⁵Caleph, ⁶Mored, Gad, ⁷Gomer,
     ⁸Etrochius, ⁹Bel, Bobel ¹⁰binn,
     ¹¹Ossi, ¹²Iessu, ¹³Iochim,

57. ¹Hidomus ²is ³Ordmor ard,   265
     ⁴Achab ⁵is ⁶Ruben ro-⁷garg,
     ⁸Humelchus, ⁹Ionan ān,
     ¹⁰Affraim, ¹¹Srū, Iar mac ¹²Nemān.

53. ¹immuig V immaigh ED immaigh P hi maig M a muig H a maigh U   ²Sennair ED (Ṡ E)   ³imon M iarsan H iman U   ⁴ra H ⁵-ladh E -oil- P -oi?lead M -oileadh HU   ⁶an H   ⁷chaem VE caom sccoil P mor- M tren- H trom- U   ⁸isin H gusin U   ⁹cathraig V cathraich E catraig PH chathruigh D chatraid M catraigh U   ¹⁰Ibithena V Ibithenae E Ibitena P Imbithena D Hebotena M Eba tena H Gam sena U   ¹¹ro M dimdhaghud na nilberla U   ¹²foglaim V focchlaimm E fogluim D foglaim M fodlaim H   ¹³-lae E -lai P hil- M

54. ¹-laigh EU -lach PM -luich D   ²mberlo D   ³as PH *om.* U ⁴bladh P   ⁵binn PD   ⁶in ergna E a n-ergnai M   ⁷rosturmim VH -tuirbim P tuirmimm D -airmim U   ⁸Fenius V Foenius D Feinus M Feinius U   ⁹-aidh V Farr- PH Farrsaich M Farrsaigh U   ¹⁰go D gan U   ¹¹brath U   ¹²Chae V Chaoi E Caidhe P   ¹³-breathach VM caoin-breath (ach *yc*) E chain- M

55. ¹Iruath U   ²Nenbhal E Noenal D Naeneal M Neanual U ³⁊ *yc* P   ⁴Gaidel V Gaoidel E Gaoidhel P Goeidel D Gaedeal M

53.   In the plain of Senar, after the Tower,
        was the fair school assembled,
        in the city of Ibitena,
        for learning the manifold languages.

54.   Those skilled in the tongues—'tis tuneful fame—
        for their cunning I enumerate them:
        including Feinius Farsaid with grace
        and Cai of the just judgements.

55.   Hiruath, Nenual brother of Nel,
        Gaedel son of Etheor,
        David, Loth of the blades,
        Saliath, Nabcodon, Forand.

56.   Talemon, Cainan, there is no concealment,
        Caleph, Mored, Gad, Gomer,
        Etrochius, Bel, tuneful Bobel,
        Ossi, Iessu, Iochim.

57.   Hidomus and lofty Ordmor,
        Achab and very rough Ruben,
        Humelchus, brilliant Ionan,
        Affraim, Sru, Iar son of Nema.

Gaeid. H Goedel U   ⁵ Eithiuir EPMHU   ⁶ Dabhi E ·   ⁷ nalland E
na lann PDM   ⁸ Sailiath H   ⁹ -codon E Nabgodon P Nabcadon
D Nabhcadon M -godon U

56. ¹ Tailimon P Dalamon M Talumón H Tailemon U   ² cain MH
caem U   ³ nocho MU nocha H   ⁴ cél PH   ⁵ Calep E Saleph P
Quiliph M Pilib U   ⁶ Moriath M mor iath U   ⁷ Goimher E Goimer H
⁸ Etrochius (o *sprs. yc*) V Etroichus P Etroichiuss D Eochrochuis M
Etroichus H Etrocus U   ⁹ Bel babebind M Belbobel U   ¹⁰ bind VEHU
¹¹ Osse ED Ose M Osu U   ¹² Iasu EU Isiu M   ¹³ Iocim E Iochimm
D Iachim M Iacim U

57. ¹ Hidomius VED Hidmius P Domu; M Idonius U   ² *om.* MU
³ Oirdmor E Ordmor P Ordonus M Adramus U   ⁴ Achap P Acab U
⁵ Sru MU   ⁶ Ruiben EP Rumen U   ⁷ gharb E   ⁸ Humelcus EPH
Umelchus M Imelcuus U   ⁹ *ins.* is U   ¹⁰ Affraim is Iar VEPH
Affram P Affraim Isiar D Efraum M Eaffraim U   ¹¹ *om.* Sru MH
(is Iar H) Iarinach (*or* -mach) is Neaman U   ¹² Nemain VDH

58. ¹Nēl mac ²Fēiniusa ³nīr ⁴bfann
⁵luid ⁶i ⁷nĒigept, ⁸co ⁹Forann;   270
¹⁰i ¹¹ferann ¹²Ēigipt ¹³īartain,
¹⁴rucad ¹⁵Gāidel ār n-athair.

58. ¹ Niuil U   ² Feinus P Foeniusa D Feiniusa M   ³ nar MH
⁴ bfamd VPH fann D fann MH fand U   ⁵ luidh E luig H   ⁶ an EH
⁷ Eigipt EHU Eigipit P Egipt D Eigep M   ⁸ go D re M iar U

VI.

R³ ¶ 28 (B 8 γ 53: M 265 a 40).

1. ¹Tobar ²Parrduis, būan a ³blad
⁴dīanaid ainm ⁵Nuchal nīam-glan;
⁶sīnit as, nī ⁷thrūag a ⁸threōir   275
ceithri srotha ⁹sōer-cheneōil.

2. ¹Fison ²*sufflatio* arfas,
Geon ³*felicitias*,
uelocitas Tigris trēn,
is *fertilis* ⁴Eufraiten.   280

3. ¹Fison sruth ola, ²sair suairc,
Tigris in fīn, sīar ³sōer-chuairt,
⁴Eufraites in mil, ⁵fodess,
Geon in loim, ⁶thuaid ⁷tibes.

1. ¹ tobur B   ² Parrtuis B   ³ bladh B   ⁴ dianadh B   ⁵ Nuchul B
⁶ sighnit ass B   ⁷ truag MSS.   ⁸ treoir·B   ⁹ saer M -cheineoil B
2. ¹ Fisson B   ² suflatio B suflaitio M   ³ *sic* M (*which must be
retained for the metre*): -itas B   ⁴ Eofraten M

VII.

R³ ¶ 66, 89 (β 34.20; β¹ 34.39; β² 10.21; M 267 δ 6;
H 102 a 35).

¹Cēt ²aimsir ³in ⁴bethad ⁵bind   285
⁶ōthā Adam co dīlind,
sē ⁷bliadna ⁸cōicat, ⁹rād nglē,
¹⁰ar ¹¹sē ¹²chētaib ar ¹³mīle.

¹ cead β   ² aimser MH aimsior β   ³ an Hβ   ⁴ beath H
bheatha β bhethadh β¹²   ⁵ bhinn β⁰¹²   ⁶ ota M ató H ata o Adhamh

58.   Nel son of Feinius who was not weak
went into Egypt, to P.arao;
in the land of Egypt thereafter,
was born Gaedel our father.

[9] -and EPMU   [10] hi bf. E hi f. D, a f. MH   [11] -nd EHU   [12] Eigipti
V Eigipit P Egipt D Eigeipti H Egeapt U   [13] iardtain E iartoin
Diardain U   [14] rucadh V rugad EH rucc̄ P rugadh U   [15] Gaedeal
VMH Gaoidel EP Goeidel D Gaedhel U

VI.

1.   The spring of Paradise, lasting its renown,
whose name is Nuchal of clear brilliancy;
there extend from out of it, not miserable is its
      strength,
four rivers of free nature.

2.   Phison was revealed as *sufflatio*,
Geon as *felicitas*,
strong Tigris as *uelocitas*,
and Euphrates as *fertilitas*.

3.   Phison a river of oil, gently eastward,
Tigris wine, a free circuit westward,
Euphrates honey, southward,
Geon milk, which laugheth northward.

3. [1] Fisson B   [2] saer B   [3] saerchuart M   [4] Eofrates M
[5] fodhes B fodeas M   [6] tuaidh B   [7] tibhes B thibeas M

VII.

The first age of the tuneful world
from Adam to the Flood,
fifty-six years, a clear saying,
over six hundreds and a thousand.

go dilinn β^{012} [7] bliadhna β [8] caecad M caogad β^{012} [9] radh β
rangle β^{12} [10] air β^{01} [11] se β^{12} [12] ceadaibh β chedaib β^{12} (ced- β^{2})
[13] mili H mhile β^{012}

VIII.

R³ ¶ 66 (H 98 a 3).

Dia Haine docuas inti,
isa n-airc comlain chinti.　　　　　　　　　　290
Dé Mairt dolodar amach
asin lestar chaem-chlarach.

IX.

R³ ¶ 68 (H 98 a 21).

1.　　Ceatrar as (s)ía saegal slán,
　　　indisis Cánoin chomślan,
　　　Adam, Iareth, ailli ⁽ᵃ⁾geal,　　　　　　295
　　　Náe nar is Mathasalem.

2.　　Tricha ar noi cetaib can ail
　　　saegal airmidnech Adaim;
　　　a dó´sescat noi cet cain,
　　　saegal Iareth abrad-chain.　　　　　　300

3.　　A noi sescat ar noi cet
　　　do Maithisailem, ni breg:
　　　caoga ar noi cet, nir bo liach,
　　　saegal Naee meic Laimíach.

(a) geall MS.

VIII.

On Friday there was the ingoing
into the ark complete, appointed.
On Tuesday they came out
from the fair-boarded vessel.

IX.

1.   Four who are longest of complete life,
the perfect Canon hath related :
Adam, Iareth, a bright praise,
noble Noe and Mathasalem.

2.   Thirty over nine hundreds without reproach
the venerable life of Adam :
nine hundred sixty and two fair,
the life of Iareth of the fair brows.

3.   Nine hundred sixty and nine
to Mathasalem, it is no falsehood :
nine hundred and fifty, it was not pitiful
the life of Noe son of Lamech.

NOTES ON SECTION I.

Prose Texts.

First Redaction.

(For the explanation of the asterisk see the beginning of R².)

1, 1*. *Fecit* shows that ∞ R¹ worked on an ante-Hierony-man text of Genesis. The Vulgate has *creauit*, as in R³ ¶ 20.

The gloss in R¹ is of some critical importance. It is absent from ¶ 1*, therefore it was not incorporated in the text of *Q. In LF it appears in the form ꝗ *nī fil . . . . fairseom,* to which F (and L *sec. man.*) add *fēin*. The version in *X is preserved in R³ ¶ 20; there we have the older *feisin*. In LF *nā foircend* precedes *fairseom,* in *X it follows *fairseom feisin*. Such a shifting about of words is practically diagnostic of the incorporation of a superscript gloss, therefore *nā foircend* must be a further glossarial addition made after the incorporation of the original gloss with the text. The history of the interpolation was therefore as follows :—

(1) The gloss existed, interlined or marginal, in √LF*X*Q in the simple form .i. *nī fil tosach fairseom* : a very natural comment—"In the beginning God made . . . . (note, that *He* hath no beginning)."

(2) ∞ *Q was copied, without the gloss, or at most with it in an interlineation.

(3) There must have been a MS. √LF*X in which the gloss was incorporated, and to which *nā foircend* was added glossarially. (In R³, these words must have been still inter-lined in √BMH, for B has them in a different place from the other two MSS. of R³.)

(4) From this MS. √LF and *X derive. But as F generally displays closer affinities with *Q than with L, we must suppose that L has undergone scribal distortion or editorial manipulation in deriving from √LF. If we had more of *X, we should probably find it nearest to ∞ R¹ : F and *Q must on the whole be good copies of √LF *X *Q,

as they are in close agreement : L is the farthest away from
∞ R[1].

2, 2*. Here again we find evidence that *Q represents an
older text; in 2* we have *cētumus, olchena, Āendidin* as
contrasted with *chētus, archena, Āine,* in 2. *Dorigne* and the
consistent spelling *-nd-* are also older than *doringne* and the
spelling *-nn-*. In these readings F shows a closer affinity to
*Q than to L.

Soillsi aingel is an attempt at a solution of the old puzzle,
as to how light could have been created before the luminaries :
see Augustine, *Civ. Dei* xi. 9.   The creation of the angels
upon the First Day is usually described in summaries of the
Creation such as this : for example, in the Arabic *Book of
the Rolls* :[1] ''The Holy First Day, chief of Days : early in it
God created the Upper Heaven and the Worlds, and the
highest rank of Angels . . . and the Archangels,'' etc. So in
Isidore, *Etym.* v. 39 : *Prima aetas in exordio sui continet
creationem mundi.   Primo enim die Deus in lucis nomine
condidit angelos.* And in the old English *Lyff of Adam and
Eve* (ed. Horstmann, *Sammlung altenglischer Legenden,*
p. 220 ff.) : ''God as his wille was behihte to make liht : and
þo he made angelus.''

Firmament. The absence of the definite article shows
that the writer took the word, which he found in his Latin
Bible, for a proper name.

The reading in F, *neam .i. firmamaind,* is a misplacement
of a gloss, for *neam* must originally have explained the
difficult word *firmament,* and not *vice versa.* The gloss must
also have been in *X, for in R[3] ¶ 20, third interpolation,
it has displaced *firmament* altogether.   That *X, and not
*Q, is the source of this passage is shown by its use of
nem-chruthaig as against the *n-ēchruthach* of F* Q. This
excerpt from *X is further instructive, as it shows that all
the dates are interpolations. They *precede* the works in *X,
but *follow* them in the other MSS.   The original text was
therefore a bald list of the works of creation—''He made first
the formless mass. He made Firmament. He made Earth
and Seas,'' etc.   The names of the days were interlined as

---

[1] Ed. Gibson (Camb. Univ. Press), transl. p. 3.

glosses, and taken in at different times and in different places. They were not securely in the text even in L, for at least three of them have been inserted *séc. man.* in that MS.

After *tondaitecha,* the words *in mara* in LF and *na fairrge* in *Q kill one another. They are both glosses, inserted independently by readers who knew or discovered for themselves that *marine* creatures were created on the Fifth Day. It follows almost inevitably that *ind āeoir* and *in talman* are glossarial also.

Dīa after *ro chumsain* is correctly omitted by E; as it has entered the text before *īarom* in *Q, and after it in √LF*X, it is suspect on the principle already set down. Most likely it remained as ꝺ till late in the R² tradition. In the original text, the verb *ro chumsain,* like *dorigni,* had no subject expressed.

Oipriugad for *foirbthiugad* is another mark of affinity between F and *Q.

⁊ *nī ō follomnacht itir* may perhaps have been suggested by the OL text *requieuit ab omnibus operibus suis quae inchoauit Deus facere* (cf. LXX, ὧν ἤρξατο ὁ θεὸς ποιῆσαι)—an implication that the Divine energy continued after the accomplishment of the Creation. As it occurs in F*Q it must be original, or a very early interpolation; more probably the latter, as it is absent from *X.

⁊ *dorad bendachtain foraib* in R² must have been inserted after the incorporation of the first leaf of *Q with that text. It is unknown to LF*X, and breaks awkwardly into the sense.

Foraib is almost certainly a copyist's mistake for *fair*: he forgot that the blessing was upon the rest-day, not upon the creatures (Gen. ii. 3).

2ᴀ (in R²). A group of three late interpolations (y^1, y^2, y^3), which (like the gloss at the end of 2* just noticed) entered the *Q tradition independently, after its first leaf had been separated from the rest of R¹. The first two were borrowed by yR³, but the third was ignored: as yR³ was nothing if not acquisitive, we infer that *Z, his copy of R², did not contain it. Y^2, which is a natural pendant of ¶ 2, was the first of the three to make its way into the text: but y^1 y^2 must both have been no more than marginal notes in *Z, for yR³ has inserted y^2 *before*, not after, the list of the works of Creation, and has taken in y^1 at a different place (¶ 25).

ᚁ *a allus* is a gloss: it is not found in R^3, and therefore was unknown to *Z.

The original purpose of y^2 was to show that Adam was made from the four elements. A further interpolator has confused this by inserting the specification of the countries from whose earth Adam was fashioned. YR^3 (¶ 25) has discovered anew the purpose of the passage, and has expressed his discovery by adding the comment *is amlaid . . . in gach duini*.

For parallels to the ideas here expressed as to the materials from which Adam was made, see Stokes, *Three Irish Glossaries* p. xl: idem, *Man Octipartite* (*sic*), in R.C., i, p. 261. The formation of Adam from the four elements is thus described in the Syriac *Cave of Treasures*:[2] "The angels saw the right hand of God opened out flat and stretched out over the whole world: and all creatures were collected in the palm of His right hand. And they saw that He took from the whole mass of the earth one grain of dust, and from the whole nature of water one drop of water, and from all the air which is above, one puff of wind, and from the whole nature of fire a little of its heat and warmth"—and therewith made Adam. In the same work Budge quotes from a Coptic tradition preserved in *The Discourse of Abbatōn the Angel of Death*, by Timothy, archbishop of Rakoti (Alexandria), to the effect that the clay of which Adam was made was brought by the angel Mûrîêl "from the land of the East." More specific but mutually contradictory information is afforded by various Jewish Rabbis on the subject. Eisenmenger[3] quotes Rabbi Meir as saying that the dust from which Adam was made was brought together from the whole earth; ingeniously deducing the fact from a combination of Ps. cxxxix [Vulgate cxxxviii] 16 and 2 Chron. xvi. 9. Rabbi 'Oshaya declares that the body of the first man came from Babel, his head from the land of Israel, his limbs from the other countries. Other theories are given in the same place, but none so specific as the version which has reached the Irish interpolator.

---

[2] Tr. Budge, pp. 51-2.   [3] *Entdecktes Judenthum*, vol. I, p. 364.

For Garad, Arabia, Lodain, Agoria the homily on Creation in *Lebor Brecc*[4] substitutes Malon, Arton, Biblon, Agore respectively. I can make nothing of these, unless "Agoria" be a misreading for "Moria": in some forms of Irish script capital *M* is not unlike *Ag*. Mount Moriah is alleged to have been the site of the altars of Solomon, David, Noah, Cain, and Abel as well as of Abraham, and is specified by Maimonides (*Beit Abachria,* c. 2) as being the source of the earth from which Adam was made. According to *The Dialogue of Salomon and Saturnus,*[5] Adam was made of eight pounds weight of materials, which are specified, but here irrelevant.

The same authority agrees with y^3 in saying that Adam was created as at the age of thirty, but the age of Eve is not specified. According to the *Lebor Brecc* homily, Adam was created nine months before Eve.

3. 3*. The legend of the Fall of the Angels, here introduced as a necessary preliminary to the Fall of Man, is part of the complicated angel-demon mythology that was absorbed from Persian sources and developed in post-exilic Judaism: quite likely it has its roots in the myth of the combat of Marduk and Tiãmat, which is the prologue to the Babylonian legend of Creation. Brought to shape by false exegesis of such scattered passages as Isaiah xiv. 12, Luke x. 18, Revelation ix. 1 ff., the story was taken over into early Christian tradition. The first of these passages, foreshadowing the downfall of the King of Babylon, and addressing him ironically as "Morning Star," has given the name "Lucifer" to the leader of the revolting angels: see Augustine *Civ. Dei,* xi. 15. The story appears in most early paraphrases of the Biblical history, as for instance in *Saltair na Rann,* no. vi, and in the fourteenth century *Cursor Mundi.*[6] None of the LG texts knows of the *second* fall of the infernal angels, after the temptation of Eve, referred to in the hymn *Altus Prosator,* verse G.

In both F and L this paragraph is desperately difficult to decipher: impossible indeed, at least for me, without the

---

[4] Ed. MacCarthy, Todd Lectures, iii, p. 48.

[5] Ed. Kemble (Aelfric Society, 1848), p. 180.

[6] Ed. Morris, E.E.T.S., line 473 ff.

help of ultra-violet photographs prepared by Professor Ditchburn. But the page is so badly rubbed in both MSS., that the photographs do not recover the whole text: it is, however, clear that L here stands by itself, and F and *Q, though not identical, are related. L's reading looks like a scribal guess at an illegible passage in √L. Comparison between the two texts reveals two or three minor interpolations, indicated by the marks ‡–‖ on the printed page, but not calling for special remark. *Imbe* in *Q as against *Nime* in LF is probably right. I take ⁊ *do Eua cona chlainn* to be a double interpolation. In the original, Lucifer and Adam were in partnership. Then someone, forgetting that Adam was at the time expected to be a virginal immortal, added *cona chlaind*. After that someone else slipped in ⁊ *do Eua*, and forgot to make the consequential change *cona cclaind*.

In R², *do Neimi* is anomalous, but it is certainly what it looks like in V. It is very worn and obscure in this place.

The "Nine orders" of the Angels are very frequently specified in Apocryphal literature, as in *The Book of the Secrets of Enoch*, xx. 1.[7] The following enumeration is given by Solomon, bishop of Basrah:[8] "The angels are divided into nine classes and three orders. The upper order contains Cherubim, Seraphim, and Thrones, and these are the bearers of God's throne: the middle order contains Lords, Powers, and Rulers: the lower order contains Principalities, Archangels, and Angels." Isidore (*Etym.* VII. v. 4) gives a similar enumeration, but in a different sequence.

[*Ro*]-*diumsach intī Lucifer*, though appearing both in *Q and in LF, is probably an early interpolation, seeing that the words of the Almighty are habitually reported in Latin. It is probably nothing more than some reader's personal opinion on Lucifer's proceedings.

The words *Venite*, etc., are a reminiscence of the sentence upon the builders of Babel—*Venite et confundamus linguam eorum* (Gen. xi. 7). The words *ut uideamus*, imported into

---

[7] Charles, *Apocrypha and Pseudepigrapha of the O.T.*, vol. ii, p. 441. See also Colossians i. 16: *Irish Liber Hymnorum* (Henry Bradshaw Society edn.), vol. ii, p. 155.

[8] As quoted by Budge, *Cave of Treasures*, p. 45.

the *Q tradition from the preceding verse 5 of the Babel narrative, are also found in the quotation from the Babel story in *Auraicept na nĒces*.[9] The Irish translation there given, *mutatis mutandis,* is identical with that found here in *Q. Obviously the annotator of R² was familiar with the *Auraicept* : we find further evidence of this on a later page.

4, 4*. That the envy of Satan for his supplanter was the reason for the Temptation and the Fall of Man, is the usual belief, derived ultimately from that popular apocryphon, *The Book of Adam and Eve.* The passage, which it is needless to quote here, will be found in Charles, *Apocrypha and Pseudepigrapha,* ii, 137. The Irish historian has, however, missed the contrast between the *Paradisus spirituum,* from which Lucifer was cast out, and the *Paradisus corporum* (not "heaven") which was to have been the portion of Adam : even the glossators in R³ overlooked this, though they could have learnt of it from Comestor, *Historia Scholastica,* chap. xxi. Our text knows nothing of the refusal of Lucifer to do homage to Adam : a very common incident in Creation stories. It is related in the Lebor Brecc *Homily.*

Doluid Iofer Niger. The subject of the verb must originally have been *Lucifer,* carried through from the preceding sentence. "Iofer Niger" is beyond question an intrusive gloss, written in by someone fresh from reading the *Life* of the fourth-century St. Juliana.[10] The name is there given as an alternative for Belial son of Beelzebub, *totius mali inuentor* : but so far as I have been able to find out for myself, or through enquiries which the Rev. P. Grosjean, S.J., has most kindly made on my behalf, the name does not appear to be recorded in any other text. Bespelled by Juliana, this being is compelled to confess his own misdeeds, the first of which is *Ego sum qui feci Adam et Euam in Paradiso praeuaricari.*[10a] The editors of *Acta Sanctorum* quote variant forms—Iophin, Iofet, Iofen, Tophet, and they suggest an (improbable) etymology (Hebrew שָׁחֹר, *šaḥōr,* "black").

---

[9] Ed. Calder, p. 12.

[10] Acta Sanctorum, February, vol. ii, esp. p. 875.

[10a] Alluding, of course, not to the original transgression, but to the subsequent subterfuges of the culprits. Our glossator has overlooked this : so has the Irish translator of the Juliana text.

The relevant passage is quoted in the glosses to *Fēilire Oengusso* :[11] the name there appears as Iafer, Iofer, and (in *Lebor Brecc*) Ethiar. Of all these forms, "Tophet" is the most comprehensible, but is not on that account necessarily the most authentic. The critical history of this interpolation usefully supplements that of the gloss in ¶ 1. It was absent from *X, as will be seen by reference to ¶ 31 : R³ cannot have taken this from *Z, because that MS., being dependent for its opening words upon *Q, would have included the demon's name. It is also absent from F, which here shows itself earlier in tradition even than *Q. In L it has become distorted by corruption : the form there found, *Iarngir*, may be compared with *Ifírnaig*, the form which the name has assumed in the Irish text of *Vita Iulianae* (R.C., xxxiii, p. 316) under the influence of the word *Ifernd*.

The occasional superiority of F and *X to *Q is further illustrated in this ¶ ; *Q contains two other interpolations, not in *XF. *I ffochraic dō* is an attempt to fill in what someone took for a lacuna after *dobērtha*; and *co curp sēim* is a cheville borrowed from Poem V, line 93.

The detached part of this paragraph, which follows ¶ 5A in R², contains an unintelligible expression ⁊ *cenn fri cotlud.* Though a guesswork rendering for it is offered in the translation, I suspect that it is really nothing but an early misreading of *cen forcend*, "without end."

5, 5*. This ¶ was no part of ∞ R¹. It must have been a marginal gloss in √R¹ ; it was taken into the text before the words *Conid aire sin*, etc. in *Q, and after them in √LF*X. Moreover, the differences between the texts in the two traditions cannot be explained except on the assumption that when it was in the marginal-gloss stage *it was in Latin throughout*, and that what we have are two independent attempts at a translation. The renderings into Irish of the words of the Deity are later still. Those in *Q are obviously quite independent of those in LF.

On the whole the texts are Old Latin. *Terra es et in terram ibis* is OL : Vulg. has *Puluis es et in puluerem ibis*. Sabatier's restoration of the OL of the second quotation is *In sudore faciei tui edes panem tuum* : Vulg. has *In sudore*

---

[11] R.I.A. edition, p. 52; H. Bradshaw Soc. edition, p. 74.

uultus tui uesceris pane. Our text lies between the two; but Sabatier in his notes quotes an identical version from Hieronymus *In Isaiam.* The OL of the third quotation is *Multiplicans multiplicabo tristitias tuas et gemitum tuum; in tristitiis paries filios.* Vulg. has *Multiplicabo aerumnas tuas et conceptus tuas; in dolore paries filios.*

It is worth passing notice that the biblical order of the three texts is reversed. Almost certainly the original glossator quoted them from memory.

We note as a contribution to the genealogy of the MSS. that the unauthorized addition *et filias tuas* is omitted in F, inserted without translation in L, and inserted with translation in *Q. We have no excerpt from *X at this point, so we do not know what was in that MS.

Sasam in R¹ may also be read *sasad,* in the obscurity of the page.

5A. (in R²). I cannot find the reading *Ecce os* in any of the Latin versions, but it is presupposed by all the redactions.

Is cuma, which is absent from E, does not seem to make any reasonable sense: the suggested translation is a mere makeshift. I suspect that the words have no glossarial or other connexion with the text at all; that they were originally a marginal scribble conveying a surreptitious communication from one student to another on some subject of transient interest—"Never mind"; "It doesn't matter."

In chēt-ghaire, here adopted from P as against VE, is certainly right: the gloss was clearly suggested by line 84 of the poem no. V. The change to *choibche* is arbitrary, made by someone who did not understand the original reading.

It is obvious that this ¶ is an interpolation, quite irrespective of its absence from R¹. It makes the creation of Eve follow the Fall!

6. This paragraph is the most difficult to read of the whole obscure first page of L. Here again *Q gives a better text, though there are several interpolations, especially the alternative version of the death of Abel.

There are numerous speculations as to the instrument of Abel's murder. *The Book of Adam and Eve* does not enlighten us. *The Book of the Rolls* says that a sharp stone was used. In the Old English versions, it is commonly said that the instrument was an ass-bone : thus, in the *Lyff of Adam and Eve* we read "wiþ þe cheke-bon of an asse he smot him on þe hed"; and in *Cursor Mundi* (1073) we are told—

> Wit the chafte ban of a ded has
> Men sais þat þar wit slan he was.

This was presumably suggested by the exploit of Samson against the Philistines. *Saltair na Rann,* which follows *The Book of Adam and Eve,* has nothing to say on the subject : and there does not appear to be any authority for the idea that a camel-bone was used. Did the old Irish historians fully comprehend the difference between an ass and a camel? In Cashel Cathedral there is a quaint carving of an elephant, of a much later date, which reveals a very rudimentary conception of the appearance of an exotic animal : and as in ancient Ireland the camel and the ass were equally unfamiliar,[12] it is quite possible that they were supposed to be similar or identical.

"*Lasin* cnāim chamaill" is the best that I can make of the faint traces in L. It seems to be different from the *do lecain chamaill* of R² and the *fid chnama* of FR³ (§ 87). The version of this paragraph in F is glossarial, and has ousted its lemma : the original form (with some minor verbal variations) is preserved by L*Q. The F version has been written after R² attained its present form, in which the Flood is stated to be a punishment for the murder of Abel. One of the glossators of R³ has copied it in ¶ 87, directly from F or perhaps √F; this late and corrupt version cannot come from the early MS. *X, which is the source of most of the R¹ glosses in R³.

Fo intamail marbtha na n-idbart is a gloss which has come into the *Q tradition after its incorporation with R² : it refers to Exodus xiii. 13, xxxiv. 20.

7. The folio torn from *Q to complete √R² comes to an end just before ¶ 7. The mutilated MS. still remained, to form the basis of R³ : the *Q equivalent of this paragraph will be found in R³ at ¶ 88. The text of L is thus revealed as

---

[12] See *Proceedings,* Royal Irish Academy, xxxiii, section C, p. 530.

corrupt. *Mac Adaim* has become *imorro* : *aireagda ro bāi ac*
has dropped out, almost certainly by oversight of a *cor fā
chasān* (these words are in a *cor fā chasān* in F)[13] : *acca mbāi
cland* is a gloss. In these respects F follows *Q exactly. The
genealogy breaks the sense awkwardly, and is doubtless an
early interpolation : it appears in all three MSS. Most likely
it was first written by an annotator in the margin. The
second interpolation of L is not in F, which substitutes
the *Imroimadar . . . . Olībana* also found at the end of ¶ 88.

The remainder of the text of this part of R[1] is
genealogical, giving the following particulars—

(i) Seth to Noah, a genealogy at first assumed rather than
expressed, but early interpolated into ¶ 7.

(ii) The three sons of Noah, with their inheritances (¶ 8).

(iii) The sons of Japhet (¶ 9).

(iv) The descendants in Ireland of Magog son of Japhet
(¶ 10). Everything outside this brief scheme may be taken
as interpolated matter.

Acca mbāi claind, shown by its absence from F*Q to be
glossarial in the L tradition, is interesting, as it proves the
acquaintance of a glossator in that tradition with poem no. V
(see line 185 of that poem). There are two quatrains from
this poem quoted in R[1], from a version widely different from
that which appears in R[2], R[3].

In tAdam tānisi has grown out of a confused and
inaccurate recollection of 1 Corinthians xv. 45.

The second interpolation is otiose, as it merely repeats
what has gone before. F has a different interpolation here,
which must come from a MS. of R[2] (¶ 10, 11) : *g*R[3] has copied
it, like the preceding paragraph, from F or from √F. Note
that the discovery that the wives of Noah and his sons were
their respective sisters had not been made when the MS. of R[2]
used by *g*F was written. Also note that the expression *na
hairci sin,* which appears in the L interpolation, postulates a
previous mention of the Ark which, in fact, does not occur
in the present context.

---

[13] An illustration of the fact that the *external form* of the texts is
of considerable importance in criticising MSS., and especially in
determining their affinities.

The almost complete absence of the Flood story from R¹ contrasts notably with the emphasis laid upon it in R², R³, and is one of several indications of the primitive simplicity of that text.

The names of the women of Noah's family were themes for endless vain speculation. According to *The Book of Jubilees* Noah's wife was called 'Emzârâ, and the wives of his sons were respectively Sêdêqêtêlĕbâb, Nê'êlâtamâ'ûk, and 'Adâtan'êsês. Various Jewish and other apocryphal authorities name Noah's wife Noria, Noema, Bath-Enos, Tithea, and Haical; Eutychus names Salit, Nahlat, Arisisah as the wives of his sons.[14] The poem *Athair cāich* gives Cata Rechta, Cata Chasta, Cata Flauia as the sons' wives (quatrain 39). Olla, here named as Shem's wife, there becomes the wife of Seth. Comestor gives similar names—Phuarpara for Noah's wife, and Pharphia, Cataflua, Fliva as the sons' wives. Cata Flauia or Cata Flua, expanded into Cata Folofia, appears in the compilation known as *Banśenchus* as the wife of *Cain*—confusion between Cain and Cam or Ham is not infrequent—as we may see in the *Book of Leinster* facsimile 136 b 32. In the *Dialogue of Salomon and Saturnus*[15] this tradition is combined with that in the text before us. Noah's wife is there called Dalila: those of Ham and Japhet are respectively Jatarecta and Catafluuia, but, the author adds, "by other names are they named, Olla, Ollina, and Ollibana." Shem's wife does not appear: indeed, Shem himself has become the wood of which the ark was made. In the fifteenth century *Master of Oxford's Catechism* the omission was rectified: Noah's wife is called Dalida, and the sons' wives are Cateslinna, Laterecta, and Aurca, otherwise Ollia, Olina, Olybana.[16] In the Pseudo-Berossus of Johannes Annius[16a]—for what that absurd document may be

---

[14] Fabricius, *Codex Pseudepigraphus Vet. Test.*, p. 277.

[15] Ed. Kemble, p. 184.

[16] Ibid., p. 218. The confusion of D and L (Δ, ʌ) in these last two versions of the name of Noah's wife shows that it must come ultimately from a Greek source.

[16a] On this worthy see *Proceedings* R.I.A., viii, p. 354 ff. The only reason for quoting him here is the fâct that he had somehow become acquainted with these names: the use which he made of them concerns no one but himself.

worth—we read how "Noah taught astronomy, division of time, and astrological predictions, and he was considered as being of divine origin : therefore was he called *Olybama* and *Arsa,* which mean 'heaven' and 'sun' wherefore the Scythians of Armenia have towns Olybama and Arsa Ratha and the like."[17]   In the Caedmon *Genesis*[18] the names of these women are given as Percoba, Olla, Oliua, Olliuani.   Gollancz, in his introduction to the sumptuous facsimile of the Caedmon MS.,[19] considers that the passage containing these names is an interpolation, on the ground that elsewhere the MS. closely follows the Biblical text.   He suggests that they have been picked out more or less at random from some Onomasticon of Biblical names, in which Aholah, Aholibah, Aholibamah (Vulgate *Oolla, Ooliba, Oolibama*) occurred together.   This is quite admissible, assuming the early existence (and local availability) of such an Onomasticon ; but the compiler can hardly have taken the trouble to look up the unsavoury connexion in which the first two of these names are found (Ezekiel xxiii).   His suggestion that Percoba is a corruption of "Berseba" seems, perhaps, less happy.   Percoba figures in *Bansenchus* along with her daughters-in-law, thus characterized (*Book of Leinster* facs. 136 b, 35–40).

> Percoba ben Noe co n-nāri,[20]
> Cen choi, cen gāri—ba gand![21]
> Copa sēim ba comse a cāem-t̃ir,[22]
> Toirsech ca cōiniud a cland.
> Olla setig Sēim blāith bithi,
> Ben Chaim Oliuan o hāis,
> Commām Iafeth Olīuane,
> Na tarat barr for bāis.

"Percoba the wife of Noe with shame,[21] without weeping, without laughter—how dull![22]   That she was modest suited

---

[17] Fabricius, *op. cit.,* p. 245.

[18] Also in *Saltair na Rann,* ed. Stokes, lines 2485–2488.

[19] Published 1927 by the British Academy.

[20] Referring, presumably, to the episode of his drunkenness.

[21] Lit., "it was niggardly"!   The translation adopted is a perhaps . supererogatory attempt to endow the cheville with some semblance of sense.

[22] Ba comsech cā caem-t̃ir MS., which is unmetrical.

her fair husband, sad in lamenting her were her children. Olla the spouse of Sem, smooth and feminine, the wife of Ham Oliuan of free-will: the wife of Japhet Oliuana, that won not the goal over death." Epiphanius (*Adv. Haeres.* I ii 26) gives us a long and silly story about "Noria wife of Noah" who burnt the Ark while it was a-building. This is irrelevant here: but it may not be a mere accidental coincidence that he makes reference immediately afterwards to a certain prophet, one *Barkabba,* whose name he describes as suitable, Καββᾶ γὰρ ἑρμηνεύεται ʻπορνεία' κατὰ τὴν Συριακὴν διάλεκτον. For completeness' sake we may add that the poem beginning *Redig dam a Dē do nim,* contained in the Irish *Sex Aetates Mundi,* has the same names, Copha, Olla, Oliua. It also gives Olla as the wife of Seth, along with Pibb and Pithibb, the wives of Adam's other married sons (cf. Poem V, line 188).

8. The *Q version of this ¶, much farced with glosses and interpolations, appears in R³, partitioned between ¶ 89 *ad fin.* and ¶ 92. Its principal contribution to criticism is the close relationship which once more it shows between that MS. and F, as both have a glossarial addition correcting the number of the sons of Shem (but in different words). On the other hand it does not show some careless omissions of F.

The world was supposed, on the basis of the data supplied in Genesis x, to have been divided into 72 nations or linguistic groups: see for instance Isidore, *Etym.* IX ii. The total of 30 + 30 + 15 is 75, which is three too many: the glossarial note just referred to corrects this.

The names of Shem's sons here specified are the *first three* of those enumerated in Gen. x. 22. It is not clear why they should be reversed in order. "Persius" corresponds to the Biblical Elam.

Cush and Canaan are the *first and last* of the sons of Ham enumerated in Gen. x. 6.

The sons of Japhet are more disguised. Dannai presumably means *Dodanim* (recte *Rodanim*) at the end of the list in Gen. x. 4. *Grēgus* no doubt is the same as *Javan* (= Ionians). *Hispāinius* is *Tarshish,* the leading town in Southern Spain. This, like "Dodanim," appears in Gen. x. 4 as a son, not of Japhet, but of his son Javan. The equation *Gomerus* = the Biblical *Gomer* needs no comment.

9. The *Q version of this ¶ appears is R³, partitioned, owing to later interpolation, between ¶ 94 and ¶ 98. It became the common property of early historians, and appears also in *Sex Aetates Mundi,* from which another version of it has entered the text of H, in the long extract from *Sex Aetates* which forms our ¶ 95. It is also found in Nennius. Leaving for the moment the general question of the text and its origin, let us concentrate our attention upon the LG version, as it appears in LF*Q. It is unknown to R². The irrelevance of the passage to the main purpose of LG shows that it can be no part of the original text: but as it appears in *Q it must have been an early interpolation. The oldest form of it, however, happens to be preserved by a late interpolation in H (¶ 93): *Iathféth dono mac Náe, is úad tuaiscert-leth na Haissia ┐ lucht na Heorpa uile.* This must derive from a tradition earlier than the extant R¹ texts: in these, the obviously glossarial *.i. Aissia Becc, Airmen, ┐ Fir na Scithia* had already become incorporated after *Haissia,* making it necessary to repeat *is úad* before *lucht.* L makes the further addition of *Media,* and corrupts *tuaiscert-leth* to *síor-deise.* "*Mac Náe*" was probably also glossarial, and I suspect that it was still interlined when ∞R³ dealt with the text: it does not appear in H in the "full-dress" form in which we find the passage in ¶ 94, though BM both contain it.

I take it that these words, and the preceding quatrain (*Tricha mac mín*) were set out in √HMB as follows:—

To the margin of this MS. someone added against these words *is iad a cland-sem lenfamaid,* which appears in all three derivatives. M, and B as presented by its eighteenth-century copyists, follow the text with this addition, and display no more than unimportant orthographical variations. But ∞H started a vicious tradition by overlooking the words in the *cor fā chasān* (line 2 of the above figure) at the end of the quatrain. He proceeded from the quatrain to line 3; thence, misled by the continuity of the sense, to line 4; and did not notice the omitted words till he came to *Alaxandrach*. So he inserted them in his transcript at the place which he had reached, allowing the repetition of the words *is ūad* .... *Alax.* to remain, to save himself the trouble of making erasures. As he wrote *Greg Beg* .... *Greg Mōr* in the first of these repetitions (¶ 94) and reversed the order in the second (¶ 98) it follows that the scribe of his exemplar (√HMB) must have accidentally omitted *Greg Mōr*, and inserted it as an interlined correction. Large interpolations were subsequently made piecemeal in the H tradition—¶ 93 after the quatrain, and ¶¶ 95–97 before *Grecus mac Iafeth*. From this point onward the two texts, R¹ and *Q, are virtually identical, and we need notice no more than that *Q justifies the insertion of *mac* after *Hisicon imorro in tres*, where L has left it out.

Taking now the paragraph in detail: the first few lines, and probably the only original part of the paragraph, enumerate the peoples descended from Japhet in Western Asia and Europe. The first interpolation enlarges on these details, assigning various peoples to the sons of Japhet from whom they are descended. These sons are the same as those enumerated above, in ¶ 8, excluding "Dannai," who is here disregarded. *Grēcus* and *Essbāinus* correspond to the Biblical *Javan* and *Tubal*. Isidore helps us to link them together: "*Iauan a quo Iones qui et Graeci, Thubal a quo Iberi, qui et Hispani*.[23] Gomer, according to Isidore (*loc. cit.*), is the ancestor of the Galatae or Galli, so it is natural to affiliate to him two personages, Emoth and Ibath, who are in the traditional Teutonic and Celtic ancestry respectively; even although these have no warrant either in Genesis or in Isidore. The important son Magog does not appear: but that is because the following interpolations have divorced him from his context. Properly speaking, ¶ 10 should follow on immediately after the first interpolation, to which it belongs.

The second interpolation is an Irish version of the Frankish "Table of Nations," published first by Grimm,[24]

---

[23] Etym., IX, ii, 28–29.
[24] *Teutonic Mythology*, Eng. Tr. by Stallybrass, vol. iv, p. 1734.

and afterwards, with a much more extensive *apparatus criticus*, by Müllenhoff.[25]   This document must date from about the year 520, as Müllenhoff has shown—basing his conclusions on the names included and (what is equally important) omitted.   The genealogy starts from the statement for which Tacitus is our oldest authority,[26] that the god Tuisto had a son Mannus, from whose three sons are descended the three branches of the Germans, the Herminones, the Istaevones, and the Ingaevones.   The Frankish Table gives eponymous names, Erminius, Inguo, Istio, clearly postulated to explain the names in Tacitus: and these are the Armen, Negua, and Isicon of the Irish version.   Two MSS. of the Frankish Table give Alanus or Alaneus as the father of these three eponyms. These MSS. (E and F in Müllenhoff's enumeration) appear from the forms which the names assume to be of Irish origin. In the others, the parentage of the three brothers is not specified, though Alanus appears in the document as "the first king of Rome"!   In "Alanus" Grimm recognized long ago a miswriting for the "Mannus" of Tacitus.

To Erminius the Frankish Table assigns the Goths, the Walagoths or Goths of Italy, the Vandals, the Gepidae, and the Saxons: to Inguo, the Burgundians, Thuringians, Langobardi, and Baioarii or Bavarians, who are here referred to in literature for the first time.   This distribution somehow became disjointed when the document reached Ireland. There, in *Sex Aetates Mundi* (see *Book of Ballymote*, p. 3 of facsimile a 50, also LG ¶ 95 N); in LG, in the present paragraph; in the Reichenau MS. of the Table, lettered F in Müllenhoff's edition; and in Nennius, who has certainly derived his copy from an Irish source; the Burgundians and Langobardi are transferred to "Airmen" or Erminius, and the Vandals given to "Negua" or Inguo in exchange.   All the versions agree in assigning Romanus, Britones, Francus, and Alamannus—the Romans of Central Gaul, Britons (of Brittany), Franks, and Alemanni, the four peoples who in or about the time when the table was drawn up were under the domination of the Frankish King Chlodwig) to Istio or

---

[25] "Die fränkische Völkertafel" *Abhandlungen* der Ak. zu Berlin, 1862, p. 532.
[26] Germania, § 2.

Isacon, the third of the three brothers. (Naturally Romanus, Francus, etc., in the Irish text are to be regarded as representing Latin *accusative plurals*.)

The table also appears in *Sex Aetates Mundi* and in Nennius; the latter version, as Zimmer has shown[27] must have been taken from an Irish source. But we cannot follow Zimmer in concluding that that source must have been either LG or *Sex Aetates*—Zimmer prefers the former hypothesis. In fact, all three compilations must have borrowed it from some common source unknown; for all three treat the genealogy differently. LG links it on to Gomer, son of Noah: *Sex Aetates* to Magog: and Nennius to Javan. The last named gives us a long genealogy, back to the antediluvian patriarchs, impinging in one or two places only on the much shorter pedigree in R^1: we find Nennius's version, however, in another connexion, in R^2 (see below, ¶ 16).

The peculiar pendant which is found in LG only, must be an addition by some philomath within the LG tradition itself. "Albanus" should of course be "Alemanus": the miswriting is a very simple matter. Our glossator thought of "Alba," and associated "Britus" with Britain (instead of Brittany). So he seemingly invented this story of the Britons having driven out the "Albans" across the English Channel, in order to secure the monopoly of the Island of Britain; and he seeks to account for similar ethnic names on the continent—Albanians, Alba Longa, or what not—as the result of this manoeuvre. *Sex Aetates* has something similar, in saying that from Albanus come the "Albanians of Asia."[28]

10. (*Q version in ¶ 99, 100, much inflated with glosses.) As has already been noted, this paragraph is properly a continuation of the first interpolation in ¶ 9. The names in the form in which they appear here, from F, are very corrupt.

Tancatar Ērinn, in which the verb of motion is used without a preposition, is a favourite construction in this text, and may possibly indicate the influence of a text originally in Latin (as in Vergil's *Italiam uenit*).

---

[27] *Nennius vindicatus,* p. 234 ff.
[28] See Zimmer, *op. cit.,* p. 237 ff.

Second Redaction.

11. This ¶ hints that in the original form of R² there was an antecedent in which the unions of Sethites and Cainites were denounced. It is more fully preserved in R³, to which we may postpone the discussion of the subject. The three sentences, in which a singular conception of the family of Noah is suggested, are clearly glossarial interpolations. They have made no impression on R³—except in the late MS. M, at ¶ 188, where the idea implied is referred to. It is probably inspired partly by a desire to draw an exact analogy between the households of Adam and of Noah, partly to insinuate that only by such irregular unions could the contamination of Cainite blood be avoided. I have found no authority for it in apocryphal or pseudepigraphic literature. The Syriac *Cave of Treasures* says that Noah married Haykel d. Namūs d. Enoch, brother (*sic*) of Methuselah.[28a] It is referred to (probably borrowed from the text before us) by the compiler of the prose version of *Banšenchus*.

The statement that the Flood was a penalty for the crime of Cain has here arisen fortuitously, owing to the accidental juxtaposition of ¶ 6 from *Q and ¶ 11 from R². It is possible to find it elsewhere in Apocrypha: thus *The Book of the Rolls,* to give but one example, makes Adam prophesy to Seth in these words: *Know, my son, that there must come a Flood to wash all the earth, on account of the children of Cain, the wicked man who slew his brother.* But this is not really parallel: the Flood is here a punishment for the *children* of Cain [and their union with the Sethites] not for the crime of Cain.

12. Here we have definite proof of what we suspected in the preceding paragraph: that the Flood, according to R² in its original form, was the penalty for the sinful marriages of Sethites and Cainites, and not for the crime of Cain itself, as the text in its present form suggests. The theory is based upon a misinterpretation of Genesis vi. 1, 2.

[28a] Tr. Budge, p. 99, who quotes (ibid., p. 97) the Book of Enoch, ch. x, for a marriage between Noah and Enoch's daughter: I cannot find this in Charles's translation.

The copyists of R² have here and there made a bad muddle of the story: conspicuously so in this paragraph, especially in the laboured arithmetical disquisition inserted at the end. The account of the Flood was developed by the copyists of the R² tradition: the R¹ copyists took little interest in it. The R² version has carelessly admitted certain discrepancies with the biblical history. The forty days of downpour, and the 600 years of Noah's life, come from Genesis vii. 12, 11. That there were "three pairs" of clean beasts is a lapse of memory: *no sechta* is a reader's correction. The month of May is named in the Irish text: the Hebrew and all the versions say "the second month." On the hypothesis that the Creation took place at the Vernal Equinox, April would be the first complete month, and so May would be the second. That the biblical months were lunar was hidden from the compilers. The date (seventeenth) agrees with Heb. and Latin: LXX: has "twenty-seventh." A careless glossator seems to have misread the date as "seventh," and to have rushed in with the information that the embarkation took place on the nones (seventh) of May. I take the sentence beginning *In tan tarnaic* to be a gloss, as it breaks the sense: *dēda do inglan*, etc., is a further gloss upon that: and *nō sechta* is an additional gloss. Lower down, ⁊ *cona ingenaib* is obviously glossarial, as it is superfluous before *sēitchib*, and indeed makes nonsense.

"Twelve cubits," which is given by all MSS. for the height of the water level above the loftiest mountain-tops, is an error: the biblical text in all versions says "fifteen," and (later in the ¶) E and P have given the correct figure. So, apparently, did √V, as is suggested by the form *cubait* for *cubat*. Early in the history of the text—or even in the history of the document from which the R² compilers derived their information—.xii. must have been misread and mis-written for .xu., as often happens. It is indeed *possible* to read .xu., as the number is written, in both V and E; but inadmissible, as it dislocates the arithmetic of the following interpolation. The Ark, we are told, drew ten cubits (there is no biblical warrant for this): its keel was two cubits above the highest summit: therefore the water-level was twelve cubits above them. This note further contradicts the orthodox version of the height of the Ark (30 cubits, Gen. vi. 15): ten cubits below water and fifteen above make only twenty-five.

Something has been lost from the sentence, .*xii. cubat diu ūas na slēibtib atā airdiu*: I suggest *diu < don usce > uas*, which would be an easy haplography.

13. The irrelevance about Enoch and Fintan is clearly a reader's note. Of the latter we shall hear more on a later page. On the legend that Enoch is reserved to fight against Antichrist, along with Elijah (and even to perish in the fighting), see *Revue celtique*, xxvi, pp. 164–5, and references there.

14. The waters began to dry after 150 days (Gen. viii. 3), but the Ark was floating for 7 months 27 days (Gen. viii. 4, LXX and Vulg.: Hebrew says 17 days). The waters continued to dry until the tenth month (Gen. viii. 5). An early loss by homoiotes at this point has affected all the MSS.: before *dechmud mīss* we must supply the words *dechmad mīss: i ccēt lō don*. The raven was sent out after 40 days (Gen. viii. 6, all versions): the 47 of the Irish text is a mistake. There is no Biblical warrant for sending forth the dove *on the following day*: it is derived from ὀπίσω αὐτοῦ (LXX) or *post eum* (Vulg.) which represent a Hebrew original meaning *from him* (i.e. from Noah). The seven days' intervals of the missions of the dove follow the Biblical story.

15. The date of the exodus from the Ark, in all the Biblical versions, is given as "The twenty-seventh day of the second month" (Gen. viii. 14). *For pridnōin Mai* must be due to the same glossator as the author of the similar gloss in ¶ 12, who believed that the voyage occupied exactly a solar year, which, in fact, was approximately true.

The passage *tossuch . . . ocht ccētaib* is an interpolation, as it breaks the sense. It must come from some historical treatise (not *Sex Aetates Mundi*, but resembling it). The opening words are clearly a chapter heading. The double article NA *hāeisse* IN *domain* may be accounted for by "age-of-the-world" having come to be regarded as an indivisible technical term. The figures are not accurate: the Hebrew reckoning should be 390, not 292; the Septuagint reckoning 1170, not 842.   (See the table in Skinner's *Commentary on Genesis*, p. 233.)

The statement that Noah's altar was the first built after the Flood is preceded by the mark .i., which is usually diagnostic of an interpolated gloss.   The passage *anmand mac Nōe* to the end of the annexed poem is also no part of the original text.   It likewise interrupts the sense, which is a description of the divisions of the world : and it gives names for the wives of Noah's sons not in accordance with the tradition followed by R².   This tradition is summed up in poem V, and if the original redactor had named these women, he would presumably have followed its lead.   See note on ¶ 7. The last sentence is a relic of the original abstract of the Biblical history, rendered obsolete by the elaborate genealogical matter which has been superposed upon it.

16. Riphath, to whom the pedigree in this paragraph is traced, comes from Gen. x. 3.   The original meaning of the name is obscure : in 1 Chron. i. 6 it appears as "Diphath," the discrepancy being due to the similarity of the characters for D and R in both the older and the later Hebrew scripts.   The addition "Scot" has of course no Biblical warrant, but conceivably it has arisen from some copy of the Latin version in which the name was given as *Riphaz* or *Rifatz* (as in two of the MSS. on which the Vatican *variorum* edition is based). The *z* we may suppose to have become separated from the rest of the name, resolved into *sc* or *st,* and then expanded into "Scot."

The genealogy is obviously quite different from that given in R¹ : but it is of equal if not greater antiquity, for it was in the document used by Nennius.   The ancestry of "Alanius" as given by Nennius is practically identical with that before us.   See ¶ 9 above.

The interpolation at the end is an attack on an opinion, presumably held by many men of learning at the time, but now of insignificant importance!   But it illustrates the difficulty which the compilers had, in reducing their chaotic materials to order.

17. We have here the first of the Synchronistic disquisitions, chiefly founded upon the Chronicle of Eusebius, which form an important but probably intrusive element in R², R³. The figures of Eusebius are not correctly reproduced. He allows only 853 years between the beginning of the reign of Ninus and the end of that of Tautanes (the Tutanes of our text) : whereas R² has 874. As for Tautanes, we must take him as we find him. It has proved impossible to reconcile the names of Mesopotamian kings, derived by Eusebius from Berossus, with the names recovered from the monuments.

The interpolator in this paragraph reckons 40 years from the Tower to Feinius Farsaid : he must therefore be a different person from the author of the otherwise very similar inter-polation in ¶ 16, who makes Feinius the sixteenth in descent from Rifath of the Tower.

¶ 17 allows two years from Feinius to Ninus, and from Eusebius we learn to consider Ninus a contemporary of Abraham. But we have already seen that on the lowest estimate there were 292 years from the Flood to Abraham : a long period must therefore be assumed from the Flood to the Tower, to be bridged by three generations only—Japhet, Gomer, Rifath.

The animadversion on the *Auraicept* is a fatuity : on referring to that text (ed. Calder, line 126) we find that the Latinus of the Tower was quite a different person from Latinus son of Faunus.

18. "Cincris" is the *Akenkheres* of Eusebius, the *Smenkh-ka-ra* of modern Egyptology. He is of no importance in Egyptian history : a mere ghost-king who reigned for a brief space c. 1360 B.C. immediately before the now famous Tutankhamun. The glossarial addition, explaining the name of Scota, has arisen from a later passage in the same redaction (see vol. ii, ¶ 129, and note thereon). It was primarily an attempt to explain the relation of Scota II, daughter of Nectanebus, to the name "Scota," and to *differentiate* her from Scota I, daughter of "Cincris," who is the person before us at the moment.

Dobreath a ingen is in all the MSS., and in the R³ appropriations of the text. It should be *dobretha a ingen*, as the corrector of E has noted in a very bad hand, which has induced the misreading, critical note (15) *ad loc.*

Third Redaction.

At the beginning of the text in B is written in an eighteenth-century hand "Accounts partly authentic and partly fabulous of the first Inhabitans (*sic*) of Ireland." At the top of the first page in M is written in a hand contemporary with the text *An toibrechan selaithi annso sis.* This has been partly cut through by a bookbinder, and is in consequence not perfectly easy to make out.

20. The gloss *isin Mac,* which has entered the text of M as an interpretation of *ar tūs* or *in principio* (critical note no. 5), is an exegesis as old as Irenaeus, who saw what he presumably thought was the Hebrew word *bar,* "son" (it is really Aramaic), in the opening words of Genesis, *B'rēshīth barā,* "In the beginning of creating."[29]

The Irish annotator probably borrowed the idea from Petrus Comestor, whose influence is obvious throughout the glosses in R³ : *Verbum erat principium in quo et per quod Pater creauit mundum . . . Creatus autem est in principio, id est, in Filio.*[30]

With regard to the interpolations, we have seen above (note to ¶ 2A) that y^2 does not come from *Q, the MS. of R¹ used by ∞ R³, nor from *X, the MS. of R¹ used by yR^3, but from *Z, the MS. of R² used by yR^3, in which MS. it was still a recent interpolation in the margin. Y³ comes from *X. That it was added later than the others is shown by the reversal of the blocks of material, for the matter of y^3 precedes y^2 in R^2. The first interpolator knew that the Creation was fully described in the following text : the second interpolator rushed in where his predecessor had thought it at least unnecessary to tread. The following differences

---

[29] See Gwatkin, *Early Church History to A.D. 313,* vol. i, pp. 196–7. The Armenian (the only extant) version of the Irenaeus text, at p. 692, translates these words "The Son in the beginning." See also Augustine, *De Civitate Dei,* xi. 32.

[30] *Historia Scholastica,* cap. i.

between this passage and its cognates in the other MSS. are
noteworthy :

> (i) The statements are inverted, each day being named
> before its work.   (The significance of this has already
> been pointed out in the notes to ¶ 2.)
> (ii) The month-dates are inserted (possibly a still later
> interpolation).
> (iii) Adam is mentioned before the beasts in the sixth
> day's work.
> (iv) There are some differences of Vocabulary : *neam*
> for *firmament* (on which see note to ¶ 2). "*muir*" *ina
> timchell, rēltanda* for *renna, anmanda muiridi* for
> *tondaitechu.* A few passages have all the appearance of
> intrusive glosses, and are marked as such in the text.

The date assigned to the *beginning* of Creation—fifteenth
of the Kalends of April, i.e., 18th March—is obviously
determined by the Vernal Equinox.   The *completed* Universe
is set upon its course on that day, the natural beginning of
the year, solar and agricultural.   Though not stated, it is
presupposed by the Flood story in R^2 : see note to ¶ 12.
 With the description of the Matter of Creation compare the
following, from *Cursor Mundi* (1. 348) :—

> The mater first ther of he mad,
> That es the elementes to sai,
> That first scapless al samen lay . . .
> This elementz that al thinges bindes,
> Four er thai als clerkes findes,
> The nethermast es watur and erth,
> The thrid es air, and fir the ferth.

The gloss *ni locdacht*, etc., may be borrowed from some
commentary or homily, though I have not succeeded in tracing
its origin.   But it reads more like the interpolation of a
copyist, anxious to reassure himself that the transcription of
the words which he has just written down did not constitute
an act of unpardonable sin.   If this were so, we must assume
that the major interpolations had already established themselves in the text, concealing from the writer the fact that he
was dealing with a text which had scriptural warrant.

21. It is important, as will appear presently, to note that the words dropped by homoiotes in B (⁊ *fodlad na n-usci*) contain 14 letters.

The subject of *ro fogail* may be either *Dīa* or *firmamint*—probably the latter, as it carries on the command "let it divide . . . it divided." The ambiguity exists even in Heb. : LXX has removed it by inserting ὁ θεός. The Irish translator is not quite emancipated from the idea of his predecessors responsible for R¹, R², that *firmamentum* is a proper noun, and does not require the article.

22. Here there is another haplography in B, caused by the homoiotes of *clandaiged.* The mistake existed in √B; for *s*B has observed the gap in the sense, and has inserted a full stop after the *clandaiged* which has survived. His intelligence did not, however, carry him to the further step of realising that he was copying a biblical text, so that had he chosen he could have filled the lacuna by referring to a copy of the book of Genesis, and translating the equivalent of the missing words.

Note that 43 letters are lost, practically the exact triple of the loss noted in the preceding ¶ : this indicates (i) that √B was written in narrow columns of short lines, with an average of 15 letters to the line, and (ii) that some of the carelessnesses for which the Book of Ballymote is notorious must be laid to the account of the exemplar from which it is copied.

23. *In grēin, ind ēsca,* which have no authority in any version of the biblical text, are evidently old ·glosses, interlined in √BMH and incorporated with the text after the separation of the B, M (and H) traditions, in different relative contexts.

24. *Barnimdaighter* is an illustration of the use of the possessive pronouns to supply the place of the missing first and second persons of the passive : but it is probably an artificial archaism in this place. One distinguished Celtist to whom I showed it called it "a monstrosity."

25. *In Tuismeadh* is another old gloss, earlier than √BMH. The omission of verse 25, which is almost a repetition of verse 24, may have been intentional; but Tr. is on the whole too conscientious for this, and it is more likely a piece of carelessness or laziness on the part of a copyist.

On the interpolation, see notes to ¶ 2A.

27. This paragraph begins the J-source of the Hebrew *Genesis.* Although Comestor calls special attention to the critically important word *Dominus,* which here begins to appear in the Divine name—adding an exegesis with which we need not trouble ourselves—the glossators have not shown any special interest in it; nor has the Irish translator made any endeavour to maintain the distinction, which is found in the Hebrew and all ancient versions.

The story of the finding of a name for Adam, contained in the long interpolation at the end of the paragraph, appears first in *The Book of the Secrets of Enoch,* written in Egypt somewhere about the beginning of the Christian Era, and brought to its final form by a Hellenistic Jew.[31] It survives to-day in a Slavonic version only: but in its time it had a considerable influence upon Early Christian literature. In chap. xxx. v. 13 ff. we read: And I [God] appointed him [Adam] a name, from the four component parts, from east, from west, from south, from north, and I appointed for him four special stars, and I called his name Adam. Charles cites parallels from *The Sibylline Oracles* (iii. 24–6); Pseudo-Cyprian, *De Montibus Sina et Syon* iv; Bede, *Exposition of Genesis,* iv; which in one form or another narrate the same story; others might be added. In *Cursor Mundi* we read (line 592)—

In this nam er four letters laid
That o the four ȝates er said:
Sua micul es Adam for to muth
Als est and west and north and south.
And thou mai ask, wit-outen blam,
Qui God him gaue sua mikel a nam . . .
It takens Adam and his sede
Ouer al the werld than suld thai spred.

[31] See R. H. Charles, *Apocrypha and Pseudepigrapha of the Old Testament,* ii, p. 425 ff.

So we find in *The Dialogue of Salomon and Saturnus* (Ed. Kemble, pp. 178, 194)—

"Whence was the name of Adam formed?—Of four stars. How are they called?—Arthox, Dux, Arotholem, Minsymbrie."

In illustration of which Kemble quotes the following elegiac couplet from MS., Harl. 3362, fol. 6—

Anathole dedit A, Disis D, contulit Arctos
Et Mesembrios M : collige, fiet ADAM.

The *Master of Oxford's Catechism* (op. cit., p. 217) gives Artax, Dux, Arostolym, Momfumbres as the names of the four stars. None of these versions of the story refers to the mission of the angels, which, however, appears in the Old English *Lyff of Adam and Eue* : this text gives us the closest parallel to the Irish version—

"þo after he made mon of erþe in flesch and bon, in þe vale of Ebron . . . þer-aftur God bad foure angelus þat heo schulden seche þulke monnes nome þat he hedde imaad. Seint Mihel wente in to þe est : he seih þer a sterre þat was swiþe briht, Anatalim was þat sterre ihote, wiþ þe furste lettre A, and soone he com aȝeyn. Gabriel in to þe west-half wente; and he seiȝ in þe firmament a sterre þat hihte was Dysus : þe furste lettre D þer-of soon he brouȝte. Raphael com to þe north : he say þer a sterre þat is iclepet Arcis; anon he fleyh aȝein, wiþ þe furste letter A þat he con wiþ him bringe. Forþ him wente Vriel riht in to þe souþ. Messembrion hihte þe sterre þat he sih þere; wiþ þe furste lettre M he wente swiþe aȝeyn & brouht hit tofore God wiþ þe oþur þreo. God took þeos foure lettres & bad Vriel rede & he radde : Adam."

28. *Parrthus na Toile* is a rendering of *Paradisus Voluptatis*, the Vulgate equivalent of the Garden of Eden. OL. has simply *Paradisus*, to which the *Parrthus* of R[1] corresponds.

The Rivers of Paradise were a favourite subject for speculation : it is therefore not surprising to find this paragraph farced with glosses.   The conceptions that lie behind them are set forth most simply in *Cursor Mundi* (line 1032)—

> Midward that land [Paradise] a wel springes,
> That rennes out with four strandes,
> Flummes farand in fer landes . . .
> The first es Tigre and sithen Gyon,[32]
> Sithen Eufrates and Fison.

Some hints at the characters attributed to the Rivers of Paradise are given by Comestor (borrowing from Isidore XIII. xxi, 7). *Unus dictus est Phison, qui a Gangaro rege Indiae dictus est Ganges . . . Tigris animal est uelocissimum, et ideo fluuius a sui uelocitate tigridi equiuocatus est . . . Euphrates frugifer uel fructuosus.*[32a]   The *Master of Oxford's Catechism* comes close to the statements in Poem no. VI :

> "Whate hight the iiij waters that renneth through Paradise?—The one hight Fyson, the other Egeon, the iijde Tygrys and the iiijth Effraton.   Thise be milke, hony, oyll, and wyne."

There is a similar passage in *Salomon and Saturnus*.   These ideas are forced, in Christian tradition, into an analogy between the four streams and the four evangelists : *Cursor Mundi* at line 21,293, likens the words of the Evangelists to water, wine, milk, and honey respectively.   They are, however, of Jewish origin.   Rabbi Yehosha ben Levi is quoted in *Yalkut Shimoni* as saying, in the course of a description of the terrestrial paradise, "And there flow out from it four rivers, one of milk, one of wine, one of balsam, and one of honey."[33]

We have already seen that 𝑉/B had about 15 letters to the line.   The haplography in the last interpolation in B is evidently due to a careless copying of words arranged thus—

---

[32] In some MSS. *Ganges.*

[32a] *Hist. Schol.*, Liber Genesis, cap. xiv (all quotations from this book are from the section on Genesis unless otherwise stated).

[33] Eisenmenger, *Entdecktes Judenthum*, ii, p. 310.

ꝼoꝺeꝛꞃcānꝺiꝶiuch
cheíꝺꝛíꝺe coꝶoích
cꝶeLaꝶꞁꞇꝺbaíbíLoꝶe

—the central line of the three being omitted, because either its end was similar to the end of line 1, or its beginning to the beginning of line 3.

Bdellium was the name of a gum, used for medicinal purposes. But Tr. or his copyists having turned the word into *Boellium,* the glossator identified it with the Latin *opalus.* His note is obviously a description of the opal set in the volcanic matrix (andesite or what not) in which it is found in nature. I have not traced the source of his information, but what he says about the stone seems to be a confused recollection of some description of the play of colours seen when it is contemplated from different angles.

29. That Adam was created first and afterwards transferred to the Paradise was the general belief, following Genesis iii. 7, 8. Damascus is named as the scene of Adam's creation, and of his retreat after the Fall : see Comestor, ch. xiii. This tradition is followed by gR^3, ¶ 38.

The glosses upon *oipriged* and *coimetad* are obviously suggested by Comestor. *Tulit ergo Deus hominem de loco formationis suae in Paradisum, scilicet terrestrem, ut operaretur ibi. Non tamen laborando ex necessitate, sed delectando et recreando, et sic Deus "custodiret illum," scilicet hominem. Vel utrumque refertur ad hominem, ut scilicet homo custodiret Paradisum et "operaretur" ut dictum est.* (Hist. Schol. xv.)

The interpolation y^1 is meant to explain away the discrepancy between the threat of *immediate* death upon eating of the fruit, and the fact of Adam's survival for over 900 years.

Comestor, again, is the source of y^2 : *Praecepitque ei dicens,* etc.; *ut homo sciret se esse sub Domino, praeceptum accepit a Domino* (loc. cit.).

30. It is impossible to decide whether the string of adjectives after *suan* and *ben* in this ¶, which is anticipatory of the vicious style of the later romance-writers, is due to Tr. or to his copyists. But see the note to the following ¶.

The idea that Adam's sleep was mantic rather than anaesthetic seems to be another borrowing from Comestor: *Non somnum, sed exstasim, in qua creditur supernae inter-fuisse curiae; unde et euigilans prophetauit de coniunctione Christi et Ecclesiae, et de diluuio futuro, et de iudicio per ignem* (Hist. Schol. xvi). It was, however, a common idea: Epiphanius (*Adv. Hæres.* II i 48) ingeniously proves it by pointing out that Adam spoke of the past (*os ex ossibus*), present (*ex uiro suo sumpta est*) and the future (*homo adhaerebit uxori sui*)! In the Old English Paraphrase of *Genesis and Exodus*[34] we read—

> God dede ðat he on sweuene cam,
> And in ðat sweuene he let him sen,
> Mikal ðat after sulde ben.

Many other quotations to the same effect might be taken from various sources.

The note *is ī seo cēt faitsine* appears to be due to a dullard homiletic glossator who has made several comments of the same kind on the text, and who is also probably responsible for the silly note *arāi grāda*, etc. He did not observe that a predecessor had already called Adam's words, *Ecce os* etc., "the first *coibche* and the first prophecy which Adam made." The longer gloss is older than the shorter statement, as it comes later in the text. This is a very important critical principle, of not infrequent application in the text before us. The annotator was in such a hurry to "hold his farthing rushlight to the sun" that he had not the patience to read a line or two further, when he would have found that he had been anticipated. In fact, both wiseacres have been misled by careless reading of Comestor, who definitely asserts that the passage which follows (*Quamobrem*, etc.) is the real prophecy (*Hist. Schol.* xix).

---

[34] Ed. Morris, E. E. T. S. (1865), lines 224–6.

31. There is evidence in the beginning of this ¶ that the adjectival exuberance of the biblical translation is to some extent glossarial. The superlatives attached to the Serpent in the original text have been multiplied by an annotator: they appear in the two MSS. *in a different order,* which as before indicates the interpolation of an interlined gloss.

The interpolation y^1 appears to come from R^2, because Eve is represented as being the sole victim of the Serpent's temptation. Comparison with the text of R^2 (¶ 4*) shows that *co curp sēim* is an interpolation made after the leaf of *Q had come into R^2, but before the writing of *Z, the copy of R^2 used by gR^3. The omission of *Iofer Niger* is a striking feature in this version of the passage.

The envy of Lucifer against Adam is referred to by Comestor (*Lucifer enim deiectus a Paradiso spirituum, inuidit homini quod esset in Paradiso corporum, sciens si faceret eum transgredi quod et ille eiiceretur* (Hist. Schol. xxi)). For once, however, this is not the source of the interpolation: the idea had been in the text from before Comestor's time, and LG, as we have seen, has no hint at the contrast between the spiritual and the terrestrial paradise emphasized by Comestor. The interpolation y^2 has nothing to do with y^1. It comes from a different source, and is most likely due to a different annotator.

Before these interpolations were made the text probably ran thus: *Ro bāi nathair . . . ⁊ ro rāid.* As the interpolation separated the subject from the verb, a later glossator interlined .i. *in athair sin* above *ro rāid.* When the gloss entered the text *is ī* evolved out of .i. This glossator's spelling of *athair,* without the initial *n,* has survived the vicissitudes of his note after its incorporation.

32. This paragraph is much farced with glosses. After *ro hoslaicit* a leaf has been lost from B. Its matter is preserved in the eighteenth-century transcript β, which is a good, though not a perfect copy of the MS. The two other eighteenth-century copies, β^1, β^2, have been collated throughout, but (as has been shown in the introduction) their only value is as a check on β, confirming some of its readings; their own variations do not appear to possess any importance, but they are recorded in order to secure completeness.

"In the noise of a mighty wind" is a curious misinterpretation of the Latin *ad auram*.

A medhōn chrainn Pairrthus: the singular number of *chrainn* reproduces the Latin *ligni*.

33. The gloss *ō guth aingleagda* is preserved in M only, but probably is another loss in the B tradition due to the short lines of $\stackrel{v}{V}$B and the carelessness of $s\sqrt{}$B. If the text were written in $\stackrel{v}{V}$B thus

ꞃꞃ
oᵹaiꞃmeꞃ̃čꝺiaaꝺā
oᵹucꜧ aiꞃᵹleaᵹꝺa
ꞃꞃoꞃaiꝺaaꝺācaic

there would have been homoiotes at both ends—a fatal trap for $s\sqrt{}$B.

On the first leaf of **H**, which begins in this ¶, the topmost 16 lines of each column are torn away entirely, and some of the others are injured, as the tear runs obliquely. In fact, the first few of the surviving lines are reduced in this manner to a few letters only, which would be quite unintelligible if we did not possess a perfect copy in M for comparison. If this first leaf of H had been perfect, the surviving portion of that text would have begun somewhere about verse 4 of the chapter, thus extending back to slightly before the beginning of the lacuna in B.

It may be worth mentioning that the Welsh antiquary, Edward Lhuyd, according to a letter written by him on 20 December 1702, and printed in *Archæologia Cambrensis*, 1859, p. 246, was possessed of "an imperfect copy of the B[ook] of Genesis in Irish" bestowed upon him by a priest near Sligo, who told him that "in the opinion of one of their chiefest antiquitys [*sic*]" it "was very little later than the first planting of Christianity" in Ireland. This fragment does not seem to be preserved among Lhuyd's MSS. in Oxford; and as one or more of the fragments now bound up in the miscellany which includes our manuscript H were at one time in Lhuyd's possession and bear his autograph, I am inclined to suspect that this "fragment of the book of Genesis" was no other than H. If so, its Sligo provenance may possibly be confirmatory of the suggestion made above (p. 13) that the H leaves had been torn out to supplement the deficiencies of the Book of Ballymote. In that case, however, the deficiency was not that caused by the loss of folio 9, which must have taken place after Lhuyd's time, but the chasm in this text described, *loc. cit.* Further, the depredation most probably took place before 1522, when the Book of Ballymote appears to have migrated from Sligo to Tir Conaill.

Dorad domh do chrann, omitting the definite article, is a literal translation from the Latin *dedit mihi de ligno.* It adds a subtle point to the story, as suggesting that Adam professed ignorance of the tree from which the fruit had come; but unfortunately the Hebrew text disallows it.

For the curious rendering *acht mē fēin,* see the notes on the Latin text.

34. The translator seems to have missed the point of the serpent's "lying in wait," and to have understood it to mean self-protection rather than hostility.

The gloss *iomad galar mīsda dhuit* is paralleled by a Rabbinic idea (Eisenmenger, i, p. 833) that this disability is due to a union between Eve and Sammaël in the guise of the Serpent.

Further confirmation of our conclusions as to the nature of $\sqrt[\gamma]{}$B is here forthcoming. As the words *d'indearna Dia . . . ⁊ do thalmain* are absent in β^{012} we may take it for certain that they were also absent in B. They just amount to two of the short lines of which we have already found indications—

cencopaᴄaᴅčuínᵳō
ᴄaᴅinᴅepñᴅiaᴄu
oínírᴅolúaiᴄꞃᴅo
ᴄaᴅoponaᴅꞃírᵳae

The eye of $s\sqrt{}$B wandered from the beginning of the second of these lines to the beginning of the fourth.

35. Our worthy glossator seems to fear that subsequent readers, if not warned, would take Eve to be the mother of animals as well as of men!

How *g*H ascertained that the garments made for Adam and Eve were *of one colour* does not appear.

36. The perverse exegesis in the interpolation in this ¶ is from Comestor: *Ironia est, quasi uoluit esse ut Deus, sed ın euidenti est modo quod non est* (Hist. Schol. xxiv).

37. Y¹ is clearly an incorporated gloss, the lemma of which is the sentence *following*. It filled the whole interlinear space above that sentence in the ms. from which it entered the body of the text, and thus it was taken in before the words which it ought to have followed. That Adam and Eve remained virgin in Paradise was a notion suggested by the fact that Eve's name of universal mother is not recorded till after the Fall. Something of the idea will be found in Augustine, *Civ. Dei* xiii, 13, 14: and it was emphasised in the *Revelationes* of Pseudo-Methodius, according to which, *Sciendum est quod exeuntes Adam et Eua de Paradiso uirgines fuerint*; or as the Old English paraphrase expresses it,

> ʒet owt of Paradyse when þey paste
> clene vyrgenys were þey both—

Our glossators, however, show no direct acquaintance with that singular production, and probably took the idea from Comestor, who gives a paraphrase of the words of Pseudo-Methodius in his chap. xxv. According to the Syriac *Book of the Bee*, Adam and Eve remained virgins for 30 years after their expulsion (ed. Budge, chap xviii).

The interpretation of the name of Cain is borrowed in the first instance from Isidore: *Cain possessio interpretatur, unde etymologiam ipsius exprimens pater eius ait "Cain" id est "Possedi hominem per Deum." Idem et lamentatio, eo quod pro interfecto Abel interfectus sit, et poenam sui sceleris dederit. Abel luctus interpretatur* (Etym. VII.

vi. 7). We must regard *no lamentacio* as a gloss, although Isidore gives the alternative interpretation, partly because, though in a Latin context, it is introduced by an Irish conjunction, and partly because it is ignored in the subsequent matter. Both etymologies are of course wrong. *Caneithi* is the Hebrew קָנִיתִי *qanīthī*, "I have gotten," *Lamentatio* looks back to the quite independent Hebrew word קִינָה *qīnāh* "a dirge." All these early commentators overlook the fact, which a little knowledge of elementary Hebrew grammar would have taught them, that it was Eve, not Adam, who said *Possedi hominem*. But they are in the good company of Augustine, *Civ. Dei* xv. 15.

The idea expressed in y^3, following many ancient commentators and versions, that the acceptance of Abel's offering was indicated by fire from heaven, seems to go back to the version of Theodotion, in which יִשַׁע (*respexit*) is translated ἐνεπύρισεν. It is, of course, developed under the influence of the narrative in I (III) Kings xviii (Elijah on Carmel). As usual, Comestor is the proximate source of the glossator's information : *Quia placuit Deo Abel et pro ipso placuit oblatio eius, quod quomodo cognitum fuerit, alia translatio aperit. "Inflammauit Deus super Abel et super munera eius." Ignis enim de coelo oblationem eius incendit.* (Hist. Schol. xxvi).

There is no authority for the words *a ttoirsi ך in dubha,* which must be a glossarial expansion.

38. The simple account of the murder of Abel in B (as preserved in the derivatives of that MS.) is clearly the original version, being based on the Genesis text. The interpolation in M, *ro iad a dā lāim fō bragait cor ba marb* (H here unfortunately fails us) is as clearly borrowed from R². This introduces us to a further complication in the history of the text—the borrowings from earlier redactions at late stages of development. This cannot be one of the borrowings originally made from *Z, as in that case it would have been in B also.

Y^1, in one form or another, must have been in √BMH. The family had returned to Damascus where Adam was created—we need not vex the shades of the glossator by insisting that Damascus could hardly have been a *cathair* at this stage of the world's history, as he conceived it. Comestor says of the expulsion from Paradise : *Emisit eum Dominus de Paradiso Voluptatis . . . in agrum scilicet Damascenum, de quo sumptus fuerat, in quo Cain Abel suum fratrem interfecit* (Hist. Schol. xxiv).

Y^2 seems to be an extract from some homily upon Abel. The haplography attested by β^{012} must have been in B. It was easy for a scribe to commit (*Abel dō cēt marb . . . Abel in cēt martir*) but for once it cannot be laid to the account of $\sqrt{}$B, for the omitted words are too long for the 15-letter lines of $\sqrt[V]{}$B.

The variant of the question *Quid fecisti* in M is curious. Presumably it is due ultimately to a reader who, having read *Cid doroinnais?* was moved to write in the margin *Pecad ⁊ gnīm n-adbal*! (He was of the spiritual kindred of Lucifer's critic in ¶ 3.) The loss of *cid*, which might easily happen after the preceding *Cāin* (especially if it were written *Caidin*, as in P) would result in the absorption of this note by the text.

Y^4 seems to come from another homily, in which reference was made to Genesis iv. 10, xviii. 20, and Luke xviii. 7, 8.

39. Once more we have a paragraph filled with glossarial fatuities. The MS. from which ∞H, ∞M, and ∞B were copied, in this order (as shown above, p. 14) must have had *ro oslaic a bēl*, probably with an open *a* in *oslaic*. Both ∞M and ∞H independently misread this as *ro sluic Abel*: but ∞B copied it correctly, and in the derivatives from B the reading has been put beyond a doubt by inserting the prefixed *f*. We have already seen that we cannot assume a ^{n}/MH differentiated from ^{n}/B; the mistake must therefore have been made twice. In the M tradition a number of interpolations—three in this paragraph alone—have entered the text, not found in H or in B. Y^1 has been inserted by some one who did not take the trouble to observe that it contradicts the biblical story, related a few lines above. But it must have entered the M tradition before the story about Abel's being strangled with Cain's hands (¶ 38) was inserted. For we may lay it down as a general principle that when we have two contradicting interpolations (*a*) and (*b*), if they

run consecutively they may be contemporary, the glossator
setting down two opposing views between which he makes
no choice; or else (*b*), the second, may be later than (*a*),
having been interpolated by a second glossator to contradict
what was already in the text. But if the two are separated
by some lines of text, then the probability is greatly in favour
of (*a*) being the later of the two, having been inserted by a
reader who has not yet reached (*b*) and does not anticipate
it.

The perverse notion that the mark of Cain was designed
to secure a prolongation of his punishment is borrowed from
Comestor. *"Omnis quis inuenerit me occidet me." Ex timore
hoc dixit, uel optando dixit, quasi diceret: Utinam occidant
me. "Dixitque ei Deus: Nequaquam ita fiet." Non cito
scilicet morieris, "sed omnis qui occiderit Cain"—supplendum
est, liberabit eum a timore, a dolore, et miseria—"septuplum
punietur." Id est, punitio fiet de eo dum uiuet in poena.*

There have been many speculations on the mark of Cain.
For once Comestor is jettisoned by our glossators, who say
nothing about the theory adopted by him, that the mark was
a perpetual shaking of the head—that "he wagged alwey forþ
wiþ his heued" as the Old English *Lyff of Adam and Eue*
puts it. The 'lump in his forehead' goes back to a lost *Book
of Lamech,* which told how Lamech, under the guidance of his
son Tubalcain—for he was blind—shot an arrow at a wild
man covered with hair, and with a horn growing out of his
forehead, who proved to be Cain. Lamech was so distressed
by the discovery that he killed Tubalcain. The additional
"lumps" are added by *y*M under the influence of poem no. V
(quatrain 23). That Cain had no beard comes indirectly from
the same authority, which states (lines 123, 124) that Seth
was the first man who grew a beard.

40. A glossator has doubtless introduced the appellation
diamus, in order to distinguish the Cainite from the Sethite
Lamech. The interpretation of the word is most likely the
work of a still later annotator.

41. That Naamah was a weaver or embroideress was a
commonplace of mediaeval apocryphal speculation. Probably
our glossator borrowed the fact from Comestor—*Soror uero*

Tubalcain Noema, quae inuenit artem uariae texturae (Hist.
Schol. xxviii).   So also *Cursor Mundi* (line 1523)—

> A sister had this brether alsua,
> And sco was heiten Noema :
> Scho was the formest webster,
> That man findes o that mister.
> That fader was the first o liue,
> That bigam was, wit dubul vijfe.

Ro chēt-chum is a favourite construction in this text : the
composition of *cēt* with a verb, to denote "he was the first
to" perform whatever action is specified.

42. The difficult Song of Lamech has given trouble to the
translator, and apparently also to his copyists.   The rendering
as we have it does not even make reasonable sense, to say
nothing of its relation to the original text.   *Ro mharbus fer*
amuigh aniu seems to have arisen out of *Ro mharbas fer am*
guinib (the last word perhaps written *guiniu*), thus representing the Latin *occidi uirum in uulnus meum.*   The sentence
which follows is apparently a gloss, the original form of
which was most likely .i. *is inund* ⁊ *"ro chrechtnaiges" annsin.*

The word *sechtoll* does not seem to occur elsewhere in
Irish literature.

It is curious that none of our meddlesome glossators have
come forward with the information—known to the author of
poem no. V, and universally believed—that Lamech's victim
was Cain.

43. Adam's speech is thus written in β : *air Adhamh,* ⌊*ar*⌋
.i. siol, etc., indicating that the scribe was puzzled by the
word *ar.*   It can scarcely be equated with the Irish *ar,*
"ploughing" : it is perhaps a degeneration of the Hebrew
זֶרַע, *zerʻa,* "seed"—read backwards, like the Tetragrammaton in poem no. V.   This word appears in the original of
the passage, and may have reached the Irish translator by some
circuitous route.

At the end of this paragraph there comes the lacuna in
the B-tradition (see p. 13) which was there even before B
lost its leaf.   The eighteenth-century copyists were conscious of
a gap in the sense, and each in his own way made a makeshift

stop-gap, here printed as ¶ 43a. H resumes in the course of the following paragraph, and until M fails us at the end of ¶ 52 H and M are the only authorities for the text. It is here printed from M, with variants from H.

44. Y^2 like y^3, was in M only. H is here defective, but a count of words shows that there was no room for it.

According to a belief recorded by Comestor, Adam was only seven hours in Paradise (*Quidam tradunt eos fuisse in Paradiso septem horas*—Hist. Schol. xxiv). With this *Cursor Mundi* more or less agrees (line 985)—

> For he [Adam] was wroght at undern tide,
> At middai Eue draun of his side.
> Thai brak the forbot als sun,
> That thai war bath don out at none.

A poem contained in the *Book of Ui Maine* specifies $13\frac{1}{2}$ hours but the *Master of Oxford* makes the time seven years. The writer of y^2 must have copied it from some other *literary* source, as is indicated by the spelling *Eba,* by the here superfluous specification of the nature of the sin, and by the description of the forbidden tree as *Crand na Haithne* (not *Fessa*).

Of the transfer of Adam's head to Golgotha, Comestor, with a critical judgement which he does not as a rule encourage us to expect in him, writes as follows: *Ambrosius, in Epist. ad Romanos uidetur uelle quod ibi sepultus fuerit Adam, et a capite eius dictum Caluariam; et ei dictum ab apostolo: Surge qui dormis, exsurge a mortuis, et illuminabit te Christus. De qua opinione dicit Hieronymus quod fauorabilis est interpretatio, et mulcens aures, non tamen uera. Unde credimus hoc a falsariis positum in Ambrosio.* (Hist. Schol. in Euangel. clxx). Of the burial of Adam in Hebron we read in *Cursor Mundi* (line 1415)—

> Doluen he [Adam] was thoru Seth his sun,
> In the dale that hat Ebron:

and in Comestor: *Locus in quo luxerunt* [Adam and Eve, after Abel] *dicitur Vallis Lacrymarum iuxta Hebrom* (Hist. Schol. xxv, doubtless suggested by Ps. lxxxiii [Hebrew lxxxiv] verse 7). This geography is a commonplace of the Adam apocrypha. The interpolation y³ is peculiar to M, and probably came from the same literary source as y². The glossators have apparently never heard the Eastern story, told in *The Cave of Treasures*, that the body of Adam was part of the cargo of the Ark, where it served the useful purpose of keeping the men and the women apart; and that it was afterwards buried by Shem in Golgotha.

45 ff. Worthy of passing notice is a commentator, possibly of ethnological or psychological interest, who was apparently unable to conceive of large numbers except in *scores*, and had to reduce the hundreds to that unit, in order to understand them.

50. Enoch was the central figure of a vast mass of folklore and apocryphal literature. His existence "in desert places and away from common life" is doubtless an expansion of the Biblical *et non apparuit*, but it may have reached the Irish glossator from some special source.

The ten names of God are thus enumerated by Isidore (*Etym.* VII. i. 1) : El, Eloi, Eloe, Sabaoth, Elion, Eie, Adonai, Ia, Tetragrammaton, Saddai. The list given by Epiphanius (*Adv. Haeres.* I, iii, 40) is Sabaoth, Eli, Eloi, Israel, Sadadai, Ellion, Rabboni, Ia, Adonai, Iabe. On their magical use, see Budge, *Amulets and Superstitions*, pp. 369 ff.

From *ō anmandaib ēcsamlaib* in this paragraph to the end of ¶ 52, M is our only authority for the text.

52. With the end of this paragraph the great lacuna begins in M. Unlike sB, sM was conscious of the gap in his exemplar, and left the remainder of the column, upon which he was writing, a blank, in the hope of filling in the missing matter afterwards. This neither he nor the subsequent owners of M were ever able to do : and H, which now carries on the story, shows us that the space provided (32 lines in a column of 50 lines) was absurdly small.

We are still in the mutilated first leaf of H, which has lost the top lines of all its columns. The missing portions of the two texts slightly overlap, so that at this point there are a few lines of the text which are altogether lost, as well as portions of the beginnings and endings of others—covering verses V. 31 (last clause) and VI. 1, 2, of the biblical text.

In the gloss explaining the name of Noah, *is Noe* is doubt. less to be corrected to .i. *Noe.*

53. From here on to ¶ 87 our only authority is H. The first two verses of chap. VI, lost from our text, contain the fragmentary tale of intercourse between *filii Dei* and *filiae hominum.* This tantalizing story was for long the subject of speculation : and some copyist seems to have considered these speculations more interesting than the barren biblical narrative. That the "sons of God" were the Sethites, and the "daughters of men" the Cainites, was the normal mediaeval solution of the enigma. It is set forth in Pseudo-Methodius as well as in Comestor, ch. xxxi, the Old English *Lyff of Adam and Eve,* and many other authorities. The full story, as related in *The Cave of Treasures,* is to the effect that Adam, when dying, had commanded Seth and his descendants to remain on the holy mountain of Hermon, apart from the offspring of Cain, and that this injunction was repeated by each succeeding patriarch till the days of Yârêd (Jared, which means "descent"), when the Sethites broke their oaths and went down to the encampment of iniquity of the Cainites. The glossator has based his interpolation, with which the text resumes after the lacuna, upon the detailed paraphrase of this story in the Irish *Sex Aetates Mundi.* The MS. is here much injured. The inner edge of the leaf has been made ragged by tearing the fragment from its proper place (as described, p. 13 *ante*), and in consequence parts of several lines are lost. Some of the gaps can be filled up by a collation of *Sex Aetates* (Rawl. B 502 facsimile) ; but not all, for the texts, though similar, are not identical. Restorations of the text are here contained within square brackets.

The alternative explanation of the origin of the monsters, recorded here by a later glossator, will be found below, ¶ 81.

54. The glossator has forgotten that the descendants of Seth had their share in the production of the giants.

55. Here again an extract from *Sex Aetates Mundi* has been interpolated, and has ousted verses 5, 6, of the biblical text : a process facilitated by the fact that the two passages began with the same words.　The passage as it appears in Rawl. B, 502, reads *Otchonairc Dīa imorro tictain dōib dar a thimna, ro chinnistar na dōini do huili-dilgenn, coni do tucad in diliu.*　This has been expanded in our text by glossators.

The interpolation at the end of the paragraph is from another source.

57. Y² is obviously suggested by Comestor's *fuit haec arca in fundamento quadrata* (Hist. Schol. xxxii).

The interpolations y^3 a, b, are parts of a single marginal note that has become bisected, and has entered the text in two different places—in the second place breaking very awkwardly into the sense.　The information is derived in part from Comestor : *Bitumine intus et extra linita est, quod est gluten feruentissimum quo ligna linita non dissoluuntur aliqua ui uel arte nec materia uel maceria bituminata solui potest . . . In lacubus Iudaeae supernatans colligitur. In Syria limus est a terra aestuans.*　Comestor in his turn seems to have taken this from Isidore (*Etym.* XVI. ii. 1) : *Bitumen in Iudaeae lacu Asphaltite emergit, cuius glebas supernatantes nautae scaphis adpropugnantes colligunt. In Syria autem limus est passim aestuans a terra . . . Natura eius ardens et ignium cognata, et neque aqua neque ferro sumpitur . . . utilis ad conpages nauium.*

I can find no authority for the two persons who altruistically contributed to the success of an enterprise from which they themselves derived no benefit : the carpenter with the improbable name Epiphenius, and the mixer of pitch whose name, in the absence of auxiliary evidence, cannot be certainly read in the text : evidently *s*H could not read it clearly in √H, and did his little best to copy it as it stood.

buidiá añlonce

The curved line over the *n* is turned the wrong way for the usual *m* contraction.　It is a little to the right of the middle of the *n,* and is attached to the top of the following *l.* The only expansion that I can think of is *Dia-anarlaoite,* as printed in the text, or perhaps *Anarlarte.* By a perverse fate the name of the father of these brethren is torn away except the end, 13, in which the minim is most likely part of an *n.* This gives *-nus,* a termination that will not fit any antediluvian name in history or legend that I ever heard of. These names, and the details of the construction of the Ark here set forth, and the prayers of Noah and his sons, appear to come from some lost homily or apocryphon.

58. Here again a glossator tells us of the peculiar matrimonial relationships of Noah and his sons, presumably borrowing them from some late MS. of R².

59. On the importance of the discrimination between clean and unclean *birds* in this paragraph, see p. 9 *ante.* The adjectives *silteach saidbir* may be original or glossarial, it is uncertain which, and matters little.

60–65. There is little in these paragraphs to call for notice other than what is referred to in the notes on the biblical text. The glosses are more than usually naïve : note especially the expression of admiration for the Ark at the end of ¶ 61, and the description of the proceedings of the dove in ¶ 65. If the latter is not an invention, it would be difficult to say whence the glossator obtained his information. Someone has acutely observed that glosses like this express and partially satisfy a natural craving for an *illustrated* history-book. In the absence of pictures, the annotator jots down picturesque details, which fill in the mental picture suggested by the words.
That the first emission of the dove took place seven days after that of the raven is a glossator's discovery, with no biblical authority.

66. The chronology of the Flood according to the interpolation forming this and the following paragraph is not easy to follow, and the attentions of glossators have added to the confusion. But the following is clear (paying due attention to the corrections, p. 127)—

	year	month	day
Noah enters ark	600	2	10
Flood begins	600	2	17
Flood lasts 150 days = 5 months of 30 days each. Therefore grounding of ark at the end of that time takes place on	600	7	17
Mountain tops appear	600	10	1
Raven sent forth 40 days afterwards (1 month and 10 days), and therefore on	600	11	11
Noah opens ark	601	1	1
Noah leaves ark	601	2	27

Noah has therefore been in the ark 1 year 17 days—in the Irish reckoning 1 year 16 days.

The interpolators (or one of them) apparently supposed that the expression "second month" implies that the May in which Noah entered the ark was an intercalary May (*Mai atharrach*). This is interesting, as it seems to indicate the recollection of a lunar calendar like that of Coligny.[35] The calculation that he entered the ark on a Friday and left it on a Tuesday presupposes a lunar calendar with 12 months of 30 days: $12 \times 30 + 16 = 376 = 7 \times 53 + 5$. The first of these five extra days being Friday, the last would be Tuesday: on this assumption therefore the calendar works out.

It is unknown to me on what basis or authority the number of species of birds and fishes in the ark is reckoned—or for that matter, why fishes were included in the calculation at all.

67. The reference to Enoch is rendered obscure by the state of the MS.: ᴧɴᴛᴧᴅᴧᴍᵽᴧ comes at the end of a line, after which a blob of the very opaque purplish colour, with which a capital letter on the other side of the page had been decorated, has penetrated through the vellum. Underneath this disconcerting obstruction the eye of faith can discern very faint traces of a letter like an ᴌ or a ʙ. The éᵽ begins the next line; but ᵽᴧ*éᵽ is more difficult to comprehend than ᵽᴧéᵽ, the reading here adopted. The general sense is presumably that as Adam and Noah were the founders of

---

[35] Unlike those responsible for R², who thought of solar months: see notes on ¶ 12 above.

human physical life, the pious Enoch was the founder of human spiritual life.

78. The gloss ⁊ *ōna huilib ēnaib* is a good illustration of the haste of a reader, too impatient to read to the end of the sentence, where he would have discovered that the birds had not been forgotten.

80. Comestor says (on earlier authority) that the rainbow shall cease to appear forty years before the Last Judgement : *Et tradunt sancti quod quadraginta annis ante Iudicium non uidebitur arcus, quod etiam naturaliter ostendet desiccationem aeris iam incoeptam* (Hist. Schol. xxxv). This paragraph is greatly influenced by the corresponding passage in *Sex Aetates Mundi*, from which also the long passage on the history of the rainbow comes. The absence from *Sex Aetates* of the anticipation that the bow will not appear before the Judgement indicates that this is a later intrusive gloss on the LG text.

81. Here again the translation has been contaminated by an extract from *Sex Aetates Mundi*. The glosses also come from that work, so that the obvious interruption of the former by the latter is old. R³ interpolates the mutual slaying of "the children of Dardan and Ioph," which does not refer to the Trojan war, as might appear at first sight,[36] but to the destruction of the Midianites (Judges vii. 19 ff.) : *Dadan* and *Epha* appear in the Latin version of the account of the family from which this people is said to have descended (Gen. xxv. 3, 4).

We are not, however, to suppose a simple cross-copying from one book to the other. The curse on Ham, and the destruction of his descendants, were written in first : the further note, here printed in smaller type, attributing the existence of monsters to the curse on Ham, must have been added as an interlined and marginal afterthought. This is shown by its dispartition (compare the fate of the note on the composition of pitch, ¶ 57.)

---

[36] Notwithstanding the occurrence of these names, in Trojan connexion, among the descendants of Ham in *Sex Aetates Mundi.*

The word *gid* (in *tucad gid dilgend*) does not appear in
the corresponding place in *Sex Aetates Mundi* (see Rawl. B,
502, facs. p. 71 *b*, line 49).   I take it that the words in √H
were *tucad aigid-dilgend* "a death-destruction was brought"
(on the persons of the Canaanites, and confiscation on their
land).   The missing letters were in a *cor fá chasán* at the
end of the preceding line, and were overlooked by *s*H.

The accompanying diagram shows what must have lain
before *s*H in the MS. (√H) which he was copying.   The
preceding MS. (∛H) had nothing but the matter of the first
and last of these lines in sequence (omitting, of course, the
letters after *Iafeth* in line 1).   Later, someone wrote into the
margin of ∛H the note about the consequences which the
curse upon Ham had brought upon his Canaanite descendants.
After this, √H was copied from ∛H; and the copyist took
this note into the text, the writing being disposed as in the
diagram.   Still later, another scribbler, writing partly between
the lines and partly in the margin, enriched √H with the
further details about the monsters descended from Ham—an
item of special interest, apparently, as another glossator
inserted it again in √H, at ¶ 53.

When our MS. H was copied, history repeated itself.   The
new paragraph was incorporated in the text at what was
obviously the most convenient place, the period preceding
Iarsin in line 2.   The scribe pursued it as far as *dainib*, in
the margin at the end of line 5: but he failed to observe its
conclusion, tucked into the blank space at the end of the
short line 6.   He then returned to *Iarsin*: but the interlineation which he had already copied, and at which he did
not look again, screened from his vision the *cor fá chasán*,
which must have concluded the first line and contained
the beginning of the obviously imperfect word "gid."   There

must have been no more than a short sentence before *Iarsin* originally: a longer sentence would have filled up the preceding line to the end, leaving no space for the indispensable *cor fá chasán*. This is an additional argument for the secondary nature of the "monsters" gloss.

It is most fortunate that *s*H possessed in abundant measure the most valuable of all endowments for a scribe— *un*-intelligence. He copied by rote what lay before him: its meaning, if it had any, was not his concern—that was the affair of his betters. Owing to this admirable quality, he failed to identify, in the words at the end of line 6 when at last he reached them, the end of the "monsters" note which he had copied only a few moments before—although he had already copied out its whole text some time previously, when writing ¶ 53. He therefore transcribed them just as they stood, and made no attempt to insert them in their proper place. It never occurred to him that "gid dilgend" was incomprehensible nonsense. Had he realised these things, he would infallibly have made disastrous efforts after emendation, and would thus have destroyed all the clues!

R³, while copying these details, omits a censure upon the Gaedil for ascribing the monsters to the Cainites, this being a violation of the scriptural truth that all life perished in the Flood. Augustine (*Civ. Dei* XVI. 8) discusses at length whether the monstrous races of men (in which there was in his time at least a half-belief: he gives a list of these deformities of folklore) were descendants of Noah, and answers in the affirmative. He does not, however, call in the curse of Ham to account for them.

82. The genealogical chap. x is lost. The heterogeneous paragraphs which follow the Biblical translation represent various attempts to fill its place.

83. The story of the Tower of Babel is very diffuse, and departs widely, in its language at least, from the biblical text. The lacunae near the beginning are due to a tear which mutilates the inner margin of the leaf.

"Hebrew," says Augustine (*Civ. Dei* XVI, 2), "was the common language of the race of men till the time of Heber father of Peleg, when the earth was divided. Till then it did

not require a distinctive name, but after that it was called
Hebrew, after Heber.'' Nowhere can the origin of the name
Gorthigern, given to this primitive language by Irish
historians and grammarians, be discerned: we might guess
that it is a corruption of some sort of rendering of the *Vox
Domini* of the Psalter, the language being assumed to be the
speech of Heaven.

[It may be desirable to explain here, in condonation of
the use of the symbol Δ for the Latin manuscript which lies
at the basis of the biblical text which we have been studying,
that it has been chosen simply because it is one of the very
few symbols not already pre-empted by the elaborate
apparatus criticus of the Vatican edition. There is not the
slightest fear of its ever being confused with the St. Gall MS.]

---

86. The biblical extract is followed by a miscellaneous
collection of snippets, with the basal text *Q acting as framework. For an analysis of this part of the compilation see the
introduction to the present section. In these paragraphs, the
parts belonging to *Q are printed in ordinary type, the
stratification of interpolations being roughly indicated by two
varieties of smaller type. This paragraph is in H only, but
the lacuna of M ends at the beginning of the poem. The
particulars as to the place of death of the patriarchs are
doubtless taken primarily from poem no. V, quatrain 42: but
from what source it reached that authority I have not
discovered, and until it is found attempts at explaining
Rafán and Radruip would be mere guesswork. *Formeinia,*
of course, = *Armenia,* and the mountain intended is no
doubt Ararat.

87. In H and M, apparently from R², or from some text
depending thereon. The comment regarding the age of Adam
seems to come from this passage of Comestor, quoting Pseudo-
Methodius: *Et anno creationis uitae Adam decimo quinto
natus est ei Cain et soror eius Chalmana. Et si enim factus
est Adam quasi in aetate triginta annorum tamen fuit unius
diei et anni* (Hist. Schol. xxv).

88. This comes from *Q. See the notes on R¹, ¶ 7. The
appended gloss, though containing the same substance as the

corresponding gloss in ¶ 7, is differently worded and must have been introduced independently.

89. The last sentence and the appended quatrain continue the matter from *Q : but before it a passage from *Sex Aetates Mundi* has been interpolated. This includes the first verse of a poem (given in full in *Sex Aetates*) and the tabular statement of the ages of the Patriarchs. These figures agree with *Sex Aetates* against all versions of the biblical text (except the Irish translation printed above) in the case of Seth : against all versions *including* the Irish translation in the case of Mahalaleel : and with all versions against the Irish translation in the cases of Methuselah and Lamech.

90. In H only, of unidentified origin. But see below ¶ 92.
Two successive readers have appended speculations on how the Goidelic language came to be.

91. Also in H only. It is mutilated by a tear from the inner margin of the leaf, and would be unintelligible if it were not borrowed from *Sex Aetates Mundi,* with the aid of which text it can be partly restored—though with some slight verbal differences—from the copies in Rawl. B. 502 and in B. The words *acht a leigiud a fo-tasgor na cinel* appear in Rawl. (41 d 20) from which B differs only in some orthographical trifles, in the form *acht a lecud hi fothechdas na genel n-aile.* The following passage from Isidore (IX ii. 39) appears to be the basis of the paragraph : *Nam quod ex filio Cham qui vocatur Mesraim Aegyptii sunt exorti, nulla hic resonat origo uocabuli, sicut nec Aethiopum, qui dicuntur ad eum filium Cham pertinere, qui Chus appellatus est. Et si omnia considerentur, plura tamen gentium mutate quam manentia uocabula apparent, quibus postea nomina diuersa dedit ratio.* See also Augustine, *Civ. Dei,* XVI, 6.

92. The beginning of this ¶ is in BM as well as H, but it is a continuation of the matter in ¶ 90; ¶ 91 being a later interpolation. The text of *Q then resumes : note how the correction about the number of the sons of Shem has been taken over. The passage is much farced with interpolations. The formula *cia ainmigter . . . ni tabar a n-airem* comes from

Sex Aetates Mundi, as also does H's note, which has ousted its lemma, to the effect that the unnamed sons had descendants, but of no importance. The summary enumeration of the sons of Shem and of Japhet in R¹ has been expanded by reference, not to the Biblical source, but to Isidore (IX ii 26 ff.). He enumerates the sons of Japhet thus : *Gomer* (ancestor of Galatae i.e., Galli), *Magog* (supposed ancestor of Scythians and Goths), *Madai* (supposed ancestor of Medes), *Iauan* (ancestor of Ionians, who are the Greeks, and eponym of the Ionian Sea), *Thubal* (ancestor of Iberi who are the Hispani, by some supposed ancestor of the Italians), *Mosoch* (*ex quo Cappadoces, unde et urbs apud eos usque hodie Mazaca dicitur*), *Thiras* (ancestor of Thracians). By some misunderstanding the city of Mazaca (Caesarea in Cappadocia) has become an unauthorized additional son, Maisechda, whose descendants a later interpolator naturally sought in vain : see below ¶ 95 L. The variant in H (ꞇ *ni tabar . . . . tabairt forro*) is an adaptation of a similar passage in *Civ. Dei*, XVI, 3.

93. This paragraph in H only. It is borrowed from R² (¶ 15). It is not clear why the order of the sons of Noah has been reversed.

94. This paragraph, more or less mutilated, is in all the MSS. It comes from R¹, but there are some traces of the influence of R². The version before us gives some good readings. It is more probable that *Fir na Scithīa* should decline into *Farsacca*, and that this, owing to the constant association of "Medes and Persians," should develop a prefixed *Media*, than that *Farsacca* (protected by the associated *Media* from misunderstanding) should evolve into *Fir na Scithīa*. The phrase *Is ūad lucht na Heorpa uile* is now exposed as a marginal gloss, taken into the text in different places : and "Grēcus mac Iafeth" is likewise shown to be an intruder into the text of R¹.

95. For convenience of reference this very long paragraph is broken into sections, denoted by capital letters. Most of it comes from *Sex Aetates Mundi* (here referred to as SAM) : it is found in H only.

A.—The gloss *no Eōnae* and the secondary gloss .i. *an seindser*, are not in SAM. But the additional son of Japhet appears, there named Masseca.

B.—The interpolated explanation of the name Gallograeci is based on Isidore, *Etym.*, IX, ii, 68. (*Galatae Galli esse noscuntur, qui in auxilium a rege Bithyniae euocati regnum cum eo parta uictoria diuiserunt: sicque deinde Graecis admixti primum Gallograeci, nunc ex antiquo Gallorum nomine Galatae nuncupantur.*)

C.—Also based on Isidore, *Etym.*, IX, ii, 69 (*Graeci ante Thessali a Thessalo, postea a Graeco rege Graeci sunt nuncupati*).

D.—This section only repeats well-worn etymological speculations with neither value nor authority behind them. The harmonistic identification of Rifath with Ibath is perhaps worth a passing acknowledgement.

E.—Taken direct from the list of Japhet's descendants in Isidore *Etym.*, IX ii, 26 ff. (*Filii Gomer nepotes Iaphet, Aschanaz a quo Sarmatae quos Graeci Rheginos uocant, Riphath a quo Paphlagones, Gotorna a quo sunt Phryges*). "⁊ Ilia" must be a gloss.

F.—*Madai, a quo Medos existere putant* : Isidore, *loc. cit.* We shall hear of the eight Medians who ruled the world, in due course, in some of the later synchronistic insertions.

G.—A combination of Isidore and SAM. According to the former : *Filii Iavan Elisa, a quibus Graeci Elisaei, qui uocantur Aeolides. Unde et lingua quinta, Graece Αἰολίς, appellatur*; and again, *Iauan, a quo Iones, qui et Graeci;* *unde et Mare Ionium.* In SAM we read : *Iaban a quo Ioni sunt, et a quibus nominatur Ionicum Mare, ⁊ is uadib rogenatar Eolldai ⁊ a quibus nominantur Iolici. Ocus is uaidib ainmnigthir in cuiced berla na Greci .i. Berla Eolla.* There is no reference to Alexander the Great in either source.

H.—Isidore, *loc. cit.* : *Tharsis a quo Cilices, ut Iosephus arbitratur. Unde et metropolis ciuitas eorum Tharsus dicitur Cethim, a quo Citii id est Cyprii, a quibus hodieque urbs Citium nominatur. Dodanim, a quo Rhodii.* I cannot find any justification for the quoting of *Civ. Dei* as an authority, unless it be this sentence from XVI, iii, *ad init.*: *Coeptae sunt enim commemorari a minimo filio qui uocatus est Iapheth.* A poor latinist, with an ill-written MS., might mix up "Coeptae" with "Seithim," and "Iapheth" with "Ioif," and produce the reading presupposed. An absurd reading, but probably most of us have heard or perpetrated equal absurdities in our own schooldays.

I.—This comes from some other source. The islands are admittedly enumerated from memory, and the names appear to be distorted: *Rōid*, *Sicil* and *Creid* are the only ones whose identification is clear. *Corbdith* and *Ceithiria* are presumably the Cycladic islands *Carpathos* and *Cytherea*. *Rodain* I conjecture (with fitting hesitation) to be the Balearic Islands, which were colonized by Rhodians, and are roughly speaking opposite the mouth of the Rhône (*Rhodanus*).

K.—*Thubal, a quo Iberi qui et Hispani: licet quidam ex eo et Italos suspicentur.* The Irish compiler is less cautious than Isidore. The remainder of this section apparently comes from Augustine (*Civ. Dei*, VII, 4).

L.—*Mosoch, ex quo Cappadoces, unde et urbs apud eos usque hodie Mazaca dicitur; Thiras, ex quo Thraces,*—Isidore, *loc. cit.* The Irish writer does not trouble himself with the Cappadocian city of Mazaca, which, as we have already seen, has become "Maissegda" son of Japhet. SAM, while briefly enumerating the descendants of the sons of Japhet, though mentioning this fiction in the preliminary text, does not, like the author of the interpolation before us, confess that information about his progeny is missing. It gives us the extra-biblical information that Thiras had seven sons: and then enumerates the children of Gomer, as they appear in § E above. But it does not, like the text before us, duplicate the personality of Rifath.

M.—*Magog, a quo arbitrantur Scythas et Gothos traxisse originem*: Isidore, *loc. cit.* The identification of the Goths and the Gaedil follows from the historical sojourn of the former, and the legendary sojourn of the latter, in the land of the Scythians, of which we shall hear later. The matter of this section, in shorter form, appears in SAM: Isidore remarks further: *Gothi a Magog filio Iaphet nominati putantur de similitudine ultimae syllabae, quos ueteres magis "Getas" quam "Gothos" uocauerunt* (IX, ii, 89).

N.—This repeats matter which has already appeared in R¹ (¶ 9) and will be found again in ¶ 98, taken from *Q. The text here is different, and more closely in accordance with that in SAM. The paternity of Baath is differently given, and the genealogical steps between him and Elenus or Alanus are omitted. Longbardus has been duplicated, and his double has been made into a fourth son of Negua. SAM differs from R³ as to the geographical connexion of Albanus: we there read .i. *ota ind Albain airtherach isind Assia Moir.*

O.—Borrowed from SAM, with an interpolation on the descent of the Franks and the Romans from Alanus.

P.—Only the beginning from SAM. The rest is the orthodox LG tradition, though the family of Barachān is new.

Q.—Mostly from SAM but with some expansion. "Sliab Mai" can be identified with *Amanus* by the help of Comestor (*Filii Iaphet tenuerunt septentrionalem regionem a Tauro et Amano montibus Ciliciae et Syriae usque ad fluuium Tanaim*—Hist. Schol. xxxvii). Isidore testifies to the same distribution: *Haec sunt gentes de stirpe Iaphet, quae a Tauro monte ad aquilonem mediam partem Asiae et omnem Europam usque ad Oceanum Brittanicum possident.* The sentence relating to Spain appears to be corrupt. In SAM it reads: ⁊ *in Espain n-uilidi co huilinn talmain* (Rawl) or ⁊ *conice in Easpain uilide fodeis .i. treuilleach,* which is nearer our present text. Tre-uilleach is written ꞇuꞁꞁeⱯć, which suggests a possible origin for the mysterious word ꞇuꞁꞁꞃꞁıchꞇ; but *tre-uillig* also appears in the text before us, and if this excludes the explanation suggested, I can only conjecture that it is a corruption of *Astures.*

96. In H only. Ionitus, the fourth son of Noah, has obviously reached our text through Comestor. *Centesimo anno tertiae chiliadis natus est Noe filius in similitudinem.*

eius, et dixit eum Ionithum. Trecentesimo anno dedit Noe donationes filio suo Ionitho, et dimisit eum in terram Ethan, et intrauit eam Ionithus usque ad mare orientis, quod dicitur Elioschora, id est, "solis regio." Hic accepit a Domino donum sapientiae, et invenit Astronomiam (Hist. Schol. xxxvii). Comestor here follows Pseudo-Methodius,[37] whose alleged "Revelations" popularized this personage in Europe. He passed into the traditions of the founding of Rome, the greatness of which he was said to have foretold. See G. A. Graz, *Roma nella memoria e nelle immaginazioni del medio eve*, Torino, 1882, I, p. 86.[38] The legend is of oriental origin. According to the *Cave of Treasures* Nimrod learned wisdom from Yônṭôn son of Noah, but the devil afterwards perverted the teaching, which accounts for the mixture of good and evil in astrology, magic, etc. The *Book of the Bee* gives Yônatôn as the name of the post-diluval son, whom Noah loaded with gifts and sent forth "to the fire[39] of the sun" in the east.

97. In H only. A history of the beginnings of the arts, clearly an imitation—almost a parody—of the inventions attributed in *Genesis* to the sons of the Cainite Lamech. Eve's penitence in the Tigris is the central incident in the *Book of Adam and Eve* and related apocryphal documents. The twin sister of Cain is usually (following Pseudo-Methodius) called Calmana. *Is uimpi doronad an t-ēd* refers to the story that the real cause of Abel's murder was the desire of both brethren to marry this sister: a dispute in which Adam took the part of Abel, as he considered that Cain's twin consanguinity was too close for an admissible marriage. The brother 'Pendan' appears in the later redaction of *Tenga Bith-nua* (*Revue Celtique*, xxviii, p. 300) as a second victim of Cain's jealousy.

Two long interpolations have divorced Oliuana from her husband Japhet.

The erection of the pillars is attributed to Seth by Josephus, who is apparently the source of this frequently-

---

[37] See C. D'Evelyn, *The Revelations of Methodius* (Mod. Language Assoc. of America, xxxiii (1918), p. 135.)

[38] I have had no opportunity of verifying this reference.

[39] "Fire" should be "land." The corresponding Syriac words in their native script have some superficial resemblance, which might mislead a careless or astigmatic copyist.

repeated story (Antiqq. I, ii, 3). The Irish writer has missed the point of the difference in the materials of the pillars. According to Josephus, there were two pillars, one of brick and one of stone. If the anticipated destruction came by water, the stone pillar would survive, if by fire the pillar of brick.

98. On this paragraph see notes to ¶ 9.

99. This is from *Q. It is instructive to compare the two genealogies of Partholon with the corresponding text in F, ¶ 10, the only other R¹ text which has preserved this passage.

*Q (1)	*Q (2)	F
Parthalon	Parthalon	Parthalon
m. Sera	m. Sera	m. Sera
m. Sru	m. Sru	m. Sru
m. Esru	m. Esru	m. Esru
m. Gaeidil Glas	. . .	. . .
m. Niuil	m. Praimint	m. Bimbind
m. Feiniusa Farrsaig	. . .	. . .
m. Bathatha	m. Aitheachda	m. Aaithecha
m. Magog	m. Magog	m. Magoth
m. Iathfeth	m. Iathfeth	m. Iafeth

Most likely the genealogy marked *Q (1) is the original, and was the only one in *Q. In the LF*X tradition, the shorter genealogy became substituted for the *Q genealogy; and this alternative form was inserted into the tradition from some MS. of that group. When two variant forms of a statement are given, united by a conjunction which means *or*, in the overwhelming majority of cases we may assume that the first is the original form, the second an interpolated alternative.

The concluding part of this ¶, which is certainly no part of the original text, is a condensed (and confused) genealogy of the Aithech-Tūatha of Connacht. Tindi s. Conri, Eochu Dala, and Fidheg s. Fēg, who is not here mentioned, divided Connacht between them after the coming of the Fir Bolg, taking respectively the East, West, and South of the Province. See *Genealogical Tracts*, i (ed Ó Raithbheartaigh) under the various names in the index, where further aspects of the relationships of these communities will be found. They are there derived from the Fir Bolg, not, as here, from the Nemedians. One or other of the two references to Tindi s. Conri in the paragraph before us, must be intrusive: it is not certain which, as the *Genealogical Tracts* assign him to the *Fir Taiden*. These, with the Domnannaig and the Fir Cráibe, constituted the "three original Connachta." Sliab (F)uirri is in Galway, near the Roscommon boundary, and close to Ballygar.

101. This paragraph, as is explained in the introduction, begins a translation of the early Latin text. It was headed *Mīniugud Gabal nĒrenn* "An explanation (i.e. translation) of the 'Takings of Ireland'." The following words were doubtless added when the text (originally independent) was tacked on to R², to supplement the deficiencies of that version.

Ethre i mbēolo aissneisen "an end (or tail) in a mouth of relation" rendered by Thurneysen (*Zu ir. Handschr. u. Lit.* ii, 5) as "recapitulation" perhaps might rather be supposed to refer to the end of a chain of oral transmission, and be translated "tradition."

Ō thosuch in libair anūas: an editorial note, inserted to link the text to R² to which it is now appended.

Hybernia insola, etc., down to *"insola" Latine dicitur*, is probably the preface of the original text.

Then follows an interpolation derived from Isidore (XIV, vi, 6) as Thurneysen has already observed: it is not reproduced quite correctly in our MSS.: the true readings of Isidore are given here in footnotes to the text. There are two glosses, one explaining the corrupt *Hiberniam* (for *Hiberiam*) and the other contradicting the oft-quoted statement, disseminated by Solinus, as to the absence of bees.

Scoti autem a Scota . . . . . . adnotentur is an additional interpolation, suggested by the reference to the *Scotorum gentes* in the excerpt from Isidore.

The sentence beginning *Phoeni autem* is a further interpolation, interrupting the remarks about the Scots. Their identification with the tatooed Picts in this passage is contrary to all the orthodoxy of the LG tradition.

With *Heriu dono* the original passage resumes: this follows on naturally to the etymological speculations interrupted by the intruded excerpt from Isidore.   Here again an unusual idea is suggested.   The comment s. q. l. is a frequent formula of complaint regarding a passage which a reader found it hard to understand.   It is equivalent to the *difficilis est haec pagina* of the Saint-Gall *Priscian*.

Quasi scissi is another etymological interpolation, a guess by some wiseacre at the origin of the word *Scoti*.

VERSE TEXTS.

I.

Metre: the two quatrains forming this composition are probably, in origin, independent compositions, as is suggested by their diversity of metre.   The second is in. *casbairdne* ($7^3 + 7^3$) with trisyllabic rhymes between lines 2 and 4; the first is in *snām sebaic,* a variety in which the third line ends with a monosyllable.

The text has been greatly corrupted by scribes, who tinkered with it unrestrainedly in the vain hope of extracting more sense out of it than the author or authors ever put into it: as the verses are mere displays of metrical gymnastics, the meaning is of minor importance in an endeavour to restore the text.   In addition to the rhymes, there is assonance between the first two lines of each stanza, and an alliteration in every line, which the attentions of the scribes have to some extent suppressed.   This is the chief help toward restoring the text.   The MS. P has been re-inked unintelligently.

1. *Slūag* has evidently been changed to the plural after the incorporation of the second quatrain, bringing another "host" into view.   Both alliteration and meaning help us to choose *cūa-chel* "a winter (or rainy) death" as the true reading, although it happens to be found only in the three inferior derivatives from B.   *Conad* has arisen from a misreading of a mark of prolongation as an abbreviation for *n*: the same mistake is probably at the base of F's *ecnad*. In *snām sebaic* there is no necessity for vowel-assonance between lines 1 and 3, and therefore we can read *cel*, "death, fate" instead of the less tractable *cēl* "an omen."

2. The insertion of *ac* in MH (not in B) is an attempt to mend the metre, after Noë had come to be pronounced as a monosyllable, Nāi. The alliteration decides for *niath-lēn* against rival readings.

3. The evidence for the infixed pronoun (*ronglēad*) is hardly strong enough to justify us in adopting it, though it may be right.

4. *Iatafen* in E is an attempt to mend the metre, the name having sunk into a dissyllable.

8. The rhyme with *dībada* teaches us the pronunciation *Olīuăna*.

II.

Metre: *debide imrind.*

Apparently a variant of poem V quatrain 40, not found in any complete text of the poem—or more probably from another poem on similar lines, as V is in *debide scāilte*, and has only two quatrains (23, 49) in *debide imrind.*

III.

Metre: *debide scāilte.*

A variant of poem V quatrain 41, likewise not found in any complete text of the poem. In Min these two quatrains run continuously, as though forming one extract: this may be original, the matter which separates them in the other Redactions being editorial. Naē is here still a dissyllable, but Iafēth is no longer trisyllabic. The variant *do dec* in the last line has obviously arisen from a misreading of the numeral sign .u.

IV.

Metre: *crō cummaisc etir casbairdne ⁊ lethrannaigecht.* There should be alliterations in the first two lines at least, but in a poem so full of proper names this is impossible to maintain consistently. The language is Middle Irish.

20. This cheville may also be translated something like "well seen was his authority," but the rendering chosen makes little difference to the sense.

22. *Ōen* used absolutely, as a rhyme to *sōer*.

32. *Meic*, inserted before *Ebaith* by numerous MSS., though desirable, is hypermetric and must be rejected.

33. *Iardain* must be read instead of *Iarboneil*, for metrical reasons, though the last is the more orthodox form.

36. *Esrū* and *meic* must be omitted, for metrical reasons. Compare line 32.

39. This refers to the magical apparition of the Tūatha Dē Danann: the "plain" is Mag Tuired.

V.

Metre: *debide scāilte*. The versifier began by making alliterative linkages (*conachlann*) between the end of every quatrain and the beginning of the next, but after the seventh quatrain abandoned the effort: no re-arrangement of the quatrains can establish the device after this point, and we must assume that the few cases to be found in the latter part of the poem are accidental.

There are two versions of this long composition, contained in not a few modern MSS. I have collated several of these in the Royal Irish Academy[40] without finding anything of importance: no version contains the isolated variants which

---

[40] 23 A 40, F III 2, 23 M 18, C vi 1, 24 P 13. Of these 23 A 40 23 M 18 and C v 1 belong to the M group and show nearly all of its peculiar readings and arrangements of the quatrains. Except for scribal mistakes (as *abartar* for *abar*, line 98 (23 A 40)) or the peculiar spelling *Caidin* for *Cain* in 23 M 18, they show no particular individuality. A later hand has inserted into 23 A 40 an attribution of the poem to Eochaid ua Floind: 23 M 18 is content to say *Ollamh eigin cct.* F III 2 and 24 P 13 are closer to the printed version. F III 2, which attributes the poem to Colum Cille, closely follows EP in its readings. The following variants may be worth noting: line 58 (this spurious quatrain is present, as in EP) *dib gan Chaim*: line 68 *Agānia* (for *Gogoma*): line 89, *tri trāth go leith, nī lūad saobh*: line 129, *ro fāsadh .uii. ccnoic*: line 142, *Tubadh Caoin*. Stanzas 28–30, 34, 37, 39, 45, 46, 50 are omitted. The city in line 251 is called *Imbitena*, as in D; in 263 we find *Etrosius*—one of many proofs afforded by Irish MSS. that although *c* was always pronounced hard in Irish, it was pronounced as *s* before *i* and *e* in Latin. 24 P 13 has also close affinity with EP, but has nothing of importance to tell us.

we have seen in nos. II, III above. In the MSS. before us, M may be taken as the type of the one text, R² of the other. H, on the whole, follows R², but U (*the Book of Ui Maine*), which has a fine copy in a different context, follows the M version. Referring back to the diagram, p. 14 *ante,* I am now inclined to think that the two folios, 2 and 7, disappeared together, and had both gone when ∞M transcribed the text. He recognised the torso of the poem, and found another copy from which to supply the missing quatrains (1–30). M and H appear to agree against R² more frequently in the second half of the poem than in the first.

42. *Mac maith Muire ingine* (an unconscious lapse into the heresy of Sabellianism!) is peculiar to M among the manuscripts here used. Though not in U, it is a reading of the M version of the text.

43. None of the MSS. indicate the nasalization after *ār.*

46. *Maiss,* the chaotic material out of which the universe was fashioned.

52. The "clouds" (*neōil*) are introduced to make an assonance with *eōin.* The poet takes advantage of the freedom in *debide* rhyme to unite the long vowel in *glē* with the short vowel in *Dardāine.* Some peculiar minor verbal differentiations appear in the M text in this quatrain.

54. The assertive interjection *Debrad* is here left untranslated, in view of the uncertainty attaching to its etymology. As everyone knows, an over-indulgence in this expletive was one of St. Patrick's few human weaknesses.

57. This stanza breaks the *conachlann,* which has not yet been abandoned; and as it appears in two MSS. only it is probably spurious, even although it is a necessary supplement to the preceding stanzas, which describe the works of creation. It is here printed as in E, with the addition of punctuation and prolongation marks only. *Deg-dāil,* the company listening to the narrative. *Anmann* must be for *anmunna* (the a elided before the following vowel); this, and the accusative *deilb,* are governed by *aisneidfed.* Note the article with a noun depending on a proper-name genitive in the last line.

61 ff. The poet is here dealing with a body of apocrypha differing from that followed in the prose text, as may be shown by the following table :—

	Prose (¶ 2ᴀ, 25)	Verse
Head from	Garad	Malōn
Breast „	Arabia	Arōn
Belly	Lodain	Babylon
Legs „	Agoiria	Laban, Gogoma

—disregarding the variant forms in the different MSS.

This, however, does not bring us nearer to discovering the origin of the Irish version of the story. Verses which appear to be a rather remote variant of these quatrains, found in *Codex Palatino-Vaticanus* (Todd Lectures, III, p. 24) revert to the prose version (Garad, Arabion [or Aradon, or Adilon], Laban, and Dagaria [or Gagaria]). The poet has also his own views as to the course of the rivers of Paradise. *Tairis* is the reading of all the MSS., but we should doubtless emend this to *tairse* : the rivers ran through the (fem.) *land*, not the (masc.) *head*. In this stanza we note an important deviation in the M text.

69. *Trāth*(a) means "days," as is more usual in this text, not (canonical) hours, on account of the reference to Christ's three days in the tomb. The first couplet of this quatrain is metrically faulty, as both lines end in a dissyllable. That Adam was for some time without life is a popular belief in apocryphal literature : but it is quite independent of the three-days' sojourn of Christ in the tomb, with which it is here typologically connected. In fact, the stories vary as to the length of time which elapsed before the body of Adam was quickened. A Muslim legend shows some affinity with the ideas here expressed. "Allah formed Adam out of a handful of dust . . . which . . . had been collected from different parts of the world, and consisted of various kinds of soil, which accounts for the divers colours of men and women. When Allah had formed Adam, He left the figure lying lifeless forty days—some say forty years—while

notice was sent to the Angels, the Jinn, and the Jan, to be
ready to worship and do him honour as soon as Allah had put
breath into his nostrils.[41]

73. *Triar* presumably means the three Persons of the
Trinity, who are represented as collaborating in the creation
of Adam—another variant from the conception in the prose
text. To make any sense of the cheville at the end of line 75
we should have to read *ba dia ndeδin* "by Their good will":
but no ms. supports this.

77. An abridged translation of quatrains 10–13, 15 will
be found in Archdeacon Seymour's paper, *The Book of Adam
and Eve in Ireland*,[42] which should be in constant reference
in studying the apocryphal Adam matter in this compilation.
Pairtech, the "great mountain" of Paradise, is new: it
appears again in the form *Pariath* in the *Lebor Brecc* history
of the creation (Todd Lectures, III, p. 48). Adam's hymn
of praise is a commonplace of apocrypha. In *Pirqe Rabbi
Eliezer*, chap. II, we read "And as [Adam] saw the creatures
which God had made he began to praise God his Creator, and
said: O Lord, how great and many are Thy works!"

81-2. Another metrically faulty couplet, both lines ending
in a monosyllable.

83. According to the Syriac *Cave of Treasures* "God took
a rib from the loins on the right side of Adam and He made
Eve: and when Adam woke up and saw Eve he rejoiced in
her greatly. And Adam and Eve were in Paradise, clothed
with glory and shining with praise, for three hours." (Tr.
Budge, pp. 59–60).

87-8. This apparently refers to the naming of the birds:
at least I can find no other story connecting Adam with birds.
Syncellus, *Chronography*, gives the dates of the incidents of
Adam's life thus: 1st day of week [3rd day of Creation of
Adam, 8th of Nisan, 1st of April, 6th of Phamouthi] Adam
named wild beasts: 2nd day, named cattle: 3rd day, *named
fowls*: 4th day, named creeping things, etc., etc.

---

[41] J. E. Hanauer, *Folklore of the Holy Land* (London, 1907), p. 9.
[42] *Proceedings*, R.I.A., xxxvi, section C, p. 121.

91. All the MSS. read *do nim,* which is unmetrical, and incidentally nonsense. It seems best to emend it to *do-gnīm* (gen. plur.) "of evil deeds," the complementary formation to *so-gnīm,* "a good deed."

96. These words spell the letters of the Tetragrammaton יְהֹוָה the Hebrew divine name *Yahweh,* inaccurately rendered "Jehovah" in European popular speech. The notion that the Devil was the first to invoke the name of God reappears in *Salomon and Saturnus* (*ed. cit. antea,* p. 191)—

"Who first named the name of God? the devil first named the name of God."

We find the statement repeated in the *Colloquy of Adrian and Ritheus* (ibid., p. 204), and also by the *Master of Oxford*—

"Who cleped first God?—The devyll."

The basal idea doubtless is that the devil acquired power over the Deity by knowing and using His secret name.[43] The poet's knowledge of Hebrew was limited to the letters of the alphabet and their names, possibly learnt from the section-headings in Ps. cxix (Vulgate cxviii); and to the external appearance of the Tetragrammaton. He did not even know that Hebrew is written and read from right to left, so that when he spelt out the letters of the divine name he enumerated them in the reverse order—the left-to-right order in which he was accustomed to read or write Latin or Irish.

97. An aetiological myth to account for the superiority of the right hand to the left. In an account of the Creation and subsequent events in T.C.D. MS. H 2 5, most of which follows LG closely, I find this: *Ro hiomuil imorro Adamh an t-ubhall ⁊ ro bad tarnocht dā ēis, ⁊ les ta lamh chle seochus lamh dheas ann, mar as ī an lamh chle sineadh chum an ubhaill.* "A. ate the apple and became naked thereafter [compare *Cod. Pal. Vat.,* p. 54] and therewith the left hand comes after the right hand, for it is the left hand that was stretched to the apple." I have not come across the idea elsewhere in apocrypha, though doubtless it exists.

---

[43] For analogies see Frazer, *Taboo and the Peril of the Soul,* p. 387 ff.

101. The expulsion of the errant pair to *Egypt* is unorthodox : Damascus is the usual place of their exile. The "one palm" suggests that the poet did not know the difference between dates and figs.

105. Throughout the poem the name *Cain* is treated as a dissyllable. P sometimes emphasises this by spelling it *Caidin.*

109. The poet, writing presumably from memory, has forgotten that Cain's offering was "of the fruits of the earth." Once again we see a faulty couplet, with the end words having the same number of syllables.

124. Seth was the first man to *grow* a beard, for Adam was presumably created with his beard, Abel died a beardless youth, and it was part of Cain's punishment to have no beard (as in the prose text ¶ 39). But no ancient authority known to me explains how Seth was a witness of the murder of Abel (which took place before he was born), why he "put his hand to the jawbone," or what he did with it.

127. That stones "grow" is still an article of popular belief : I have been shown, by a Co. Meath farmer, a stone with a mark upon it which, he believed, was produced by the pressure of another stone, while the marked stone was "growing." *Salomon and Saturnus* agrees with our poet that this growth had been stopped by the flow of Abel's blood. We there read—

> "Tell me why stones are not fruitful?—Because Abel's blood fell upon a stone when Chain his brother slew him with the jawbone of an ass."

Also in *The Master of Oxford's Catechism*—

> "Why bereth not stonys froyt as trees?—For Cayne slough his brother Abell with the bone of an asse cheke."

139. The tale of how Lamech accidentally slew Cain is one of the most familiar legends of Apocrypha. It is of Jewish origin, and as stated above, in the notes to ¶ 39, was probably imported into Christian tradition from a lost "Book of Lamech." See Seymour, *op. cit.,* p. 130, for references to which add the quotation from Rabbi Solomon Jarchi in

Eisenmerger's *Entdecktes Judenthum*, vol. i, p. 470. The weapon used by Lamech was, however, an arrow; not an apple, as in the text before us.

142. The name Tubalchain must be scanned as a tetra-syllable, to give a rhyme for *brīg* : we must therefore follow E′ in reading *is,* as against the *ocus* of other MSS. On the other hand it is a trisyllable in line 144, unless E is right in cmitting the following article. But D emphasizes the difference by a difference of spelling.

143. The words *in cara* are difficult to deal with. See Meyer, *Contribb.* s.v. *cor* for the meaning suggested in the translation.

145. I know of no other version of the almost nauseatingly silly story of the subsequent adventures of Abel's ram, narrated in this and the following quatrains.

148. It is common sense that this must refer to "the ram caught in the thicket," which provided a surrogate for Isaac : and that the original version ran *dar cend meic Aprām* (not *Aprāim,* which is forbidden by the rhyme: Aprām is indeclinable). Some meddler, however, older than the existing MS. tradition, oblivious of the story of the sacrifice of Isaac, assumed vaguely that the event must have been something or other in the history of the Children of Israel; so he changed the genitive singular to genitive plural.

153. This quatrain seems out of place : it probably should follow quatrain no. 15. The name of the tree is given as *Sezen* in the Ethiopic *Book of Mysteries of Heaven and Earth.* (See Budge, *Cave of Treasures,* p. 66); as *Deachuimhan* ["tithing"] in the late version of *Tenga Bithnua* (*Rev. Celt.* xxviii, 300).

155. We have heard of "the plain of Aron" before, as the region over which the rivers of Paradise flow. This looks like a confusion based on some old misreading of the Hebrew source (the ‏ד‎, *d,* in "Eden" being misread as ‏ר‎ *r*). The contrary mistake is made in the Greek version of Numbers xxvi. 36.

163. *Deich mbliadan risin uile,* i.e., ten years in addition to all the 930 years of Adam's life. That Eve survived Adam is generally agreed in apocryphal literature, but the actual length of her widowhood is very variously stated.

166. The poet has misread .d.cccc.xii. in his authority, substituting .xu. for the last letters. On the other hand, he has not docked Seth's life by three hundred years, as the prose texts have done. The M text has altered the verse text to conform with the prose.

173. Jared's life was 962 years long. Here again .ii. has been misread as .u.

177· Most of the MSS. agree on *ochtmoga,* but the variant *sechtmoga* is historically correct.

182. Lamech's life was 777 (Hebrew) 753 (Septuagint). The figure in the text 775 and H's correction 757 are both unauthorized. An owner of U has taken the trouble to look the matter up : see the footnote.

186. Adam's son Sile, and the three wives in line 188, reappear in *Sex Aetates Mundi,* but whence they reached that text I have failed to discover. Olla was Seth's wife, Pip was Cain's, Pithip was Sile's. Evidently there is some confusion between Seth and Shem, just as Cain and Ham (Cham) are sometimes interchanged. Pip and Pithip must therefore have some kinship with Oliva and Olivana, but the nature of the kinship is not clear.

193. On the names of these women see the note on the prose texts ¶ 7.

205. On this quatrain and its mysterious geography, see the notes on the prose text ¶ 86, where we find the interesting back-formation *Formenia > Armenia* on the basis of *ar < for.*

212. D spells this word *cubaat,* and writes it thus (as nearly as can be represented in print) cubɑττ, the first two τ's being really a fantastic *a.* The same peculiarity was probably also in √D, and has influenced E's *cubatat.* E was certainly not copied from D, but might well have come from

√D. This is a good illustration of the way in which the *external form* of the MSS. and their handwriting may sometimes give us some crumbs of information as to their relationship; see ante, p. xxvii. It must be admitted that this peculiar way of writing a sequence of *a*'s and *t*'s, in any combination, is a trick of Muirges ó Maoil Conaire, the scribe of D, and that it reappears in the *Book of Fenagh,* another of his productions. It is not, however, a regular habit: it looks more like an artificial affectation, in which he indulges whenever he remembers to do so, and he may have made it his own after learning it from √D.

215. The cheville *cen brōn* is more than usually meaningless here if we give to the word *brōn* its ordinary meaning "sorrow." K. Meyer, *Contribb.* gives (with a query) an alternative meaning "burden" which helps slightly, but not much. But we need not expect a poet in metrical difficulties to be intelligible all the time: our present poet is better in this respect than many of his colleagues.

218-219. In both these lines the *o* of *ro* is metrically elided. Several of the scribes have failed to notice this, and have endeavoured to emend what they took to be the faulty measure of the rhythm.

221. I know of no authority for the extravagant dimensions here ascribed to the tower.

228. The list of the heroes of Nimrod's Tower agrees with that in *Auraicept,* except that Peleg and Rabiath (= Rifath) Scot are here omitted. Dardan appears in *Auraicept* as "Bardanius." The names are selected, on some random principle which it is futile to try to determine, from a list of the immediate descendants of Noah; with such incongruous additions as Nabcodon, Latinus, and Longbardus. The first of these comes from an Ogham alphabet of names: see Calder's *Auraicept,* p. 20, and also below, line 257.

240. The sense of the couplet seems to be "though God be no respecter of persons—though the abbot and the king be all one in His sight—may He grant me the favour of a long life."

251-2. These lines appear in the order as printed in all the MSS., but as the tetrasyllable *Ibitēna* should follow the trisyllable *il-bērla* they should be transposed. The city of Ibitēna is apparently an echo of the name of the Median city of Ecbatana. As the table of *variae lectiones* shows, this name assumes a variety of forms. Keating gives another version, Eathēna, and quotes this quatrain as from *Cin Droma Snechta*—which seems to suggest that this poem was contained in that important manuscript.

257 ff. This is the Ogham-alphabet list of the chief persons of Nimrod's Tower, from which one set of names for the Ogham letters was derived. For metrical reasons the alphabetic order has been disturbed (see for the proper arrangement Calder's *Auraicept,* p. 20) and some of the names have been modified. Mored, Gad, Hidomus correspond respectively to Muiriath, Gotli, and Iudonius. Ordmor (possibly meant for *Ord.Mōr,* but the *variae lectiones* suggest that it is one word) corresponds to Ordines (Ordonus in M). Srū, the Stru of the Ogham list, has been lost from all the MSS. except M; and additional names have been interpolated (Nenual, Gaedel, Cainan, Ionan).

VI.

Metre: *debide scāilte.*

273. On the characters ascribed to the rivers in this poem, see the note on the prose ¶ 28.

274. The name Nuchal here given as the fountain-head of the four rivers, can hardly be dissociated from Nuchul, given as the name of an African river in the Geographical Poem of Ros Ailithir (*P.R.I.A.,* xvi, p. 241). Its (probably erroneous) identification with the Nile, and the identification of the latter with Gihon, may have led to the transference of the name to the well-spring of Paradise.

278. We must read *felicitias* for the sake of the metre.

284. I suspect that *tibes* is wrong, but I take it as I find it in the MSS.

VII.

Metre : *debide scáilte.*

VIII.

Metre : *rannaigecht becc.*

This quatrain, and the following poem, found in H only, are printed exactly as they appear there, with the addition of punctuation marks only.

[X.

Metre : *debide scáilte.*

296. In this poem Náe has become a monosyllable ; a fact emphasised by the spelling of the genitive Náec in line 304.

END OF VOLUME I.

IRISH TEXTS SOCIETY

—:□:—

THE IRISH TEXTS SOCIETY *was established in* 1898 *for the purpos of publishing texts in the Irish language, accompanied by such intro ductions, English translations, glossaries and notes as may be deeme desirable.*

The Annual Subscription is 21/- *(American subscribers,* $5) *payable on* 1st January. *This entitles members to receive, post free, th current volume. There is no entrance fee.*

Members whose subscriptions are not in arrear may, wher necessary, complete their sets by obtaining back volumes up to Volum XXI inclusive at the reduced rate of 10/6 *a volume. Volumes XXI and XXIII are* 12/6 *and all subsequent volumes are* 21/- *each. Th current subscription of £1 1s. 0d. should be paid for the year in whic any application is made for back volumes under this arrangement.*

The payment of a single sum of £12 12s. 0d. (colonial or foreig members, £13 0s. 0d.; American members, 65 *dollars), entitles to lif membership. Life members will receive one copy of each volume issue subsequently to the receipt of this sum by the Society. All remittance should be made payable to the Society, not to individual Officers.*

Vols. I. II. III. and XIV. are now out of print and others are rapidl becoming scarce. The ordinary sale price to non-members throug Messrs. Simpkin, Marshall, Ltd., 4 *Stationers' Hall Court, London E.C.4., is* 25/- *per volume (post free).*

The Council makes a strong appeal to all interested in the preservatio and publication of Irish Manuscripts bute to its funds.

Please Note Address.

All communications should be addressed to the Hon. Secretary, Iris Texts Society, c/o National Bank Ltd., 15, *Whitehall, London, S.W.*1

IRISH TEXTS SOCIETY.

THE THIRTY-FOURTH Annual General Meeting of the Irish Texts Society was held on Saturday, 11th February, 1933, in the Library of the Irish Literary Society.

Dr. Robin Flower, chairman of the Executive Council, presided.

The Minutes of the last Annual General Meeting, held on the 13th February, 1932, were taken as read. Mr. Maurice O'Connell, Assistant Secretary, read the

Thirty-Fourth Annual Report

Duanaire Finn. The Council are glad to report that all the poems and translations forming Part II of *Duanaire Finn* are through the final proofs. Arrangements are now being made for binding. This volume will be followed by Part III, consisting of the Preface, Notes to the Poems, Glossary, and Index of Persons and Places, etc. Both volumes are being edited by Mr. Gerard Murphy, M.A. Part I, edited by Professor Eoin MacNeill, D.Litt., was issued by the Society in 1907, and is now nearly out of print.

Instructio Pie Vivendi (Holy Life and Heavenly Thought). The first part of this interesting theological work is now nearing completion. It will consist of the Latin original and Irish translation, with a short glossary of the rarer Irish words. The Irish is a very good specimen of the early modern language. The work will be in two volumes, and volume two is in active preparation.

The Great Blasket. The Council regret that owing to illness, the result of an accident while on a visit to the Aran Islands, Dr. Flower was obliged to suspend his work on this volume for some time. He has now resumed. The volume will consist of a collection of tales dealing with the life of the Great Blasket Island, Co. Kerry, in the nineteenth century. A number of poems by a poet of the locality will also be included, with stories illustrating their subjects.

NOTE.—Part II of *Duanaire Finn* was distributed in September of this year.

The number of back volumes disposed of during the year was 94.

The Rev. P. S. Dinneen's edition of the Society's revised and enlarged Irish-English Dictionary is now nearly exhausted. The Council have under consideration the question of a reprint.

During the year an edition of the Society's smaller dictionary in Roman type was completed, and a new edition in Irish type has also been printed. Both editions are now obtainable at 3/-.

The Council regret to report the deaths of the following :—
Right Rev. Dr. Shahan, Vice-President of the Society ; Lady Gregory, Col. J. W. MacNamara, Dr. Goddard Orpen.

Members who joined during the year were :—Dr. Gerard Coyne, Ballinasloe ; Miss Anna Irene Miller, Baltimore, U.S.A. ; Maire Ni Locain, Dublin ; Fergus Patterson, Putney, London ; Convent of St. Louis, Monaghan ; Minnesota University Library, Minn., U.S.A.

J. C. Sprott, Esq., Glasgow, resigned.

The adoption of the Annual Report was moved and seconded. During the discussion which followed, Dr. Joyce referred to the slow rate of production of the Society's books. It was explained that the delay in every case was occasioned by illness or pressure of other business that obliged the editors to postpone their work on the Society's volumes. On a show of hands the Report was adopted.

The Financial Statement was explained by the Treasurer and adopted on the proposal of Mr. Buckley, seconded by Dr. Joyce.

The re-election of the Officers and outgoing members of the Council, Mrs. Banks, Mr. Buckley and Dr. Flower, was proposed by Mr. O'Keeffe, seconded by Mr. FitzGerald, and carried.

A hearty vote of thanks was accorded to Mr. R. W. Farrell, F.L.A.A., for auditing the accounts, and his appointment as auditor for the year 1933 was agreed upon.

IRISH TEXTS SOCIETY.

RECEIPTS AND PAYMENTS ACCOUNT FOR THE YEAR, 1932.

DR.	£	s	d	CR.	£	s	d
Brought forward from 1931	1115	12	1	Trade Distribution ...	7	3	1
Donations to Editorial Fund	1	11	0	Storage	7	10	0
Sales of Larger Dictionary	398	8	9	Printing and Binding ...	275	17	1
Sales of Smaller Dictionary	82	19	0	Postage, etc.	12	1	4
Interest, etc.	167	1	7	Income Tax	27	10	0
Postage			6	Insurance	4	10	0
Subscriptions and Sales of Volumes	191	13	10	Investment, 5% War Loan	1016	14	3
				Royalty	53	2	6
				Editors' Expenses ...	20	0	0
				Sundry Expenses ...	72	13	2
				Balance, being Cash in Hand and at Bank ...	460	5	4
	£1957	6	9		£1957	6	9

BALANCE SHEET AS AT DECEMBER 31st, 1932.

LIABILITIES.	£	s	d	ASSETS.	£	s	d
Sundry Creditors ...	449	10	6	Cash at Bank ... 455 0 1			
Reserves :—				Cash in Hand ... 5 5 3			
Printing and Binding of Volumes under Contract	670	0	0	Cash on Deposit ... 850 0 0			
Income Tax	30	0	0		1310	5	4
Binding of Larger Dictionary	66	13	4	£2900 3½% Loan at 99⅛	2874	12	6
Printing of Annual Reports	20	0	0	£250 C.N.R. at 91 ...	227	10	0
Editorial Expenses ...	540	0	0	Sundry Debtors	355	18	2
Subscriptions paid in advance for Vols. not under Contract	226	16	0	Insurance paid in Advance	1	2	6
Reprint of Larger Dictionary	600	0	0	Office Furniture 11 13 1 Less Depreciation ... 4 10 6			
Balance	3324	15	3		7	2	7
				Stock	1151	4	0
	£5927	15	1		£5927	15	1

(*Signed*) M. C. LYNCH, *Hon. Treasurer.*

The undersigned, having had access to all the Books and Accounts of the Society, and having examined the foregoing statements and verified them with the Books, Deeds and Documents, etc., relating thereto, now signs the same as found to be correct.

(*Signed*) ROBERT W. FARRELL, F.L.A.A., *Certified Accountant.*
28*th January*, 1933.

GENERAL RULES

——:0:——

OBJECTS

1.—The Society is instituted for the purpose of promoting the publication of Texts in the Irish Language, accompanied by such Introductions, English Translations, Glossaries and Notes as may be deemed desirable.

CONSTITUTION

2.—The Society shall consist of a President, Vice-Presidents, an Executive Council, a Consultative Committee and Ordinary and Life Members.

OFFICERS

3.—The Officers of the Society shall be the President, two Honorary Secretaries and the Honorary Treasurer.

EXECUTIVE COUNCIL

4.—The entire management of the Society shall be entrusted to the Executive Council, consisting of the Officers of the Society and not more than ten other Members, to whom the Executive Council may add by co-optation not more than two members, who shall retire annually.

5.—All property of the Society shall be vested in the Executive Council, and shall be disposed of as they shall direct by a two-thirds majority.

6.—Three members of the Executive Council shall retire each year by rotation at the Annual General Meeting, but shall be eligible for re-election, the Members to retire being selected according to seniority of election, or, in case of equality, by lot. The Council shall have power to co-opt Members to fill up casual vacancies occurring throughout the year. Any Member of Council who is absent from five consecutive Ordinary Meetings of the Council to which he (or she) has been duly summoned, shall be considered as having vacated his (or her) place on the Council.

CONSULTATIVE COMMITTEE

7.—The Consultative Committee, or individual Members thereof, shall give advice, when consulted by the Executive Council, on questions relating to the publications of the Society, but shall not be responsible for the management of the business of the Society.

MEMBERS

8.—Members may be elected either at the Annual General Meeting, or from time to time, by the Executive Council.

SUBSCRIPTION

9.—The Subscription for each Member of the Society shall be £1 1s. 0d. per annum (American subscribers, $5), entitling the Member to one copy (post free) of the volume published by the Society for the year, and giving the right to vote on all questions submitted to the General Meeting of the Society. Regular members, whose subscriptions have been paid up to date, may, however, fill up gaps in their sets of back volumes, prior to volume 22, at 10/6 a volume. The payment of a single sum of £12 12s. 0d. (Colonial or foreign members £13 0s. 0d., American members 65 dollars) entitles to life membership. Life members will receive one copy of each volume issued subsequently to the receipt of this sum by the Society.

10.—Subscriptions shall be payable in advance on 1st January in each year.

11.—Members whose Subscriptions for the year have not been paid are not entitled to any volume published by the Society for that year, and any Member whose Subscription for the current year remains unpaid, and who receives and retains any publication for the year, shall be held liable for the payment of the full published price, viz. 25/- of such publication. *

12.—The publications of the Society shall not be sold to persons other than members, except at the advanced price of 25/-.

13.—Members whose Subscriptions are in arrear shall not have the right of voting at the Annual General Meeting of the Society.

14.—Members wishing to resign must give notice in writing to the Honorary Secretary, before the end of the year, of their intention to do so ; otherwise they will be liable for their subscriptions for the ensuing year.

EDITORIAL FUND

15.—A fund shall be opened for the remuneration of Editors for their work in preparing Texts for publication. All subscriptions and donations to this fund shall be purely voluntary, and shall not be applicable to other purposes of the Society.

ANNUAL GENERAL MEETING

16.—A General Meeting shall be held each year in the month of January, or as soon after as the Executive Council shall determine, when the Council shall submit their Report and the Accounts of the Society for the preceding year, and when vacant seats on the Council shall be filled up, and the ordinary business of a General Meeting transacted.

AUDIT

17.—The Accounts of the Society shall be audited each year by an auditor appointed at the preceding General Meeting.

CHANGES IN THESE RULES

18.—With the notice summoning the General Meeting, the Executive Council shall give notice of any change proposed by them in these Rules. Ordinary Members proposing any change in the Rules must give notice thereof in writing to the Honorary Secretary seven clear days before the date of the Annual General Meeting.

LIST OF IRISH TEXTS SOCIETY'S PUBLICATIONS

—◻—

(Out of print)

(1.) Giolla an Ḟiuġa. [The Lad of the Ferrule]
Eaċtra Cloinne Riġ na h-Ioruaiḋe. [Adventures of the Children of the King of Norway]
Edited by PROFESSOR DOUGLAS HYDE, LL.D., D.LITT., M.R.I.A.

(Out of print)

(2.) Fleḋ Bricrenḋ [The Feast of Bricriu]
(From Leabhar na h-Uidhre).
Edited by GEORGE HENDERSON, M.A., PH.D.

(Out of print) *See Volume* 3*a New Edition.*

(3.) Dánta Aoḋagáin Uí Raṫaille [The Poems of Egan O'Rahilly]
Edited, chiefly from MSS. in Maynooth College, by
The REV. P. S. DINNEEN, D.LITT.

(*Volume for* 1909) (*See No.* 3)

(3a) Dánta Aoḋagáin Uí Raṫaille [New Edition of the Poems of Egan O'Rahilly]
Revised by PROFESSOR TADHG O DONNCHADHA and
The REV. P. S. DINNEEN, D.LITT.

(*Volume for* 1901)

(4.) Foras Feasa ar Éirinn [History of Ireland.] By GEOFFREY KEATING. Part I. (See Vols. 8, 9, 15).
Edited by the late DAVID COMYN, M.R.I.A.

(Volume for 1902)

(5.) Cᴀɪᴛṗéɪm Conᵹᴀɪʟ Cʟᴀɪṗɪnᵹnɪᵹ   [The Martial Career of Conghal Clairinghneach].
Edited by
The REV. P. M. MᴀcSWEENEY, M.A.

(Volume for 1903)

(6.) Virgil's Æneid, the Irish Version, from the Book of Ballymote.
Edited by The REV. GEORGE CALDER, B.D., D.Lɪᴛᴛ.

(Volume for 1904)

(7.) Ⱃuᴀnᴀɪṗe ḟɪnn. The Poem Book of Finn. [Ossianic Poems]. Part I.
Edited by PROFESSOR EOIN MᴀcNEILL D.Lɪᴛᴛ.

(Volume for 1905)

(8.) ḟoṗᴀṗ ḟeᴀṗᴀ ᴀṗ Éɪṗɪnn [History of Ireland].   By Gᴇᴏꜰꜰʀᴇʏ Kᴇᴀᴛɪɴɢ.   Part II.
Edited by The REV. P. S. DINNEEN, D.Lɪᴛᴛ.
(See Vols. 4, 9, and 15).

(Volume for 1906)

(9.) ḟoṗᴀṗ ḟeᴀṗᴀ ᴀṗ Éɪṗɪnn [History of Ireland].   By Gᴇᴏꜰꜰʀᴇʏ Kᴇᴀᴛɪɴɢ.   Part III.
Edited by The REV. P. S. DINNEEN, D.Lɪᴛᴛ.
(See Vols. 4, 8, and 15).

(Volume for 1907)

(10.) Two Arthurian Romances [eᴀċᴛṗᴀ mᴀcᴀoɪṁ ᴀn ɪoʟᴀɪṗ ᴀᵹuṗ eᴀċᴛṗᴀ ᴀn ṁᴀuṗᴀ ṁᴀoɪʟ] Adventures of the Eagle Boy and Crop Eared Dog.
Edited by PROFESSOR R. A. S. MACALISTER, M.A., D.Lɪᴛᴛ.

12.

(Volume for 1908)

(11.) Poems of David O'Bruadair. (Part I.).
Edited by The REV. J. MacERLEAN, S.J.
(See Vols. 13, 18).

(Volume for 1909—see 3a supra.)

(Volume for 1910)

(12.) Buile Suibhne Geilt, A Middle-Irish Romance.
Edited by J. G. O'KEEFFE.

(Volume for 1911)

(13.) Poems of David O'Bruadair. (Part II.)
Edited by The REV. J. MacERLEAN, S.J.
(See Vols. 11. 18).

(Volume for 1912—Out of print)

(14.) An Irish Astronomical Tract, based on a Mediæval Latin
version of a work by Messahalah.
Edited by the late MAURA POWER, M.A.

(Volume for 1913)

(15.) ⲫⲟⲣⲁⲥ ⲫⲉⲁⲣⲁ ⲁⲛ Éⲓⲣⲓⲛⲛ [History of Ireland]. By GEOFFREY
KEATING. Part IV. Containing the Genealogies,
Synchronisms and an index, including the elucida-
tion of place names and annotations to Parts I., II.,
III. (See Vols. 4, 8, 9 supra.)
Compiled and Edited by REV. P. S. DINNEEN, D.LITT.

(Volume for 1914)

(16.) Life of St. Declan of Ardmore and Life of St. Mochuda
of Lismore.
Edited by The REV. P. POWER. M.R.I.A.

(Volume for 1915)

(17.) Poems of Turlogh O'Carolan and additional Poems.
Edited by PROFESSOR TOMAS O'MAILLE, M.A., Ph.D.

(Volume for 1916)

(18.) Poems of David O'Bruadair. (Part III.)
Edited by The REV. J. MacERLEAN, S.J.
(See Vols. 11, 13).

(Volume for 1917)

(19.) Ṡaḃalċaṟ Ṡeṗluiṟ ṁóiṟ [The Wars of Charlemagne]
Edited by PROFESSOR DOUGLAS HYDE, LL.D., D.Litt.,
M.R.I.A.

(Volume for 1918)

(20.) Iomaṟḃáṡ na ḃfileaḋ [The Contention of the Bards] Part I.
Edited by The REV. LAMBERT McKENNA, S.J., M.A.

(Volume for 1919)

(21.) Iomaṟḃáṡ na ḃfileaḋ (Part II.)
Edited by The REV. LAMBERT McKENNA, S.J., M.A.

(Volume for 1920)

(22.) Poems of Taḋg Ḋall O hUiginn (Vol. I. Text.)
Edited by ELEANOR KNOTT.

(Volume for 1921)

(23.) Poems of Taḋg Ḋall O hUiginn (Vol. II. Translation.)
By ELEANOR KNOTT.

The Great Blasket. A Collection of tales told by Tomár O Cṗioṁtáinn and recorded by ROBIN FLOWER, D.Litt. with poems by Seán O Duinnṗleiḃe (*in the Press*).

Duanaire Finn. Part III. Containing Notes to all the Poems, Glossary, Indices, etc.
Edited by GERARD MURPHY, M.A.

Instructio Pie Vivendi—Holy Life and Heavenly Thought. Part II. English translation of the Irish version, with Notes, etc.
Edited and translated by REV. JOHN MacKECHNIE, M.A., B.D.

The Harrowing of Hell and other New Testament Apocrypha.
Edited and translated from Irish Manuscripts of the 15th century, with a critical study of the sources and with notes. By ROBIN FLOWER, D.Litt.

Irish versions of three tales by Montalvan, with the original Spanish text and synopsis in English.

Cinn-Lae Amhlaoibh Uí Shúilleabháin. Humphrey O'Sullivan's Diary, 1827-1835. Two volumes.

The revised edition of the Society's Larger Irish-English Dictionary (1340 pp.), edited by REV. P. S DINNEEN, D.Litt., (price 12/6 net ; post free 13/-) can be purchased from The Educational Company of Ireland, Ltd., 89 Talbot Street, Dublin. The Smaller Irish-English Dictionary (240 pp.) by the same editor, can be had of Messrs. M. H. Gill & Son, 50 Upper O'Connell Street, Dublin, and of Messrs. Simpkin, Marshall, Ltd., 4 Stationers' Hall Court, London, E.C.4. (price 3/- net.).

LIST OF MEMBERS.

(N.B.—Members are earnestly requested to send Notice of any Chang of Address to the Hon. Sec., Irish Texts Society, c/o National Bank, Ltd. 15, Whitehall, London, S.W.1., to avoid loss of books and notices).

Honorary Life Members :

NAMES.	ADDRESSES.
Hull, Miss Eleanor, D.Litt. ...	2, Gloucester Gardens, (58) Richmond Hill Richmond, Surrey.

Life Members :

Bradley, The Rev. Michael, P.P. Knockloughrim, Co. Derry.
Braunholtz, Prof. G. E. K., M.A. 22, Old Road, Headington, Oxford.
Byrne, G. P. ... ... 24 College Square North, Belfast.
Byrne, The Rev. J. ... ... Castlehead, Grange-over-Sands, Lancs.

Crotty, The Rev. Michael, P.P. Abbeyside, Dungarvan, Co. Waterford.
Curran, The Rt. Rev. Monsignor Irish College, Rome, 24.
  M. J.

Dalton, J. P. ... ... 19 Belgrave Square, Monkstown, Co. Dubli
De Paor, Eamonn ... ... Fatha, Eadarghoil, Bantry, Co. Cork.
Diolun, Maolra, M.A., Ph.D. ... University College, Dublin.
Donnellan, J. P. ... ... Killeany, Aran Isles, Co. Galway.
Doolan, Thomas ... ... 31-32 Great George's Street, Waterford.
Dowling, Frank ... ... 950 South Street, Roslindale, Mass., U.S.A

Farrell, R. W., F.L.A.A. ... ... Clonbrone, Arundel Road, Durrington Worthing, Sussex.
FitzGerald, T. D., B.A. ... ... c/o National Bank, Ltd., 15 Whitehall London, S.W.1.
Fleming, The Rev. R., PH.D. ... Rathmines, Dublin.

Gahagan, F. Evatt ... ... 31, Harrington Sqr., London, N.W.1.
Goblet, Professor Yan M. ... 178 Rue de la Pompe, Paris, xvi.
Gourley, C. E. ... ... 70 Claremont Road, London, E. 7.

Hackett, J. D. ... ... 132 East 16th Street, New York, U.S.A.
Harley-Walker, The Rev. C. T. The Yews, East Hanney, nr. Wanstead Berks
Havard-Jones, The Rev. H. T., The Vicarage, Spaldwick, Huntingdon.
  M.A.
Haynes, Miss Muriel Sturgis ... 22, Embankment Road, Boston, Mass U.S.A.
Horsford, Miss C. ... ... 27 Craigie Street, Cambridge 38, Mass U.S.A.

John, E. T. ... ... 63 Warwick Square, London, S.W.1.

NAMES.	ADDRESSES.
Kelly, Paul Herrick ...	... 132 Cheapside, London, E.C.2.
Kennedy, Chief Justice Hugh ...	Newstead, Clonskeagh Road, Dublin.
Kennedy, Patrick J., M.A.	... 17 Irishtown, Clonmel, Co. Tipperary.
Lewis, The Hon. A. L. ...	... The Hill, Abergavenny, Mon.
MacErlean, Andrew A., LL.B. ...	119 East 57th Street, New York, U.S.A.
MacFhinn, An t-Athair Pádraig Eric, D.D.	Coláiste na h-Ollsgoile, Gaillimh.
MacLoughlinn, James L.	... 60, Waterloo Road, Pembroke, Dublin.
McInnes, Wm. MacArthur	... c/o McLaren, 55, Randolph Road, Broon hill, Glasgow.
Malone, Prof. Kemp. ...	... Johns Hopkins University, Baltimor Maryland, U.S.A.
Mitchell, The Rev. Joseph, Canon	President, St. Mary's College, Galway.
OBuacalla, Micheál ...	... 108, Rock Rd., Booterstown, Co. Dublin.
OCarroll, Jos., M.D. ...	... Lynwood, Dundrum, Co. Dublin.
OCasaide, Séamus, M.A., B.L., M.R.I.A.	Bóthair Lorcáin, Clontarf, Dublin.
OCianáin, S. F., M.B. ...	... Ballinalee, Edgeworthstown.
OCorcura, Micheál ...	... 2 Mulgrave Road, Cork.
ODubhgaill,The Rev. T.,B.A.,B.D.	St. Columb's College, Derry.
OSullivan, The Rev. T.	... 173 Botanic Road, Dublin.
Perry, Miss A. M., M.A. ...	... 79 South End Road, Hampstead, N.W.
Sheehan, The Most Rev. M., D.D.	Archbishop of Sydney, Juverna, Homebus Sydney, N.S.W.
Ua Concheanáin, Tomás	... Lios na Mara, Bothar na Tragha, Galwa
Ua Corcra, Domhnall ...	... 1 Auburn Villas, Ashburton, Cork.
Ua Cuileamháin, Seán ...	... Dun Cormac, Wexford.
Van Hamel, Dr. A. G. ...	... 19, Prins Hendriklaan, Utrecht.
Walker, Charlton, B.A. ...	... 16 Seaton Avenue, Plymouth.

Ordinary Members :

Andrews, Mrs. Edmond	... 561 Surf Street, Chicago, Ill., U.S.A.
Ashbourne, Lord... ...	... 17 Rue des Domeliers, Compiègne, Ois France.
Banks, Mrs. M. M. ...	... 16, Hornton Court, Kensington, W.8.
Bartholomew, J. ...	... Nunholm, 9 Victoria Circus, Glasgow, W.'
Béaslaí, Piaras, Major General	8, Eden Park, Sandycove, Co. Dublin.
Bell, S.	... 3, Southdean Gardens, Wimbledon.
Bergin, Prof. Osborn J., D.LITT.	10, Grosvenor Place, Rathmines, Dublin.
Beynon, The Rev. E. D.	... 8475 Dearborn Avenue, Detroit, Michigar U.S.A.
Boland, John P. ...	... 4, Stone Buildings, Lincoln's Inn, W.C.2.
Boswell, C. S.	... Gatcombe, nr. Seaton, South Devon.
Boyd, E. A.	... 131 East 19th St., New York City, U.S /

NAMES.	ADDRESSES.
Bradley, W., M.D.	Nevonstown House, Navan, Co. Meath.
Brady, Very Rev. J. Canon, P.P.	Keady, Co. Armagh.
Breathnach, Caitlín	23 Main Street, Carrick-on-Suir.
Breathnach, Cormac	Central Model Schools, Dublin.
Breen, The Rev. D.	Dingle, Co. Kerry.
Bright, William, LL.D., T.C.D. ...	Willowdale, Glenageary Rd., Dunlear Co. Dublin.
Briley, W. P.	18, Temple Park, Blackrock, Co. Dublin
Brophy, Michael M.	48, Approach Road, Margate.
Brown, Professor A. C. L.	Northwestern University, Evanston, U.S.
Brown, Thomas	20, Nassau Street, Dublin.
Brown, Prof. W. Edward ...	Lafayette College, Easton, Pa., U.S.A.
Buckley, James, M.R.I.A. ...	11, Homefield Road, Wimbledon, Surrey
Burns, Samuel	13 Warrington Road, Newcastle-on-Tyn
Byrne, O. A.	Villa Faraldo, 3, Rue Bel Respiro, Bea Soleil, A/M., France.
Calder, Rev. Geo., B.D., D.LITT.	4, Oakfield Terrace, Glasgow, W.
Clarke, John J.	57 St. Aubyn's Place, Lr. Newtowr Waterford.
Coffey, Brian MacMahon, M.D.	12, Denny Street, Tralee, Ireland.
Cohalan, The Most Rev. Dr. ...	Bishop of Cork, Farranferris, Cork.
Costello, Thomas, M.D.	Bishop Street, Tuam, Co. Galway.
Coyne, Dr. Gerard	Mount Pleasant, Ballinasloe, Co. Galway.
Cox, Prof. Edward G., PH.D. ...	University of Washington, Seattle, Wash ington, U.S.A.
Creed, The Rev. C. M.	Durrus, Bantry, Co. Cork.
Crone, J. S., M.D., J.P., M.R.I.A.	Castlereagh, 34 Cleveland Road, Ealing London, W.13.
Cross, Professor Tom Peete ...	Dept. of Comparative Literature, Uni versity of Chicago, Ill., U.S.A.
Cullinan, Rev. Thos.	P.O. Box 89, Cradock, S. Africa.
Curran, C. P., M.A.	15, Garville Avenue, Rathgar, Dublin
Curtis, Prof. E.	37, Trinity College, Dublin.
De Barra, Liam	Beech Walk, Roscrea, Co. Tipperary.
De Bhál, An t-Athair Tomás, S.P., PH.D.	Cill Curnáin, Co. Limerick.
De Bharra, Seán	61, Patrick St., Drumcondra, Dublin.
De Blacam, Aodh	Lios Gréine, Artane, Co. Dublin.
De Blaghd, Earnán	6 Temple Villas, Palmerston Road, Dublin S.W.1.
De Lury, Alfred T.	University of Toronto, Canada.
Digby, Everard W.	47, Charleville Rd., London, W.14.
Diolún, Thomas	Teach an Daingin, Galway.
Dobbs, Miss M. C.	Port na Gabhlann, Cushendall, Co. Antrim
Donnellan, P., M D.	St. Mary's, 13, Mayfield Rd., Terenure Dublin.
Dowley, Miss Brigid	Westgate, Carrick-on-Suir, Co Tipperary
Dowling, Mrs. D.	Ard na Gréine, Ballymacelligott, Tralee.
Doyle, Miss M.	56 Hunter St., London, W C.1.
Dunn, Professor Joseph... ...	Catholic University, Washington, D.C. U.S.A.
Dunne, The Rev. J.	Rathroe, Tullow, Co. Carlow.

NAMES.	ADDRESSES.

Eadie, Lieut.-Colonel J. Inglis, D.S.O. ... c/o. Messrs. Grindlay & Co., 54, Parliame Street, London, S.W.1.

England, Thomas A., LL.D. ... 11a Caithness Rd., London, W.14.

Enschedé, M. Johannes ... Huize, Ipenrode, Heemstede, The Nethe lands.

Esmonde, Sir T. Grattan, Bt. ... Ballynastragh, Gorey, Co. Wexford.

FitzGerald, M. J. ... ... 18, King St., Snow Hill, London, E.C.1.

FitzGerald, Rev. Wm., C.C. ... Thurles, Co. Tipperary.

FitzSimmons, B. ... ... Sheepshead N. School, Kilcrohane, Bantr

Fitzsimons, Patrick J. ... ... 48, Longstone Street, Lisburn.

Flower, Robin, D.LITT. ... ... Dept. of MSS., British Museum, Londo W.C.1.

Flynn, Francis ... ... 4, Avon Place, Bothwellhaugh, Bothwel Scotland.

Franklin, M. ... ... 74, St. Lawrence Rd., Clontarf, Dublin.

Freeman, A. Martin ... ... 166, Lauderdale Mansions, London, W.9

Fynes-Clinton, O. H. ... ... Weirglodd Wen, Bangor, N. Wales.

Gaffney, J. S., B.A., Solicitor ... 86, O'Connell Street, Limerick.

Gaidoz, Professor Henri ... 22 Rue Servandoni, Paris vi.

Gates, H. C. ... ... 24, Bayswater Terrace, Skircoat Greei Halifax, Yorks.

Gill, Mrs. M. ... ... Castle Street, Carrick-on-Suir, Ireland.

Gogan, L. S. ... ... 373, North Circular Road, Dublin.

Green, J. S., Lt.-Col., R.A.M.C., M.R.I.A. ... Air Hill, Glanworth, Co. Cork.

Griffen, Harold D., M.A. ... ... William Woods' College, Fulton, Missour U.S.A.

Griffin, Henry Farrand ... ... Barnstable, Massachusetts, U.S.A., pe Stevens & Browne, Ltd.

Grosjean, The Rev. Paul, S.J. ... 24, Boulevard St. Michel, Brussels.

Gwynn, Dr. Edward ... ... Provost's House, Trinity College, Dubli

Haran, Dr. J. A. ... ... 15, Shelley Road, Beechen Cliff, Bath.

Hayden, The Rev. E. M. ... St. John's Rectory, Clinton, Ill., U.S.A.

Headlam, M. F., C.B. ... ... 5, Tedworth Square, London, S.W.3.

Healy, A. Collins, B.A. ... ... 521 West 124th Street, New York City U.S.A.

Heggarty, The Rev. J. M. ... 114E, 2nd St , Los Angeles, Cal , U.S.A.

Henry, Prof. Robert Mitchell, M.A. Queens' University, Belfast.

Hickey, The Rev. B. ... ... St. Mary's, Wellington Road, Ashton under-Lyne.

Hodges, Figgis & Co. ... ... 20, Nassau Street, Dublin.

Hogan, John ... ... 7 Prince Arthur-Terrace, Leinster Square Rathmines, Dublin.

Hogan, The Rev. Stanislaus, O.P. Holyrood, East Camberwell, Melbourne

Houlihan, The Rev. M. J. ... 43 Maple St , Hyde Park, Mass , U.S.A.

Hull, Vernam E. ... ... 29 Randolph Hall, Cambridge, Mass.,U.S A

Hurley, The Rev. T. A. ... ... The Monastery, Killarney, Co. Kerry.

Hyde, Professor Douglas, D.LITT., 65 Adelaide Road, Dublin.

NAMES.	ADDRESSES.
Jarcho, Saul W.	... 303 West 106th Street, New York, U.S.
Jennings, Rev. T. A., M.A.	... St. Jarlath's College, Tuam, Co Galway.
Johnston, J. P., SC.D. ...	... Royal College of Science, Upper Merrio Street, Dublin.
Joyce, Francis, M.B. ...	... 190 Camberwell Road, London, S.E.5.
Joyce, Wm. B., B.A. ...	... 1 Effra Road, Rathmines, Dublin.
Joynt, Ernest E.... ...	... Kingston, ...Tyrconnell Road, Inchicor Dublin.
Keappock, The Rev. Thomas ...	Parochial House, Collinstown, Co. West meath.
Keenan, L. F., M.D. ...	... 58 Upper Clapton Road, London, E.5.
Keliher, Thomas ...	... 134, Upper Thames Street, London, E.C.
Kiernan, T. J., M.A., PH.D.	... Office of the High Commissioner, Iris Free State, 33-37 Regent St., Londo S.W.1.
King, Michael J., B.A. ...	... Borrigone, Co. Limerick.
Lankford, J. R.	... 7 Ashburton Hill, St. Luke's, Cork.
Leslie, Shane	... Glaslough, Co. Monaghan.
Lewis, Timothy	... University College, Aberystwyth, Wales.
Liddell, M. F.	... 35, Trinity College, Dublin
Lloyd, Joseph H., M.R.I.A.	... Buaile na Gréine, Stillorgan Park, Dublin.
Lynam, E. W., B.A., M.R.I.A.	... British Museum, London, W.C.1.
Lynch, M. C.	... 20 East Bank, Stamford Hill, London, N.16
Lynch, Timothy ...	... Sun Lodge, 65 Sunday's Well, Cork.
Macalister, Prof. R. A. S., M A.	18 Mount Eden Road, Donnybrook, Dublin S E.1.
MacAoidh, Ian	... 33 Curzon Rd., Muswell Hill, London, N.10
MacAoidh, Micheál ...	... Teach Druim, Drum Amharc, Dun na nGall
MacBhloscaidh, P. ...	... 17 Sráid Caitrín, Limerick
MacBride, A., M.D. ...	... Infirmary House, Castlebar, Co. Mayo.
MacBride, Joseph M. ...	... Mallow Cottage, Westport, Co. Mayo.
MacCana, Peadar ...	... 25 Mary Street, Drogheda.
MacCarrthaigh, Tadhg ...	... N.S , Kinnegad, Co. Meath.
McCarthy, P. J , N.T. ...	... Shannon View, Glin, Co. Limerick.
MacClintock, Major H. F.	... Red House, Ardee, Co Louth.
MacColuim, Fionán ...	... Department of Education, Dublin.
MacCosgair, Liam T. ...	... Beechpark, Templeogue, Co. Dublin.
MacDermott, The Very Rev. J. Canon	Croghan, Boyle, Co. Roscommon.
MacDiarmuda, An t-Athair M.	Keady, Co. Armagh.
MacDomhnaill, F. S. ...	... c/o. Barclays Bank, 9 Russell Square London, W.C.1.
MacDonald, The Rev. Archibald	Kiltarlity Manse, Beauly, Invernesshire.
MacEochagáin, Stiobhán Pádraig	Lorne House, Coleham, Shrewsbury.
MacGinley, P. T. ...	... 108, Drumcondra Road, Dublin.
MacGiolla Seannaigh, an t-Athair	Spiddal, Galway.
McGrath, Patrick ...	... 20 East Essex Street, Dublin.
McGreevy, Thomas ...	... 15, Cheyne Gardens, London, S W.3.
MacGrianna, D. ...	... 60, Lindsay Road, Glasnevin, Dublin.
MacKay, Donald ...	... c/o Miss M. MacKay British Bank of Sout America Ltd., Caixa Postal, 83 Sa Paulo, Brazil
MacCarvill, Mrs Eileen...	... 8 Fitzwilliam Square, Dublin.

NAMES.	ADDRESSES.
McKenna, The Rev. L., s.j. ...	Rathfarnham Castle, Co. Dublin.
McLees, William H.	379 Grant Avenue, Brooklyn, New York U.S.A.
MacLennan, The Rev. Malcolm, D.D.	6 Polwarth Terrace, Edinburgh.
MacLeod, The Rev. Malcolm, M.A.	United Free Church Manse, Lochgilphead Argyllshire.
MacLoingsigh, The Rev. Peadar	St. Columb's College, Derry.
MacLysaght, E.	Raheen, Tuamgraney, Co. Clare.
MacMurnaigh, Micheál	St. Anne's, Anne St., Dundalk.
Macnaghten, The Hon. Helen ...	Runkerry, Bushmills, Co. Antrim.
MacNeill, James	Dundrum, Co. Dublin.
MacNeill, Patrick Charles ...	27, Edenvale Road, Rathmines, Dublin.
MacNiocaill, S.	46 Oakley Road, Ranelagh, Dublin.
MacSeáin, The Rev. Seán ...	Omagh, Co. Tyrone.
MacSuibhne, Pádraic	5 Highfield Avenue, Cork.
MacSwiney . of Mashanaglass, The Marquess, M.R.I.A. ...	39 Upper Fitzwilliam Street, Dublin.
MagFhloinn, Liam	Newtown School, Waterford.
Mahony, J. J.	Suite 608, Ashland Block, Chicago, U.S.A
. Meaghar, The Rev. J. R. ...	St. Thomas of Canterbury, Waterloo Liverpool.
Meehan, Francis	Leitrim, Ireland.
Merriman, Professor P. J., M.A.	President, University College, Cork.
Mhic Chathmhaoil, Mairéad, Bean	Westpoint House, Strand Rd., Sutton Co. Dublin.
Micheál, an t-Athair, O.S.F.C. ...	Fr. Mathew Hall, Queen St., Cork.
Miller, Miss Anna Irene ...	2426 Eutaw Place, Baltimore, Maryland U.S.A.
Miller, C. R. D.	301, Craigie Hall, Cambridge, Mass., U.S.A
Miller, The Rev. W.	Braganza House, Carlow.
Moloney, Francis	74 State Street, Boston, Mass., U.S.A.
Moynihan, James	34 Dunbar St., Cork.
Mühlhausen, Prof. Docktor Ludwig	Ruldolfstr, 48, Hamburg, 34.
Mulcahy, Timothy, B.A.... ...	2 Tivoli Terrace, Clonmel.
Mullen, The Rev. E. J., C.C. ...	Carrick, Tirconaill.
Munn, Dr. James Buell ...	58 Garden St., Cambridge. Mass, U.S.A.
Murphy, F. T.	4 Highland Park, Roxbury, Mass, U.S.A.
Murphy, J. J. Fintan	16 Effra Road, Brixton Hill, London, S.W.
Murphy, William, N.T.	53 Harbour Row, Cobh, Co. Cork.
Murphy, Dr. Philip	Main Street, Carrick-on-Suir, Co. Tipperary
Murray, Sir Hubert	Government House, Port Moresby, Papua
Murrin, James B.	Carbondale, Pennsylvania, U.S.A.
Nesbit, Mrs. M. K.	Montilly, Sion Mills, Co. Tyrone.
Newlin, Nicholas...	1804 Pine St., Philadelphia, Penn., U.S-/
Ní Bhruadair, Gobnait ...	Baile an Chongnaimh, Cuan an Chaisleain Cill Airne, Co. Ciarraidhe.
Nic Dhonnchadha, Lil. ...	116, Lower Baggot St., Dublin.
Nic Eochagáin, Seosaimhín ...	87 Upper Dorset St., Dublin.
Nic Mhathghamhna, Lil. ...	Listellick, Tralee, Co. Kerry.

NAMES.	ADDRESSES.
Ni Dhunlainge, Sighle ...	... 19 Finglas Rd., Glasnevin, Dublin.
Ni Locain, Máire... ...	... 136, Upper Drumcondra Rd., Dublin.
Nilsen, Eugene	... 20, Ekebergueren, Christiania, Norway.
Ni Raghallaigh, Máire	... 87 Upper Dorset Street, Dublin.
Ni Shuilleabháin, Eibhlín	... Baile h-Éil, Co. Kilkenny.
Nolan, P. J.	... 624, Roosevelt Avenue, York, Penna, U.S.A.
OBeagáin, R. S.	... 2, Wilmont Avenue, Sandycove, Dublin.
OBraoin, D.	... 5 Ennismore Villas, Magazine Road, Cork
OBriain, Art.	... 15 Mecklenburgh Square, London, W.C.1
OBriain, Pádraig ...	... Ballyferriter, Dingle, Co. Kerry.
OBriain, Seán, B.A., B.COM., H.D.E.	... Céimín, Dorgan's Rd., Glasheen, Cork.
OBrien, The Rev. Denis, D.PH., D.D.	Effin, Kilmallock, Co. Limerick.
OBrien, Michael	... Ballymakeera, Co. Cork.
OBrien, Edward, M.A. ...	... Falmore House, Moville, Derry.
OBrolcháin, Pádraic ...	... Dún Bride, Nashville Park, Howth, Co Dublin.
OBrosnacháin, an t-Athair D. ...	Colaiste Bhreannáinn, Cill Airne, Co. Chiarraidhe.
OByrne, William ...	... Eascrach, Cruimghlinn, Co. Bhaile Atha Cliath.
OCadhainn, Liam ...	... Les Buissonnets, Bridgemount, Castlebar Co. Mayo.
OCadhlaigh, Cormac, M.A.	... 5 Hill View, Cross Douglas Rd., Cork.
OCallaghan, Jeremiah ...	... 121 Duke Street, Sheffield.
OCaoimh, Micheál... ...	... 3 Ashbourne Villas, Limerick.
OCarroll, J., B.A....	... 2 The Terrace, Arklow, Co. Wicklow.
OCarroll. J. T.	... 129 Queen's Road, Richmond, Surrey.
OCeallaigh, Seán ...	... Ros Cathaill, Cill Mhine, Westport.
OCeallaigh, Seán T. ...	... c/o. *The Nation*, 91 St. Stephen's Gree Dublin.
OCeileachair, The Rev. Seán	... Coláiste Naoimh Eóin, Portláirge.
OCeocháin, Domhnall ...	... Coolea, Macroom, Co. Cork.
OCinnéide, An Bra. S.M.	... Mainistir na mBrathar, Dún Dealgain.
OConchobhair, Diarmuid	... Carrignaveeah, Sunday's Well, Cork.
OConchobhair, Risteárd	... 7, George's Quay, Cork.
OConnell, Maurice, A.C.I.S.	... Hill View, Marion Rd., Mill Hill, Londo N.W.7.
OConnor, Denis Hayes	... Monster House, Charleville, Co. Cork.
OConnor, Michael ...	... Clooncurra N.S., Lispole, Co Kerry.
OCriocháin, an t-Athair Brian ...	Grange, Sligo.
OCuill, Seán	... 44 Mountjoy Street, Dublin.
OCuinn, The Rev. Seamus ...	Bessbrook, Co. Armagh.
OCúrnáin, The Rev. Tadhg	... The Presbytery, Dingle.
ODalaigh, R.	... 63 Handside Lane, Welwyn Garden Cit' England.
ODea, The Rev. D., B.A.	... Newmarket-on-Fergus, Co Clare.
ODomhnaill, an t-Athair M.	... Teach na Sagart, Castlerea, Co. Ro common.
ODonachu, an t-Athair D.	... Tracton, Co. Cork.
ODonnchadha, Prof. Tadhg, D.LITT.	Croata, Glasheen Road, Cork.

NAMES.	ADDRESSES.
ODonnell, The Rev. M.	... Kilronan, Aran, Co. Galway.
ODonnghaile, an t-Athair N.	... Galway.
ODonovan, J. J. ...	... 2 Eden Terrace, Limerick.
ODonovan, T. J., B.A. ...	... An Cappach, Bréan Traigh, Co. Cork.
ODubhda, Peadar ...	... Bothar Dealgan, Dún Dealgan.
ODubhshlaine, F. ...	... Customs and Excise Office, Glenamadd Co. Galway.
ODuibhir, Antoine ...	... Roinn Josef, Coláiste Phádraig, Maynootl
ODwyer, Professor R. ...	... 9 Upper Leeson Street, Dublin.
OFionnachta, S.	... 6, Warrenpoint, Clontarf, Dublin.
OFlaherty, The Rev. Michael	... Summerhill College, Sligo.
OFlynn, John	... Kirwan's Hotel, Carrick-on-Suir, Co. Tipperary.
OFearghaill, Rev. A., s.j.	... Coláiste Iognáid, Gaillimh.
OGabhláin, Pádraic ...	... Cloongoonaugh, Aughamore, Co. Mayo.
OGallagher, M.	... 1430 Plaisance Court, Chicago, U.S.A.
OGlasáin, Séamus ...	... Barry's Hotel, Rath Droma, Wicklow.
OGorman, The Rev. J. J., D.C.L.	193 Fourth Avenue, Ottawa, Canada.
OHalloran, The Rev. P., c.c.	... St. Mary's Nenagh.
O h-Annracháin, Peadar	... Dun Aoibhinn, an Scibrin, Co. Cork.
OHanrahan, T. W. ...	... Altamount, Kilkenny.
O h-Aodha, Seamus, M.A.	... Ive-Le-Bawn, Fermoy, Co. Cork.
OHegarty, P. S.	... Highfield House, Highfeld Road, Rathga Dublin.
OHegarty, The Rev. T., c.c.	... Quigley's Point, Derry.
OKeeffe, The Rev. David	... St. Colman's Cathedral, Queenstown.
OKeeffe, J. G.	... 1, Dynevor Rd., Richmond, Surrey.
OKelly, Thomas ...	... 40 Hilldrop Road, London, N.7.
OKiely, Laurence, M.A. ...	... Crehana, Carrickbeg, Carrick-on-Suir.
OLoughlin, Colm ...	... 5-6 Fleet Street, Dublin.
OMahoney, D., M.B. ...	... Glasnevin Lodge, Glasnevin, Dublin.
OMáille, Prof. Tomás, M.A., PH.D.	Roigne, College Rd., Galway.
OMaolcathaigh, Pádraig	... Coláiste Chnuic Mhelleri, Ceapach Chuin Co. Waterford.
OMaolchatha, Séamus ...	An Ghráinseach, Clonmel. Co. Tipperar
OMaoldhomhnaigh, an t-Athair Mairtín	Killaloe, Co. Clare.
OMeachair, Pádraig ...	... 2184, Valentine Avenue, Bronx, Ne York, U.S.A.
OModhráin, The Rev. S.	... St. Jarlath's College, Tuam, Co. Galway.
OMoghráin, Pádraig, M.A.	... Knockloughra N.S., Westport, Co. Mayo
OMoráin, The Very Rev. P. S., Canon	Claregalway, Ireland.
OMuimhneacháin, Conchubhair	Béal Atha an Ghaorthaidh, Co. Cork.
OMuirthile, An Br. D.L.	... Coláiste Caoimhghin, Glas Naoidhean, Ba Atha Cliath.
OMuimhneachain, Aindrias	... Coláiste Caomhghin, Glas Naoidhean, Ba. Atha Cliath.
OMurchadha, Colm ...	... Leinster House, Kildare St., Dublin.
OMurchú, Micheál ...	... 33 Home Farm Rd., Drumcondra, Dubli
ONeill, Seán	... Customs and Excise, Swinford, Co. May
ORaghallaigh, Criostoir, M.A.	... 269 Clonliffe Road, Drumcondra, Dublir
ORahilly, Professor T. F., D.LITT.	Ballincurrig House, South Douglas Ro Cork.
ORayla, Proinsias ...	... 19 Munster Street, Phibsborough, Dubl

NAMES.	ADDRESSES.
OReilly, The Rev. J. M.	... Bekan, Ballyhaunis, Co. Mayo.
OReilly, The Rev. Robert	... Prior, Ballinskelligs.
ORiain, Liam P. ...	... 15 Kempshott Rd., Streatham, London S.W.16.
ORiain, The Rev. Nioclás	... Tipperary.
ORiain, Art.	... 3, Páirc Cille Muire, Dublin.
ORioghbhardáin, Domhnall, o.s.	Tamhain, Oran Mor, Co. Galway.
ORioghbhardáin, M., B.A., F.R.G.S.	N.S. Abbeydorney, Co. Kerry.
ORiordan, E. F., M.A. ...	... Suite 608, Ashland Block, Chicago, U.S.A
ORiordan, J. P. ...	... 59, Harberton Rd.,Highgate, London, N.19
Ormond, The Rev. W., Adm.	... Carrickbeg, Carrick-on-Suir, Co. Tipperary
OSeaghdha, Muircheartach, o.s.	Ard na Gréine, Eadar Goil, Bantry. .
OSeochfhradha, Pádraig	... 119, Morehampton Road, Donnybrook Dublin.
OShaughnessy, J. ...	... Gifford Park, Bronxville, N.Y.. U.S.A.
OShea, The Rev. John	... Carrick-on-Suir, Co Tipperary.
OSuilleabhain, Seán ...	... Kinnard, Lispole, Co Kerry.
OSullivan, D. J.	... Cairn Hill, Foxrock, Co. Dublin.
OSullivan, D. K.... ...	... 89 Emmet Rd., Dublin.
OSullivan, Jerh.	... St. John's, Port Glasgow.
OSullivan, John	... Beni Suef, Egypt.
OSuilleabhain, Tomas, Cigire	... 9 Geraldine Villas, Traghli.
OTighearnaigh, P. S. ...	... 57 Palmerston Road, Dublin.
OTreasaigh, an t-Athair M.	... St Michael's, Pery Square, Limerick. .
OTuathail, Eamonn, M.A.	... 15, Lower Kenilworth Park, Harold' Cross, Dublin.
Parker, The Rev. P., P.P.	... Cushenstown, Ballynabola, Co Wexford.
Patterson, Fergus ...	... Stella Polaris, Westleigh Avenue, Putney London, S.W.15.
Perry, The Rev. J. F. ...	... Hern's Nest, Rugeley, Staffs.
Phléimoinn, Máire Bean	..; An Sgoil, Síl Eiligh, Co. Wicklow.
Porter, Mrs. Valentine Mott.	... Box 211, Carmel, California, U.S.A.
Probsthain, A.	... 41, Great Russell St., London, W.C.1.
Purcell, Joseph ...	... 2 Glenmalure Villas, Castleview Garden Limerick.
Redmond, Owen J. ...	... 13 Lomond Avenue, Fairview, Dublin.
Reinhard, J. R.	... 328E. Huron St., Ann Arbor, Michigan, p B.H. Blackwell, 50 and 51 Broad St Oxford.
Rice, The Rev. James	... St. Joseph's, Headley Road, Hindhea Surrey.
Rice, Ignatius J. ...	... Roselawn, Ballybrack, Co. Dublin.
Robinson, Prof. F. N. ...	... Harvard University, Cambridge, Mass U.S.A.
Roche, Miss K. ...	... Mater Dei Gymnasium, 59 Batavierenw Nijmegen, Holland.
Rohan, T., M.A.	... 84, St. Lawrence Road, Clontarf, Dublin.
Ross, The Rev. Neil, M.A., B.D.	The Manse, Laggan, Kingussie.

NAMES.	ADDRESSES.
Saurin, C. J.	... 23 Grosvenor Road, Ilford.
Seton, Sir Malcolm ... · ...	... 26 Upper Park Rd., Haverstock Hill,N.W.
Sheehan, John	... William Street, Fermoy, Co. Cork.
Sloane, C. Gordon ...	... Platten Hall, Drogheda, Co. Meath.
Smith, J. A., LL.D. ...	... Magdalen College, Oxford.
Smith, Prof. Roland M.	... Dept. of English, Wesleyan Universit Middletown, Conn., U.S.A.
Smyth, F. Acheson ...	... 71 Harcourt Street, Dublin.
Suipéal, an t-Athair T., B.D.,B.A.	Lixnaw, Co. Kerry.
Taylor, Barry	... 5124 Calumet Avenue, Chicago, U.S.A.
Thompson, Lady ...	... 39, Steele's Road, Hampstead, N.W.3.
Thurneyson, Prof. Dr. L. Rudolf	Bonn. Mechenheimer Allee 55, Germany.
Tierney, Rev. John, D.PH.	... Edenderry, Offaly.
Townsend, E. R., Paymaster-Lieut., R N.	Boundary Oak, Waterlooville, Cosha Hants.
Ua Buachalla, Domhnall	... Maynooth, Co. Kildare.
Ua Ciaráin, Rev. A. ...	... Ballincondan, Ballina, Co. Mayo.
Ua Fearachair, D. ...	... 17 Grattan Square, Dungarvan, Co. Wate ford.
Ua Gadhra, Proinsias ...	... Ceibh na gCeannaidhe, Limerick.
Ua Mathghamhna, Seosamh	... Patrick Street, Listowel.
Ua Tuama, D.	... Kincora, Moreton, Cheshire.
Ui h-Ainnín, Máire, Bean	... Crecora, Patrickswell, Co. Limerick.
Ui Chuinn, Máire, Bean...	... National School, Killala, Co. Mayo.
Vendryes, Professor J. ...	... 85 Rue d'Assas, Paris.
Walsh, The Rev. Paul ...	... Stamullen, Co. Meath.
Walsh, The Rev. R. F., C.C.	... Draperstown, Co. Derry.
Walshe, M. C;, J.P. ...	... 2b, Bickenhall Mansions, Gloucester Plac London, W.1.
Walsh, Miss Róisín ...	... Cypress Grove, Templeogue, Co. Dublin.
Walshe, Rev. J. A. ...	... Rossmuck, Maam Cross, Galway.
Waters, Eaton W., M.D.	... Brideweir, Conna, Co. Cork.
Webster, K. G. T.	... Gerry's Landing, Cambridge, Mass., U.S.
Weisweiler, Dr. Phil. Josef.	... Frankfurt a.M., Kurhessenstr, 68.
Whitehill, Walter Muir, Jr.	... c/o Barclay's Bank, (France), Ltd., 33 ru du iv Septembre, Paris.
Williams, Professor Ifor.	... Y Wenllys, Menai Bridge, Anglesey.
Williams, T. W. ...	... Woolcombe, St. Mary's, Uplyme, Lym Regis.
Woulfe, The Rev. Patrick, C.C.	Kilmallock, Co. Limerick.
Wulff, Miss Winifred P., M.A., PH.D.	Cypress Grove, Templeogue, Co. Dublin.
Young, Miss Rose M. ...	... Portnagolan, Cushendall, Co. Antrim.

Libraries, Societies, Colleges, and Schools

Aberdeen, University Library ... per Librarian.

Aberystwyth, Library of University College of Wales — per Librarian.

Albany, U.S.A., New York State Library — per Stevens and Brown, 28-30, Littl Russell St., London, W.C.1.

Baltimore, Maryland, U.S.A., Enoch Pratt Free Library ... — per E. G. Allen & Son, Ltd., 14 Grape St Shaftesbury Avenue, W.C.2.

Baltimore, Maryland, U.S.A., Johns Hopkins University Library — per E. G. Allen and Son, Ltd.

Belfast Central Public Library — per G. H. Elliot, Chief Librarian, Roy Avenue, Belfast.

Belfast, Clonard Monastery ... — per The Rev. Fr. Rector, C.SS.R.

Belfast Library and Society for Promoting Knowledge (Linen Hall Library) — per F. J. P. Burgoyne, Librarian, Donega Square North, Belfast.

Berlin, Indogermanisches Seminar (Indo-germanic Department) of the University of Berlin. — per Dr. Pokorny, Berlin, Charlottenburg, Stuttgarter Platz. 21.

Birmingham Public Library ... — Librarian, Reference Dept., Ratcliff Plac Birmingham.

Boston Public Library, Mass. ... — per Bernard Quaritch, 11 Grafton Stree New Bond Street, London, W.1.

California University Library ... — per Stevens and Brown, 28-30 Littl Russell St., London, W.C.1.

Cardiff Central Library ... ... — per Harry Farr, Librarian, Cardiff.

Carnegie United Kingdom Trust — See under Coleraine, Dublin, Kilkenn Lifford, Sligo, and Wicklow (below).

Carrick-on-Suir, Convent of Mercy — per The Reverend Mother.

Chicago, Newberry Library ... — per Stevens and Brown, 28-30 Littl Russell St., London, W.C.1.

Chicago Public Library ... — per Stevens and Brown.

Chicago University Library ... — per Stevens and Brown.

Cleveland Public Library ... — per B. Quaritch, 11 Grafton St., London W.1.

Clongowes Wood College ... — per Rev. C. Mulcahy, s.j.

Coláiste Bhrighde, an Fálcarrach, Tír Chonnaill — per An Priomh-Oide.

Coláiste Caoimhin, Glas Naoidhean, Baile Atha Cliath — Do.

Coláiste Einne, Teach Talbóid, Baile Atha Cliath — Do.

Coláiste Ide, Baile an Ghoilín, Daingean — Do.

Coláiste Moibhi, Glas Naoidhean, Baile Atha Cliath — Do.

Coláiste Muire, Leitir Ceanainn,   per An Priomh-Oide.
  Tír Chonnaill
Coláiste na Mumhan, Magh Ealla,   Do.
  Co. Chorcaighe

Coleraine, Co. Derry, Carnegie   County Book Repository, Coleraine.
  Libraries
Concord State Library ...   ... per Arthur H. Chase, Librarian, Concor
    N.H., U.S.A.
Copenhagen, Royal Library   ... per Haase and Son, Levstroede, 8, Cope
    hagen.
Cork, Public Library   ...   ... per Librarian, James Wilkinson, F.L.A.
Cork Co. Council Carnegie   25, Patrick St., Cork.
  Library Service.
Cork, University College Library per Librarian.

Derry, Convent of Mercy   ... per The Superioress.
Dresden, Saechsische Landes-
  bibliothek   ...   . Dresden, Saxony.
Droichead Nuadh : Co. Kildare,   per The Very Rev. The Prior, O.P.
  Dominican College
Dublin, " An Fáinne "   ...   ... per An Rúnaidhe, 25 Parnell Sqr., Dubli
Dublin, Carnegie United King-   32, Merrion Square, Dublin.
  dom Trust
Dublin County Council Library   The Courthouse, Kilmainham.
Dublin, King's Inn, Hon. Society per Hodges, Figgis & Co., 20 Nassau Stree
    Dublin.
Dublin, National Library of   per Hodges, Figgis & Co.
  Ireland.
Dublin, Oireachtas Library   ... per Controller, Stationery Office, Dublin
Dublin, Royal Irish Academy ... per Hodges, Figgis & Co.
Dublin, Royal Dublin Society ... per Hodges, Figgis & Co.
Dublin, Trinity College Library   per A. de Burgh, Librarian.
Dundalk, Free Library   ... per Town Clerk, Town Hall, Dundalk.
Dundalk, St. Joseph's   ...   ... per The Rev., The Rector, C.SS.R.

Edinburgh Public Library   ... per E. A. Savage, Principal Librarian.
Edinburgh University Library   per J. Thin, 54-55 South Bridge, Edi
    burgh.
Esker, Athenry, St. Patrick's   ... per The Rev., The Rector, C.SS.R.
Evanston, Ill., U.S.A., North-   per Stevens and Brown, 28-30 Littl
  western University Library   Russell St., London, W.C.1.

Galway, University College Lib-   per Hodges, Figgis & Co., 20 Nassau St
  rary   Dublin.
Glasgow, The Mitchell Library... per S. A. Pitt, City Librarian, North St
    Glasgow.
Glasgow University Library   ... per Jackson, Wylie & Co., 73 West Georg
    Street, Glasgow.
Gottingen University Library ... per Librarian, Prinzenstrasse 1 Gottinger
    Germany.

Hamburg, Seminar für Verg-   Hamburg, Universität.
  leichende, Sprachwissenschaft
Harvard College Library   ... per E. G. Allen & Son, Ltd.

Iowa City, Ia, U.S.A,. The Library, Library Annex, State University of Iowa.	per Stechert & Co., 2 Star Yard, Care Street, London, W.C.2.
Ithaca, N.Y., U.S.A., Cornell University Library	per E. G. Allen & Son, Ltd.
Kilkenny, Carnegie Free Library	per Ed. McSweeney, Librarian, John Quay, Kilkenny.
Kilkenny Carnegie Library Service	Book Repository, John's Quay, Kilkenn
Leeds, Central Public Library ...	per T. W. Hand, Librarian.
Leipzig, Borsenverein .der Deutschen Buchhändler	Konigstrasse, 35, Leipzig.
Leipzig, Universitäts-Bibliothek	Beethoven Strasse 6, Leipzig, Germany pε A. Probsthain, 41 Gt. Russell Stree London, W.C.1.
Lifford, Tirconaill, County Library	The Librarian, County Book Repositor Lifford, Co. Donegal.
Limerick, Carnegie Free Library	per J P. McNamara, Director.
Limerick, Connradh na Gaedhilge	per The Secretary, 17 Thomas Stree Limerick.
Limerick, Mary Immaculate Training College	per The Principal.
Limerick, Mount St. Alphonsus	per The Rev. Fr. Rector, C.SS.R.
Listowel, Co. Kerry, Presentation Convent	per Sister Michael.
Listowel, Carnegie Free Library	per Veritas Coy., Ltd., Dublin.
Liverpool Public Library ...	per G. H. Parry, Librarian.
London, Connradh na Gaedhilge	per The Secretary, 31 Red Lion Square London, W.C.1.
London, Irish Literary Society	per The Hon. Secretary, 39 Grosveno Place, London, S.W.1.
London Library	per C. J. Hagbert Wright, Librarian, St James's Square, London, S.W 1.
London University College ...	per Librarian, Gower Street, W C.1.
London, University Library ...	per The Goldsmiths' Librarian, Universit Library, South Kensington, London S W.1.
Los Angeles Public Library ...	per Stevens & Brown.
Louvain, Belgium, Bibliothèque de l'Université Catholique	per Dr. E. Van Cauwenbergh, Chie Librarian.
Louvain, Collège de Saint-Antoine	per Rev. Fr. Guardian.
Lund, Sweden, University Library	per A. B. Gleerupska, Universitet. Bokhandeln.
Manchester Reference Library ...	per Librarian, Piccadilly, Manchester.
Manchester, John Rylands Library	per H. Guppy, Librarian, Deansgate, Manchester.
Manchester,Victoria University of	per Librarian.
Maynooth, Co. Kildare, Cuallacht Chuilm Cille (St. Columba's League)	per The Secretary, St. Columba's League St. Patrick's College, Maynooth.
Meadville Theological School Library	per Stechert & Co., 2 Star Yard, Carey Street, W.C.2.

Melbourne, Public Library ... (E. C. Armstrong, Librarian), per Sotheran Ltd., 43 Piccadilly, W.1.

Michigan University Library ... per Sotheran, Ltd., 140 Strand, W.C.2.

Minnesota University Library ... Minneapolis, Minn., U.S.A., per Steche & Co.

Monaghan, Convent of St. Louis per Sr. M. Laurentia.

Munich, Bavarian State Library per Asher & Co., Behernstrasse, 17, Berlir

New York Public Library ... per Stevens & Brown, 28-30 Little Russe Street, W.C.1.

New York, Columbia University Library per Stevens &-Brown do. do.

North Carolina, University of, Chapel Hill. per Stevens & Brown, London, .W.C.1.

Nottingham Public Reference Library per Librarian, Central Public Library, She wood St., Nottingham.

Oslo University Library ... per Cammermeyers boghandel, Oslo.

Ottawa, Library of Parliament... per E. G. Allen & Co., Ltd., 14 Grape St Shaftesbury Avenue, W.C.2.

Oxford, Meyrick Library, Jesus College per L. B. Cross, Librarian, Jesus Colleg Oxford.

Oxford, Taylor Institution ... per L. F. Powell, Librarian.

Paris, Bibliothèque de l'Université à la Sorbonne per C. Klincksieck, 11 Rue de Lille, Pa

Paris, Bibliothèque Nationale ... do. do.

Pembroke Urban District Library, Ballsbridge per City Treasurer, Dublin.

Philadelphia Free Library ... per Stevens & Brown, 28-30 Little Russe Street, London, W.C.1.

Philadelphia, Mercantile Library per T. Wilson Hedley, Librarian, 10th St above Chestnut Street, Philadelphi Pa., U.S.A.

Philadelphia Philo-Celtic Society 1504 N. Gratz St., Philadelphia, Pa., U.S.

Princeton University Library ... per Sotheran, Ltd., 140 Strand, W.C.2.

Rathmines, Co. Dublin, Public Library. per Librarian.

Ring, Co. Waterford, Iol-Scoil na Mumhan per Seumas Ó h-Eochadha.

San Francisco Public Library, Civic Centre per Stechert & Co., 2 Star Yard, Care Street, London, W.C.2.

Sligo, Carnegie United Kingdom Trust County Book Repository, Sligo.

Stanford University Library, California per Stechert & Co., 2 Star Yard, Care Street, London, W.C.2.

Strasbourg, Bibliothèque Universitaire et Regionale per M. Le Directeur.

Swansea Public Library (Welsh and Celtic Dept.) per Librarian.

Swansea, University College Library. Singleton Park, Swansea.

Thurles, Co. Tipperary, Carnegie Libraries	per Librarian, County Book Repository Thurles.
Toronto Reference Library ...	per Messrs. Dawson & Son, Cannon House Pilgrim Street, E.C.4.
Uppsala Kungl. University Library	Uppsala, Sweden.
Urbana, University of Illinois, U.S.A.	per Stechert & Co., 2 Star Yard, Care Street, London, W.C.2.
Washington, Library of Congress	per Stechert & Co., 2 Star Yard, Care Street, London, W.C.2.
Waterford Public Free Library	per Librarian, Lady Lane, Waterford.
Wicklow, Carnegie Libraries ...	County Book Repository, Wicklow.
Yale University Library ...	per E. G. Allen & Co., Ltd., 14 Grape St. Shaftesbury Avenue, W.C.2.

Lightning Source UK Ltd.
Milton Keynes UK
UKHW02f1813251018
331211UK00008B/73/P